GAME
DEVELOPMENT
WITH BLENDER®

DALAI FELINTO AND MIKE PAN

Cengage Learning PTR

CENGAGE
Learning·

Professional • Technical • Reference

Australia • Brazil • Japan • Korea • Mexico • Singapore • Spain • United Kingdom • United States

CENGAGE
Learning·
Professional • Technical • Reference

Game Development with Blender®
Dalai Felinto and Mike Pan

Publisher and General Manager, Cengage Learning PTR:
Stacy L. Hiquet

Associate Director of Marketing:
Sarah Panella

Manager of Editorial Services:
Heather Talbot

Senior Marketing Manager:
Mark Hughes

Acquisitions Editor: Heather Hurley

Project Editor: Marta Justak

Technical Reviewer: Mitchell Stokes

Copy Editor: Donna Poehner

Interior Layout Tech: MPS Limited

Cover Designer: Mike Tanamachi

Indexer: Sharon Shock

Proofreader: Sam Garvey

© 2014 Cengage Learning PTR.

CENGAGE and CENGAGE LEARNING are registered trademarks of Cengage Learning, Inc., within the United States and certain other jurisdictions

For product information and technology assistance, contact us at
Cengage Learning Customer & Sales Support, 1-800-354-9706

For permission to use material from this text or product, submit all requests online at **cengage.com/permissions**

Further permissions questions can be emailed to
permissionrequest@cengage.com

Blender is a registered trademark of Blender Foundation. The Blender logo has been used with permission of Blender Foundation. All other trademarks are the property of their respective owners.

Library of Congress Control Number: 2010922107

ISBN-13: 978-1-4354-5662-4

ISBN-10: 1-4354-5662-9

Cengage Learning PTR

20 Channel Center Street

Boston, MA 02210

USA

Cengage Learning is a leading provider of customized learning solutions with office locations around the globe, including Singapore, the United Kingdom, Australia, Mexico, Brazil, and Japan. Locate your local office at: **international.cengage.com/region**

Cengage Learning products are represented in Canada by Nelson Education, Ltd.

For your lifelong learning solutions, visit **cengageptr.com**

Visit our corporate website at **cengage.com**

Printed in the United States of America
1 2 3 4 5 6 7 15 14 13

To my niece for being such a special little princess.
— Dalai

To my mom and dad, who have done everything for me.
— Mike

ACKNOWLEDGMENTS

The driving force of an open source project is its user community. We want to start by thanking our user community for the overall support they have shown for Blender and specifically to us for this book.

We would also like to thank the Blender Foundation and its chairman, Ton Roosendaal, for facilitating the development of this amazing software, Blender. We are grateful for a remarkable team of developers, who have tirelessly worked to improve the Blender game engine: Benoit Bolsee, Brecht van Lommel, Campbell Barton, Daniel Stokes, Mitchell Stokes, and many others.

From the vast Blender community, we would like to thank three people in particular. Mitchell Stokes, for tech reviewing this book and for helping to ensure that the game engine bugs we reported during this book were squashed in time for this release. Yorik van Havre for helping us by peer reviewing half the book and providing valuable feedback. Stephen Danic for bringing us the embryonic project of this book and entrusting it to us, resulting in what you have in your hands.

Lastly, our deepest appreciation goes to our families and friends who have supported us on this journey.

FOREWORD

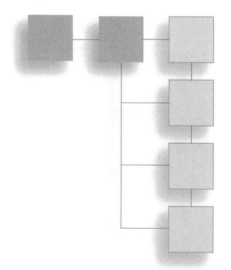

It must have been sometime in 1998 when I first downloaded a copy of a strange and unknown 3D application called Blender. It wasn't a particularly good experience—it didn't look like anything I had ever seen, there was no documentation available at all, and there was no way to get in touch with other users. I got in touch with Ton Roosendaal, and in the years that followed I wrote tutorials, worked for Ton at his company, Not a Number, and founded BlenderNation, which is still the main news site for Blender.

During that time, what has fascinated me most was the Blender community—a worldwide loose band of artists, teachers, software developers, and 3D lovers in general—all of them attracted by the notion of this high-quality, powerful, open-source, free 3D package.

Unlike the communities of many similar but closed applications, the people in this community tend to be very open to each other as well: ask a question, and you will receive an answer. Mention a bug in the software, and someone may fix it for you before the day is over. Ask to become involved, and we will find a place for you. And this generosity is not limited just to the hobbyist users—it extends to the many professionals as well.

And professionals they are, especially during the last few years. Blender is gaining popularity fast in environments like movie studios, special effects companies, advertising agencies, and schools. The community is rife with examples of their outstanding work, which in turn convinces more people of Blender's qualities.

The fact that Blender has a built-in game engine (or rather, a fully embedded interactive environment) is one of its lesser-known features. But like the other aspects of the software, it has seen a huge leap in quality: it now has a very capable scripting environment, GLSL rendering, and node-based materials. It is an extremely useful tool, not just for making games but also for creating interactive simulations of any kind.

Seeing people like Dalai and Mike invest their time in the huge undertaking of writing a book about the Blender Game Engine gives me courage that it will earn the popularity it deserves.

—Bart Veldhuizen

Bart is a long-time Blender evangelist who has actively participated in the education and dissemination of Blender. He was known for his work as a community manager for Blender before it was even open source. More recently, Bart founded BlenderNation and BlenderNetwork, two of the central hubs for Blender users around the world.

ABOUT THE AUTHORS

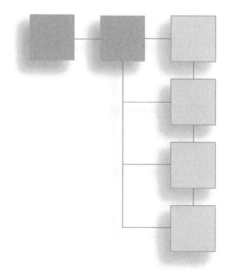

Dalai Felinto, who is currently living in Vancouver, Canada, was born in sunny Rio de Janeiro, Brazil. He has been using Blender since beginning his under-graduate studies in Architecture and Urban Planning in 2003. His participation in the Blender Community includes papers, workshops, and talks presented at events such as BlenderPRO in Brazil, Che Blender in Argentina, Blender Conference in Amsterdam, View Conference in Turin, BlenderVen in Venezuela, and Blender Workshop in Canada. He has contributed patches and code to Blender since version 2.47. Dalai uses Blender and the game engine in his work as a science communicator at the University of British Columbia, Canada. However, his day job doesn't stop him from doing freelance Blender projects around the world. His latest works have been for Italy, England, and the Netherlands.

Dalai's dream career move is to land a job in the movie industry, working at Pixar. Follow his adventures at dalaifelinto.com.

Mike Pan is a CG generalist who started using Blender 10 years ago, before it was open sourced. Mike's interest in Blender includes everything from special effects to compositing, and from real-time graphics to scripting. He has given talks at the Blender Conference in Amsterdam, hosted workshops at the View Conference in Turin and Blender Workshop in Vancouver, and conducted a three-day Blender course in Kerala, India. Mike is currently the lead programmer for a two-year project at Harvard Medical School to develop a biomolecular visualization software using Blender. Before that, he worked at the University of British Columbia with Dalai on a marine ecosystem visualization project.

Mike lives in the always-raining Vancouver, Canada. You can find him at mikepan.com.

Contents

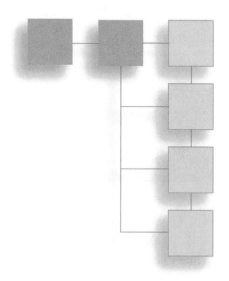

INTRODUCTION

There is an old Chinese proverb that says:

"When you plan for a year, sow rice.

When you plan for a decade, plant trees.

When you plan for a lifetime, educate people."

In this always changing technology-driven world, one can't plan any farther ahead than five years. Perhaps we would have been better off farming rice instead of writing this book. Nevertheless, we felt that is was our duty to pass along the torch for all the knowledge that we have been so gently taught.

This book is the result of two long-time Blender users and friends wanting to share what they know about the game engine: Dalai Felinto, an active developer of Blender, who will offer insights into the game engine from the unique perspective of a coder, and Mike Pan, a long-time Blender artist, who will approach Blender from a more practical perspective.

When both of us started, there wasn't much material out there for teaching the way into the Blender game engine. This is getting better over time, but we still believe there is a gap between the available material and the current needs of the professional market.

We hope this work will be well received and help pave the way to a new era of creative interactive projects with the game engine.

WHAT YOU'LL FIND IN THIS BOOK

Chapter 1, "Game Blender in a Nutshell," starts off by giving you a brief introduction to 3D computer graphics, as well as Blender in general. This serves as a foundation for the rest of the book. If you haven't used Blender before, there should be sufficient information in this chapter to get you familiar with the terminology and interface.

Chapter 2, "First Game," is written in a "do-as-I-say-and-don't-ask questions" style. You will follow a lengthy tutorial to create a small but complete game. This might actually be the most demanding chapter in the book if you haven't used Blender before. If you are discouraged, don't be. It only gets easier from here.

The bulk of the book is organized into chapters focusing on a single component relevant to the game creation process: **Chapter 3, "Logic Bricks," Chapter 4, "Animation," Chapter 5, "Graphics," Chapter 6, "Physics,"** and **Chapter 7, "Python Scripting."** These chapters are made to be as independent as possible, but since the game engine is a system, sometimes it is difficult to talk about certain features in isolation.

Chapter 8, "Workflow and Optimization," talks about polishing and optimization. At this point, you should have a pretty good idea of how the game engine works. This chapter will expand that knowledge by talking about the game creation process as a whole.

Chapter 9, "Publishing and Beyond," deals with the final milestone before your work is seen by everyone: the technical aspects of packaging and releasing a game created with Blender.

Chapter 10, "Case Studies," contains a selection of games that people have made using the Blender game engine. The aim is to give you a glimpse at the possibilities of Blender.

The goal of this book is not just to teach you the game engine, as that would make this a software manual, but also to share our experiences of using Blender by giving you tips, hints, and work-arounds to common problems and questions.

WHO THIS BOOK IS FOR

This book is designed for anyone who has an interest in using the Blender game engine to make games. While having some Blender experience is ideal, we tried really hard to make sure that this book is accessible for everyone. The book works best when you have access to a computer with Blender installed at the same time, because this isn't a book that you can just read from cover to cover on the beach.

As this is a book about the Blender game engine, topics such as advanced modeling and animation techniques are beyond the scope of this book. If you are looking for a book that teaches you how to move your character in a game, welcome! If you are looking for a book that teaches you how to animate your characters so that they walk realistically, numerous other books are better suited to that task. Likewise, Python programming in Blender will also be taught without assuming any prior Python knowledge, but this book is not a replacement for a full-fledged Python manual.

This book is written for Blender version 2.66. Any of the other Blender 2.6x releases should also be compatible with the book, but you can expect minor changes if the version of Blender you use deviates from our target version number.

COMPANION WEBSITE DOWNLOADS

This book comes with numerous tutorial files that will be needed throughout the book. You should download the companion files from www.cengageptr.com/downloads before you start with the book. While the book will inevitably have omissions or mistakes, we will strive to keep the online files accurate and up-to-date.

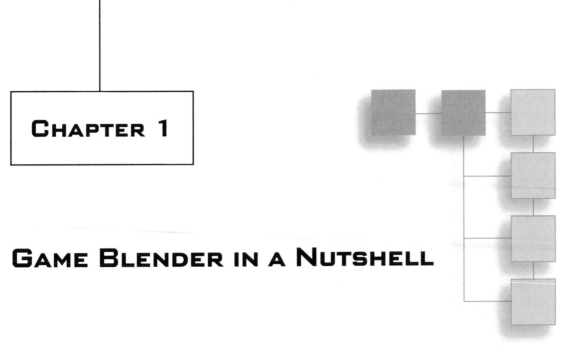

CHAPTER 1

GAME BLENDER IN A NUTSHELL

We can't start a book with a negative comment or a question, can we? So let's try a self-deprecating joke instead. Here is something you don't know about Mike. He has read more Linux books than he cares to admit. Unfortunately, Mike rarely makes it past two chapters. Given that the first two chapters usually contain not much more than a warm introduction and a rich history of the software, this practice has two profound consequences. The first is that Mike can articulate the history of Linux far better than almost anyone. The second is that he still does not know anything about Linux. Granted, the former happens to be far more useful at a party than knowing the difference between "tar cvfz" and "lshw."

In keeping with this tech book tradition, this book won't be any different. In this chapter, you will learn of Blender's history and be introduced to the very basics of this application.

BLENDER HISTORY

Every open source project has its own unique history. Some were started as academic projects and were quickly embraced by a passionate community of users. Other projects originated as commercial ventures that only later found their way into the open source community. The Blender community is made of people who have made their living by using Blender since its early days as a commercial project and also people who adopted Blender after it became an open source software. By understanding the hiccups Blender encountered in its development over the past 20 years, you may get a better idea of what may come next.

Blender Begins

It was the mid-1990s, and the personal computer was taking off faster than anyone had anticipated. With it, there arose the advent of animated graphics and 3D games. It was at this ripe time that Blender came into being. Blender started off as an in-house 3D animation software created by a small Dutch animation studio called Neo-Geo. Perhaps it was because of the lack of a cheap and capable substitute; perhaps it was due to sheer ambition, but for whatever reason, NeoGeo decided to create its own animation software from scratch rather than using what was available. The chief programmer of Blender was Ton Roosendaal, who was responsible for writing a large part of the core Blender functionalities.

For the next few years, Blender remained the internal tool of a very successful animation studio (see Figure 1.1). The software became so good that in 1998, Blender was made available to a wider audience. A new company, Not a Number (NaN), was formed to oversee the development and distribution of Blender. Largely via the Internet, Blender was distributed as two separate versions: a free version with limited functionality and a version that was not free (called Blender Publisher) that had a few additional features. Being the only complete 3D animation and game creation package available for free at a time when computer graphics was still in its relative infancy, Blender started gaining popularity, and many online communities developed that allowed artists to share knowledge and their work.

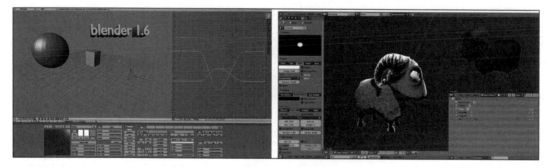

Figure 1.1
Left: Blender 1.6. Right: Blender 2.65.
Source: *Blender Foundation.*

The Dark Nights

Alas, with the collapse of the Internet bubble and some other unfortunate circumstances, Not a Number (NaN) filed for bankruptcy in 2002. Since Blender was the intellectual property of the company at the time, dissolving the company meant an uncertain future for Blender. The Blender community did not want to see their favorite software go down with NaN. So a deal was struck in which NaN would release the source code of Blender to the public for a payment of €100,000. A "Free the Blender" fundraising campaign was started. The online community responded very generously. A few months later, enough money was collected to convince NaN to re-release Blender as an open source software to the newly established Blender Foundation. The foundation was created specifically to manage the now open source Blender. Ton Roosendaal, the original creator of Blender, heads the foundation.

Blender Rises

Located in beautiful Amsterdam, the Blender Foundation now oversees the development, distribution, and marketing of Blender. But because of the open source nature of the software, its development has been driven largely by volunteer contributors from across the world.

The Blender Foundation also created the Blender Institute, an animation and game studio that focuses on movie and game development using Blender. The Institute produced the movies *Elephants Dream*, *Big Buck Bunny*, *Sintel*, *Tears of Steel*, and the game *Yo, Frankie!* See Figure 1.2. These projects serve two main goals: The production process is an opportunity to improve Blender in a real studio environment, and the end result (be it a movie or a game) also serves as an advertisement for the software itself.

Figure 1.2
From top: *Elephants Dream, Big Buck Bunny, Sintel, Tears of Steel,* and *Yo, Frankie!*
© *2014 Blender Foundation.*

In its 10-year lifespan as an open source software, the biggest change came with the release of Blender 2.5, which changed much of how Blender looked and behaved. This refactoring, as it was called, took years of planning and coding. Blender 2.5 marks a significant milestone in the history of Blender. For users coming from the Blender 2.4x series, the entire interface looks radically different: menus items are rearranged, keyboard shortcuts are altered, even the default color scheme has changed from a boring gray to a slightly less boring shade of gray. (That was a joke.) Blender 2.5 is designed to be more intuitive, faster to use, and easier to learn than its predecessor. If you are new to Blender, Welcome! You probably picked the best time to start learning this wonderful application.

Blender uses the Python programming language for scripting. With Python, you can customize the behavior of Blender, extend its functionality, and, more importantly, use Python in the game engine. Knowing how to program is not a requirement for using Blender, but knowing Python will make you a far more capable game-maker.

The year 2012 marked the tenth anniversary of Blender going open source. During these 10 years of open source development, more than 150 people have contributed something to the source code, totaling 50,000 contributions ("commits," in SVN techno-jargon), averaging nearly 30 commits every day over the past year. Needless to say, the program has improved much over the years, and it shows no sign of slowing down. Figure 1.3 shows the Blender development statistics gathered from the official SVN repository including Blender trunk and all its branches.

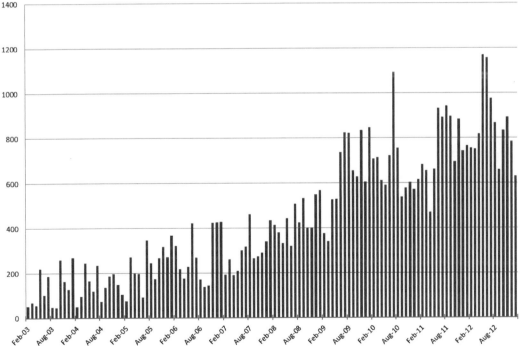

Figure 1.3
Blender SVN statistics.

Of course, software exists to serve the users—that's you. Every time a Blender user creates a piece of artwork, it justifies, even if just a little, the enormous amount of time that went into creating the software. I hope that by picking up this book, you are on your way to creating something amazing to share with the world.

ABOUT BLENDER

Chances are, you already know that Blender is an open source 3D software that is capable of modeling, animation, rendering, compositing, and producing a game all in one package. Even if you are not sure what each of those term means, don't fret!

Let's break down the term "open source 3D animation software."

"Open source" means that Blender's source code is available for anyone to access and modify. The most obvious advantage to open source software is that as an artist, you can use Blender for free, for non-commercial as well as commercial work. As a developer, you are allowed to modify Blender in any way you want to suit your specific needs. But open source does not mean that anyone can make malicious changes to the Blender code without approval. Blender is licensed under the GNU Public License v2 (GPL2). In a nutshell, it means that Blender can be copied, modified, and if re-shared, the changes in the source code have to be available and licensed in an equivalent license.

Caveat

Before you publish a game using Blender, you should understand the limitations of the GPL. This topic is covered in Chapter 9, "Publishing and Beyond."

The term "3D" means three dimensions. The world we live in is 3D because it has height, width, and depth. Compare this with 2D software programs such as Photoshop, GIMP, or Flash—the content-creation process in Blender is done in a 3D space, not on a 2D canvas (see Figure 1.4).

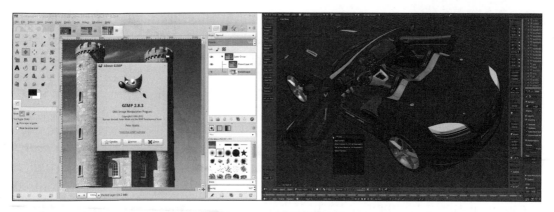

Figure 1.4
2D vs. 3D.
Source: *Blender Foundation. Art © 2014 Mike Pan.*

The term "animation" is perhaps a misleading one. Although we tend to attribute the term "computer animated" to any film that is done by a computer, we should remember that Blender isn't limited to just creating animation. Blender is capable of modeling, rendering, compositing, and making games just as well as it can animate.

The term "software" suggests that Blender is a tool—a tool that allows you to create animations and games. So this book will treat it as such—merely a means to an end. We will help you understand each of Blender's features, so you will know how to use the software to achieve what you want.

However, this is not a book on game design. Topics such as storyline, art direction, and game playability are beyond the scope of this book. Blender is merely a platform that enables you to make art.

ABOUT THE GAME ENGINE

Blender is a multi-faceted tool. This book will focus on one aspect of it: the game-creation process. If you are new to Blender, learning the game engine means you will pick up basic modeling, animation, and other necessary skills along the way. If you already have Blender experience, great! The skills you already know will make transitioning to the game engine much easier.

Compared to some of the commercial game engines available today, the Blender game engine (BGE or GE for short) is relatively simple. Is that a bad thing? Not necessarily. A simple platform like Blender is very easy to learn, and yet it's flexible enough to do a lot.

To give you some idea of what the game engine is capable of, Chapter 10, "Case Studies," is dedicated to projects that were done in the GE. You can skip ahead to get a glimpse of the various applications that people have created using this platform.

FUTURE

If you are one of the early birds who pre-ordered this book (thank you, by the way), you might have noticed the numerous delays this book has gone through. One downside to writing about software is that it's constantly improving, so that it's hard to decide when to stop writing about upcoming features and just publish. At the time of publication, many experimental features had not made their way into the official release. Blender SVN branches with a heavy focus on game-engine improvement include Cucumber, Candy, and the Harmony branches. Test builds for these branches are available online for you to explore. To keep yourself always on top of the latest features of Blender, remember to read the release log pages of the future Blender releases.

Test Builds

Many non-official test builds of Blender are available from graphicall.org. Additionally, you can find official snapshot builds on builder.blender.org.

3D BASICS

If you haven't used any 3D application before, the terms modeling, animation, and rendering might be foreign to you. So before you go off to create the spectacular game that you always wanted to make, let's have a quick refresher on the basics of computer graphics. You don't have to endure the boring section below if you are already know what RGB stands for and the difference between Cartesian and Gaussian.

The knowledge in this section is universal and applies to all other 3D applications. So even if you are coming from a different application, the same concepts drive all of them.

Coordinate System

We live in a three-dimensional world that has width, height, and depth. So to represent anything that resembles real life as a virtual world inside a computer, we need to think and work in three dimensions. The most common system used is called the Cartesian coordinate system, where the three dimensions are represented by X, Y, and Z, laid out as intersecting planes (see Figure 1.5). Where the three axes meet is called the *origin*. You can think of the origin as the center of your digital universe. A single position in space is represented by a set of numbers that corresponds to its position from the origin: thus (2, –4, 8) is a point in space that is 2 units from the origin along the X axis, 4 units from the origin along the –Y axis, and 8 units up in the Z direction.

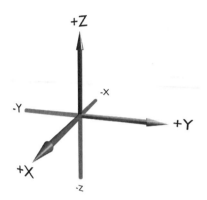

Figure 1.5
The three axes illustrated.
© 2014 Cengage Learning®. All Rights Reserved.

Points, Edges, Triangles, and Meshes

Although we can define a position in space using the XYZ coordinates, a single point (or a "vertex," as it's more commonly known in computer graphics) is not terribly useful; after all, you can't see a dot that is infinitesimally small. But you can join this vertex with another vertex to form a line (also known as an "edge"). An edge by itself still wouldn't be very visible, so you create another vertex and join all three vertices together with lines and fill in the middle. Suddenly, something far more interesting is created—a triangle (also known as a "face")! By linking multiple faces together, you can create any shape, the result of which is called a "mesh" or "model." Figure 1.6 shows how a mesh can be broken down into faces, then edges, and ultimately, vertices.

Figure 1.6
Teapot, cube, face, edge and vertex.
© 2014 Mike Pan.

One Moose, Two Meese

The plural of vertex is vertices.

Why is the triangle so important? Turns out, modern computer graphics use the triangle as the basic building block for almost any shape. A rectangular plane (also known as a *quadrangle,* or more commonly a *quad*) is simply two triangles arranged side by side. A cube is simply six squares put together. Even a sphere is just made of tiny facelets arranged into a ball shape.

In Blender, a mesh can be made from a combination of triangles, quads, or n-gons. N-gons are a relatively new addition to Blender 2.6; they allow you to create faces with more than four edges. The benefit of n-gons is their ability to retain a clean topology while modeling. Without n-gons, certain areas of a model (such as a window on a wall) would require a higher number of triangles or quads to approximate, as shown in Figure 1.7. While n-gons make modeling easier in some cases, Blender still converts them to simple polygons (that is, triangles and quads) when you run the game.

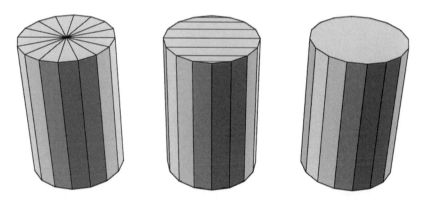

Figure 1.7
The same cylinder cap can be made up of triangles, quads, or an n-gon.
Source: *Blender Foundation.*

The process of creating a mesh by rearranging vertices, edges, and lines is called *modeling.* Blender has many tools that help artists define the geometry they want.

It is worth noting that unlike the real world, polygonal models do not have volumes. They are just a shell made of interconnected faces that take the shape of the object, but the inside of the object is always "hollow."

Another concept that a modeler will likely encounter is surface normals, or "normals" for short. Normal is a property of each face that indicates the direction a polygon is facing. Because normals are used for shading computation of the surface, ideally all the normals for a mesh should be pointed "outward." Wrongly oriented normals can cause the mesh to show up as black or invisible. Fortunately, there is a Make Normals Consistent function in Blender that can usually resolve the issue. Figure 1.8 shows how normals are presented in Blender.

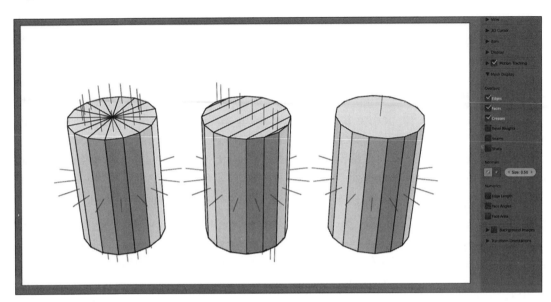

Figure 1.8
Surface normals are displayed as cyan lines protruding from the faces.
Source: *Blender Foundation.*

Beyond Polygons

Technically, there are other approaches to computer graphics that do not rely on triangles or polygons, such as NURBS (Non-uniform rational B-spline) and voxel (short for VOlumetric piXEL). But polygon modeling and rendering is by far the most common, and it is the only supported method in the game engine.

Basic Transform

The three basic transforms that you should be familiar with are:

- **Translation:** The moving of an object in any direction, without rotating it.
- **Scaling:** The resizing of an object around a point.
- **Rotation:** The rotating of an object around a point.

These three are the most common manipulations you will encounter. They are illustrated in Figure 1.9.

Figure 1.9
Translation, scaling, and rotation.
© 2014 Cengage Learning®. All Rights Reserved. Art © 2014 Mike Pan.

Materials and Textures

Using polygons, you can define the shape of a mesh. To alter the color and appearance of it, you need to apply materials to the object. Material controls the color, shininess, bumpiness, and even transparency of the object. These variables ultimately all serve to add details to the object.

Often, changing the color is not enough to make a surface look realistic. This is where textures come in. Texturing is a common technique used to add color and detail to a mesh by wrapping the mesh with an image, like a decal. Imagine a toy globe: if you carefully peel off the paper map that is glued onto the plastic ball and lay it out flat on the table, that map would be the texture, and the plastic ball would be the mesh. The projection of the 2D image onto a 3D mesh is called *texture mapping*. Texture mapping can be an automatic process, using one of the predefined projections, or a manual process, which uses a UV layout to map the 2D image onto the 3D mesh. Figure 1.10 illustrates how an image is mapped onto a model.

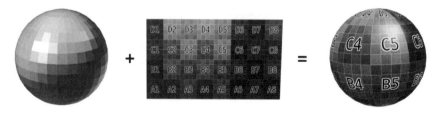

Figure 1.10
Meshes with texture applied.
© 2014 Cengage Learning®. All Rights Reserved.

Texturing can be thought of as an extension of material.

Traditionally, a texture changes the color of a surface. But that's not all it can do: textures can also be used to alter other properties of the surface such as its transparency, reflectivity, and even bumpiness to create the illusion of a much more detailed surface. Figure 1.11 shows the different kinds of textures that represent a brick surface.

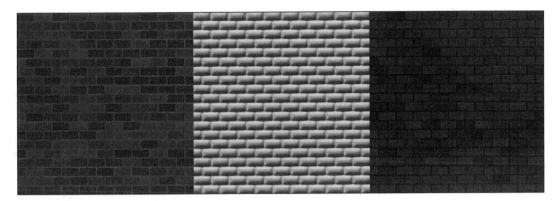

Figure 1.11
From left to right: diffuse map, normal map, and specular map.
© 2014 Cengage Learning®. All Rights Reserved.

A diffuse map controls the base color of the surface. A normal map controls the surface normal of an object, creating a bumpy effect by changing the way the light is reflected off the object. A specular map controls the specular reflection of an object, making it look shiny in certain places and dull in others. A texture map can also have transparent pixels, rendering part of the object transparent.

Generally, textures are image files. But there are also other ways to texture a surface, such as using a procedural texture. Procedural texture differs from an image in that it's generated by an algorithm in real time, rather than from a pre-made image file. The Blender game engine does not support procedural textures yet.

Lights

Everything you see is the result of light hitting your eyes—without light, the world would be pitch black. Likewise, light is just as important in a virtual world. With light comes shadow as well. Shadow might not be something that you think about every day, but the interplay of shadow and light makes a huge difference in how the scene is presented.

In most 3D applications, there are several different types of light available to the artist; each type has its advantages and disadvantages. For example, a Spot lamp approximates a lamp with a conical influence; a Sun lamp approximates a light source from infinitely far away. Lamps in Blender are treated like regular objects: they can be positioned and rotated just like any other object. Figure 1.12 shows how different lamps look in Blender.

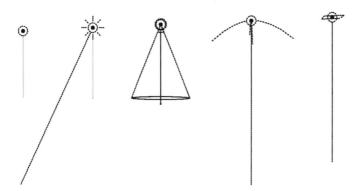

Figure 1.12
From left: Lamp, Sun, Spot lamp, Hemi lamp, and Area lamp.
Source: *Blender Foundation.*

Think of lighting as more than something that makes your scene visible. Good lighting can enhance the purpose of the scene by highlighting details while hiding irrelevant areas in shadow. Skillful placement of lighting also adds drama and realism to the scene, making an otherwise boring scene look visually exciting.

Camera

When you are creating a 3D scene, you are looking at the virtual world from an omniscient view. In this mode, you can view and edit the world from any angle—just like a movie director walking around a set in order to adjust things. Once the game starts, the player must view the game through a predetermined camera. Note that a predetermined camera does not mean the camera is fixed; almost all games have a camera that reacts to a player's input. In an action game, the camera tends to follow the character from behind; in a strategy game, the camera might be hovering high above, looking down; in a platformer, the camera is usually looking at the scene from the side.

A camera is also treated as a regular object in Blender, so you can manipulate its location and orientation just as you can with any other object. (You can manipulate a camera's size, too, but it is meaningless to do so, since the virtual camera's size does not change the image it produces.) Figure 1.13 shows a camera object as seen from different views.

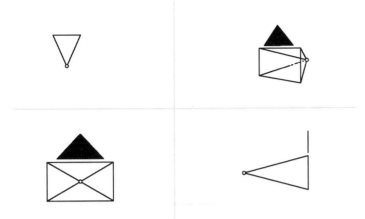

Figure 1.13
Camera objects.
Source: *Blender Foundation.*

Drawing and Composition for Visual Storytellers

Speaking of lights and cameras, this is the part where we point out the wonderful book by Marcos Mateu-Mestre called *Framed Ink*. The book uses tons of beautiful drawings to illustrate the many key principles in visual storytelling.

Animation

In this context, *animation* refers to the technique of making things change over time. For example, animation can involve moving an object, deforming it, or changing its color. To set up an animation, you create "keyframes," which are snapshots in time that store specific values pertaining to the animation. The software can then automatically interpolate in between those values to create a smooth transition. Figure 1.14 shows keyframing using Blender's Dope Sheet Editor. The Dope Sheet allows you to see the various properties that change during an animation: the horizontal axis represents time; the vertical axis shows the various properties, such as location or rotation that are keyframed.

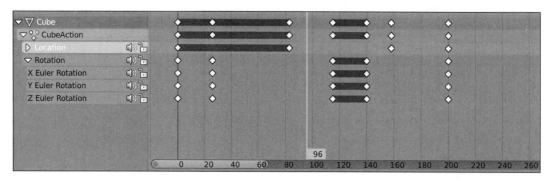

Figure 1.14
Dope Sheet Editor: each diamond shape is a keyframe.
Source: *Blender Foundation.*

The easiest way to animate is to alter the location, rotation, and scaling of an object over time. For example, by altering these variables, you can realistically animate the movement of a bouncing ball, as shown in Figure 1.15.

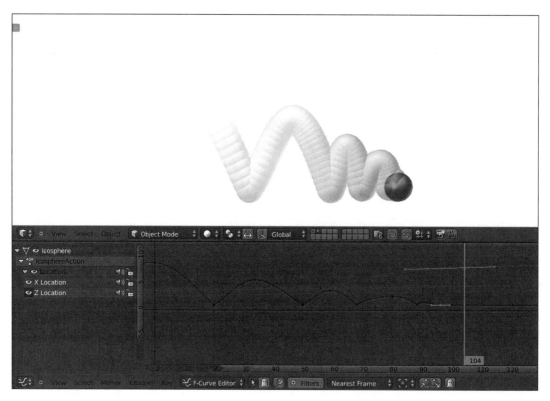

Figure 1.15
LocRotScale animation.
Source: *Blender Foundation.*

To animate something more complicated, such as a human, it's not enough to just move, rotate, and scale the object as a whole. This is where armatures come in. Armatures are skeletons that can be "inserted" into a model to control the model's deformation. Using this system, you can create complex yet organic-looking animations like Figure 1.16.

Figure 1.16
Armature animation.
Source: *Blender Foundation.*

A third way to animate is using shape keys. Shape keys are snapshots of the mesh in different shapes. They are often used to animate nuanced changes that cannot be otherwise easily animated with armatures, as shown in Figure 1.17. Using shape keys to animate is covered in Chapter 4.

Figure 1.17
Shape keys animation.
Source: *Blender Foundation.*

Finally, keep in mind that making objects move doesn't always have to be a manual process. You can also make objects move by using the physics engine, as shown in Figure 1.18 (see Chapter 6).

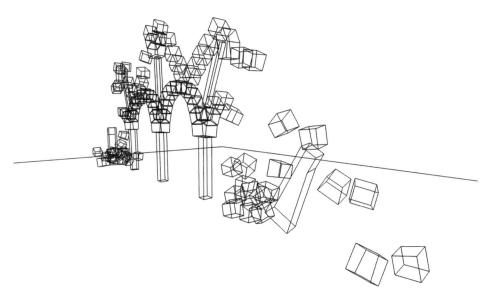

Figure 1.18
Procedural physics-based motion.
Source: *Blender Foundation.*

Game

So far, we have talked about 3D at length. But how does the game engine fit into it? Well, a game engine simply takes the existing 3D assets and attaches a "brain" to them so the objects know how to respond to events. The "brain" can be in the form of logic bricks (which can perform different actions depending on the user input), scripts (which can extend the functionality of logic bricks), or other physical properties of an object (such as rigid body settings to make an object tumble and fall realistically). See Figure 1.19.

3D Object   +   Game Logic   =   Game

Figure 1.19
Game = Object + Logic.
© 2014 Cengage Learning®. All Rights Reserved. © 2014 Mike Pan and Dalai Felinto.

A game engine is made up of many distinct components:

- **Rendering Engine:** Turns the 3D scene you've built (including models, lights, and camera) into an image to be displayed onscreen.
- **Physics:** Handles collisions and physical simulations of objects.
- **Logic/Scripting:** The brain behind a game—it reacts to the user input, makes decisions, and keeps track of what's going on in the game.
- **Sound:** Produces the audio events.

The above list is not meant to be exhaustive, but it should give you an idea of what a game engine does. The Blender game engine gives you a lot of control over each of these components, which you will learn one by one in later chapters.

Quality vs. Performance

Making a video game is a constant balancing act between quality and performance. As artists, you want to make the virtual world as rich and detailed as possible; on the other hand, you need to make sure the game can run smoothly for people who might not have top-of-the-line computers. Throughout the process of game-making, you will run into cases where you have to make a decision whether to prioritize the visual quality or the performance of the game. You will also learn tricks to achieve high-quality visual without compromising the performance, as well as how to optimize the game by identifying what is slowing it down.

QUICKSTART

This concludes the crash course on 3D graphics. It's finally time to dive into Blender! From now on, you may be better off reading the book with the computer at your side. In this section, we will give you a short tour of Blender, just enough to get you familiar with the software.

Installation

Blender runs on Windows, Mac OS X, and Linux, and is available in both 32-bit and 64-bit. You can find the Blender installer for your operating system from www. blender.org. The complete Blender download size is less than 70MB.

When I'm Sixty-Four

The 64-bit version of Blender is generally faster than the 32-bit version and can let you use more than 4GB of memory. If you are using a 64-bit OS, there is really no reason to get the 32-bit binary.

Go ahead and install Blender. Start the application once it's installed.

Technically, Blender does not need to be installed before it can be used. The installer is available for convenience only. Blender will run from any location. You can even copy it to a USB storage device and carry it with you, so you'll never be apart from your favorite program. Although, by default, Blender saves some user settings to the user directory.

Even though you need Blender to develop the game, Blender games can be packaged as stand-alone applications, so that others playing it don't need to install anything. See Chapter 9, "Publishing and Beyond," for more details.

System Requirements

Blender has no explicit system requirement. The performance of the software is dependent on the complexity of the project. Needless to say, the faster your computer is, the better Blender will run.

Blender uses hardware video acceleration to display the main interface and the 3D Viewport. As a result, running Blender on an older "onboard" or "integrated" video card might yield suboptimal performance. An AMD Radeon or NVIDIA GeForce video card is recommended. Older video cards also might not support all the advanced OpenGL 2.0 features that Blender uses. This might result in reduced graphic capabilities when it comes to fancy shader-based effects.

Interface

If you are starting Blender for the first time, don't be intimidated by its interface. The interface is probably unlike most applications you have used, but it's very logically grouped once you learn them. Furthermore, since this book is focused on the game engine, you will only have to learn a small subset of all the features available to you.

On the splash screen, there is an option to change the user interaction preset to Maya. This will alter the keyboard shortcuts and mouse behavior to match that of Maya. Although you are welcome to do that if you are a Maya user, in this book, we will assume you are using the default Blender preset.

Once the initial splash screen disappears, you are presented with an empty workspace similar to the one shown in Figure 1.20.

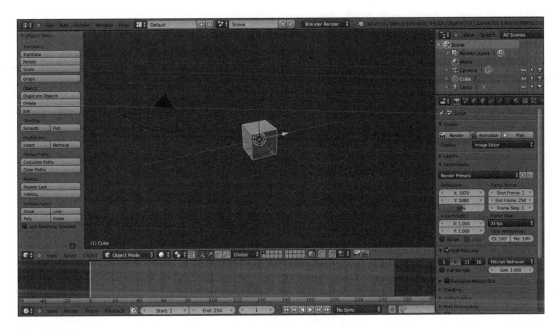

Figure 1.20
Blender default workspace.
Source: *Blender Foundation.*

The Blender window is divided into Editors. Each Editor region can be resized, moved, and changed to display a specific set of content. For now, let's focus on the default setup as shown in Figure 1.20.

Main Menu

At the top of the screen is the main menu, which offers basic functionalities such as Open, Save, and Help. Furthermore, the main menu controls the view for the rest of the Blender window. The Render Engine option in the middle of the menu controls how the interface is configured. By default, Blender Render is selected. In this mode, the interface is configured for doing 3D modeling, animation, and rendering. But let's switch it to the Blender Game mode. Click the drop-down menu and select Blender

Game from the list. This setting will unlock certain features that are not visible when Blender is in the Blender Render mode, and, to reduce clutter, it also hides features that are not available in the Blender game engine.

Game Engine First Setup

Always make sure that the Blender game engine is selected in the main menu when you are working on a game project (see Figure 1.21).

Figure 1.21
Selecting the game engine.
Source: *Blender Foundation.*

3D Viewport

Occupying the majority of the screen is a 3D Viewport. Here you can see the 3D world you created and test the game. For now, feel free to explore the 3D Viewport by holding down your middle mouse button over the 3D Viewport and dragging the mouse; the view should rotate with the mouse movement. (Mac users can do the rotate gesture on the Trackpad or the Magic Mouse.) The default scene contains three objects: a cube, a camera, and a light. To select one of the objects, right-click on it. The selected object is highlighted in yellow.

Basic Navigation Controls

Press and hold the middle mouse button to rotate the 3D view. Scroll the mouse wheel to zoom in the 3D view. Right-click to select a 3D object. Selected objects are highlighted in yellow.

Another common setup for the 3D Viewport is to split the view into four quadrants: top view, side view, front view, and a perspective view. You can turn on Quad view by pressing Ctrl+Alt+Q with the mouse over the 3D Viewport (see Figure 1.22). Press the same key combination to go back to the single view.

Figure 1.22
Quad view.
Source: *Blender Foundation. Art © 2014 Mike Pan.*

To quickly snap to one of the predetermined views (side, top, front, and so on), the number pad is the way to go. Figure 1.23 shows the keyboard layout on the number pad.

Num Lock	/	*	- Zoom Out
7 Top	8 View Up	9	+ Zoom In
4 View Lft	5 Perspective	6 View Rgt	
1 Front	2 View Dwn	3 Side	Enter
0 Camera	. Centre		

Figure 1.23
Number pad keyboard layout.
© 2014 Cengage Learning®. All Rights Reserved.

Outliner

Back to Figure 1.20. To the right of the screen are two editors. The top portion is the Outliner, which contains a listing of all the data in the current Blender file. For a large project, the Outliner is an indispensable tool for organizing your scene. For now, you can safely ignore it.

Properties Editor

Under the Outliner on the right, you have the Properties Editor. Here you can access global settings for the file, as well as settings for individual objects. This is one of the most frequently used panels in Blender, after the 3D view perhaps. The Properties Editor is context sensitive, which means it will automatically display different content, depending on the object that is active. Take a closer look at the row of icons at the top of the Properties Editor, as shown in Figure 1.24. These tabs organize the properties into groups, with the more general settings on the left-most tab, and the more specific settings on the right.

Figure 1.24
Properties Editor icons.
Source: *Blender Foundation.*

Timeline

At the very bottom of the screen is a timeline window, which will be useful when you start making animations.

Workspace Customization

The default screen, as described previously, is set up for general use. At some point, it becomes necessary to change the screen layout to accomplish other tasks. To select a different layout, use the Screens layout drop-down menu from the main menu.

Apart from the predefined screen layouts, you can customize the screen layout however you like. You can either split an existing editor into two or merge two adjacent editors together.

Editor, Region, and Area

A region within the Blender windows is called an *editor*. An editor displays a specific set of content and tools. Common areas include: 3D View, Properties Editor, UV/Image Editor, and Logic Brick Editor.

Figure 1.25 shows one area split into two. You can do it by dragging the top corner of the area to the right or bottom

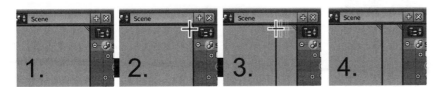

Figure 1.25
Area splitting.
Source: *Blender Foundation.*

To merge two adjacent areas into one is exactly the same as shown in Figure 1.25, but it is done in reverse order. Optionally, you can click with the right mouse button in the edge of the area you want to split or join, and select the option in the Area Options pop-up menu.

Each editor contains a header, which is found on either the bottom or the top of that editor. They contain tools and menu options relevant to the editor. Figure 1.26 shows some headers for the different editors.

Figure 1.26
Headers (Action Editor, 3D Editor, Image Editor, Properties Editor).
Source: *Blender Foundation.*

Not only can you change the size and layout of the editor, but the type of editor can also be changed. As you can see in Figure 1.27, the left-most icon in the header can be used to change the editor type.

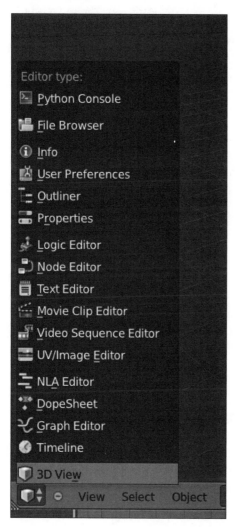

Figure 1.27
Editor selection.
Source: *Blender Foundation.*

Almost everything a studio needs to create the game is integrated into a single interface: you can create the game, test the game, and play the game all from the same
program. This means that, as an artist, you can create a game in the shortest time
possible, without having to worry about importing and exporting files between different applications. As a programmer, you won't have to switch back and forth between
different software just to test your code. Figure 1.28 shows some screenshots of different editors that you will be using throughout the book.

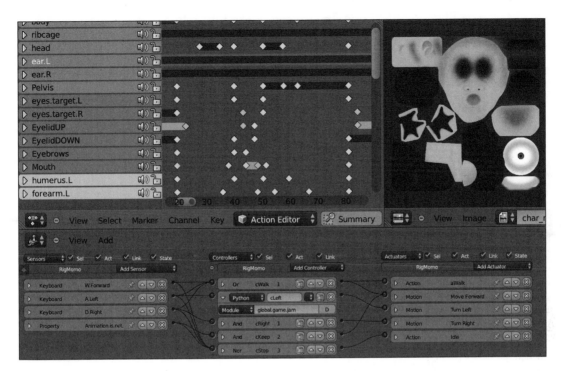

Figure 1.28
Dope Sheet, Image Editor, and Logic Brick Editor.
Source: *Blender Foundation.*

User Preferences

To further customize Blender, you can use the User Preferences panel to adjust Blender's settings. User Preferences can be accessed from the File main menu.

More on the 3D View

The 3D view is where you will spend most of your time, so let's take a look at it in a bit more detail. You've already learned a few ways to navigate around the scene earlier in this chapter, using both the mouse and the keyboard.

Viewport Shading Modes

Let's look at the four different Viewport Shading modes available in the 3D view. As shown in Figure 1.29, they are used to change the way the scene is displayed onscreen. The four modes are:

- **Bounding Box:** Represents all objects as a wireframe boundary. Useful for when the scene gets really complex.

- **Wireframe:** Draws all objects as wireframe, which allows you to see through objects.

- **Solid:** Draws all objects as solid faces, which is commonly used when modeling.

- **Textured:** Draws all objects as solid faces, also with texture and accurate lighting. This is useful for previewing the scene.

Figure 1.29
The four Viewport Shading modes.
Source: *Blender Foundation.*

The two most commonly used Shading modes are Wireframe and Solid. Therefore, they are assigned to a keyboard toggle for easy access. Press the Z key to toggle between Wireframe and Solid View modes. Additionally, you can Press Alt+Z to toggle between Solid and Textured view modes.

Standing Out

Individual objects can also override the Viewport Shading mode via a setting under the Properties Editor → Object → Display → Type.

Editing Modes

To the left of the Shading mode selector is the Editing Mode selector.

- **Object Mode:** The default mode, which allows the manipulation of objects in the scene as a whole. From this mode, you can select any of the objects in the scene, and move, rotate, and scale them. In fact, almost everything apart from modeling can be done from Object mode.

- **Edit Mode:** This mode can be seen as the counterpart to Object mode. It allows you to edit the underlying geometry of the object. If you are modeling, you'll probably want to be in Edit mode. For this reason, Edit mode is not available when a non-editable object is selected (for example, a camera or lamp).

To switch between Object mode and Edit mode, press the tab key.

In addition to the two editing modes we just discussed, there are a few other modes that are less commonly used.

- **Sculpt Mode:** Only available for Mesh objects. Allows modifications to the mesh as if it were clay.
- **Vertex**, **Weight,** and **Texture Paint Mode:** Only available for Mesh objects. These modes allow the assignment of color or weight to the mesh.
- **Pose Mode:** Is used to animate bones in an armature.

Edit mode and Object mode are by far the most commonly used editing modes, so we will refrain from diving too deeply into the other modes for now.

Keyboard and Mouse

The joke is that to move an object in Blender, you have to press the G key, which stands for "movinG." This gag stems from the fact that to a beginner, many of the shortcuts in Blender seem counterintuitive. However, there is a very good reason why "G" is preferred over "M." In this case, the G key can be easily accessed on the keyboard by the left hand while the right hand is on the mouse. Also, officially, G stands for Grab.

Think Different

By default, the Mac keyboard uses Command instead of Control as the default modifier key. So whenever you see Ctrl+something in this book, mentally map it to Cmd if you are using a Jobsian product.

Additionally, Blender has good support for multi-touch gestures on OS X. You can pinch to zoom, rotate to orbit around, and pan around.

Let's start with some shortcuts that work the way you would expect:

- **Ctrl + S:** Save
- **Ctrl + O:** Open
- **Ctrl + N:** New File
- **Ctrl + Z:** Undo

- **Ctrl + Shift + Z:** Redo
- **Ctrl + Q:** Close Application

The above shortcuts work anywhere within Blender: they are effectively global. Unfortunately, the familiarity ends here.

To manipulate an object in the 3D view, generally you have to select it at first:

- **Right-click:** Select object
- **Shift + Right-click:** Extend selection to multiple objects
- **A:** Select all

All of the actions above are "reversible." If something is already selected, right-clicking on it will deselect it. If all the objects are already selected, pressing A will deselect all.

Once an object is selected, you can start manipulating it. The keyboard shortcuts below correspond to the three most basic transforms:

- **G:** Start Grabbing
- **S:** Start Scaling
- **R:** Start Rotating
- **Move mouse:** Carry out transform action
- **Left-click:** Confirm transformation
- **Enter:** Confirm transformation

Pressing one of the keys will start the transformation, and then you can move your mouse to control the degree of the effect. To finalize the transformation, left-click the mouse or press Enter.

Search

The final tip that you will learn is the search functionality in Blender. If you are unable to recall how to invoke a certain operation, whether through a button or a keyboard shortcut, a quick way to find it is by using the search functionality. Key in a few letters of what you are looking for, and the result should appear as shown in Figure 1.30.

Tapping on the spacebar from anywhere will bring out a search box that contains a list of actions.

Figure 1.30
The search box.
Source: *Blender Foundation.*

A word of caution, though: the current implementation of the search is not very context-aware, so sometimes operations that are not permitted in the active context might show up.

BLENDER PHILOSOPHY

Blender is designed with certain philosophies in mind. Understanding these will allow you to use Blender the way it is intended, which allows you to navigate around Blender faster and work more efficiently.

Let the brainwashing begin!

Interface

Because Blender was originally created as an in-house software, its interface is designed to maximize speed and efficiency for users who have mastered it. Since Blender 2.5, a lot of work has been done to make the interface more user-friendly. That said, Blender is probably unlike any other program you've used before, including other kinds of 3D software. Luckily, the Blender interface is very consistent within the application. This means that once you learn to do something, you'll be able to use it in another part of the program.

Keyboard

Because of the large number of commands Blender is capable of performing, invoking a function through a quick tap on the keyboard is generally faster than using the mouse to find the menu entry. As you follow through the rest of this section, pay special attention to the shortcut keys that are used, because Blender is designed to let you work fast once you learn the shortcuts.

Blender's keyboard shortcuts are optimized for a full-sized English QWERTY keyboard. The number pad (which, unfortunately, is not present on many laptops) is used to quickly navigate around the 3D scene. Laptop users usually have to press extra keys on their keyboard (such as the Fn key or a toggle) in order to simulate a number pad key. Alternatively, Blender also has an add-on called "3D Navigation" that provides an easier way to navigate around the world for people without a number pad.

To enable the 3D navigation plug-in to help you navigate around the 3D Viewport quickly, go to File → User Preferences → Add-Ons, and turn on 3D Views: 3D Navigation. Then you can switch views quickly from the 3D view's Toolshelf, as shown in Figure 1.31.

Figure 1.31
3D Navigator.
Source: *Blender Foundation.*

Mouse

Blender is designed for a three-button mouse: a mouse with two buttons and a scroll wheel. Although there is an option to emulate the middle-mouse button (when you click on the scroll wheel), this book will assume that you are working with a three-button mouse for convenience.

How to Emulate a Three-Button Mouse

If you don't have a three-button mouse, you can use the Alt+Left mouse button combination to emulate the middle mouse button. To enable this feature, go to File → User Preferences → Input and turn on Emulate 3 Button Mouse.

Context

In Blender, the actions you can perform at any given time are limited to the current state of Blender, also known collectively as the "context." For example, certain operations can only be invoked when you have an object selected; the Property Editors change, depending on which object is selected; the effect of the keyboard shortcuts even changes, depending on where your mouse is positioned. This context-sensitive nature lets you focus on the task at hand by only providing you with options that make sense at the time. This is Blender's way of preventing the interface from getting too cluttered.

The "context" usually refers to one or a combination of the following:

- **Active rendering engine:** Blender Render, Blender Games, and Cycles Render are the default three.

- **Active editor:** The active editor is defined as the window subdivision that the mouse cursor is hovering over. Shortcut keys often have different effects, depending on which editor the mouse is over.

- **Active object:** The active object is defined as the object that is most recently selected.

- **Selected object:** All the objects that have been selected (highlighted). Keep in mind that there can be more than one selected object, but only one active object.

- **Editing mode:** Blender has six different modes of editing. Two of the most commonly used are the Edit mode and the Object mode. In Object mode, you can manipulate objects as a whole. In Edit mode, you can change the shape of a mesh. In each mode, there is a unique set of tools and options at your disposal. You will learn about the other four modes (Sculpt, Vertex Paint, Texture Paint, Weight Paint) in later chapters.

Datablocks

Often, a single Blender file contains hundreds of objects, each with different colors, textures, and animations. How is all this organized?

Blender uses "datablocks" to represent content stored within a Blender file. Each datablock represents a collection of data or settings. Some common datablock types you will encounter are Object datablock, Mesh datablock, Material datablock, Texture datablock, and Image datablock.

In order to reduce the apparent complexity of the program, Blender further organizes datablocks into hierarchies. At the top level are scenes, which can have a number of worlds, each of which can have any number of objects (objects can be a mesh, a lamp, a camera, and so on). If the object is a mesh, then a Mesh datablock is attached to it. If the object is a lamp, then a Lamp datablock is attached to the object.

An example of a datablock hierarchy chain is shown in Figure 1.32: Scene → Object → Mesh → Material → Texture → Image

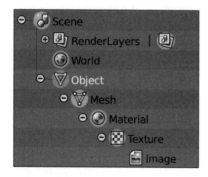

Figure 1.32
Datablock hierarchy.
Source: *Blender Foundation.*

Throughout the Blender interface, you will run into many datablock managers. They all look like Figure 1.33.

Figure 1.33
Datablock manager.
Source: *Blender Foundation.*

Because datablocks can be shared, copied, and reused, large scenes can be managed efficiently through the use of shared datablocks. Figure 1.33 shows a datablock that has been shared by three "users," as denoted by the number next to its name.

Parenting and Grouping

Grouping and parenting both allow you to introduce some form of order to the scene by setting up arbitrary relationships between different objects. But grouping and parenting work in different ways.

Parenting is used to establish links between multiple objects so that basic transformations like location, rotation, and scaling are propagated from the parent to its children. This way, any transformation applied to the parent is automatically applied to all the children. Parenting is a useful way to "glue" different objects together so they behave as one.

To parent one object to another, simply select the object you want to be the child first. If more than one object is to be a child, select all of them now. Lastly, select the object that you want to be the parent. Then press Ctrl+P to set parent.

An object can only have one parent object, but a parent object can have many children.

Grouping can also be used to logically link objects in the scene together without any transformation constraints to the objects. Unlike parenting, grouping does not have a parent-child relationship; objects are simply members of a group.

Select all the objects you want to group. Then press Ctrl+G to add them to a new group. You can also manage group membership from the Object Properties Editor.

Grouping, by itself, is not very useful. But groups can be quickly "instanced" as group instances. Group Instance is a very useful way to create multiple copies of objects without making actual copies of the objects. Grouping will also come in handy for asset management, which will be discussed in the next chapter.

A single object can be in multiple groups. A group can have multiple objects.

Backward Compatibility

Blender is designed so that older files can be opened with newer versions of Blender. But due to the rate that Blender matures, some unexpected behaviors are to be expected when you least expect them.

Due to the Blender Python API change in Blender 2.5, old scripts written for 2.4x will be broken in later versions of Blender. But by the time you are reading this, there should be enough new content available for you to find.

ONWARD

This concludes the crash course on Blender and the game engine. By now, you should have a cursory understanding of the function of a game engine and be familiar with the Blender interface. In the next chapter, you will get your hands dirty and build a simple game by following the step-by-step tutorial.

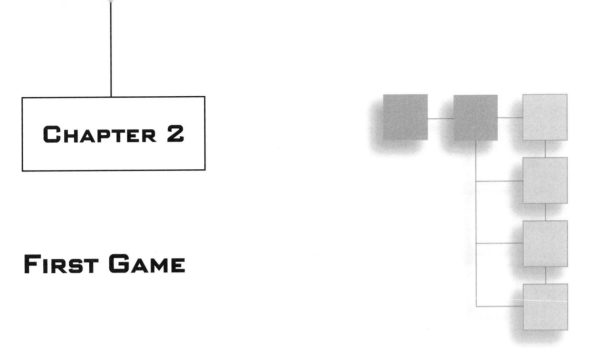

CHAPTER 2

FIRST GAME

In this section, we are going through the steps of making a simple game, from start to finish. The first goal is to keep your Blender knowledge up-to-date. Second, this is a chance to present an overview of the game's workflow. From this point on, you should be able to read the chapters in this book in any given order, according to your needs.

Welcome to *Feed The Shark,* the game.

GAME IDEA

The shark population has been depleted worldwide. Studies suggest that overfishing and the illegal marketing of shark fins has impacted not only the top predator of the oceans but also brought imbalance to the whole ecosystem.

It is payback time!

Although we're tempted, we can't really make a gory game here. Because of the risk of losing our teenage audience, we need to make some compromises in developing the story line:

Struggling for survival, sharks need to eat as much as possible to escape the risks of extinction.

Sure, who doesn't like sashimi? Simply put, we will need a swimming shark that has to eat fish and is controlled by the player (as shown in Figure 2.1). Every time the shark eats a fish, it gets bigger and bigger.

To make it more like a game, we will wrap it with a score system and an omnipresent ticking, counting-down clock.

Figure 2.1
Feed The Shark, the game.
© 2014 Dalai Felinto.

GAME ELEMENTS

This minimalistic game will consist of:

1. Animated shark controlled by keyboard

2. Underwater environment

3. Schools of fish controlled by AI

4. Interface

We are not covering all the topics extensively. We will, however, walk you through some of the basics of modeling, animating, and other Blender-specific tasks.

If you are already familiar with Blender as an asset-making tool, you might skip some of those steps. On the DVD, you will find incremental snapshots for all the individual parts.

FILE ORGANIZATION, DATABLOCKS, AND LINKING

Starting with the right fin...

It's important to plan ahead and to know how to organize the files we will be creating. For this project, we will try to make the files as self-contained as possible. You should be able to open the shark file and test the swimming animation—without having to worry about the other fish, the terrain, or the interface.

Having independent files allows for a big team to work together on separated assets. It also helps for individual versioning control. It may seem like overkill for a small project, but it's a good practice that scales up pretty well.

Version Control

> Version control is any system you can find to organize the version of your files. If you keep daily backups of your production files in a separate folder, then you are doing version control. In practical terms, there are more modern ways to accomplish this, without having to handle file renaming and manually filled log files—namely SVN, Git, and Bazaar.
>
> Blender files are not optimal when it comes to merging. (Given that they are binaries, you either roll back a file entirely or do it manually.) Thus, working with individual components can help you overcome that.

Datablocks

In the previous chapter, we introduced you to the concept of datablocks. Linked datablocks (for example, a Texture datablock used by a Material datablock) don't even need to be part of the same file. In our project, we will use it to a certain extent. What are the criteria here?

Taking material and textures as an example, you need to consider how you will be using them in your workflow. Those two are often edited together: You adjust the influence of a texture channel in your material, tweak the material diffuse color, and get back to the texture. In this case, it's best to have both datablocks in the same file.

Now let's look at armatures and actions. Only after you are done with your rigging, do you start the animation. Even if you change your armature after you start the animation, you may want to keep them separated. If you need to go back to an earlier version of the armature but want to keep the new animations, separated files are the way to go. That said, we could keep the actions separated from the main armature files. We could, but for the sake of simplicity, we will not.

But how do we keep them linked while in separate files?

Linking and Appending

There are four ways of adding new objects and other datablocks to your Blender file. You can build them from scratch; you can import them from a different format (Collada or FBX, for example); and you can link or append them from another Blender file.

Linking and appending are quite similar. They both allow you to import part of a Blender file into your current file. Here, the concept of data block should become

even clearer. In Figure 2.2, you can see the link/append dialog. Whether you are linking or appending, it will depend on the link option in the load window.

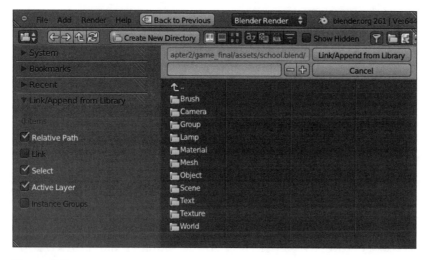

Figure 2.2
Blender file structure.
Source: *Blender Foundation.*

The difference between linking and appending is what happens after you bring the
new data into your file. If you append a file—let's call it *library*—the new elements
will keep no reference to the original library file. You can literally delete the library
file, and it will not result in any changes in your work file. That also means that any
change you do in your library file will not be synced back into your working file.

If you want to keep the files in sync (and you do most of the time), you then need to
set "Link" while importing the library file. By doing this, you will not be able to edit
the file in your working Blender file. Instead, you need to go back to your library file,
change it, save it, and then open the working file again.

As you will see from our file structure (explained next), we will be using mostly linking between the files.

You don't simply dump the whole Blender file inside yours. Instead, you can navigate inside the file structure and bring in only an object, or a group, material, or
even an entire scene. We will be linking the shark, interface, environment, and
other fish in the main file. We could also do nested linking, by having one of the
library files link another file inside it (for example, the actions could be linked in
the armature files).

How to Use the Chapter Files

On the Book files, you can find the complete game/exercise in the folder \Book \Chapter02\game_final\.

For simplicity's sake, we will use Blender relative path syntax to refer to the files inside this folder. In this case // refers to the base folder and //interface/score.blend stands for \Book\Chapter02\game_final\interface\score.blend.

To play the game inside Blender, open the file game.blend. This file is only a part of the game and depends on the external files that are organized as:

- **//game.blend**
- **//assets/shark.blend**
- **//assets/school.blend**
- **//level/seabed.blend**
- **//interface/score.blend**

To follow the progress of the instruction steps, we have other folders. Copy the whole folder onto your computer to work from there. These are the folders we will be using:

- **\Book\Chapter02\game_my**—The semi-empty folder structure to be filled as you advance in the chapter.
- **\Book\Chapter02\game_progress**—The same folder structure but filled with files of different snapshots. Every file is named after the original name plus a progress number—for example, game.2.blend //assets/shark.8.blend. To use them, you need to rename the file to the original name and copy to the right folder in "game_my" folder.
- **\Book\Chapter02\game_final**—The final as of the end of this exercise; use for reference.
- **\Book\Chapter02\references**—Files to support the making of the game.

For the rest of the chapter, we will refer to the files from your //game_my/ top folder.

MODELING

Open Blender and save the default file as //assets/shark.blend.

We will model the outline of the shark based on reference images. To set up your working environment, follow these steps:

1. Split your 3D view into four views (Ctrl+Alt+Q).

2. Open the 3D view Properties panel (N)—remember that the mouse needs to be over the 3D view in order to call the commands for it.

3. In the bottom of the panel, you will see the Background Images option. Turn it on.

4. Add three images for the three Axis/Views: Top, Front, and Right. They can be found in the reference folder named shark-top.png, shark-front.png, and shark-right.png.

5. Change their size to 1.50.

The current file, as seen in Figure 2.3, can be found under the name //assets/shark.1. blend.

Figure 2.3
Background images setup.
Source: *Blender Foundation.*

To start the model, remove the initial cube (X) and add a cylinder into the scene (Shift+A → Mesh → Cylinder). New objects are always added to the 3D cursor location, so make sure that it is in the center of the scene [0,0,0] (Shift+S → Cursor to Center). The default cylinder doesn't match the dimensions or the orientation of the reference model. The quick way to change that is to access the redo last menu (F6) and tweak the cylinder parameters. As you can see in Figure 2.4, we used 12 Vertices, Radius of 0.4, Depth of 1.0, Location Y 0.5, and Rotation X 90 degrees.

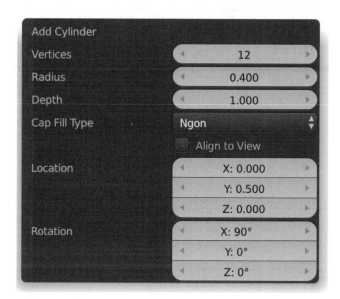

Figure 2.4
Redo last menu.
Source: *Blender Foundation.*

This will be the base for the shark. We will roughly model from the front and side views, trying to match the picture. To work with more freedom, let's customize the screen. Since we will be modeling with side- and front-view references only, it helps to toggle off "quad view" in the Properties panel in the 3D view. Instead, we will split the screen in half (dragging the triangle from the bottom left edge of the 3D view editor).

Enter the Edit mode and, in the top view, remove half of the mesh (leaving the vertices from the middle). Since the shark is symmetrical, we don't need to model its two halves. Switch back to the Object mode and in the Properties panel add a Mirror Modifier. Set clipping to on and make sure that the mirror axis is X. The other default options are fine. Thanks to the modifier, you should now see the cylinder complete again. Back in the Edit mode, any change you make will be automatically mirrored in the other half, as you can see in Figure 2.5.

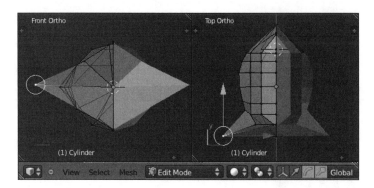

Figure 2.5
Mirror Modifier.
Source: *Blender Foundation. Art © 2014 Cengage Learning®. All Rights Reserved.*

We can't do much with the current mesh. We need more vertices to model the shark, and we will use the Loop Cut tool for that. In Edit mode, press Ctrl+R. This will show a purple edge on top of the cylinder. If you move your mouse over the mesh, you can choose where to slice it. In our case, we want a cut parallel to the base of the geometry. To confirm the command, right-click in the window and either move the mouse to slide the new edge loop, or press Esc to cut through the middle of the cylinder. If you scroll your mouse wheel before you confirm (click), you can do multiple slices at once, as shown in Figure 2.6.

Figure 2.6
Loop cut.
© 2014 Cengage Learning®. All Rights Reserved.

We will slice the cylinder on every section where the outline of the shark has a significant change in its slope. Remember to save the file, and if you want to compare your progress, check the file //assets/shark.2.blend.

Since this is a shark and not a sausage, we need to accommodate the new mesh arcs to follow the reference image. The B key will turn box selection on and let you select one or more vertices at once. Another useful shortcut is Alt+RMB on one of the edges of the loops to quickly select the edge loop.

With the arcs selected, you can grab them and move around (G). When necessary, you can use the S key to scale them around. The transformations (Rotation, Scaling, and even Grabbing) always happen relative to/around a pivot. By default, the pivot is the 3D Cursor. You can change it, for example, to pivot around the center of the selected vertices. To change the pivot, use the shortcuts comma and period (current selection and 3D cursor respectively) or the menu by the Shading mode. In fact, a lot of the other options in the 3D View header are important for modeling (such as snap, proportional editing, vertex/edge/face selection) and can be found in Figure 2.7.

Figure 2.7
3D View header.
Source: *Blender Foundation.*

At this point, you can start exploring the top view as well. For quickly switching to top view, use NumPad7 or toggle quad view on and off. Sometimes you need to transform the geometry only in one axis. In Figure 2.8, you can use the handler to pull if you want to move an edge in a specific axis. You can also use the keyboard for that. To restrict the transformation, press X, Y, or Z after the command and slide in the specified axis. Shift+X, Y, or Z works in the opposite way. It locks the transformation for the opposite axis (so you can only move/scale/rotate in a plane). This is really useful—we use G with Shift+Z all the time.

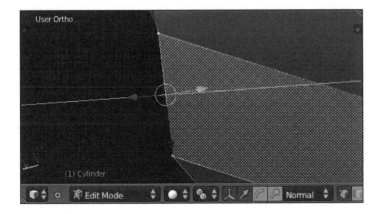

Figure 2.8
Locked axis transformation.
Source: *Blender Foundation. Art © 2014 Cengage Learning®. All Rights Reserved.*

You can also use the Proportional Editing tool, as shown in Figure 2.9. Sometimes you don't want to move individual vertices/edges/faces, and edge loops and box-selected areas are too big to be transformed as a single unified block. To use proportional editing, press O (or go to the icon in the 3D View header) to toggle it on and off. Now if you move a vertex, all the neighboring vertices will tag along. The influence of the tool is determined by the circle around the pivot. (Again, see how important the pivot is?) You can increase the size of the circle of influence by scrolling the mouse wheel up and down.

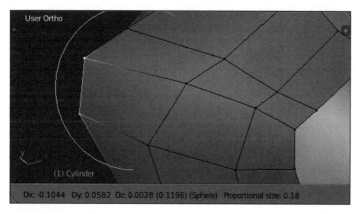

Figure 2.9
Proportional Editing tool.
Source: *Blender Foundation. Art © 2014 Cengage Learning®. All Rights Reserved.*

With these tools, you can get to the stage of the file //assets/shark.3.blend. Also in this file, there are some sketch lines on top of the 3D view; these are made with the Grease Pencil tool to help block out the shape before modeling. They are temporary markers and nothing more. Therefore, they were removed once the model was finished in shark4.blend. Although we can already add a tail to the shark, this poor shark still can't swim. To finish the modeling instructions, we will extrude those missing bits. In this context, extruding means to pull a piece out of the base geometry while keeping it connected. It's easier to show than to say. In Edit mode, select the face on the side of the shark and extrude it by pressing E, as shown in Figure 2.10.

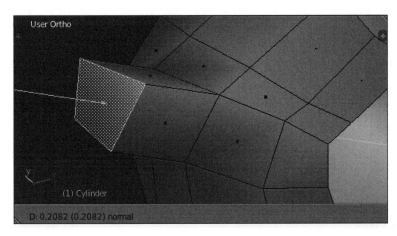

Figure 2.10
Extruding.
Source: *Blender Foundation. Art © 2014 Cengage Learning®. All Rights Reserved.*

Once you enter the extrude command, a new face is created. This face is connected to and in the same position as the original face. Additionally, it automatically puts you in the Grab command with the movement locked to the normal axis (no more the X, Y, or Z but the face normal instead). Pull the face as far as needed (in our case, the front reference image should be the guide) and click to finish it. If you press Esc, you will cancel the Grab part of the command but will still have the new face.

Transform Orientation

If an object or its parts is rotated in relation to the global axis, you will find the default axis locking hardly useful. Therefore, Blender allows you to quickly set a different alignment mode in the 3D View header (the default is Global). To switch to it, enter the desired axis twice (for example, X+X).

By changing the global orientation, you are actually changing the orientation of the Transform controllers (Translate, Rotate, Scale).

One exception to this system (and broadly used) is that when Global is set as the global orientation, you get Local transformations when double-typing your locking axis.

Additionally, an advanced resource is to add custom Transform Orientations. This is accessible at the end of the 3D View Properties panel.

Because the Mirror Modifier has both "Merge" and "Clipping" options turned on, the extrude will not simply be constrained to the normal (the axis perpendicular to the face) initially. Instead, the extruded face will be locked to the normal, but half of it will be locked in with the mirror plane. Therefore, it will behave as if locked vertically (Z axis).

To save time with the modeling, we will add a head from the built-in meshes in Blender. While in the Edit mode, go to the Add Mesh menu (Shift+A) and choose Monkey. You will need to scale (S), rotate (R), and grab (G) it to make it match the reference image. And they match perfectly—what a happy coincidence.

You will need to remove some faces from the neck to connect it with the top part of the body. To delete faces, use the X key. This will bring up the menu shown in Figure 2.11—pick your option wisely. To connect vertices and edges, use the F key. (They need to be selected, and no more than what can fit in a face.)

Figure 2.11
Delete menu.
Source: *Blender Foundation.*

To finish the model, you can add the swimmers on the sides. Start by selecting one face in the lateral of the mesh and extruding it until necessary. As we did for the main body of the shark, we should add more sections to the swimmer with the Loop Cut tool.

You can refine your model as much as you want. The current model is in //assets/shark.4.blend.

TEXTURING

The next step shouldn't take much time. To add the skin of the shark, we will use an image projected into the faces. Images are two-dimensional, while our models are three-dimensional. In order to match them both, we need to do the equivalent of peeling an orange and flattening the peel onto a flat plane. The peel in the plane will be our image of the orange skin, allowing us to use a 2D image for our 3D model. Another example is the representation of the world map where a sphere is projected onto a plane, as you can see in Figure 2.12. The process of mapping the 3D geometry to a 2D plane is called *UV texturing*.

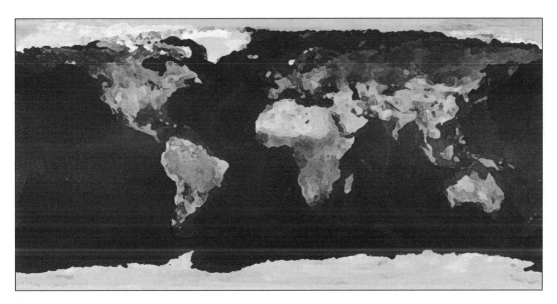

Figure 2.12
World Map: 2D surface equivalent of a 3D geometry.
Source: *NASA*.

Before we start, go to the Modifiers panel and apply the Mirror Modifier. If you don't do that, the shark can't have a different texture for each of its sides—instead, it would use the same texture flipped in the model. Also, you will no longer need the background images. You can turn them off or remove them from the file—both options can be found in the Background Images panel in the 3D View Properties menu.

To start creating a UV texture, you need to switch to Edit mode and call the UV Mapping menu (U). This menu has different mapping options. We will be using the first one, Unwrap, which is a semi-automatic way to calculate the optimal stretching for the 2D texture. The result can be seen and edited in the UV/Image Editor.

In the Editor menu, click Image → New, and in the pop-up menu, set UV Test Grid and confirm. This will produce a sample image where you can check in the 3D model as to how stretched the map image (texture) will be, once it is re-projected onto the shark model. If you look at Figure 2.13, you should spot a problem with the default unwrapping: the image on the side of the shark is too stretched and does not have enough resolution. While the shark tail has a high resolution, that doesn't correspond to its need (the tail is small after all)—the smaller the squares of the UV test grid, the higher the pixel-per-face ratio.

Figure 2.13
Bad "default" unwrapping.
© *2014 Cengage Learning®. All Rights Reserved.*

To solve this problem, go to the 3D view and select the edge loop that splits the side-swimmer from the body. With this "ring" selected, go to the Edge menu (Ctrl+E) and select Mark Seam. Now redo the UV Mapping → Unwrapping, and you will have a more distributed stretching along the mesh. This can be seen in Figure 2.14 and in the file //assets/shark.5.blend.

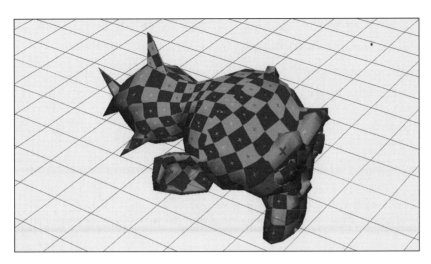

Figure 2.14
Final UV mapping.
Source: *Blender Foundation. Art © 2014 Cengage Learning®. All Rights Reserved.*

Your model is now ready for proper texturing. In the 3D view, switch to the Texture Paint mode and have fun. Once you are done painting, save the image from the UV/ Image Editor to your computer in //assets/textures/shark.png.

No Paint, No Pain

There is more to texture painting than we can cover here. But it's important to know that the feature is there, and it works great for 3D touch-up painting of your game textures.

Thus, if you don't want to paint the model, you can use the reference image as texture. Turn back to the side view and in the UV Mapping menu (U), set Project from View. In the UV/Image Editor, select the image you used for reference. For the side-swimmers, go to top view and, selecting only them, repeat the procedure and choose the top reference image.

Another option is to use the simple "shark tattoo" texture I painted for the final game file. This fish is a small part of the texture, because the texture corresponds to the UV layout of the whole mesh. If the image looks strange in your shark, you will have to edit your UV layout to make it match the UV of the //assets/shark.6.blend. You will find the texture in \Book\Chapter02\game_final\assets\textures\shader.png.

The texture needs to be part of a material. Select the object, and in the Properties Editor, open the Material panel. Create two materials—one for the eyes and one for the rest of the shark. In Edit mode, you can assign a material for the selected faces. The material for the eyes is shadeless and uses white as its diffuse color. The body material is also shadeless, but needs a texture for the color information. With the body material selected, switch to the Texture panel and add a new texture. The texture type needs to be "Image" or "Movie," and you need to pick the image you prepared as a texture. Finally, go to the Mapping tab and select UV as Coordinate. This way, the texture will be mapped according to the UV you just created.

If you are not familiar with materials in Blender, refer to Chapter 5, "Graphics." You can also import the materials Shark and SharkEyes from the current file at //assets/shark.6.blend.

RIGGING

Animate the shark...

In order to make the shark swim, we need an armature with bones. Similar to real bones, the Blender bones will deform the mesh, producing the animation for our game.

The base file is here: //assets/shark.6.blend

The first thing to do is to add an Armature object (Shift+A → Armature). It's important to have the armature center at the "center of mass" of the shark, which happens to be the right place for the shark mesh origin as well. (In our case, it's in the center of the scene at coordinates [0,0,0]). To make sure you got this right, in the 3D view look at the big dot representing the center of the shark or try to rotate it using its center as pivot. If the center is slightly above the side-swimmers and centralized in the short side of the shark, you are good to go. Otherwise, you need to reset its origin with the Shift+Ctrl+Alt+C option:

1. Move the 3D cursor to the approximate location (or to skip the next step, put it in [0,0,0] or use Shift+C).

2. Set its X coordinate to 0—the Property panel shows the 3D cursor's exact location.

3. Set Origin → Origin to 3D cursor.

With the 3D cursor in the center of the object, add the armature (Shift+A). In the Edit mode of the armature, select this bone (A or RMB on it) and move it −1 unit in Z. Now the tail of the bone is in the center. The tail is the small extremity of the bone, opposite to its head. This will be our root bone, the one bone that controls all the others.

With the 3D cursor still in the center, add a new bone (Shift+A). Select this bone tail and move (G) it until it matches the mouth location, as you can see in Figure 2.15. Now select this bone and the root bone and parent them without linking them (Ctrl+P → Keep Offset). This way the bone can still move freely, although it is parented to the root bone.

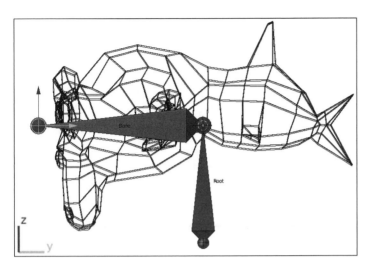

Figure 2.15
Bone editing.

Back to the root bone: select its tail and extrude it (E). This is another way of adding bones, automatically connecting them. Move the extruded bone to the beginning of the shark tail. Now repeat the procedure for the new bone, extruding it all the way to the end of the shark tail. Figure 2.16 shows the current bones as seen in //assets/shark.7.blend.

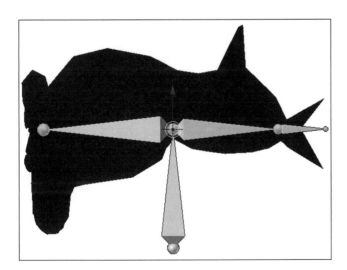

Figure 2.16
Armature Bones.

Before animating the shark, we need to link the armature with the mesh. This is done with the Set Parent To operator:

In the Object mode, select the shark mesh and then the shark armature and Ctrl+P → Armature Deform → With Automatic Weights. This will try to automatically set the influence of each bone in the mesh. For fine-tuning, select the armature, set it to Pose Mode, and then select the mesh and set it to Weight Paint mode. Now you can select the bones individually and paint their influence over the vertices as shown in Figure 2.17.

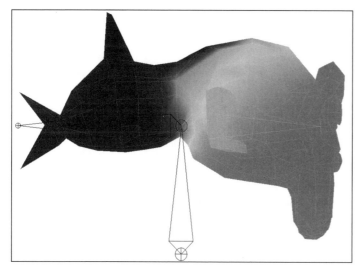

Figure 2.17
Weight painting.
Source: *Blender Foundation. Art* © *2014 Cengage Learning®. All Rights Reserved.*

X-Ray and Auto-Normalize
_____

With the armature selected, go to the Properties Data panel and set X-Ray on in the armature display—this will make the bones always be visible. Also, while weight painting, you can set Auto Normalize in the Tool panel—this ensures that all bone-deforming vertex groups don't add up to 1.0 while weight painting.

_____

To test the bone weighting, move the bones around (in the Pose not Edit Mode) and see if the mesh goes with it. The file is ready for animation and can be found here: //assets/shark.8.blend.

ANIMATION

To create an animation, you need to define the individual poses that will build up the illusion of movement. As an artist, you can define the poses frame by frame or work in a few moments of the animation. For example, you can define just a few frames, and Blender will automatically calculate the missing frames for the animation. It depends on how much control you want.

When 206 Bones Are Too Many

The animation complexity is also directly related to the number of bones created in your rig. For this game, we are not using many bones for simplicity's sake. In Chapter 4, "Animation," you will find more robust examples.

We will create a swimming cycle—an animation where the first and the last poses are the same and can be played seamlessly in a loop. Let's start by the following these steps:

1. Set the current frame to the initial one (Shift+Left).

2. Select the armature.

3. Change to the Pose mode.

Rotate the tailbone 50 degrees clockwise in the Z axis. Rotate the head bone 5 degrees counter-clockwise in the same axis. Select all bones (A) and insert a keyframe (I→LocRot). This will be our pose for the first frame. The current file is at //assets/shark.9.blend and is shown in Figure 2.18.

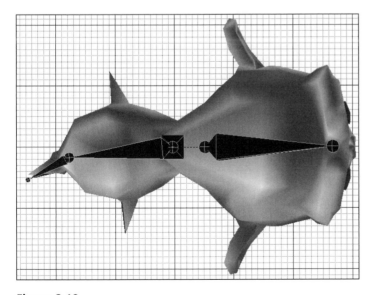

Figure 2.18
Initial pose.
Source: *Blender Foundation. Art © 2014 Cengage Learning®. All Rights Reserved.*

To create a cycle, you need the beginning and end frames to match. Move to frame 31 (through the Timeline or Shift+Up six times) and add a new keyframe for the same pose.

There are different ways to see your animation in Blender. Change your current screen to Animation (in the header menu where you see Default). This screen shows the three animation editors: Dope Sheet, Graph Editor, and Timeline, as you can see in Figure 2.19.

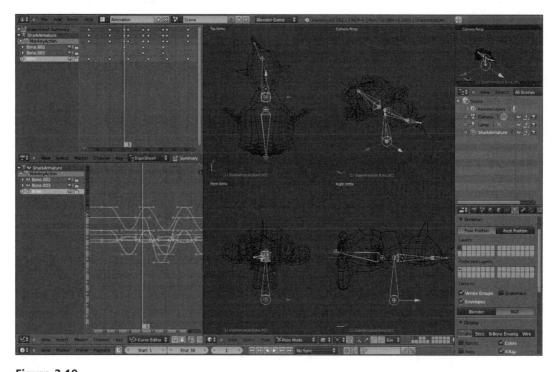

Figure 2.19
Animation screen.
Source: *Blender Foundation. Art © 2014 Cengage Learning®. All Rights Reserved.*

In the Dope Sheet, you can see where we have added keyframes so far. The two points and the line connecting them mean that there is no change between the two poses. The other way of adding a new pose is by selecting the keyframes in the Dope Sheet and duplicating them. As with the other editors in Blender, you can grab (G), scale (S), copy (Shift+D), and toggle all selection (A) using the same shortcuts you are used to.

The middle pose of the animation cycle should be opposite to the initial (and final) pose. Blender has a simple way to flip poses. In Figure 2.20, you can see the Paste Flipped option in the 3D View header.

1. Change to the Pose Mode.

2. Select all bones (A).

3. Click on Copy Pose in the 3D View header.

4. Go to frame 15.

5. Click on Paste Flipped Pose.

6. Store the keyframes (I).

Figure 2.20
Copy and paste Flipped Pose buttons.
Source: *Blender Foundation.*

Bones Mirroring

If your rigs have bones bifurcating from the main bone chain, there is a special way to make them mirror. By default, Blender will try to paste the pose of the same bone mirrored relative to the Y axis. Sometimes, however, you want to swap the transformations between two bones—a left and right. The classic example is walking animations when you need to animate only half of the strides.

To have Blender interpret the bones as two sides of the same bone, you need to name them L (for left bones) and R (for right bones). This way, the bone Swimmer.001.L will be treated as the pair of Swimmer.001.R, and their poses will be swapped and mirrored when using the Pose Flip Paste option. To learn more about this, refer to the walking cycle tutorial in the Chapter 4.

The swimming animation is now finished. In the Timeline, set the final playback frame to 30. Playing back the animation (Alt+A) will reveal our lovely and clumsy swimming cycle. In the Dope Sheet, switch the Display mode to Action Editor. There you can change the name of the current action to "SharkSwimming," as shown in Figure 2.21.

Figure 2.21
Action Editor header.
Source: *Blender Foundation.*

The current snapshot of this file is //assets/shark.10.blend.

You can also do a "SharkAttack" animation. For a smooth transition, make the new action with the same initial and final poses as the "SharkSwimming." If you go with that, use the attack animation when the shark eats a fish.

CAMERA AND KEYBOARD

After all the hard work of setting up your main character, it's time to bring in the game. If you play (P) the game now, you will see nothing but the shark standing still.

Playing and Quitting the Game

> Every time you need to test the current status of the game, you can launch it from the Game menu (available when the engine is set to Blender Game) or by using the shortcut P. To quit the running game and go back to the regular Blender environment, use the Exit key set in the game Render panel (Esc by default).

We will now set up the logic bricks. You'll learn more about logic bricks in the next chapter. They are the visual components of the logic and interaction of the game. The shark animation and movement will be controlled with logic bricks. We will also set up the camera control and motion.

The shark will always be swimming. Thus, we will be playing the swimming animation constantly:

1. Change your screen from animation to game logic.
2. In the Logic Editor, add an Always sensor (Shift+A → Sensor → Always).
3. Add an Action actuator and connect it with the sensor.
4. In the Action actuator: mode Loop Stop, action SharkSwimming, start frame 1 and end frame 30.

Now that the shark can swim, you want it to move around. The controls of the game are simple: use the spacebar to swim forward; left and right to rotate; up and down to emerge and submerge. You have to add a Keyboard sensor for each of those keys and connect them as such:

- **Left key** → **Motion actuator:** RotZ = 1° and disable L for rotation
- **Right key** → **Motion actuator:** RotZ = −1° and disable L for rotation
- **Up key** → **Motion actuator:** RotX = 1°
- **Down key** → **Motion actuator:** RotX = −1°
- **Space key** → **Motion actuator:** LocY = −0.05

Test your progress inside the game (P) and remember to always save. If your file is showing a different result than the file at //assets/shark.11.blend, check the logic bricks in Figure 2.22.

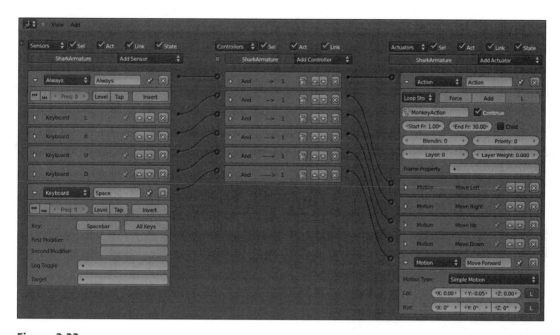

Figure 2.22
Motion actuators.
Source: *Blender Foundation.*

This simple setup allows the shark to swim freely away from the camera. To have the camera following the shark, select the camera and do the following:

1. Add an Always sensor.
2. Add a Camera actuator and connect it with the sensor.
3. In the Camera actuator, set SharkArmature as object, height 5.0, axis –Y, min 5.0, max 20.0, damping 0.10.

This camera will be behind the shark, always trying to stay inside the specified distance (from 5 to 20 Blender units). The damping will set how fast you want the camera to adjust to the new position while the shark swims away.

If you are modeling everything from scratch, you should tweak the speed and angle of the shark Motion actuator and the damping and distance of the camera to better accommodate the scale of your work.

With the shark alone in the scene, it's hard to tell how it is moving. It's time to add other objects to the scene so you can make sure that the camera settings and the shark motion are well adjusted. Thus, the next step is to add the world (the SeaBed et al). In the meantime, you can compare the status of your file with: //assets/shark.12.blend.

WORLD AND ENVIRONMENT

We will leave the shark file for now and put the game pieces together. Open the file //game.1.blend. This empty file will be the main file of the game. If you want to start a file from scratch, open the Blender default file, delete everything from it (press A to select all and then X to delete), and change engine to Blender Game and Shading mode to GLSL.

You need to bring the shark model into this file. Start by linking in the SharkMesh and the SharkArmature objects from the shark asset file. Go to the menu File → Link, navigate to the shark blend file, and once in it, navigate inside "Object," select the SharkArmature and SharkMesh objects, and press OK. A screen capture of the linking options is shown in Figure 2.23. The default options are good for now.

Figure 2.23
Linking options.
Source: *Blender Foundation.*

It's important to save your file first; otherwise, the Relative Path option will have no effect. Linking keeps your shark file as an external asset. Any changes you make in the shark.blend file will be transferred over to the game.blend file, once you save it. That also means you cannot make changes in the asset objects through the game.blend file. If you linked before you saved the file, no worries. You can change all the file paths by going to the menu File → External Data → Make All Paths Absolute.

The camera doesn't need to be linked. In fact, it's better to keep it as a local object, given that you will certainly adjust its parameters later. To append (not link) the camera, use the menu File → Append and use the default options to import the camera. This will be the main camera for the game. Select the camera and in the 3D View header, choose View → Cameras → Set Active Object as Camera. If everything went right, you can now play your game, and it should behave just as in the shark.blend file.

Good news. The SeaBed was already prepared and is ready for the game (and in your game_my asset folder). Repeat the linking steps once again for the SeaBed group inside the file //level/seabed.blend. You now have the shark, the camera, and the set prepared for the game. The progress shown in Figure 2.24 can be checked at //game.2.blend.

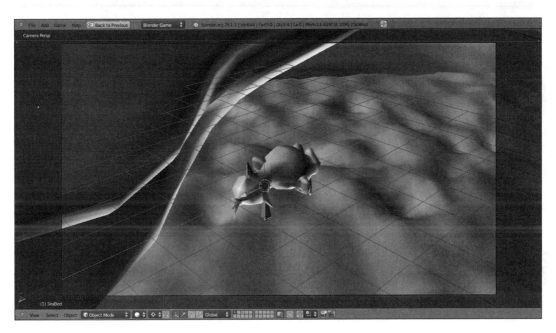

Figure 2.24
Shark, camera, and SeaBed.
Source: *Blender Foundation. Art © 2014 Cengage Learning®. All Rights Reserved.*

To simulate the water, we will add a blue mist effect. This produces an effect similar to fog and gives a nice water attenuation effect (where everything eventually fades to blue). Follow these steps:

1. Switch to the World panel in the Properties Editor.
2. Create a new World.
3. Set Horizon Color to Hex: 264A6B.
4. Turn Mist on and set Start 0.0 and Depth 50.0

In order to preview the color and the mist effect in the 3D Viewport, you need to set Viewport Shading to Texture (Alt+Z), as shown in Figure 2.25. The World is now finished and part of the //game3.blend file.

Figure 2.25
Mist effect—preview in 3D View.
Source: *Blender Foundation. Art © 2014 Cengage Learning®. All Rights Reserved.*

Play your game and swim around with the shark. However, there is one basic element missing in our survival shark game: the food.

ARTIFICIAL INTELLIGENCE

While the shark is 100 percent interactive, controlled by the player, the fish will be controlled through a simple AI (artificial intelligence) mechanic. The principles are simple: the fish's swimming cycle is handled by logic bricks, while the fish's constant spawning inflow is controlled by an individual "program" (a script) responsible for the following components:

- Populating the game with fish schools.

- Making the fish follow a "fish leader."

- Killing some fish when the shark attacks.

Speaking of Scripts

Scripts can also be used to complement the functionality of a component of the game. The score scene is using logic bricks to handle the score, but it needs a script to handle the time out, the game over, and to change the resolution of all the text objects. We'll explain more about that in the "Scoring System" section of this chapter.

Once again, we will take advantage of a system with linkable assets. Instead of creating the fish school yourself, you will bring it inside your game, ready to use.

Start by reopening the current version of the file //game.blend. Now you need to link the group FishSchool from the file //assets/school.blend. (This time, instead of navigating in the Object subfolder, go to Group.) If you link a group in with the "Instance Groups" option enabled, you will end up with an instance of this group added to the scene. This "group instance" is nothing more than an empty object that is used to place a Blender group in the scene. The group is linked from the original file, thus changes made there are kept in sync with your game file.

In Figure 2.26, you can see the game with the school of fish around the shark. If you open the file school.blend, you can see an empty (FishLeader) in the visible layer and an object (Fish) in the second layer (which is and has to be hidden by default). The empty is always rotating and adding more of the fish model into the scene. A fish is added every second or so until the limit specified in the FishLeader game property, maxFish, is reached. Change this number from 30 to 100 and fish will flood you. Decrease to 5, and you make the game even harder. Select the FishLeader, and you will see some new logic bricks. Pay particular attention to the Python controllers.

Figure 2.26
School of fish.
© 2014 Cengage Learning®. All Rights Reserved.

The script allows for more direct manipulation of your game elements, complex math computations, and a denser logic for your game play. If you look at the scripts in this file (in the text editor), you'll see you have nothing to be scared of. This is a simple textual way to describe interactive behaviors for your game. And it's far simpler than the hardcore task of programming an entire game engine. Cheers for the compromise. In Figure 2.27, you can look at the game property and logic bricks (including the script controllers) of the FishLeader.

Art Versus Math

"But I'm an artist and don't understand math." Sure, we get that a lot. But bear in mind that here you only need to understand the mechanics of when to rely on a script and what you can do with it. For a more in-depth overview of this topic, see Chapter 7, "Python Scripting," later in the book. Also, the math you need for Python scripting is more accessible than most people assume. Unless, of course, you are planning to run for Miss U.S.A. http://youtu.be/9QBv2CFTSWU

If you want to do your own customizations, try to animate the fish with bones. You can follow all the steps we did for the shark. Additionally, remember to change the object being added by the FishLeader "AddFish" actuator (see Figure 2.27). Instead of adding the fish, you will have to add the fish parent (the FishArmature object you will create). The armature child (the fish itself) will be added together automatically.

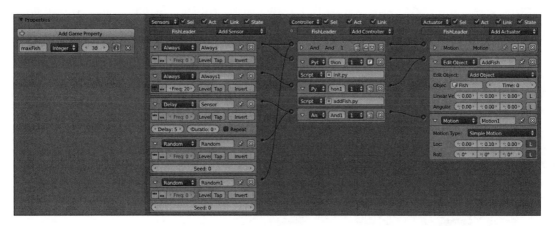

Figure 2.27
Logic bricks and game property of the FishLeader.
Source: *Blender Foundation.*

The current checkpoint is at //game.4.blend. If you changed your //assets/school.blend file, you need only replace the one in the sources with yours. As we mentioned (three times already, anyone counting?), the new data will be automatically synced in the game. Play your game, and get ready to wrap up the shark feeding.

ALL YOU CAN EAT

If you try to catch the fish with the shark, you will see that the shark pushes the fish away. For the game, we need three things to happen: (1) the fish needs to die, (2) the shark needs to get bigger, (3) a score on the screen needs to tell how many fish we caught and how much time we have left.

The score system will be made in the next section. For now, we will focus on making the shark and the little fish interact.

The school of fish is, in fact, already set up. But let's look at what we have there. Open the file //assets/school.blend. In the second layer, select the fish and look at the logic bricks, shown in Figure 2.28.

Figure 2.28
Fish school logic bricks.
Source: *Blender Foundation.*

We have a Collision sensor that will only be active when touching an object that has a "shark" property. We don't want to know when one fish collides with another or with the seabed, for that matter. This filter addresses that. The sensor is connected to a Python controller "killMe.py" that takes care of some housekeeping. It tells the FishLeader that we will need a new fish soon. The controller also activates two actuators: one to kill the fish, and the second to send a message indicating a fish went down.

This message is like spam mail. It doesn't matter if you have a mail-only sign in your mailbox. It doesn't even matter if you don't have a mailbox. You will receive the McDonald's coupon you never asked for. (And you will end up eating there—damned spammers!)

And so will the shark. Once the shark receives a message, it can act accordingly. In our case, we want to make the shark big. To do so, open the file shark.12.blend again. Until now, we have been adding all the logic bricks to the armature. Now let's put the armature aside and use the mesh:

1. Select the SharkMesh object.

2. Add a keyframe to the size (I → Scaling).

3. Go to frame 100, scale up the shark, and repeat the previous step.

4. Open the Logic Editor.

5. Create a Boolean game property named "shark."

6. Create an Integer game property named "size."

7. Add a Message sensor with the subject "Sharked."

8. Add a Property actuator: mode Add, property "size," and value 1.

9. Add an Action actuator: mode Property, action SharkMeshAction, and property "size."

10. Connect the sensor with both actuators.

The final shark file is at //assets/shark.13.blend. In Figure 2.29, we have a screen of the logic bricks setup.

Figure 2.29
Shark ready to grow.
Source: *Blender Foundation.*

We started by creating an animation for the shark. This animation is played according to a game property (size) that will increase every time a message is received. The message gets to the shark every time a fish is eaten (for example, collides with the shark). Thus, we have a good synchronization between fish disappearing and the shark getting bigger.

Apart from that, the shark needs the "shark" game property to be detected by the fish school. This will trigger the collision. The Collision sensor simply checks if the object has a property with a given name, so the type and value of the property are arbitrary (in our case, we are using a Boolean property, but it could be any other property type). Now one by one, we can eat the fish. And it's time to count sheep.

Scoring System

The score system of the game is part of its interface built on top of the 3D view. In Figure 2.30, you can see the main elements of the interface: the score on the top left, the time countdown on the top right, and the title of the game on the bottom right.

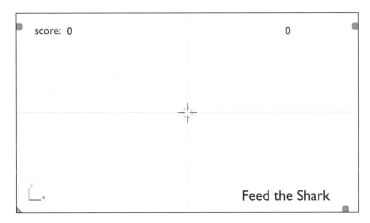

Figure 2.30
Interface elements.
Source: *Blender Foundation.*

The user interface is independent from the game file, objects, and events. Thanks to the messaging system of the game engine (the combination message actuator and message sensors), you can implement the interface as a separate file with its own logic. Open the interface file in //interface/score.blend. The diagram in Figure 2.31 illustrates the dynamic of its elements and the message flow.

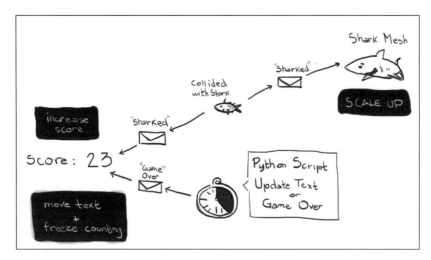

Figure 2.31
Message system diagram.
© 2014 Dalai Felinto.

Now you have two sets of independent and concurrent events. On the one hand, you can update the score every time a message comes from a fish saying it got "sharked" (a fish collided with the shark). This is pretty straightforward and happens for as long as the game is not over.

The game is over when you run out of time, which is part of the second set of events. The time system is an independent countdown timer (using a timer game property). It updates the time in the interface and sends a message to all the game elements when the time is up, and the game is over. This message is used to freeze the fish-counting and trigger an action to move the score to its final position, as you can see in Figure 2.32.

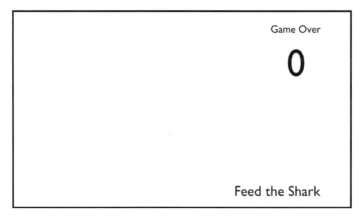

Figure 2.32
Game over interface.
© 2014 Cengage Learning®. All Rights Reserved.

This scene will be imported without changes into your game file. Once again, the linking system of Blender allows you to keep components separated and synced. Open //game.4.blend and link (not append) the "Score" scene from the //interface/score.blend file. Although the scene is now in the Blender file, you still need to load it into the game:

1. Add an empty object (Shift+A → Empty).

2. Select the object and open the Logic Editor.

3. Add an Always sensor.

4. Add a Scene actuator: mode Add Overlay Scene, scene "Score."

5. Connect the sensor with the actuator.

Now the game is a combination of two scenes that work as separate layers. The file is at //game.5.blend. In Figures 2.33 and 2.34, you can see the user interface integrated within the game.

Figure 2.33
Game start.
© 2014 Cengage Learning®. All Rights Reserved.

Figure 2.34
Game over.

MUSIC FOR YOUR EARS

A game is not complete without sound effects. There are three sounds under //sounds/: the ambient sound (water.m4a), the eating-fish effect (sharked.m4a), and the ending sound (gameover.m4a). This is the farewell set of instructions for this chapter and a prelude for the following chapter (entirely on logic bricks). Speaking of the lack of images, those are sound samples. Feel free to whistle along.

- **Ambient sound:** Add a Sound actuator; load the sound file (water.m4a). Mode: Loop End, Volume: 2. Connect it to the Always sensor you created to load the UI. This will play the ambient sound through the whole game in an eternal loop.

- **Eating-fish sound:** Add a Message sensor with subject: "Sharked" and a Sound actuator; load the sound file (sharked.m4a). Mode: Play End, Volume: 2. Connect the sensor with the actuator. Every time a fish is eaten, the sound effect will be played.

- **Ending game sound:** Add a Message sensor with subject: "GameOver" and connect it to a new Sound actuator; load the sound file (gameover.m4a). Mode: Play End, Volume: 0.3.

There is a catch here. You are sending the GameOver message not once but continuously. That would make the GameOver sound play in loop, which you don't want.

You can fix this in the score.blend scene file (by sending the message only once). Or else you can do it here, as follows:

You need a Boolean game property that tells you what the status of the game is: when gameover is False the game is running; if gameover is True the game is over. When you receive a message with the subject "GameOver," you need to change the value of this property. You do this by connecting the Message sensor with a new Property actuator—Mode: Assign, Property: "gameover," Value: True.

Next you add a Property sensor named GameIsNotOver to detect if the game is running (if the gameover game property is True or False). Set Evaluation Type to Equal, Property to "gameover," and Value as False.

Connect this sensor to the And controller of the game over Sound actuator. Optionally, you can also link this sensor to the And controller of the eating-fish Sound actuator. This will make the sound effects stop after the game is over. The ambient sound should still play; thus, there is no need to connect the GameIsNotOver sensor with the And controller of the ambient Sound. The final logic bricks can be seen in Figure 2.35.

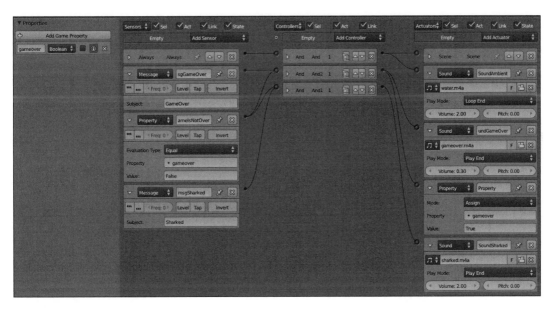

Figure 2.35
Sound logic bricks.
Source: *Blender Foundation.*

The final file is at //game.6.blend.

Where to Go from Here

The game is complete: the final files are in \Book\Chapter02\game_final\game.blend.

The modular approach we took allows for easy customization of the individual elements of the game. As you advance in the book, you should try to keep evolving the games files. Create a new user interface. Create multiple shark animations. Change all your assets.

If you want to share your version of the Feed the Shark the game, please host it online and send us a link. If there are enough contributions, we will make them available on the book's home page.

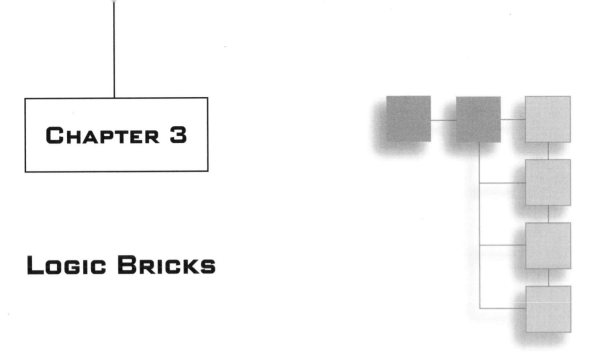

CHAPTER 3

LOGIC BRICKS

What makes a game different than a movie? Let's see. In both you can find yourself buried in a comfortable seat eating junk food and alienated from the world. And funny 3D goggles are not exclusive to either. But what about interactivity? In a game you can control a player and interact with the world and the game elements. The story can be dynamically created in front of your eyes.

Therefore, as a director and content creator you will play different roles in a movie or a game. In a movie, for example, you have to direct the flow of the story, but for a game, you have to direct how the player controls and experiences this flow. Those are the times of super computers—ode to Watson, IBM's Jeopardy "intelligent" machine. More than ever, it's time to narrow the gap between what technology can deliver and what the public can experiment with and assimilate as part of their own nature. As Kevin Flynn praised in *Tron* and *Tron Legacy*—the Disney game-related movie and prequel—*all the power to the user.*

Traditionally, to design your game interaction in the past, you would have needed coding expertise and a highly technical background. If, as a creative artist, any words such as *technical, code,* or *programming* scare you, be afraid no more. Logic bricks is here to rescue you. Logic bricks is a visual set of tools responsible for integrating the game components together. By using logic bricks, you can determine what to do after a mouse click, when to play an animation, how to move your character, and so on, as shown in Figure 3.1.

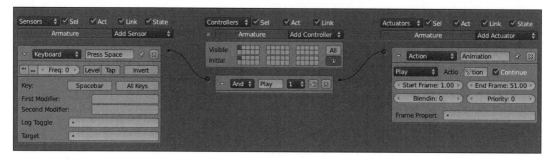

Figure 3.1
Example of playing an animation when pressing Space.
Source: *Blender Foundation.*

The logic brick system is composed of three main elements: sensors, controllers, and actuators. Sensors are an event system used to trigger an action upon a specific event (for example, an object collides with another object or the joystick is used). Once one or more sensors is triggered, you can use a controller to control whether or not this set of events will produce an event in the game (and which effect). Controllers work as logic pipes, evaluating sensors through simple logic conditions, such as And, Or, and Not. Finally, when a controller validates a set of sensors, it will activate an actuator. An actuator is responsible for a specific action of the game (such as ending the game, moving an object, and so on).

In this chapter, we'll cover sensors, controllers, and actuators in detail—specifically, how and when to use them. Additionally, you will learn about object game properties, the state machine system, how the interface works, and the architecture of the system as a whole. As a system used to build new worlds, this is no place for *do's* and *don'ts*. It will be up to you to find the best set of features that fits your project and creativity. Nevertheless, when possible, we'll present suggestions of when and how people have used the tools in the past, but you don't have to feel constrained by that. Treat logic bricks as small Lego pieces and surprise us and yourself.

Leave Your Python at the Door

Logic bricks are really easy and quick to use. You can make entire games with them with absolutely no need for coding.

General Overview

Thus far, you know that this whole system will allow you to create those little pieces that compose the interaction of your game. There are multiple ways to put those little parts together and even more ways to combine them. It's impossible to show all the possibilities, but there is a common principle as to how they operate that we can look at.

Simple Example

From the book files, open *\Book\Chapter3\bowling_base.blend*.

In this file, you have a small bowling game that includes the bowling ball, the pins, and the rink for the ball to roll around in. The goal here is to launch the ball and keep it rolling as much as you can. If you go to the Blender game menu and start the game, you will see that nothing much seems to happen. Here are some things you may need:

- Keyboard sensor to react when keys are pressed.
- Actuator to move the ball.
- Controller to activate the actuator when the sensor is positive.

Select the ball, and you will see that some of those logic bricks are already there, as pictured in Figure 3.2. Click in the socket by the Keyboard sensor and drag the line all the way to the socket by the Motion actuator. If your aim was good, this will create a controller to bridge the sensor with the actuator. Start the game again and press the spacebar a few times to roll a strike.

Figure 3.2
Simple bowling sample game.
Source: *Blender Foundation.*

To make things more interesting, there is also a timer that will start when the game begins. If you connect the Property sensor (already in the file) to the same controller as the Keyboard sensor, you will only be able to move the ball for a few seconds. The Property sensor will be positive as long as the timer is inside a specified range. So the

And controller will be positive only when both the Keyboard and the Property Sensors are positive.

This is a simple example, but it should get you started so that you can experiment with the available options and other logic bricks. Go ahead and change a few things. Don't worry because nothing will break. In Figure 3.3, you can see how your final linked logic bricks may look. Notice that there are some logic bricks pre-created for the camera and the first pin. If you connect them as shown, the camera will animate as soon as the ball hits the pin.

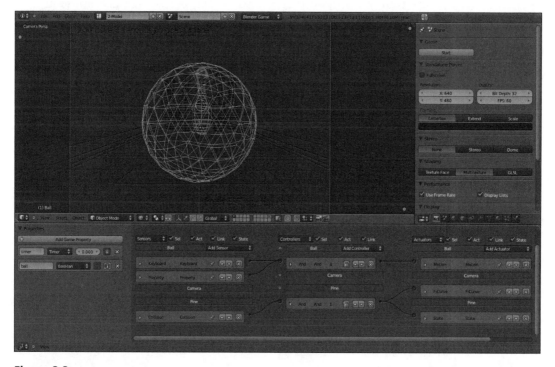

Figure 3.3
Bowling logic bricks.
Source: *Blender Foundation. Art © 2014 Cengage Learning®. All Rights Reserved.*

ARCHITECTURE

The game engine was designed to revolve around game objects. Fifteen years ago, when it was first developed, this was a breakthrough design. The idea of having events controlled per object, as opposed to a central controller, worked well for the early days of 3D engines. Nowadays, some people may advocate that controlling elements per object is less scalable and more difficult to manage. That will be up to you to decide. Regardless of your thoughts on that subject, the game engine still allows you to emulate a centralized controlling system, while giving autonomy to each object to deal with its own business. Part of this flexibility is due to the hooked-up Python layer and the logic brick system. Through the Python interface, you can replace or at least control most of the effects and logic setups you create with logic bricks. With logic bricks, you can quickly set up a system that is easy to visualize, implement, and test. The strength of the game engine comes from the trade-off between the two sibling systems. A flexible design may lack features and performance compared to specific engines. Nevertheless, the different kinds of applications you can prototype and develop quickly with the game engine make up for the compromise.

If you look at a level deep into the object structure, you will find that the architecture of the logic bricks system is "controller-centric." It revolves around the controllers of the game because they are the ones to determine what do to with the sensors and what actuators to activate. This doesn't have to be followed strictly, but based on this design, you will want to keep your sensors and actuators to a minimum and optimize their usage with the controllers. Actually, in order to optimize the performance, the game engine disables any sensor and actuator that is unlinked to a controller or linked to a controller in a non-active state. This is one of the (many) reasons why Python controllers are so popular. They allow you to replace the use of multiple sensors and actuators by direct calls to their equivalents in the source code. Chapter 7, "Python Scripting," is entirely dedicated to that aspect of the game engine, and will complement the applications of logic bricks discussed in this chapter.

INTERFACE

Logic bricks has its own editor inside the Blender interface. While other game settings are spread all over the panels and menus, editing logic bricks can be done entirely inside the Logic Editor.

You can see that logic bricks are sorted per object and organized according to your own needs. For each individual object, the controllers are executed from top to bottom, as presented in the interface. Nevertheless, there is not much control as to which of the object's logic bricks runs first. The criteria of organization for the logic bricks tend to reflect more personal preferences and visual clarity needs than internal requirements.

Here are some instructions on how to use the Logic Editor interface.

2.50 Is the New 2.49

For those used to the Blender 2.49 interface, you may need some time to get used to the enhanced new design of Blender. The first thing you will notice is that the Physics panel has been moved to the Physics tab at the Properties Logic Editor. If you jumped straight to this chapter and are a bit lost navigating Blender interface, then Chapter 1 should help you find your way.

Add

To add new logic bricks is only possible for the active object—the one always displayed as first in the Logic Editor list. You can see the Add Sensor/Controller/Actuator button right after the name of the active object on its respective column, as shown in Figure 3.4.

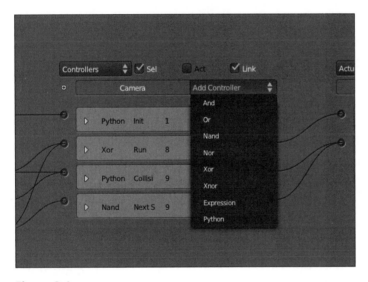

Figure 3.4
Add controller.
Source: *Blender Foundation.*

When you click in the button, a pop-up list will show you all the available logic bricks that are compatible with this kind of object (for example, Armature sensors are only available for Armature objects). Selecting the desired type will create a new logic brick with the default parameters for this particular type (which you will likely need to change). The name of the logic brick is automatically created, based on its type, for pure convenience.

Quick Ways to Add a Logic Brick

As a quick alternative, you can use the Add Menu (in the Logic Editor header bar) or press Shift+A.

Remove

In order to delete individual logic bricks, you need to click the "x" icon present in the header of each logic brick. By doing this, you are unlinking each logic brick with any connected logic bricks and removing it. Although this action can be reverted with Undo, simply unlinking a logic brick or moving it to an inactive state (for controllers) is enough to disable it. The game engine will not compute unlinked and disabled logic bricks. Thus, it can be handy to have testing sensors and actuators hanging around for later use with no performance impact.

Move

When you add a new logic brick, it will show up in the bottom of the logic bricks stack of the active object. You can move it up and down according to your need. In order to rearrange them, you need to set the logic brick to be unexpanded and use the up and down arrow icons.

Link

Every logic brick has a connector used to link it with other logic bricks. Sensors show the connector on the right side of their header, while actuators show it on the left side. Controllers are placed between the sensors and actuators, so the connectors are presented on both sides. Drag the connector from a logic brick and drop it in the connector you want to link to.

Kill Two Birds with One Stone: Linking and Adding a Controller

Try to link a sensor directly with an actuator on the same object. Blender will automatically create an And controller and link it between them.

You don't need to keep the logics self-contained in single objects. When you select more than one object at the same time, you will see all of them in the Logic Editor. That feature allows you to connect a sensor from one object to the controller of another one and again to the actuator of yet another object. This is one of the key elements for group instancing—an advanced way of sharing logic bricks, which is covered at the end of this chapter.

Message System

> If you found that cross-linked objects can easily become hard to keep track of, welcome to the team. Before getting desperate, make sure that you read about the elegant alternative presented by the Message sensor and Message actuator. Be aware that if you decide for the messaging system, your events will always be delayed by one logic tic, since it will only trigger the sensor in the next logic loop.

Unlink

Drag the mouse holding the left mouse button and the Control key to use the Unlink feature. This will activate a knife system to cut the links between logic bricks you want to unlink. It works the same way as the Node Editor in Blender.

Expand/Show/Hide

Visual organization is a key aspect of working with logic bricks. You don't need to edit the values of a logic brick all the time so you can often keep most of them hidden. You can hide/show one particular logic brick using the arrow to the left of its header. If you want to hide/show all the sensors or controllers or actuators of one object, simply click in its corresponding header.

Hide and Show Menus

> On the top of the Logic Editor, you can access a menu to quickly hide or show the bricks for sensors, controllers, and actuators for all the selected objects, as seen in Figure 3.5.

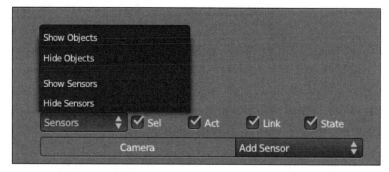

Figure 3.5
Show/Hide drop-down menu.
Source: *Blender Foundation.*

Move

When you add a new logic brick, it will show up in the bottom of the logic bricks stack of the active object. You can move it up and down according to your need. In order to rearrange them, you need to set the logic brick to be unexpanded and use the up and down arrow icons.

States

Above the list of an object controller, you can see a small but important plus icon. It shows and hides the States control. You can also set initial game states and the ones you want to see at that moment in the interface. In order to learn how to use the State system, look ahead to the end of this chapter in the "State Machine" section.

States Layers

When you play the game, the active states of a controller are the ones in the bottom row shown in Figure 3.6, known as *initial states.* The states present in the top row, namely visible states, are a tool to help you visualize different states without messing with the Initial States set. They are reset to the Initial States every time you reopen your file.

Figure 3.6
Controller states.
Source: *Blender Foundation.*

The States interface works like the layer system in Blender—click to select one state and Shift+click to select more than one. As with the Blender layers, states have no individual names for the time being.

Properties

The left panel in the Logic Editor allows you to add and edit your object game properties (see Figure 3.7). Unlike the logic bricks, the visible game properties are those of the current active object only. As with other editor areas in Blender, you can hide/unhide this area with the property panel shortcut (N).

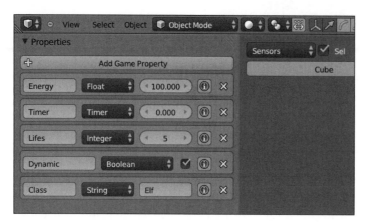

Figure 3.7
Game Properties panel.
Source: *Blender Foundation*.

Properties are often used to store a variable characteristic of a game object (for example, life, energy, or speed). In this case, you will be using Property actuators to change the values of a property when hitting an enemy, accelerating, and other sorts of events. On top of that, Property sensors or Expression controllers can invoke different actions when you get to certain values (for example, end the game when life and energy are zero).

Another way of using the properties is to determine how other objects will react to each one. As we will see later on this chapter, there are a few sensors that rely on the existence of a property to interact with an object. Those Physics sensors (Near, Collision, etc.) work regardless of the property value; they check only for the property name, which can't be changed inside the game.

The available properties are: Float, Integer, Timer, Boolean, and String.

Now let's move ahead and look at the functionalities you can use.

Sensors

Sensors are the first layer of interaction between your game objects and the game itself, so they need to be planned carefully to avoid overhead on your logic performance. It's usually a trade-off between maintainability and work speed. For the first stages of your project, you may be able to have multiple sensors for the same tests (for example, individual collision sensors for different property and material checks). Later on, when and if performance becomes an issue, you can replace them for a more elegant solution with the same functionality. But for now, you should just focus on playing and experimenting with the presented tools.

The next part of the chapter is structured to serve both as a continuous reading and reference guide. If you read it through, you will capture the big picture of the system, what you can do, and when you might use the specific features. I recommend you read it all at least once. Later, you can revisit this chapter for a deeper perspective on the presented functionalities.

Header

In the first part of this chapter we mentioned some options present in all the logic bricks. Now we will see with more details the properties that are specific for sensor headers, as shown in Figure 3.8.

Figure 3.8
Sensor header.
Source: *Blender Foundation.*

- **Name:** Can be used to identify your sensor, even when it's not expanded. You will refer to it from inside the Expression and Python controllers.

- **Pulse Positive:** Continuously sends positive pulses to the controller while the sensor is active.

- **Pulse Negative:** Continuously sends negative pulses to the controller while the sensor is not active. A negative pulse will not be sent before the sensor is positive at least once or the level is enabled.

- **Frequency:** Sets how often the pulse will trigger the sensor. The frequency is actually the number of logic tics that will be skipped before triggering the sensor again. Keep it at zero to have the sensor pulsing for every logic tic.

- **Level:** Triggers the controller at the beginning of the game or when the controllers are activated from a disabled state. With this option, you can force negative signals (for example, a property is not inside a range, a mouse is not over your object, a key is not pressed) to trigger the controller, even if it never turns positive. Mostly used as part of a state system to force a sensor to be evaluated right after the state of an object changes.

- **Tap:** Triggers the sensor only once, even if the sensor remains active. It works opposite to the pulse, and is especially useful for Physical sensors, Keyboard sensors, and Mouse sensors.

- **Invert:** Still triggers the sensor as it would normally, but sends a negative signal when it starts and a positive one when it stops being valid (for example, when a key is no longer pressed). If you need the sensor to send a negative signal before ever being positive, remember to turn on Level.

Always

Always, as shown in Figure 3.9, is the simplest and most often used sensor. There are basically two ways of using it. When Pulse is off, it will run once when the level starts and never again. When Pulse is on, the sensor will run repeatedly, triggering controllers according to its frequency.

Figure 3.9
Always sensor.
Source: *Blender Foundation.*

Always sensors are commonly used to initialize actuators, such as Filters 2D, Motion, Scene, Sound, and so on. When combined with the Python controller, this sensor is often used to call scripts that need to be initialized first (when the frequency is zero) and scripts that handle global events (with the frequency set according to the needs of a particular script).

Delay

Similar to the Always sensor, the Delay sensor allows you to postpone the initialization of some actions by some logic tics (see Figure 3.10). You will notice three options here: Delay, Duration, and Repeat.

Figure 3.10
Delay sensor.
Source: *Blender Foundation.*

Delay is the initial waiting period before the sensor is triggered. *Duration* stands for how long (once triggered) the sensor will be positive/active. If you want this to happen cyclically, you can set Repeat on. It's important to note that the Pulse option works on top of those three parameters.

In combination with the Python controller, this sensor is often used to call scripts that require other scripts to run first.

Actuator

Here comes a chicken-and-egg situation. In order to understand this sensor, you may need to get more familiar with actuators first. The Actuator sensor is triggered when the selected actuator changes its status (active/inactive), as shown in Figure 3.11. A typical application of it is with the Action actuator. If you use an Expression controller to check for the Actuator sensor status (for example, actsensor=false), you can trigger another action right after an animation is done.

Figure 3.11
Actuator sensor.
Source: *Blender Foundation.*

Actuator Sensor and the Messaging System

In the online files, you can find a file that illustrates how this sensor can be used with the message and the animation system: \Book\Chapter3\sensor_actuator.blend.

Joystick

Don't listen to those Kinect fanboys, joysticks are still here to stay (see Figure 3.12). Start by selecting your Joystick Index, which means you can work with multiple joysticks in the same game. For every Joystick sensor, you can control one of the following: Hat, Axis, Button, and Single Axis.

Figure 3.12
Joystick sensor.
Source: *Blender Foundation.*

Keyboard

You don't want to map your keyboard, key by key to individual Keyboard sensors (see Figure 3.13). Yet you can. In order to provide flexibility for game developers, the game engine can control actions on an individual key basis, capture modifiers (traditionally Alt, Ctrl, Shift but extended to any key), or on no particular key. For the latter, the option All Keys linked to a Python Controller is the way to go, although for a full Python approach, you don't even need the Keyboard sensor.

Figure 3.13
Keyboard sensor.
Source: *Blender Foundation.*

Log Toggle and Target work together. When the Log Toggle property value is True and a String is set as Target, you can keep track of all the pressed keys by a given sensor. It can be used for debugging or even for direct input of texts for a property.

In the online files, you can see a sample of that: *\Book\Chapter3\sensor_keyboard. blend*

Keys Status on Python

The Keyboard sensor will send a positive pulse when the specified key is pressed down and a negative one when it is released. The status of the key is represented by Python constants:

bge.logic.KX_INPUT_JUST_ACTIVATED right when it's pressed,

bge.logic.KX_INPUT_ACTIVE while it's being held, and

bge.logic.KX_INPUT_JUST_RELEASED right after it's been released.

Its status can only be accessed from a Python controller.

Mouse

The Mouse sensor is used to control the mouse input in the game. It can be used entirely with logic bricks or integrated with Python. Be aware that individual sensors are needed to handle different mouse events and most of them are not handled per object (see Figure 3.14). The mouse events are separated in two different types commonly combined together:

- **Mouse inputs**—general input: Movement, Wheel Down, Wheel Up, Right Button, Middle Button, and Left Button.

- **Mouse actions**—per object: Mouse Over and Mouse Over Any.

Figure 3.14
Mouse sensor event types.
Source: *Blender Foundation.*

If you run an actuator when a mouse input is triggered (for example, Left Button), the action will happen, regardless of where the click is. If you need an actuator to happen when you click on one particular object, then you need a Mouse Over and a Left Button linked through an And controller.

Collision, Physics and Mouse Click

> In order to be clickable, an object must have collision enabled in the Physics Panel.

Armature

Armature is an advanced sensor to help you detect error threshold on bone constraints (see Figure 3.15). It was created as part of the IK solver implementation integrated by the developer Benoit Bolsée.

Figure 3.15
Armature sensor.
Source: *Blender Foundation.*

The original goal of this set of functionalities was targeted at robotic studies, so it may rest outside the scope of your project. If you are going to use iTaSC (instantaneous Task Specification using Constraints), this sensor will help you keep track of your armature constraints. For more information, please visit: http://wiki.blender.org /index.php/Dev:Source/GameEngine/RobotIKSolver.

To Caesar What Is Caesar's

> The Armature sensor is only available for Armature objects. If you copy this sensor to non-Armature objects, the panel will show "Sensor only available for armatures," and the sensor will be inoperative.

Touch

The Touch sensor is a subset of the Collision sensor. Actually, they share the same code internally. It's likely to be deprecated in the future.

Collision

The Collision sensor can be used to detect collisions between a game object and other objects or the environment (see Figure 3.16). You can filter the collision to only trigger the sensor when the object hits a face with a specific material or an object with a particular property (use the M/P button to toggle between them). As with the Physics sensors, this sensor is dependent on the Physics properties of the objects involved in the interaction (collision, ghost, bounding box, and so on). Look at Chapter 6, "Physics," to read about the physics settings for the objects and the game.

Figure 3.16
Collision sensor.
Source: *Blender Foundation.*

This sensor is often used with collision proxies, which are invisible low-poly meshes created to spare your heavy graphic objects from the expensive collision tests.

Use It Moderately

Together with the other Physics sensors, this sensor is considered to be expensive computation-wise, so use it reasonably and use physics proxies whenever possible—a topic discussed in Chapters 6, "Physics," and Chapter 8, "Workflow and Optimization."

Near

For more advanced control over the physics interaction of your game, you can trigger actions based on the distance of the objects in your scene before they even collide. Unlike the Collision sensor, the Near sensor is only sensitive to property detection (see Figure 3.17). Leave the Property blank, and it will detect all the objects.

Figure 3.17
Near sensor.
Source: *Blender Foundation.*

This sensor will be triggered when a detected object is closer than the Trigger Distance. Once triggered, it will only stop being valid after the object is farther than the Reset Distance.

The Amazing Near Sensor

The Near sensor detects all directions. It's the game engine equivalent of the Spider-Man sense.

Radar

The Radar sensor creates a detection cone locked up to one direction (see Figure 3.18). You must choose the axis, the distance, and the angle of your detection radar. Similar to most of the other Physics sensors, you can filter the detection per property.

Figure 3.18
Radar sensor.
Source: *Blender Foundation.*

Troubleshooting and Debugging

In order to easily debug your radar settings in the game, you can turn on the Show Physics Visualization option in the Game Menu. The result is shown in Figure 3.19.

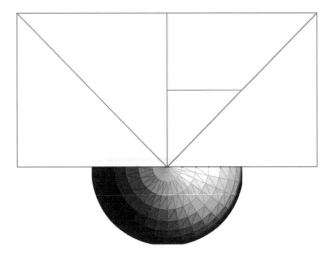

Figure 3.19
Radar Sensor Physics Visualization.

Ray

The Ray sensor can only cast rays in a specified axis (relative to the object) and as far as the determined range distance goes. Although it may seem limiting, this makes it the fastest Physics sensor available (see Figure 3.20).

Figure 3.20
Ray sensor.
Source: *Blender Foundation.*

In order to get more data from the casted ray, you can access the sensor from a Python controller. The API allows you to access hitObject, hitPosition, and hitNormal.

If X-Ray Mode is on, the ray will only stop when hitting an object with the property or material specified. Otherwise, it will stop when the first object returns None, in case of a non-match.

Random

The Random sensor generates pulses randomly (see Figure 3.21). Its use is so generic that it is misleading to define one specific application for it. You can change the Seed property to produce pseudo-random pulses. When the seed is zero, it works as a regular Always sensor.

Figure 3.21
Random sensor.
Source: *Blender Foundation.*

Do Not Use It Randomly

Use the Random sensor together with other sensors to add an organic dynamic to them. It's especially useful for environment behavior and artificial intelligence (AI).

Message

The Message sensor receives a message sent from a Message actuator or from a Python controller (see Figure 3.22). A game object will receive any message sent specifically to it or broadcast to all the objects. To achieve another level of control, you can use the optional Subject field to filter the messages of a particular subject (not triggering it otherwise). Take a look at the Message actuator for a longer explanation.

Figure 3.22
Message sensor.
Source: *Blender Foundation.*

Extra Message Information

The extra information available in the message (subject, body) can be accessed only by a Python controller.

Property

The Property sensor helps you use properties effectively for your game objects (see Figure 3.23). A game property usually does not change any aspect of your game directly (see the note "Expressions"). Instead, they store a value (for example, life points) to be interpreted and to invoke specific actions and effects.

Figure 3.23
Property sensor.
Source: *Blender Foundation.*

This sensor has different evaluation types that allow you to detect specific values, track ranges, or sense any property change. Respectively, they are: equal, not equal, interval, and changed. Be aware that the interval option should not be used by Strings and Booleans, but it is the only one recommended for Timer properties.

The exceptions are properties used by Python scripts, those used by Filters 2D, and Text strings used by Bitmap Texts.

Expressions

Instead of direct values, you can use an expression in the value fields for this sensor. Take a look at the Expression controller for more details.

CONTROLLERS

Sensors can't do much for themselves without controllers. As explained in the architecture section, controllers are the central piece of the logic bricks, because all events pass through them, as well as the actions of the game. Yet, they are simple to understand and use. For games using only logic bricks, you will be using one or two types of controllers most of the time. Indeed, until a few Blender versions ago, we didn't have more than four kinds of controllers.

In this section, the Expression controller deserves special attention due to the possibilities that it brings. The Python controller, on the other hand, is the shining star of another section of the book, as it reveals a world of complexity and promises. It can be skipped for now and revisited once you get to Chapter 7, "Python Scripting."

Using States as Organization Layers

The controller state system was designed to help in building advanced state machine systems. But as it turned out, it works great as a way to organize your logic bricks. You can use different states as layers, to group controllers and their linked sensors and actuators. The initial state of the controller needs to include all the states you set. But while working, you can alternate the visible states to show only a small parcel of them at a time.

Header

Similar to the sensors, each controller carries a unique set of information, regardless of its type. Pay special attention to the State and Mark options, both unique to controllers. In Figure 3.24, you will find all the options available on their headers.

Figure 3.24
Controller header.
Source: *Blender Foundation.*

- **Name:** Unlike the sensors and actuators, the name here has no importance other than to keep your controllers easy to identify when not expanded.

- **State:** Set the state (from 1 to 30) of the controller. To read about the state machine system, check out the "State Machine" section in this chapter.

- **Mark:** Forces the controller to run before non-marked controllers.

Booleans

When you have one single sensor that has to call an actuator, there is not much to worry about. In this case, a simple And controller will make it work. If instead you need to activate the actuator only when the sensor is False, you can use the Invert option to keep using the same Add controller. Too simple? Let's complicate it a bit then. What if you have two sensors and only one of them needs to be True? You could create two And controllers linked to the same actuator. It's not elegant, but it would work.

How Many Times Can You Activate an Actuator?

If you think that the setup above would call the actuator twice, then have fun testing it. An actuator is activated only once per frame, regardless of the number of controllers calling it.

But what if you wanted to use only one controller to handle those two sensors? In this case, it would be the Or controller, created specifically for that. That's not all, though. Either for convenience or for more advanced control, you could simplify your controllers by using the other Boolean controllers. Together with And and Or, those are the other logic switches to use when combining multiple sensors and their outcomes.

- **And:** True if *all* the sensors are True. False if *any* of the sensors is False.

- **Or:** True if *any* of the sensors is True. False if *all* the sensors are False.

- **Nand:** True if *any* of the sensors is False. False if *all* the sensors are True.

- **Nor:** True if *all* the sensors are False. False if *any* of the sensors is True.

- **Xor:** True when *only one* sensor is True. False if *more than one* sensor is True or if *all* the sensors are False.

- **Xnor:** True if *more than one* sensor is True or if *all* the sensors are False. False when *only one* sensor is True and *all* the other sensors are False.

Expression

Sometimes logic switches don't give you enough control to evaluate your sensors. You may want to compare the value of more than one property at once, or maybe even to check for specific arranges in your sensors, calling the actuator only when some sensors are positive and others negative. Or why not (it's your game after all) do all of this together? As you have guessed, expressions can handle all of those situations and a few others.

Before going into all of the options, let's first take a look at some examples:

First case: We want to eliminate your player when the energy is zero, and there are no lives left. So we create two game properties, named "energy" and "life," and control them with the expression:

```
energy<=0 AND life==0
```

Simple, right? But what if you want to finish the game when you type "quit"? Now you need a keyboard sensor with all keys logged to a text property. The expression would be:

```
text=="quit\n"
```

End of Line

Here we are using \n to identify a Return (Enter) right after the word. You can see this last technique combined with other actuators and different objects on: \Book\Chapter3\controller_expression.blend.

This is especially powerful for quick prototyping and debugging of your game.

Expressions tend to be as simple as the examples presented. They can grow big, however, and the following parts will show how to combine simple expressions to create more advanced controllers. Keep in mind that expressions are actually used also in the Property sensor and Property actuator. The difference is that for them the result will be directly used as the property value. Therefore, there you will use mostly Values and Arithmetic Operations. For the Expression controller, the expected value is always a Boolean, so you end up using Comparison Test and the Boolean Operations more often.

Error Checkpoint

Always check the console for errors. If the expression is incorrect, the game engine will print an error when you call the controller.

Values

The simplest expression contains no more than a single value. If you want to check if a Boolean property is true, you only need to use its name as a value:

```
my_property_that_may_be_true
```

For the Expression controller, you will only use the lonely value when dealing with Booleans; however, for the Property sensor, Property actuator and as part of big expressions, you can also use the following types as values:

- **Boolean:** True, False
- **Number:** 5, −7, 3.5, 40, 3.5—integers and floats, positive, negative, and even zero.
- **String:** "text"—always within quotation marks.
- **Property:** propertyName—gives the property value.
- **Sensor:** sensorName—gives True or False according to the sensor status.

A single value is not exactly an expression. Let's move on and see what kind of expressions and operations we can make when combining them together:

Sensors in an Expression

In order to use a sensor name, the sensor has to be linked to the Expression controller. Sensors can't be used in the expressions for the Property sensor and the Property actuator.

Comparison Tests

If instead of testing a single variable, you need to compare two values, there are five different comparison tests you can use. The test can be between a variable (property or sensor) and a value, two values, or two variables:

- **Equal:** fruit = "jabuticaba"
- **Greater:** 2.5 > 2.49
- **Lesser:** energy < 37
- **Greater or Equal:** speed >= 100.0
- **Lesser or Equal:** timer <= 2011

The result of a comparison test will always be a Boolean. If you need to return a value other than True or False, then what you are looking for is:

Condition Statement: IF (frame < 0, −1, 0)

The syntax is: IF (Condition, ValueWhenTrue, ValueWhenFalse). If you use the above expression as a value for the Add mode in a Property actuator, it will decrease the counter (for example, frame) if the value is greater than zero.

Arithmetic Operations

If your value is numeric, you can also manipulate it a bit. This can be used to assign a value based on a variable (for example, speed * time) or as part of a test (for example, energy + potion > 0). The most basic math operations are supported to operate your value:

- **Addition:** 1 + 3.8
- **Subtraction:** 10.5 – 5
- **Multiplication:** 23 * 1000
- **Division:** 37/400
- **Modulus:** 10 % 3

Boolean Operations

Finally, you have the capability of combining Boolean tests together. A Boolean test can be a simple Boolean value (for example, a sensor or a property value) or the result of a comparison test. They work as aggregators through which you can compile big expression tests.

- **And:** `potionKeyboardSensor AND numberPotions > 0 AND energy + 30 < 60`
- **Or:** `speed <= 0.0 OR stopKeyboardSensor`
- **Not:** `jumpKeyboardSensor AND NOT floorCollisionSensor`

The Boolean operations are not commutative or associative when grouped together. For example, try to read the following expressions:

```
1 = 2 AND 3 > 4 OR 5<6
False AND False OR True
```

They are intentionally ambiguous. Are we testing the AND or the OR first? In order to solve this issue, you can use parentheses to isolate your expressions. The previous expressions are evaluated as:

```
(1 = 2 AND 3 > 4) OR 5 < 6
(False AND False) OR True
```

Those expressions will result in true (false or true = true). If the expected result was false, we should have grouped it as:

```
1 = 2 AND (3 > 4 OR 5 < 6)
False AND (False OR True)
```

You can find an elegant use of the Boolean operators to create a toggle mechanism on: \Book\Chapter3\controller_expression_toggle.blend.

Fake Flipper Animation with Expressions

In the accompanying material, you can see a simulation of the Flipper animation mode implemented using the Property mode instead. This is done in two different ways: one with an Expression controller, and another with Nand and And controllers and an Expression in a Property actuator. It shows the flexibility of the system and is a nice way to regulate the speed of your animation:

\Book\Chapter3\controller_expression_flipper.blend.

Python Controller

With a Python controller, you can evaluate sensors and activate actuators just as you would do with the other controllers. You can indeed replace any of the tests (logical switches or expressions) by an equivalent in Python. Actually, not only can the other controllers be replaced by this, but also most of your logic bricks as well. Chapter 7 is entirely dedicated to how and when to use this controller. Even if you are not into programming, we recommend you read the introduction sections of this chapter to understand its differences and advantages.

There are two types of Python controllers: Script and Module.

- **Script:** This will take an internal Text datablock and run it as a script.

- **Module:** This will call a module from a script file inside or outside your game file. The Module mode has a Debug option that forces the module to be recompiled every time you call it. This is really slow, but allows you to do changes in your script while your game is playing.

Which Came First, the Controller or the Controller?

For scripts, the order in which the controllers is executed matters. In cases where you need a script to run before the others, you can use the Mark option present in the Controller header. This is commonly used for Python controllers running scripts that are responsible for the initialization of your game variables and settings.

ACTUATORS

Last, but not least, there are the actuators. The trouble you've taken setting up sensors, controllers, and noodle linking will finally pay off. The actuators are grouped per themes (scene, game, object, actions, and so on), and their names and applications may surprise you. (For example, did you know the Camera actuator doesn't have to be used by a camera object?) We recommend that you familiarize yourself with all the options and sub-options and experiment with them as much as you can. While some effects work by themselves (for example, the Game actuator), some will be more useful when combined together (for example, Motion and Action actuators). Have fun!

Header

The header of the actuators is similar to the sensors. Like the sensors, the Name is an essential element when using the actuator with a Python controller. In Figure 3.25, you can also see the Pin, a special option available to be used with controller states.

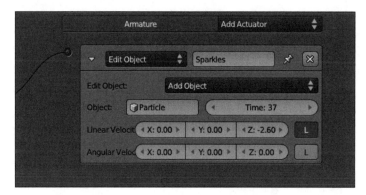

Figure 3.25
Actuator header.
Source: *Blender Foundation.*

- **Name:** This can be used to identify your actuator, even when it's not expanded. It's also used from Python scripts to activate it.

- **Pin:** When working with the state machine system, you can use the State option on top of the actuator list to show only the actuators linked to controllers from visible states. With the Pin option in the actuator header, you can set your actuator to be always visible.

Action

Camera, lights, action! And let the animation begin. Whether you want to animate your armature or you want to play a pre-recorded action, you will end up using this actuator. An action can contain different F-Curves, controlling various object properties. If you split your property curves in different actions, you can control them one at a time. For example, leave Size and ObColor in the same action, and you can have a banana that is green when it's still small and turns yellow while growing.

You can also have the same property present in multiple actions and use individual actions to store different animations.

Short Actions in the Long Run

Before the animation system redesign in Blender, it was only possible to have multiple actions for armatures and shape keys. Therefore, for any other animated action, people would create one really long action with different animations in different frame ranges. This still works well, but it's hard to manage if you ever need to change the length of one of the animations—you would have to update the start and end of all the actuators that were playing the other subanimations. You may find yourself still using this technique in order to organize your file; however, sometimes a long action can be easier to manage than multiple small ones.

The actuator will let you pick an action, set the frame range, and configure how you want to play it (see Figure 3.26). If you are planning to reuse this actuator—for example, for linked/shared logic bricks—you can leave the action blank and set it through the Python API during the game engine. In Chapter 4, "Animation," we will use this actuator in a series of tutorials.

Figure 3.26
Action actuator.
Source: *Blender Foundation.*

What Can Be Animated

Some of the animations you create in Blender can be used in the game engine. The same result you see in the viewport when you play them back with Alt+A, you can also get in the game engine. That includes armature poses, shape keys, and some of the properties of object, material, light, and camera as following:

- **Pose:** Any recorded sequence in an Armature object can be played. It's common to have different animated cycles—walking, running, jumping, tired walking, taking a break—and to alternate between them during an event. When using multiple action actuators, you may have an action currently playing when you start a new one. To make the transition smoothly, you can set the Blend In and Priority to respectively blend the animations for a certain number of frames and to play the new animation on top of the old one.

- **Shape Keys:** Similar to poses, you can play the shape key actions created in the Dope Sheet Editor with control over the blending, priority, frames, and so on. There is even a Continue option common to both that allows you to start the animation where you left the last time you activated it. Remember that you don't play the individual shape keys but rather the action that stores their influence on each other over time.

- **Object Properties:** Location, Rotation, Scale, Color, and Physics properties (Location and Rotation Damping, Anisotropic Friction).

- **Material:** Diffuse Color.

- **Light:** Energy, Color, Distance, Attenuation, Spot Size and Spot Blend.

- **Camera:** Start/End Clipping and Focal Length.

What Cannot Be Animated

Unfortunately, not everything we can animate inside Blender can be animated in the game engine. More specifically, the following elements can't be animated with the Action actuator: Drivers, Scene, World, remaining Object, Material, Camera, and Light properties.

Be aware that this may change in the near future. And some of these settings behave differently, depending on the render mode (GLSL, MultiTexture).

Animating More Elements via Scripting

Some Scene settings, such as Shading Mode, Mouse Cursor, and Eye Separation, can be set through the Python API. The same is valid for World settings, such as Mist, Background Color, Physics and Logic Maximum Steps, and FPS.

Object Settings

If you are not animating an Armature Pose or a ShapeKey, there are extra options you can use, as below and highlighted in Figure 3.27.

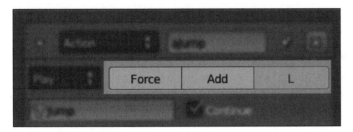

Figure 3.27
Action actuator – Dynamic Object settings.
Source: *Blender Foundation.*

- **Force:** If your object is Physical Dynamic, you can apply the transformations (for example, location) as a mechanical force. This avoids the "ghost" effect of having objects trespassing each other when their new location overlaps. With force, they will simply collide.

- **Add:** Evaluate the fcurves as relative values. This way you can add the transformations on top of each other, instead of setting a new position/size/rotation.

- **Local:** Apply the transformations in local or world coordinates.

Play Modes

The game engine, by default, plays the actions from the start to the end frame, and stops. There are times where you may want to loop the animation, play it backward, or even control the playback speed in a different way. This can be achieved by changing the Action actuator playback type, as you can see in Figure 3.28.

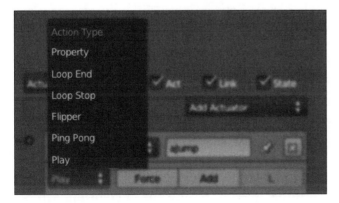

Figure 3.28
Action actuator–Play Mode.
Source: *Blender Foundation.*

- **Play:** Plays the action from start to end frames. If you want it to play again, you have to send a new positive signal to the actuator (for example, a Keyboard sensor with Pulse enabled can have the animation playing interruptedly if a key keeps being pressed).

- **Ping Pong:** Plays the animation from start to end. Next time, it will play it from end to start. Then start to end, and end to start again. And ping, pong, ping, pong.

- **Flipper:** Plays it until you keep it valid. As soon as you stop with the positive signal (for example, you release the key), it plays back to the initial frame. This happens even if the animation was only halfway through the frames.

- **Loop Stop:** Plays the animation while the actuator is valid. If the animation gets to the final frame, it loops back to the start frame. If the actuator is no longer active, it stops right away.

- **Loop End:** Plays the animation continuously going to the initial frame after reaching the final one. If you interrupt the signal in the middle of the action, it will behave like the Play mode and play it all the way until the end frame.

- **Property:** Instead of using start and final frames, you drive the animation by a game property value. You can use any number, integer or not, as the property value. That way, you can have pretty smooth playbacks. With this option, you can also simulate slow-motion, time-lapse, or even create your own Play mode by controlling the property change as you will.

Blendin, Layers, and Priority

If you need to play multiple actions for the same object, you need to configure their transitions and how they will interact. So you need to explore the remaining options in the Action actuator interface: Blendin, Layers, and Priority. Blendin works as a cross fading effect between actions, while Layer allows to have different actions playing at the same time.

- **Blendin** is necessary when you need to switch actions. More specifically, it's vital when you want to smoothly fade from one animation to another. Imagine, for example, that your character is walking and then starts to run. Even if the frames of both animation cycles start and end exactly alike, the effect will be strange. The difference in speed of the actions will make the transition too noticeable and unnatural. Thus, unless you are animating an old car with some engine problems, you don't want the transition to be so abrupt. Therefore, you can Blendin the new action (for example, to run) within the current one (to walk). Blendin works even if the old animation is no longer playing. Note that

Blendin only works between Action actuators that are in the same animation layers.

- **Priority** will determine the execution order of different actions in the same layer. If you have two or more actions playing at the same time, which one will be played? This will be up to the priority to decide. The actuator with the lowest priority will be the one played (so a low priority number equals a high execution priority).

- **Layer** allows you to have concurrently playing animations. In other words, you can stack multiple actions to be played independently. For example, you can have a base layer for the body actions and a top layer for the face animations. While the body can be playing a walking animation, the face can be playing different idle actions. Splitting actions in separate layers (and separate Action actuators) also allows for gradual blending between the actions.

- **Layer Weight** sets the ratio of influence of the previous animation layers to blend into the current Action actuator.

Armature

The Action actuator is not the only way of moving and controlling your armature. With the help of bone constraints, armatures can perform autonomous interactions with other objects. Together with the Armature sensor, this actuator was originally created for robotic simulations. Nevertheless, these kinds of non-baked/pre-done bone animations can serve multiple purposes. For a proper explanation on when this can be used and how it works, please refer to the iTaSC section in Chapter 4, "Animation."

And for more information, please visit: http://wiki.blender.org/index.php/Dev:Source/GameEngine/RobotIKSolver.

Figure 3.29
Armature actuator.
Source: *Blender Foundation.*

The actuator modes are the following:

- **Run Armature:** Runs the simulation in this armature.

- **Enable/Disable:** Takes a bone and a bone constraint as arguments. It allows you to control when this particular constraint should run.

- **Set Influence:** Sets the influence of a bone constraint dynamically.

- **Set Weight:** Sets the weight of the IK influence in a bone.

- **Set Target:** Sets the targets for a bone constraint. When using the Inverse Kinematic Constraint, you can also set the Secondary Target (also known as *polar target*).

Dynamic Constraints

This actuator only works for Armature objects. If you want to drive some of the bone parameters (for example a bone constraint influence), you need to have an active Armature actuator with the "Run Armature" option.

You can find an example of Set Influence with Run Armature in the sample file \Book\Chapter3 \influence_dynamic.blend.

Camera

The Camera actuator will move your object (usually your active camera) behind the specified axis (X or Y) of the camera object (see Figure 3.30). The front part of your object is its Y axis, because this is the one used in the final alignment. It will not act right away, though. The more you activate it, the closer you get to the specified parameters: Min, Max, and Height. After reaching the target, your object will keep "bobbing," while making sure it keeps itself inside the distance determined by the Min and Max range.

Figure 3.30
Camera actuator.
Source: *Blender Foundation.*

If You Are Looking to Change the Active Camera, Keep Looking

If you are trying to change the active camera of the scene, please look at the Scene actuator.

Constraint

The Constraint actuator takes control over your object position and orientation. You can use it to make sure that an object is always close to the ground, which is probably the most popular application of it. If you are into physics demos and sci-fi games, you might use it to simulate an anti-gravitational field. What if you want to make a bop bag? A Constraint actuator will make it for you. (Well, you do have to set it up.)

Location Constraint

With the Location Constraint option, the actuator will move your object inside the specified range (see Figure 3.31). It doesn't have to happen right away, and this is one of the beauties of it. You can set a Damping factor, which will determine how many frames it will take for the object to get in the right position; this produces very smooth results.

Figure 3.31
Constraint actuator – Location.
Source: *Blender Foundation.*

The Min and Max are global coordinates and can only restrict one axis at a time. To lock your object into a three-dimensional cage, you need three distinct Constraint actuators. This will give you full control over the range of positions where your object should be.

Distance Constraint

The Distance Constraint option compares and controls the distance between your object and nearby objects (see Figure 3.32). You first have to determine which axis you want to use for the distance check. If you toggle the **L** button, the actuator uses the object axis; otherwise, it uses the global one. The game engine will cast a ray in that direction and try to find a surface that has the game property or the material specified with the M/P option. It uses the Range to determine the maximum length of the casted ray. If the ray hits a face, the following options will be considered:

- **Force Distance:** Sets the new distance between your object and the found/hit surface.

- **Damping:** The number of frames for the repositioning to be complete.

- **N:** Turn it on, and your object will be aligned with the (normal of the) found/hit surface.

- **RotDamping:** The number of frames to complete the alignment rotation.

Figure 3.32
Constraint actuator – Distance.
Source: *Blender Foundation.*

Until a Negative Signal Do Us Part

This actuator will be active as soon as it is triggered and will remain active until it receives a negative signal or can no longer find a surface (for example, the floor) in the given range. If you want to keep your actuator active even when it doesn't find a surface to be constrained to, you can turn on the Persistency **(PER)** option. If Time is greater than zero, it will set the maximum activation period of the actuator.

Orientation Constraint

Instead of affecting your object's position, the Orientation Constraint option will restrict its rotation on individual axes (see Figure 3.33). It aligns the specified axis with the reference direction. For example, if you want to make your bop bag stay straight, you can use Z as Direction and 0, 0, 1 as the Reference direction. As with the other Constraint actuator options, you can set Min and Max angles, Damping frames, and the Time.

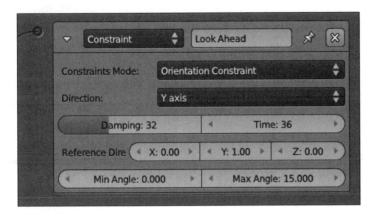

Figure 3.33
Constraint actuator – Orientation.
Source: *Blender Foundation.*

Force Field Constraint
The Force Field Constraint simulates a spring field underneath your object (see Figure 3.34). The effect is similar to hovering above water or simple buoyancy. Force fields can also be set with the Physics settings in the Material Panel (see Chapter 6 for details).

Figure 3.34
Constraint actuator – Force Field.
Source: *Blender Foundation.*

The special options are the following:

■ **Force:** Spring force of the force field.
■ **Distance:** Height of the force field.

- **RotFh:** Aligns the object axis with the normal of the force field.
- **N:** Adds a horizontal force to (the slopes of) the field.

The rest of the options behave as the ones presented for the other Constraint actuator types: Direction, M/P, PER, Time, Damping, and RotDamping.

Edit Object

There are a few actuators that feel as if they could be split into individual ones. The Edit Object is certainly one of them (see Figure 3.35). With this actuator, you can add more objects into your scene, remove your object out of it, replace its mesh, track its orientation to another object, or eventually alter some of its physics dynamics settings. Let's take a look at them:

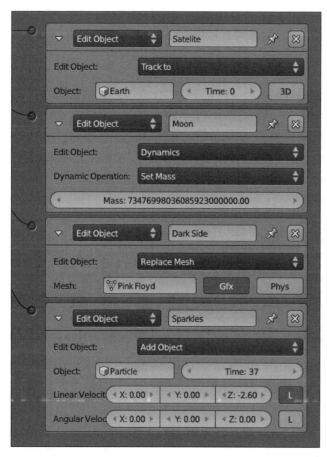

Figure 3.35
Edit Object actuator.
Source: *Blender Foundation.*

- **AddObject:** If you have objects in one of the non-visible layers, you can add them into the game with this option. The added object will be at the position and with the orientation of the object controlling the actuator. The scale, however, will be a combination of both objects. Other than that, the new object is pretty much autonomous—actually game property and logic bricks in the new object will be as good as if the object existed since frame one. The only exception is the Timer game properties that start counting only when the object gets added. You can add multiple instances of the same object, and any of them will behave as an independent duplicated copy of it.

Through the options in the interface, you can change the initial linear and angular velocity of the object and its life duration.

For More Control Go with Python

There are so many applications for this feature that it is hard to narrow them down to one example. They run from dynamically populating your game to creating short duration particle effects. You may find yourself looking for more control over added objects, and scripting may address this for you. Through the Python API, you can access the previously added object, get its life span, or even completely replace the actuator by its Python equivalent function KX_Scene.addObject().

- **EndObject:** Take a deep look at your game object. Now turn away and say bye! Not only will your object be removed from the game, but also any child object parented to it.

- **ReplaceMesh:** If your object is not an Armature, a Camera, an Empty, a Lamp, or a Text, it does have a mesh attached to it. And if it has a mesh, it can have it switched into a different one. There are two options here: to replace the graphic mesh—the one you see rendered—or to replace the physical mesh—the one used for physics interactions, viewed with Show Physics Visualization.

But Isn't This Slow? Not Really

This feature works pretty fast. All meshes in the blender file are preconverted when the game is launched. When the actuator is activated, the game engine simply swaps the current mesh for the new one. This works even if there is no visible object using the mesh you want to replace, or there is no object at all; just make sure to keep the mesh alive with the "fake user" option.

This option can be used to implement what is known as level of detail: you swap your object mesh based on its distance to the camera. Whether the extra stress on your logic and eventual scripting makes up for the gain in rasterizer performance will be up to your particular game.

- **TrackTo:** Unlike the Camera actuator, this Edit Object option will not move your object but rather change its rotation. Your object will work as a security camera tracking the object specified in the Object field. The 3D tracking option allows for three degrees of freedom in the tracker object. If Time is bigger than zero, it will determine how long a tracking lasts before the actuator is reactivated. To change the tracking axes, go to the Relations Extras options in the Object panel.

- **Dynamics:** Rigid Body and Dynamics can be turned off and back on here. That doesn't make a static object into a Rigid Body or Dynamic. It works to temporarily (or permanently) disable the physics behavior of one. The mass of the object can be changed here as well.

Message

There are different ways to coordinate actions between different objects. As presented earlier, one of them is through linking logic bricks from different objects. That is not only messy, but also limiting; you can only link objects if they are both present in the game altogether (ruling out dynamic added objects); nor can you broadcast an action over multiple objects without linking them manually. A good alternative is to use the Message actuator to send a message for other objects (or for itself). The three optional available fields are: To, Subject, and Body. You can see them in Figure 3.36.

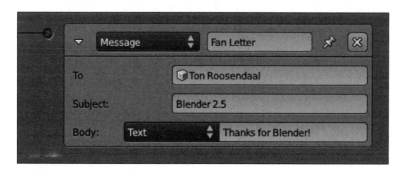

Figure 3.36
Message actuator.
Source: *Blender Foundation.*

If you don't know which object to send the message to (or want to send it to more than one), you can broadcast it instead. For that you simply have to omit the To parameter. A Message sensor—the other part of the story—can filter messages by their Subject. The Body can only be retrieved by a Python script, and it is commonly left blank when you only want to trigger an event, not to pass a value. The Body can be either a text or the value of a property.

The Real Thing About Real-Time Is That It Has a Delay

Be aware that messages are only going to be detected by the Message sensor in the next logic cycle. Therefore, it's not a full replacement for linked logic bricks.

Motion

"My body move, move, my body …move!"—hippo dance/pickup line (one of the best moments of DreamWorks' *Madagascar 2*).

It moves, but it does it in distinct ways. For example, an animated character will use an Armature actuator to control the bones and a Motion actuator to control the general movement of the object into the scene—its orientation and position. So unless the game character is doing a windmill exercise, your walking cycle will need this actuator. As a matter of fact, any object—with or without an action assigned to it—may need to rotate and move around. Therefore, this is one of the most important actuators and vastly used for a game. Let's take a deep look at the two available methods: Simple Motion and Servo Control.

Rotate It Just a Bit

Once activated, this actuator will keep playing until it receives a negative signal or until it stops receiving the positive ones. So if you want to rotate your object a few degrees only when you press a key, you must use the Tap option in the Keyboard sensor.

Simple Motion

The simplest way of moving an object is by changing its location in a specific direction. You can determine the offset in the X/Y/Z axis and in the next frame, your object will be that far from its original position. You can apply a rotation the same way, by considering the angle you want to rotate each of the axes every time. In Figure 3.37, you can see the barebones for this actuator.

Figure 3.37
Motion actuator – Simple Motion.
Source: *Blender Foundation.*

But what happens if your object is a dynamic one? If the object is already being controlled by the rules of physics, you can interact with it on that instance as well. Dynamic Object Settings allow you to apply physical changes into your object and let it react to them. Instead of displacing it a few units away, you can actually push it with some force into a given direction. What will stop the object from moving in this direction forever? As in the real world, the reaction from the other objects will produce resistance through surface collision (also known as *friction*). There will be times when you want to move your object regardless of the other game actors' physics meshes. For those, you can still rely on the Loc and Rot options.

When your object is a dynamic one, you will see new options in the actuator (see Figure 3.38). Force, Torque, Linear and Angular Velocity, and Damping were all explained earlier. The difference between Force, Torque, and Linear and Angular Velocity is simple: when you use Force and Torque, you are adding physical momentum that will be applied to the object mass and result in a specific velocity. When you set the velocity directly, you have the game engine making sure the applied momentum will result on that velocity. There is also an option to Set or Add the Linear Velocity on top of the existent one and specify the Damping Frames to simulate acceleration; those are the number of frames that it will take to reach the target velocity.

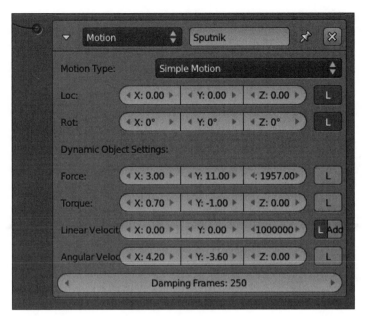

Figure 3.38
Motion actuator – Dynamic Object Settings.
Source: *Blender Foundation.*

Local and Global Again

In Blender, there are two main coordinate systems: Local and Global. Whenever you refer to an axis, you should be aware of the system you want to use. The default one is always the Global (also known as *World*) and will use the absolute X,Y,Z reference of your scene. When you want to use the Local one, which is shown as an L in the interface, the axis used will always be relative to your object's current orientation.

Servo Control

This is a more complex and complete method for controlling your object's linear movement. The Servo Control option enables you to control speed with force. It will apply a variable force in order to reach the target specified speed. It can be used to simulate the most varied effects, such as friction, flying, sliding, and so on.

The Servo Control can (and should) be used for any object, regardless of its dynamic/ physics properties (see Figure 3.39). It replaces both Location and Linear Velocity from the Simple Motion option. The produced result is a more fluid and continuous movement for your object. This also doesn't affect the behavior of collision and other physics interactions—as opposed to using Location in the Simple Motion. The latter makes the object do "jumps into space," ignoring whatever is between its original and final position.

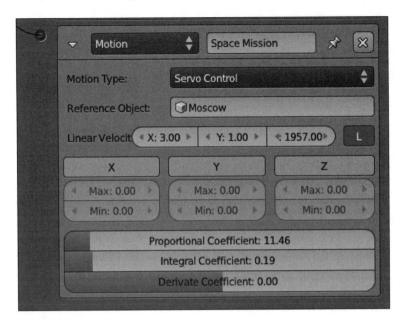

Figure 3.39
Motion actuator – Servo Control.
Source: *Blender Foundation.*

- **Reference Object:** Albert Einstein once said that everything is relative. One of the breakthroughs of his scientific findings originated from his observation of a train from different reference points (a station, the same train, another train). The Reference Object here works as such, relativizing the new velocity from its position and velocity.

- **Linear Velocity:** The target velocity used in the Servo Control calculation.

- **Force Limit X, Y, Z:** It can control the minimum and maximum of the force applied in the object. The target velocity will eventually be reached so this option works toward speeding up or slowing down the acceleration.

Advanced Motion Control

PID Servo Control System: The following options help you to control the responsiveness and the reaction of your movement. In simple English, this is known as a "control loopback mechanism," and it is a constant evaluation procedure that shapes the characteristics of your movement.

This is a generic (non-Blender specific) system; for more information, look at external references such as: http://en.wikipedia.org/wiki/PID_controller

- **Proportional Coefficient:** You don't need to change this parameter unless you know what you are doing. It will adjust itself to be 60 times the Integral Coefficient, so if you want a different value, remember to update it after making any adjustments there.

- **Integral Coefficient:** The default value (0.5) will give you a fast response into the system. Values as small as 0.1 will produce very slow responses.

- **Derivate Coefficient:** This parameter is not required and has a direct effect on the stability of the movement. High values can cause instability.

Character Motion

Last and more recent is the actuator to work with character objects, which is covered in Chapter 6. This actuator will only work if the object physics type is set to Character.

As you can see in Figure 3.40, most of the options are already familiar to us. The only addition is the Jump option, used to simulate a physically accurate jump from your character.

Figure 3.40
Motion actuator – Character Motion.
Source: *Blender Foundation.*

Parent

Dynamically setting the parent of your objects allows you to make small components behave as a unity. Think of a Rubik's Cube game as a good example of this. Every time you rotate a face of the cube, the small pieces will be linked to a different rotational axis. In terms of implementation, you will reset the parent relation of the individual pieces on every rotation. Now, thanks to the Parent actuator, you only have to worry about the face's movement as a whole, instead of the pieces individually.

Figure 3.41
Parent actuator.
Source: *Blender Foundation.*

The UI options are presented in Figure 3.41. If the parent object shape is a compound (set in the Physics panel), you can merge the shapes with the Compound option. From an opposing standpoint, when you don't want your object to interfere with your parent physics geometry, you can check the Ghost option to make it behave as such.

If You Go with Physics, Don't Parent It!

Some of the physics interactions, such as Rigid Body, will behave erratically or not work at all when your object is parented.

Property

There are a few ways of changing your game properties. You can change them through a Python script, a logging option from a logic brick (for example, a Keyboard sensor), or by using the Property actuator (see Figure 3.42). Let's take a look at the available options.

Figure 3.42
Property actuator.
Source: *Blender Foundation.*

- **Add:** Increments or decrements of numbers can be done with this option. Remember to use the minus sign to decrease a number, although when adding a number to a String property, that number will get added to the text, regardless of its signal.

- **Assign:** This option allows you to specify a new value for your property or to copy it from another property of the same object. When your property is a String, you can enclose the new value in single or double quotes.

- **Copy:** Copy a property from a different object. See the note that follows on different data type conversions.

- **Toggle:** When the property is a Boolean, it will toggle from True to False and vice versa. When it's a number (integer, float or timer), it will toggle from 0 to 1 and anything different than 0 to 0.

Mixing Types

When your properties are of different types, Blender will try to accommodate them. Booleans are converted to 0 or 1 when assigned to numbers, and floats are always rounded down.

Remember the Expressions?

Instead of direct values, you can use an expression in the value fields for the Property actuator. Take a look at the Expression controller for more details.

Random

Controlled randomness is one of the keys for a decent AI (artificial intelligence). As you can see in Figure 3.43, the Random actuator has 10 options to generate pseudo-random numbers. They are divided by types—Boolean, integer, and float—and they use a seed for consistent results over time. A seed allows an algorithm to generate the same random numbers every time you start the interaction.

Figure 3.43
Random actuator.
Source: *Blender Foundation.*

The generated number is stored in a game property indicated in the Property field. Booleans are converted to 1 or 0 when assigned to a numerical property, and to a TRUE or FALSE text when assigned to a String property. Integers or floats are converted to False when they are zero and are assigned to a Boolean property; they are converted to True otherwise.

Sound

Soundtracks and sound effects—the possibilities are endless and definitely a key aspect of your game. You will use this Sound actuator when you play a "click" sound for the UI (see Figure 3.44). You will also use it to announce steps from surrounding enemies. In fact, the opening music, the main track, and the credit sounds all are musical—music, music, and music. You may love music, but if they all play together at the same time, you get the cacophonic experience of an indie garage band. On the other hand, to sync the events of your game with its sounds, you can use these options: Play, Volume, Pitch, and 3D Sound.

Figure 3.44
Sound actuator.
Source: *Blender Foundation.*

Spatial 3D Sound

If the sound has only a single channel, you can use it as a 3D sound source. That means the sound will be played using your game object position as reference; it gets louder the closer it gets to the camera, and lower when it's farther away. The 3D options cover the distance range of the volume influence of your sound, the audio cone extension, and its angles.

State

The state machine in the game engine works like a layer system on which every controller can belong to one or more state. As with the Blender layers, you can have none, one, or multiple states active at a time. If you disable a state, you will disable the logic bricks that are exclusively linked to this state's controllers. You need a way to change the active states and that's what the State actuator is for (see Figure 3.45).

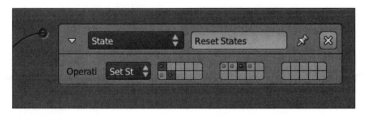

Figure 3.45
State actuator.
Source: *Blender Foundation.*

- **SetState:** Replace the current state mask entirely with the one supplied.
- **AddState, RemoveState:** Act on individual states by adding/removing the select ones.
- **ChangeState:** Toggle the selected states reversing their values.

States Continued...

Read more about how to use the states in the "State Machine" section, later in this chapter.

Visibility

In the physics buttons, you can choose the initial visibility of your object and whether or not it's an occluder object. The Visibility actuator allows you to change those properties dynamically during the game, as shown in Figure 3.46. The extra option, Children, replicates the visibility and occlusion recursively for all its children objects.

Figure 3.46
Visibility actuator.
Source: *Blender Foundation.*

Scene

While most of the actuators act on top of the object, the following actuators—Scene, Filter 2D, and the Game actuator—work globally, either per scene or per game.

Multiple scenes are a common way to make a user interface (overlay scene), handle different levels (although that can be accomplished with multiple blender files as well), or even preload your game assets in the memory (adding scenes and suspending them before effectively switching between scenes). See Figure 3.47.

Figure 3.47
Scene actuator.
Source: *Blender Foundation.*

Multiple scenes are rendered as a stack, the ones in the back first, followed by the ones on top. The Scene actuator allows you to restart your scene, change the current one, add overlay and background scenes, suspend, resume, and remove them.

Also, you can change the current camera of the scene by assigning a new camera object in the Set Camera option.

Freeze! New Scene!

Every time a new scene is set or added, the game engine has to convert all the assets into its internal objects. This is the same process that occurs for your main scene when you first load up your game. Since the game engine is single threaded for most of its operations, the whole game will freeze waiting for the new scene to load.

Filter 2D

The Filter 2D actuators are post-processing effects applied to the entire screen (see Figure 3.48). They are similar to what can be done with the Composite Nodes in Blender or the filter effects from a graphics software program such as GIMP or Photoshop.

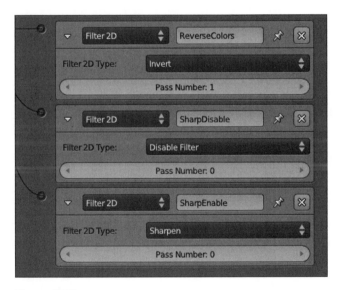

Figure 3.48
Filter 2D actuator.
Source: *Blender Foundation.*

Old Graphic Cards Support

Filters 2D require graphic cards with support for GLSL (officially included in OpenGL 2.0 or higher). Otherwise, they will not run and may crash Blender in some cases. Most of today's computers do support it, but you may have trouble running it in some old embedded graphic cards. When not supported, you will see an error report in the Blender console, and it can eventually lead to crashes on Blender. There is no harm for your system, though, so if you are not sure of the compatibility of your graphic card, you can go ahead and try it.

You may be already familiar with most of the built-in filters. They have similar implementation to traditional filters found in any digital processing software:

- **Blur:** It smudges the whole canvas. Neighboring pixels are blended together, thus existent small details are eventually lost.

- **Sharpen:** It's the opposite of Blur. The details will jump out of the screen becoming crystal clear.

- **Dilation:** While Blur averages neighboring pixels, Dilation will pick the brightest (maximum RGB value) one of the surrounding pixels and use it as the pixel color. The result is a sharper image but with a loss of details; however, it's a good compromise between Blur and Sharpen.

- **Erosion:** It works opposite to the Dilation method. This filter compares the values of all the neighboring pixels and uses the darker (minimum RGB value) one as the pixel color.

- **Laplacian:** This was originally conceived as an edge detection filter. It will produce dark regions where there are not many changes of color and bright zones when the color changes abruptly.

- **Sobel:** This is another simple edge detection formula that detects the spatial frequency of high changes in the image. It will produce images of high contrast with white lines against a solid dark background.

- **Prewitt:** Similar to the Sobel algorithm, this filter also handles edge detection. The difference is that the Prewitt algorithm is more sensitive to vertical and horizontal edges. The Sobel, on the other hand, is isotropic; it's not biased for any particular set of directions.

- **Gray Scale:** This filter discards the color information of your image, keeping the same luminance.

- **Sepia:** This simulates a photography technique to give a warmer tone for a photo and make it last longer. This effect can set an interesting mood for flashbacks or past scenes in your game. The Sepia effect is reached by first converting the image into grayscale and then mixing it with a bright, desaturated yellow.

- **Invert:** Makes a negative of the frame image. What is white becomes black, what is pure red is converted to cyan, and so on. The inversion is made on top of the RGB values of your scene (instead of the HSV, for example).

A filter can be applied on top of another one. In order to combine more than one filter, the filters have to run in a controlled order; otherwise, the effects may vary a lot. To run in the correct order, each Filter 2D actuator has a Pass Number, which will determine which runs first by an ascending order.

There are two extra filters that complement the usage of the other ones:

- **Custom Filter:** This is a more advanced option that allows you to write your own filters for your game (see Figure 3.49). There are interesting effects that can be implemented: depth of field, screen-space ambient occlusion, high dynamic range, color balance, vignetting, noise, and so on

Figure 3.49
Filter 2D actuator – Custom Filter.
Source: *Blender Foundation.*

It's still important to be aware of the Pass Number, just as for the other filters. The Custom Filter can be mixed with the others with no problems. Finally, you can select a Text datablock to use as the filter source. The filter is actually a GLSL shader, which is a whole topic on its own. Chapter 5 covers that in depth along with other graphic topics.

- **Motion Blur:** In a video camera, fast objects appear to be blurred the faster they go. It's quite a popular effect and even in real-time rendering, it can be simulated in an artistic way (a euphemism for a trade-off between quality and performance with tons of compromise).

This filter has its own option to be enabled and disabled. As you can see in Figure 3.50, there is no Pass Number there. The reason is that Motion Blur is always computed before the other filters. Therefore, it will run prior to the first of your filters. You can set the Value to adjust the sensitivity and general effect of the blur—small values will produce very little blur.

Figure 3.50
Filter 2D actuator – Motion Blur.
Source: *Blender Foundation.*

Enable, Disable, Remove

You can run a Filter 2D just like any other actuator. A positive signal will trigger it once, and the filter will run. However, the filter will keep running, even if the sensor sends some negative signals.

If you want to turn a filter temporally off, you can use the Disable option. To reactivate the filter, you use Enable. If, however, you know that you will no longer need this filter during the game, you should use Remove to remove it instead. For any of these three options, you have to set the Pass Number of the filter you want to deal with.

Why Does Filter 2D Not Follow the Rest of the Actuators' Behavior?

Although it may sound arbitrary, there is a reason behind the enable/disable design of the Filter 2D system. The filters are actually shaders, small programs that must be sent to the graphic card for them to be compiled and accessible to the game. To avoid the overhead of recompiling the shaders every time you call them, the game engine keeps them in its memory from the first moment you enable them until you finish the game, remove the filter, or remove the scene where the filter belongs. *To remove the object that called the Filter 2D will not make the filter stop running.*

Game

The Game actuator concentrates on top-level functions you can perform on each game. Its options are Start, Restart, and Quit this game, Load and Save bge.logic.globalDict, as shown in Figure 3.51.

Figure 3.51
Game actuator.
Source: *Blender Foundation.*

Start Game From File will stop the game and start/load the new file. It's used to load new levels or simply to access files with new scenes. Blender will go through the whole process of loading a new file and converting the data. That may produce some waiting time where the whole game (shaders included) seems to be frozen. All the events that happened in the game will be lost with the following exceptions:

- **Global dictionary:** The python dictionary bge.logic.globalDict (explained properly in Chapter 7) is persistent through all your gameplay.

- **Material settings:** If you change the material render mode from Multitexture to GLSL, for example, it will only be valid for the new file you load. This is very useful for loading files that help you to set up the graphic property according to the user profile.

Restart Game will load the opened file again. Since it loads the saved file, any changes made before launching the game engine will not be present.

Quit Game works the same way as if the exit key is pressed (ESC key is the default, this can be changed in the render panel). When combined with the proper sensor and controllers, this option allows the user to quit the game by clicking on a button in the game, for example.

Load and Save bge.logic.globalDict is only relevant if you are using Python scripts. Once you save the global dictionary, it will create a file in the same folder as your blend file with the extension .bgeconf.

Please Wait While Game Loads…

If the initial scene of your game is too heavy, you may consider implementing a simpler initial scene/file with the game credits, title, and a "please wait while game loads" message. This scene will then have an Always sensor linked to a Game actuator set to Start Game From File.

STATE MACHINE

"Why did the controller cross the road?—to get to the next state."

A state is a conjunct of actions to be performed by a game character. In our case, it's a set of sensors, controllers, and actuators that together represent a subset of the possible behavior the character will present. Let's say it in a simple way.

Pretend we are creating a triathlon sport game. The triathlete will be able to swim, bike, and run during the course of the game. A real athlete doesn't stop to switch modalities and neither does ours. Therefore, we need to make sure the game inputs (for example, Keyboard sensors, collision detection, and so on) will result in different actions and interactions for each modality (for example, diving, jumping, crashing, and so on). The other thing we must consider is the transition of the states. In our example, each modality/state is exclusive and sequential; they can't happen simultaneously and have a specific order to follow. The player will start swimming, then biking, and finally running. Although they are independent states, they can (and likely will) share sensors and eventually actuators. In Figure 3.52, you can see a pseudo logic bricks arrangement for the initial settings of all three modalities. As you can see, the same sensor is linked to different controllers, each one in a respective state and calling different actuators.

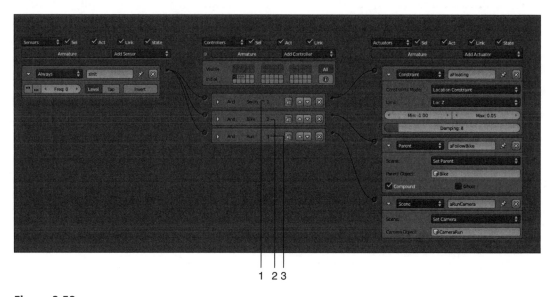

Figure 3.52
Initial settings of the triathlon state system.
Source: *Blender Foundation. Art © Cengage Learning®. All Rights Reserved.*

Although all the controllers and actuators are visible, the state 1 (Swim) is the only one that is part of the initial states. Therefore, any controllers from other states (for example, Bike and Run) will be disabled when the game starts. Indeed, sensors and actuators will only be active if the controller they are linked to are currently active. In our pseudo logic bricks, the actuator set to make the player float—a Location Constraint actuator—will be disabled automatically once the state 1 (for example, Swim) is demoted.

This is the simplest way of using states. It's not the only one, though. In more complex systems, the states don't need to be exclusive and will work more as individual components that you can turn on and off accordingly. One of the important aspects of this system is that from a controller of any state, you can completely rearrange the status of all the other states, turning them on or off.

Artificial Intelligence and the State Machine

In the artificial intelligence literature, there are multiple techniques to deal with artificial behavior. The state machine implementation in Blender is flexible enough to be used with your design, whatever you pick. Two of the most popular systems—Finite State Machine and Behavior Tree—can be implemented with the current features and the other variations might as well. The state system can also be accessed through the Python interface for a pure programming control.

SHARING AND GROUP INSTANCING

The game engine centralizes the logic components at the object level. This is at the same time a curse and a blessing. On the positive side of things, you can set up each object as a unique, independent participant of your game. The down side comes when you need to reproduce a behavior, and when the last thing you need is unique objects. Sure, you can copy over logic bricks and properties, but this is hard to maintain and doesn't scale well for more complex files. Note that we are not talking about duplicated objects—those indeed share the same logic brick. We are looking at game objects that have different individual components but need to share part of each other's functionality. We need a compromise between both systems, and this is possible with group instancing and logic bricks cross-linking.

Group instancing support in the game engine was added for the project *Yo Frankie!*—agame demo project organized and developed by the Blender Foundation in 2008. For this particular project, they had to share the logic bricks between the NPC enemies (sheeps, rats, etc.) and a different set of logic bricks for the two main playable characters (Frankie and Momo).

To Read More...

To read about their specific implementation you can look at Campbell Barton's chapter in *The Blender GameKit, 2ⁿᵈ Edition:* http://wiki.blender.org/index.php/Doc:2.4/Books/GameKit_2/12.Yo_Frankie!#Logic_Sharing.

The first and simplest usage of this feature is to replicate the same set of objects multiple times. Open the file *Book\Chapter3\group_instancing_logic_1.blend*. As you can see in Figure 3.53, here we have 10 copies of a system compound of balls and fountains. The balls will constantly roll inside the fountain and every once in a while the ball will get more of an impulse at the bottom of the fountain.

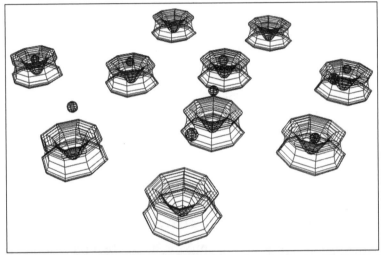

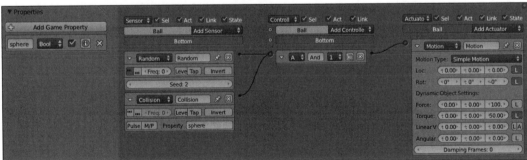

Figure 3.53
Group Instance first example.
Source: *Blender Foundation. Art © 2014 Dalai Felinto.*

There are three relevant components here: a fountain for the ball to roll in, a ball, and an invisible plane in the bottom of the fountain set to send the balls up when they collide. Since we want the objects to be alike, what we need to do is to group the three elements together and hide them in one of the non-visible layers. Now in our main layer, we can use the Add Menu (Shift+A) and select the newly created group in the Group Instance option. Figure 3.54 shows the option to be selected there.

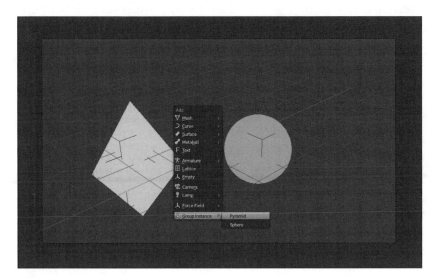

Figure 3.54
Add Menu – Group Instance.
Source: *Blender Foundation. Art © Cengage Learning®. All Rights Reserved.*

Logic Brick Duplication

There are other ways to duplicate your logic brick object. In fact, the Group Instance option from the Add Menu is simply a shortcut for using an Empty with Group as the Duplication type. Vertices and Faces can also be used there, but this will only duplicate the child object in the geometry, not an entire group.

The most obvious advantage of this is that if you need to change the logic bricks, you can at any time edit them in the original elements of the group. This will automatically be replicated to all the instances that share the same logic bricks. Group Instance also works for dynamically added objects. In other words, you can add a Group Instance by placing it in the file (as the previous example shows) or by using the Add Object option of the Edit Object actuator.

Now that you understand how Group Instancing works, let's go a step further and see a more advanced (yet still simple) example of sharing logic bricks. Please open the file \Book\Chapter3\group_instancing_logic_2.blend. In the first example, we were duplicating the same group, but here we have two different groups: Pyramid and Orbit. Both groups share one common object, the DummyMesh, and have a unique object on their own.

Now look closely at the logic bricks in Figure 3.55. The sensor and the controller are in the DummyMesh, while the actuators are in the Pyramid and the Orbit objects.

This way, a Group Instance that contains the DummyMesh and either the Pyramid or the Orbit will share similarities, allowing for individual effects on top of them. In this example, if you press the spacebar, the Pyramid rotates while the Orbit runs away from the camera.

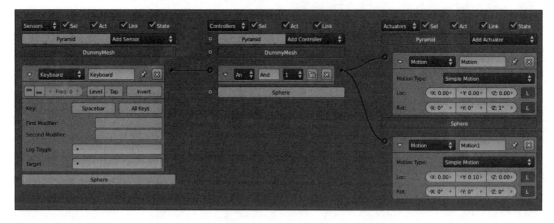

Figure 3.55
Group Instance—second example.
Source: *Blender Foundation.*

To the Infinite and Beyond

Now that we have gone over the various possibilities with logic bricks, it's time for you to put these skills into practice. Try the sample files and play with them. Rip them apart, disassemble them, and combine them. It's important to look at them creatively and use their diversity and flexibility in your favor.

In the past few years, there have been community organized game engine contests. One of the categories is specifically logic bricks-only games. It's really interesting to see what can be done without a single line of code. An online search for "Blender Game Engine Contest" should give you enough inspiration for further experimentation.

Actually, even if you are planning to use Python over plain logic bricks, it's important to understand both systems and how they work together. In the end, which tools you use will depend on the project you are working on, your team, and your workflow.

Finally, in one way or another, the next chapters all relate back to this one. You might review some parts of this chapter while learning the game engine aspects of animation, graphics, physics, constraints, and Python.

CHAPTER 4

ANIMATION

Written in collaboration with Moraes Júnior—Mango Jambo for friends—known for his work as the main character animator in the Blender Foundation open game project Yo Frankie!

Animation is the breath of life. It's the soul of your characters. And we swear we're not making that up. Take a look at the etymological origin of the word, and you will find that animation comes from *anima*, which means *soul* in Latin. Try to remember that. If for nothing else, it can help you to sound smart for the next person who wonders why you are paid to play video games. Figure 4.1 highlights what animation can be.

Figure 4.1
This chapter is about what? Hmmm? I can't see!
Source: *Blender Foundation.*

Back on the right track, in this chapter you will note a different structure than the previous chapters.

We will first talk about the main animation tools and available techniques. This part will be naturally dense, focusing on when and why to use specific animation features. Even for those experienced Blender animators, there are important aspects of the game engine system that you will need to learn because not all the resources available in Blender translate directly to the game engine.

The second part is organized as a tutorial. I worked with artist Moraes Júnior to expose his animation workflow. In this part, we will revisit the game engine animation features and learn how an artist integrates them into a production environment. For this part, it's especially important that you follow along with the steps in the book files.

Keyframing a Keyframe

Keyframe is used both as a verb and a noun in this chapter. The latter (noun) refers to the animation frames that you will manually create. The first (verb) is the action of creating those frames (through the "I" key shortcut or the Auto Recording system).

In order to use the animation system properly, it will help if you know how to produce astonishing animations. For that there is a lot of good literature available, whether it is Blender specific or not. This book will not teach you how to do nice animations. Nonetheless, we want you, the artist, to understand how to animate for the game engine.

Before You Start

If this is your first time working with animation in Blender, make sure that you haven't skipped the first chapter. The game engine uses the animations created in Blender with keyframes, F-Curves, interpolations, and so on. To learn how to master animation, you will have a better time consulting a Blender-specific book. Nevertheless, it doesn't hurt to refresh your mind regarding basic concepts and interface navigation topics covered in Chapter 1.

Every Pot Has a Cover

Every animated pot has an F-Curve.

Where do we use animations in a game? The most obvious place is for character animation; for example, whenever the player walks, jumps, or flies, you'll see game animations running. That is not the only time, though, when you'll see animations. You will also see them in cut scenes, background elements, the user interface, and so on—the list is endless. In order to cover such a wide variety of usages, there are three mechanisms that the game engine provides to animate your game elements: object transformations, armature poses, and shape keys.

- **Object transformations** enable you to change object transformations such as size, rotation, and location.

- **Armatures** let you work with a bone structure, deformed mesh, and bone special settings, such as bone constraint and bone parenting.

- **Shape keys** give you complete mesh transformation control.

These are different systems, but there is a lot of overlap among them. More importantly, you often will use them together. In the next pages, we will talk about these mechanisms individually and also see how they complement each other. In the practical aspects of how to use them effectively, we will focus on character animation, which is the most complex form of animation you can have in your game. Once you understand the concepts of character animation, you will have no difficulty in bringing life to your menu elements, shaking your environments, and directing your cut scenes.

Rousing reading awaits you. Let the fun begin. First, let's look at one fundamental concept for game animation—the animation cycle.

ANIMATION CYCLES

An animation cycle is usually a short action that when repeated produces the illusion of a continuous long movement. A classic example is the walking animation of a character. You don't need to animate the left step, then the right step, then left, then right … ad infinitum. An action with a left and right step can produce the same result. Just make sure the action starts and ends in the same pose, and you can keep playing it in a loop.

Animation cycles are at the core of the character animation in a game. A library of multiple animations can provide a diverse and rich behavior for your game character. As a reference, in a game project such as *Yo Frankie!*, the main characters—Frankie and Momo—have 87 and 70 individual unique actions, respectively. A few of the actions you can find there are: Walk, Walk Back, Walk Faster, Turn Left, Turn Right, Jump, Pick, Throw, Jump, Idle Sleep, Idle, Idle Show Off, and many others.

Moving Animation Cycles

A lot of the basic actions of a game can be expressed as moving animation cycles: to walk, to run, to spin, to fly, to roll, and to swim. You may have noticed that all these example actions express the idea of movement in space as well. However, an animation cycle does not have any influence in the displacement of the animated object. Rather, you get the final animation look and feel through a combination of external motion control (for example, a Motion actuator) and playback of an animation cycle. Indeed, if you play back only the animation action alone, you will see that it looks more like a treadmill exercise.

Still Not Convinced?

What we are doing here is splitting the bone pose animation from the object animation. We could indeed make the character move forward by moving all the bones in that direction. Although this would make the object mesh display in the right place, it wouldn't move the object's center, which would result in errors for the physics computations and eventually for the display of the object itself. The physics bounding box is calculated around the object's center, as is the camera culling test—the routine that makes sure that objects outside the camera range are not rendered.

Still Animation Cycles

There are cases where you don't need to displace your object while playing its animations, and we call them still *animation cycles*. An animation cycle without the displacement component is like a dog chasing its own tail. And if this is what you want to animate, you need the animation cycle and nothing more. In fact, any idle or secondary animations can be used directly without the need of a Motion actuator. For example, if you are doing a breath animation cycle or making your character tap his feet while waiting impatiently for you to make a move, all the animation is controlled by the armature poses. Even if your character has to move around a bit, you would not use a Motion actuator here. In these cases, make sure that the final pose is in the same position as the initial one.

Actions and F-Curves

An action in Blender is something special for animation. By its definition, an action is a collection of channels of F-Curves. It allows a property (object size, bone position, etc.) to have a different value along different frames.

But what are F-Curves? Functional Curves are curves created by control points (the keyframed positions) and interpolated to fill the void. As in Blender, in the game engine you don't need to define a keyframe for every single frame of your animation. The parts of the curve between keyframes will be calculated based on the interpolation settings and the handlers of each of the keyframes.

When we talk about the action of an object, we are referring to the current action linked to it. This is the animation that will be played when you play back the animation in the viewport, or if you render the animation from Blender. This is also the action the keyframes are stored in. To play this action in the game engine, you need to get the action name to use in the Action actuator—select the object, and you will find the action in the Dope Sheet when set to Action Editor.

Don't Lose Your Action

If you want to play different actions for the same object during a game, you need to create them in Blender. An action is a datablock that can be named, removed, imported, and linked as any other Blender datablock.

It is important to set the Fake User option (in the header of the Dope Sheet set to Action Editor) if you plan to unlink an action from an object and create a new one. Otherwise, the software will assume you no longer need that action and will remove it the next time you save and reopen your file.

Also, you can use an action created by one object in another object, proven that they are compatible. For most objects all they need is to be of the same type. For armatures, they also should have the same amount of bones with the same names. For meshes with shape key actions, the shape key channels need to have the same name.

At first we don't edit a curve directly in the F-Curve Editor. The usual workflow is to first keyframe some parameters (for example, position and rotation) in the 3D view. After the blocking of your key and in-between poses, you may want to do tiny adjustments in the curve. This is the time when you can go to the F-Curve Editor and make changes directly in the curves. With some practice you may even look at the chaos as in Figure 4.2 and see bouncing balls and smooth fade-ins and fade-outs.

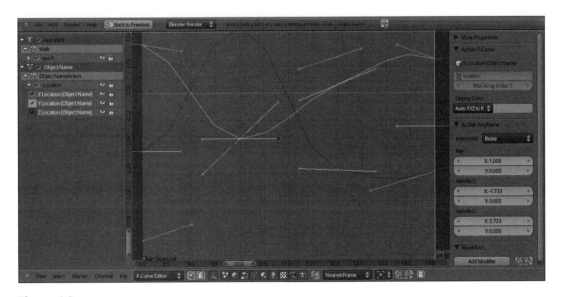

Figure 4.2
F-Curve chaos.
Source: *Blender Foundation.*

Even when you are using the Action actuator, you will be internally manipulating F-Curves (through the Dope Sheet or luckily the 3D view). The only actions that will change your object geometry are the bone pose action and the shape key actions. The former will play the bone pose action for your armature, while the latter plays a shape key action affecting the whole mesh.

Other actions can be used to animate your object as a whole without affecting its internal geometry. You can move the object, change its size, rotate it, and animate its specific type parameters. For example, you can animate a camera to follow a pre-determined path or animate a lamp to flicker a dimly colored dynamic light. Does your camera need to change the lens during the game? An action can easily do that for you.

ARMATURE AND POSES

The Bone animation system works in the game engine very closely to the way it does in Blender. You will create a Mesh object and an Armature object to deform the first.

Mesh and Armature

Both the Armature and the Mesh objects need to be present in the game for them to work. In fact, if you are adding the animated object dynamically (for example, through an Add Object actuator), you will refer to the Armature object to bring in the animated conjunct.

As in Blender, the Armature object is the parent of the Mesh object. Therefore the armature will be the game object running most of the animation sensors and actuators. Thus you may as well dump all the logic bricks of your object in the armature. An exception is the Replace Mesh option in the Edit Object actuator. In that case you need to run the actuator in the Mesh object itself.

The workflow for armature and bones resembles the NLA (Non-Linear Animation) Editor in Blender. You create individual animation actions that you want to be played at a certain time. Those are the actions we referred to when talking about the animation cycles, earlier in this chapter.

The first difference is that you don't need to predefine the order and length of all the action you want to play. For example, in the NLA Editor if you want to animate a shark turning, you will create an action for "Straight Swimming" and another for "Turning." You will alternate between them based on your script: maybe the shark turns at the same time you throw bait close by.

Speaking of NLA

Even though NLA animation is not supported in the game engine, you can still use the NLA Editor to make your animation sequences. Cut scenes or complex dialog scenes can benefit a lot from an NLA based workflow.

For example, you can combine dialog actions from a MoCap (motion capture) system with pregenerated idle body animation cycles. Once the animation editing is done you need to combine the actions into a single action with the Bake Action operator, available via the Search Menu (spacebar).

Unlike in the NLA Editor, we have a chance to play actions based on the player decisions or AI predesigned interactions. In our shark example, we can have the player controlling the shark and turning it when it gets tired of swimming in a straight line. Maybe this shark likes to chase its tail restlessly. Either way, we can play and stop playing the individual animations ("Straight Swimming" and "Turning") anytime. Figure 4.3 illustrates this.

Figure 4.3
Shark stuck in the Turning Action.
© 2014 Dalai Felinto.

The second difference is regarding the bone constraints. We will cover it in more detail later. It's important to know that not all the bone constraints that work in Blender will work in the game engine. Most of them do, so it shouldn't be much of a hassle. Also, the constrained bone and the target bone should be part of the same armature.

The third difference is the general simplicity of the armature and bone system. In general, games have simpler rigging (as the armature and bone system are known) than in animated movies. For AAA games, this is not so true—their rigs are closer to film than to traditional game rigs. In the end, the complexity of the rig is also directly related to the amount of polygons your mesh has. Therefore, as game objects naturally have fewer faces than their animated film counterparts, the rigging reflects that.

A good example is Frankie the Flying Squirrel in the animated short *Big Buck Bunny* and in the *Yo Frankie!* game. As you can see in Figure 4.4, the original model had 11,777 faces and 388 bones, while the model remade for the game has only 2,509 faces and 52 bones. Even though the role of Frankie was pumped up from a side film character to the game main character, the complexity of the game file is much simpler. (The film-file face count goes to 128,404 when you apply the Subdivision Surface modifiers.)

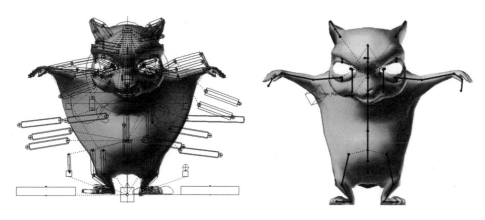

Figure 4.4
Big Buck Bunny (left) and *Yo Frankie!* (right) rigging comparison.
Source: *Blender Foundation.*

When to Use Pose Actions

Always! The main usage of pose actions is the one explained earlier when talking about animation cycles. Full animation cycles will not be the only ones in your character repertory.

You don't need to have all the bones posed in all the actions you want to play. Imagine you want to have a regular walking animation and allow the character to look back while walking. For this kind of situation, you can animate the upper-body bones in a different action than the legs and the hip. If the animations are in separate actions, you can turn the single actions (walk, look back) on and off individually. This will spare you from making an animation action for every possible combination of individual movements (blink, jump, walk, scratch the head, and so on). It also makes it simpler to control those actions. They don't need to have the same length or be called from the same actuator.

Animated characters are not the only game objects that can use the armature animation system, though. You can use armatures anytime you need more control than the Motion actuator can provide. Even a simple object like a door can use an armature to help open and close it. The problem with a door is that you often need to use the door as a colliding object—to keep the three little pigs safe from the wolf. That leads us to our next topic.

Graphic Mesh vs. Physics Shape

To animate a mesh with bones is a relatively expensive task for the computer. Therefore, when you set an object to play a pose action, you are changing only the graphic mesh of the object—the mesh used for the game render. All the physics computations, however, are done in another instance of this mesh, and are not updated with the animation. In Figure 4.5 you can see the screen when Show Physics Visualization is on and the game has an object armature animated. The original rest pose of the armature is used for the physics/collision mesh. This is the mesh with the arms lying still. Although we can see the correct pose on top of that, this is not the one used for the physics computations.

Figure 4.5
Physics mesh not updated for armatures meshes.
Source: *Blender Foundation.*

Bone Constraints

The constraints are a handy set of tools to facilitate the animation process. They are more familiar to riggers than to animators, since they are used to build easier-to-animate armatures. Thanks to bone constraints, we can build bone controllers to ease the work with complex game armatures. Because of constraints such as the IK (Inverse Kinematics), we can create poses in very simplified ways. In a nutshell, bone constraints will spare you from animating all the bones individually by setting relations between them.

The way bone constraints work in the game engine is quite similar to Blender itself. There are a few differences, though. When you define a bone constraint—for example, the copy rotation—you set one bone to be constrained to another bone, the target bone. In this case, the constrained bone will copy the rotation of the target bone for every pose, every frame. Unlike Blender, in the game engine, the target bone and the constrained bone need to be part of the same armature.

In Blender, bone constraints can be used in two ways. The first and simplest way is to use them to help with posing. For example, the Track To bone constraint helps you indirectly animate the eyes' rotations by animating the target the eyes are looking at. In this case, even though you are not directly animating the eye bones, the animation process is much more intuitive. This is how you do it in Blender, and this is how you will do it for the game engine. Another way of using them is by setting up the constraints and animating their Influence values. Each bone constraint has an influence that ranges from zero to one.

Bone Constraint Influence

When you start a game, the current influence of the bone constraints will determine the initial armature behavior. If you need to change it during the game, you can use an Armature actuator with the Set Influence option.

Bone Constraints Not Supported

Because the constrained bone and the target bone need to be in the same armature, some constraints that rely on external curves, hinges, and objects are incompatible with the game engine. In the current version of Blender, the nonsupported bone constraints are: Spline IK, Follow Path, Rigid Body Joint, Script, Shrinkwrap, and, partially, the Child Of.

Rigid Body Joint Partly Supported

Rigid Body Joint is supported as an object constraint, but not as a bone constraint. You will learn how to use it in Chapter 6, "Physics."

Bone Constraints Supported

All the Transform, Tracking, and Relationship bone constraints that were not mentioned previously can be used as you would in Blender.

In Figure 4.6, you can see the menu with all the bone constraints compatible with the game engine highlighted.

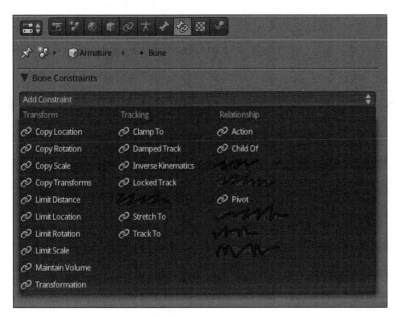

Figure 4.6
Supported bone constraints.
Source: *Blender Foundation.*

If you're not familiar with bone constraints, following is a brief overview of them and their functionalities. As with almost every other feature of the game engine, the suggested usages illustrate but do not limit their potential application.

Transform

The Transformation bone constraints help you build a bone control system. This control armature is a high-level armature, with only a few bones directly affecting the real armature.

Copy Location, Rotation, Scale

These allow you to copy part of the transformation and to set an offset for the copy. The bone doesn't get locked, allowing for further adjustments of the bone transformation (see Figures 4.7a-c).

A simple use would be building control armatures with bones duplicated between the armatures. Those bone constraints allow for syncing of the bone chains.

An artistic example of its use would be clothes or armor. The external bone chains (for clothes) can copy the base bone chain (for the body) to use as a base transformation. Since there is no locking, you can animate the external bones independently of the body animation. The offset can be used to match the real separation between the body and cloth geometries.

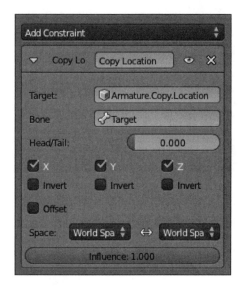

Figure 4.7a
Copy Location bone constraint.
Source: *Blender Foundation.*

Figure 4.7b
Copy Rotation bone constraint.
Source: *Blender Foundation.*

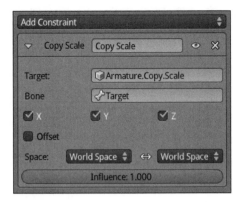

Figure 4.7c
Copy Scale bone constraint.
Source: *Blender Foundation.*

Copy Transforms

Unlike the previous bone constraints, you cannot set the bone offset in this constraint, so with influence 1.0, the constrained bone and the target bone will be exactly in the same place (see Figure 4.8).

As a rule of thumb, an influence different than 1.0 produces more interesting behaviors.

Figure 4.8
Copy Transforms bone constraint.
Source: *Blender Foundation.*

Limit Distance, Limit Rotation, Limit Scale

When you use a bone transformation to influence another bone (for example, bone control sliders or bone drivers), you are mapping a range of transformation (the position from [0,0,0] to [0,1,0] into the constrained bone—see the Transformation bone constraint). Limit bone constraints restrict the bone to transformations inside the expected range they are being mapped from (see Figures 4.9a-c).

They can also be used to complement Copy Location/Rotation/Scale bone constraints by copying the transformation but limiting some of the parameters (for example, copy location but not allow Z to be below zero—under the bone used as a ground reference).

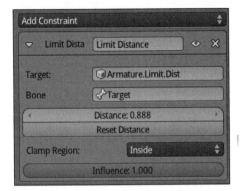

Figure 4.9a
Limit Distance bone constraint.
Source: *Blender Foundation.*

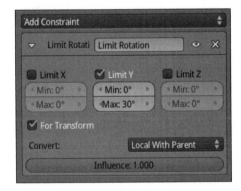

Figure 4.9b
Limit Rotation bone constraint.
Source: *Blender Foundation.*

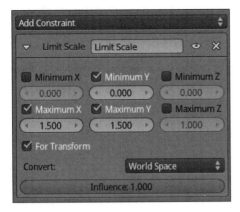

Figure 4.9c
Limit Scale bone constraint.
Source: *Blender Foundation.*

Maintain Volume

This bone constraint does not use a target (see Figure 4.10). The transformation happens only dependent on the bone itself (and within the axis opposite to the selected Free axis).

It's used for squash and stretch, the classic cartoon effect for squeezing bouncing balls.

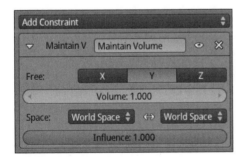

Figure 4.10
Maintain Volume bone constraint.
Source: *Blender Foundation.*

Transformation

This is the best bone constraint for sliders. It allows you to map the transformation from the target bone into a completely different transformation of the constrained bone. For example, you can map the location range of a target (slider) bone from [0,–1,0] to [0,1,0] onto the rotation of the constrained bone from –90° to 90° (see Figure 4.11).

In the book files, you can see this example of a bone slider where we are using Limit Location, Transformation, Copy Rotation, and a Limit Rotation bone constraints to set up a simple arm. It's not the optimal use of those bone constraints, but it shows how they can be set up together.

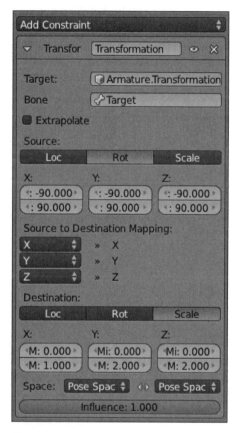

Figure 4.11
Transformation bone constraint.
Source: *Blender Foundation.*

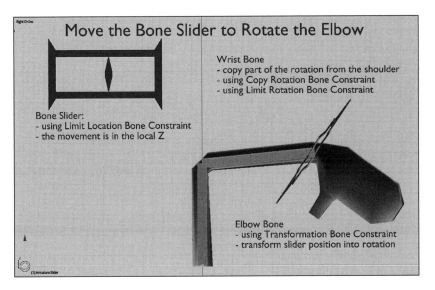

Figure 4.12
Bone slider.
© 2014 Dalai Felinto.

You can find the file in *\Book\Chapter04\1_constraints_transform.blend* (see Figure 4.12).

Tracking

A tracked bone constraint can be part of your main armature or your control bones. For example, it's common to have the Inverse Kinematics bone constraint in one bone that is part of the chain. At the same time, the Track To often uses a bone not connected to the chain and not deforming any mesh directly.

Clamp To

The Clamp To bone constraint forces the bone along a curve object (see Figure 4.13). The bone needs to be disconnected from the bone chain to properly constrain its location into the curve.

It's quite handy for cyclic environment animation of assets from your game. For example, you can make birds flying in the sky by having a predefined curve for the bones to follow along. Cars driving or even people walking in the background also can be accomplished with this technique.

Figure 4.13
Clamp To bone constraint.
Source: *Blender Foundation.*

Damped Track, Locked Track, and Track To

Those three bone constraints work in a similar way. You select a target bone—where the constrained bone will be facing—and an axis indicating the internal direction to point to that target. The difference is how much manual control over the bone rotation you need after setting up the bone constraint. While the Track To completely locks the constrained bone rotation, the Damped Track keeps it completely loose for transformations on top of the bone constraint influence.

The Damped Track gives you the most freedom between them, and it's the simplest to set up. You only have to select the axis to lock, and it allows you to adjust the rotation of any axis of the constrained bone (see Figure 4.14). You can see an example of this used in robotic eyes. The basic effect is to track a target object. But you can still spin the eye around for a cheesy, I mean, classic "droid target locked" effect.

Figure 4.14
Damped Track bone constraint.
Source: *Blender Foundation.*

Locked Track will work as a compromise between the other two trackers. It allows you to adjust the rotation of the non-tracked axis (see Figure 4.15). A security camera can be simulated with this bone constraint. A main axis is tracked by the camera (for example, doing a horizontal spin-around routine), while the other axes are independently controlled/animated.

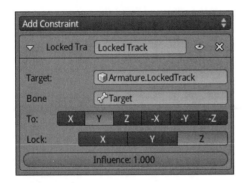

Figure 4.15
Locked Track bone constraint.
Source: *Blender Foundation.*

Track To locks the constrained bone for any rotation adjustment, leaving its rotation to be controlled entirely by the bone constraint (see Figure 4.16). By default, it rotates only one axis. However, you can track the other axis of the bone by setting Target Z in this Bone Constraint panel. The classic use of this is for eyes. Instead of rotating the eye bones directly, you can set them to track a target bone at which the eyes will be staring.

Figure 4.16
Track To bone constraint.
Source: *Blender Foundation.*

Inverse Kinematics

The IK (Inverse Kinematics) bone constraint helps you bypass the FK (Forward Kinematics) architecture of the armature bones. FK is designed for individual changes of rotation over the bone chain (from the parent to the children). In order to change a bone location, you need to rotate all the bones that lead to it and make sure the resulting rotation places the bone into the desired location (see Figure 4.17).

It's very easy to lose yourself in going back and forth to fine-tune the position of your bones. Let's look at an arm rig as an example. A simple armature would have a shoulder bone as the parent, and the arm, forearm, and hand as children. If you want to put the hand in a particular place, you need to rotate the shoulder, rotate arm, and finally rotate the hand. If you miscalculated the extension of the arm and its radius of extension, you need to go back and rotate the hand again, fine-tuning it.

With IK, you only need to move the hand to the target place. The rotation of the forearm, arm, and shoulder will be automatically calculated by Blender.

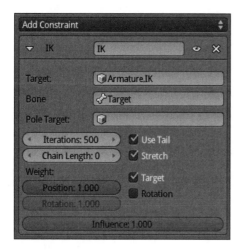

Figure 4.17
Inverse Kinematics bone constraint.
Source: *Blender Foundation.*

The target bone can't be a parent or child of any bone constrained by this bone constraint—this produces cyclic unpredictable effects. This includes not only the bone where you added the IK, but also as many bones as you set in your chain length. (Leaving it as zero influences the whole bone chain.)

Legacy Solver   By default, Blender uses the Legacy solver for the Inverse Kinematics calculations. This is how most of the animation software works and how animators are used to working.

When a bone is under the influence of an IK bone constraint, you can set specific IK settings in the Bone panel, as you can see in Figure 4.18.

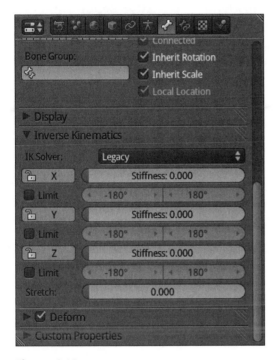

Figure 4.18
Inverse Kinematics Bone panel.
Source: *Blender Foundation.*

These parameters allow you to add some control over the otherwise automatic IK computations.

- **Limit**: In the arm, you need to make sure that the bones behave as real bones would. For example, in real life you can't twist the elbow above certain limits. In order to mimic this behavior you can force the rotation of a bone to be inside a given range. In our case, the limits would be set: X: 5° to 180°; Y: −90° to 90°; Z: 0° to 0°.

- **Stiffness:** This parameter sets how difficult it is to rotate the bone. High values make a bone rotates less. Joint stiffness can be one of the earliest symptoms of arthritis. So look after your characters.

- **Stretch:** Cartoon arms often need to stretch beyond their original sizes. The Stretch factor has to be set per bone. (Stretch needs to be enabled in the bone constraint as well, but it's on by default.)

Unlike the Stretch To bone constraint, the volume of the bone is not entirely preserved when using the IK stretch. In order words, the arm seems fat when stretched. To use IK stretching and the Stretch To bone constraint, you need to set up two bone chains separately: one for the IK, and the other—with Stretch To—to deform the mesh. The Stretch To is what preserves the correct volume for the bones. You can see a sample file in the Stretch To section later in this chapter.

Target-less Bone Constraint

If you don't select a target for the bone constraint, you can still use the IK in a special way. In this case, the constrained bone is the self-target, and as such it's free to be placed anywhere. This technique, known as *fake IK,* is really light in terms of computation. In the traditional IK, you keyframe only the target bone, thus the IK computation has to run every time you play the animation. With fake IK, the computation is valid during the transformation (when you are moving the target bone around). You have to keyframe all the individual constrained bones for this to work. (This is automatically done when AutoKey is enabled from the Timeline Editor.) Since there is no IK happening when you play the animation, the computation of fake IK is far superior to real IK.

iTaSC Solver   Additionally, you can change the IK solver in the Armature panel to use iTaSC. This name stands for *Instantaneous Task Specification using Constraints.* This IK solver was developed especially for robotics, but can be used as a more advanced replacement for the old IK (Legacy) solver.

The calculation for the armature structure is calculated on the fly, based on predefined constraints and a dynamic target. It's a very powerful system, but not directly related to the more traditional armature, bones, pose animation paradigm. No keyframes are required here.

The iTaSC solver is faster than the Legacy one and definitively better at handling real dynamic constraints (see Figure 4.19).

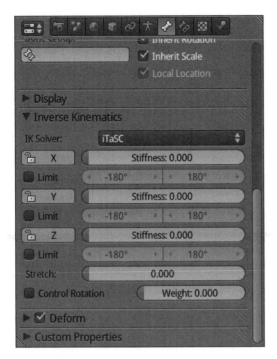

Figure 4.19
iTaSC Bone panel.
Source: *Blender Foundation.*

The other bone constraints are great to help you animate your armature, but they are not as efficient in dealing with the real-time changes in the armature to produce dynamically plausible movement. If you are into robotics or simply want to explore more advanced settings in this solver, please refer to the official documentation:

http://wiki.blender.org/index.php/Dev:Source/GameEngine/RobotIKSolver.

Stretch To

A stretched bone allows you to produce cartoon body transformations (see Figure 4.20). Different from a scaled bone, a stretched one maintains its volume. The target bone needs to be completely isolated from and not connected at all to the constrained bone. It can't be either a child or a parent.

In the book files, you can find an example of a more advanced technique that integrates Stretch To, IK, and Copy Rotation bone constraints. Study it carefully; further instructions are inside the file *\Book\Chapter04\2_cartoon_arm.blend.*

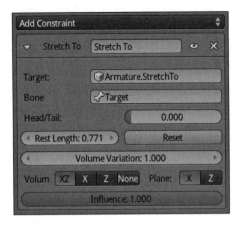

Figure 4.20
Stretch To bone constraint.
Source: *Blender Foundation.*

Relationship

The following are the bone constraints that are supported the least. Ironically, apart from the category name, there is not much relationship between them.

A bone constraint worth mention is the Action bone constraint. With it, you can play complete actions in the armature by moving one single bone around. Given the complexity of this constraint, the example part of this text evolved as a *pseudo-tutorial*. I say *pseudo-tutorial* because we are working on top of no file, although you should be able to follow the instructions and reproduce the effect yourself.

Action

With the Action bone constraint, you can play back an entire action by controlling one single bone (see Figure 4.21). Make sure that the target bone is not animated in the action you are playing; otherwise, this will produce unpredictable results. Since this is a more complicated bone constraint, the best way to show possible usages is by a pseudo-mini-tutorial as you see next.

Figure 4.21
Action bone constraint.
Source: *Blender Foundation.*

An example of using this is for *Transformers*-like animations. Let's say you need to create a character similar to Optimus Prime. The armature has two very distinct base poses: a regular car and a bad-ass robot. Some of your animation cycles will happen in the car shape and others in the robot.

You first create a separated action with two extremes—the car and the robot bones' conformation. The action itself contains the transformation between those two shapes.

Now you create a bone—disconnected from the main chain—to control the influence of this action over the bone's pose. This bone will be used as a target in the Action bone constraints you need to create for all the bones (and by that I mean create one bone constraint, set it properly, and copy over to the other bones).

Slider-like Controllers

This is indeed a classic usage of a bone controller as a slider. Since only one of the transformations of the bone (Location X) will be used to influence the played action, you can even lock the other pose transformations (Location YZ, Rotation XYZ, Scale XYZ) and create a limit location bone constraint for this bone. In Figure 4.22 you can see an example of this setup.

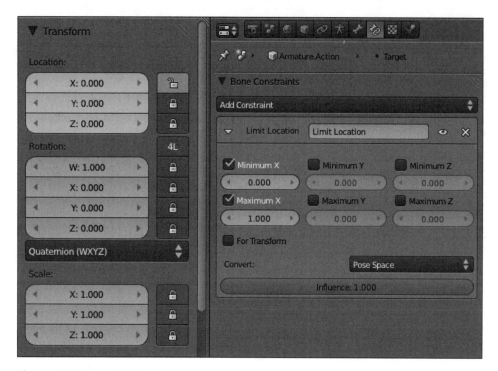

Figure 4.22
Bone constraint slider.
Source: *Blender Foundation.*

After all the setup is done, you only need to worry about the target bone when you need to switch between the poses. Move the bone to the left, and you have a car. Move it to the right, and you have a robot. Animate the bone going from left to right, and you can integrate the "*Transformers*" animation as part of any other action.

Another use for this bone constraint is to play two actions influencing the same bones at the same time. This is a work-around for the game engine's limitation of only being able to play one action that influences a bone at a time. In the book files, you can see a sample of this in \Book\Chapter04\3_action_constraint.blend. Note in the file that each Action actuator is set to its own layer, so they can be stacked together for the same object.

Child Of

It's only partially supported.

The ability to dynamically set parent relations for bones during the game is essential for some animations. Imagine that you are building a samurai game. In the nonfight moments, the sword will be inside a scabbard, and therefore it should be parented to it. During combat, the sword will move from the scabbard to the samurai's hands. From that point on, the sword should be parented to the hands so that it follows their position and rotation during the slicing-heads animation.

The bone to be dynamic parented (for example, the sword bone) needs to have no transformation in Pose mode (it needs to be in its local origin [0,0,0] and with zero rotation). It also can't have a parent, other than the ones dynamically defined by the constraint.

In Blender, you can have multiple Child Of bone constraints and alternate between the current parent for a bone. In the game engine, however, since you can't animate the Influence of bone constraint, the use is not so flexible. In the end, you will be using it as if it were the Copy Transformations bone constraints. The difference is that the Child Of allows you to select which transformations to copy over (for example, Location and Rotation), and its Set Inverse option is similar to the Offset option of the Copy Location, Rotation, and Scale bone constraints (see Figure 4.23).

Figure 4.23
Child Of bone constraint.
Source: *Blender Foundation.*

Another option for this type of animation is to use bone parenting. With that, the sword can even be a Physics object and interact with other elements of the game. This is covered in the last tutorial of this chapter, titled "Hats Off to Momo and Vice-Versa."

Not Supported Yet Useful

As with the other bone constraints not properly supported in the game engine, you can still use it fully to help with animating in Blender. However, you will need to bake the constrained bone transformations in order to see the changes in the game engine. This topic is covered later in Chapter 8, "Workflow and Optimization."

Floor

The floor allows you to create an imaginary plane to constrain your bone transformations to. It creates the equivalent of a floor, a ceiling, or a wall that cannot be transposed. The pose location from the constrained bone must be cleaned for the clamping to the plane to work (Alt+G). See Figure 4.24.

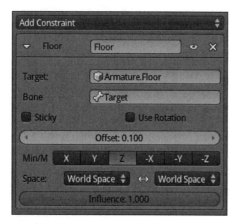

Figure 4.24
Floor bone constraint.
Source: *Blender Foundation.*

Pivot

This bone constraint helps rotate bones around a specific bone. An example would be to create a screwdriver animation. The screw position would be represented by a bone used as a pivot (the target bone in this bone constraint). The hand with the screwdriver would have its rotation locked to the pivot. To make the Influence propagate through the bone chain, you would need the hand bone to have an IK bone constraint (see Figure 4.25).

Given that often the screw will not be part of the mesh directly deformed by the armature (unless you are animating Frankenstein preparing himself for an IQ test), the Pivot bone can be the parent of an external object you use as a placeholder for the screw. More on that in the next section.

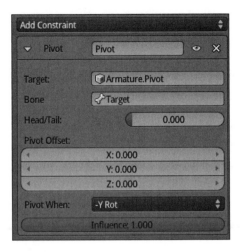

Figure 4.25
Pivot bone constraint.
Source: *Blender Foundation.*

BONE PARENTING

It's not Vegas, but what happens in the armature does stay in the armature. So, how do you make your animation affect other objects? The armature affects the deformed mesh, but that's not all.

Bone parenting allows you to sync external events with the internal animation. It's a very simple feature, similar to object-to-object parenting. The difference here is that you parent one object to a bone. Whenever you animate the armature, the bone position will be copied over to the child object. This child object actually acts as a parent for other objects. It works as an integrated extension of the armature into the game world.

Earlier, when talking about armature and poses, we mentioned that the Physics mesh of your deformed mesh is not deformed. Nevertheless, you still can use bone parenting to interact physically with your world.

Let's look at an example. Imagine that you need to pick up an element (a key, a coin) in your game with your character's hand. You start by animating your arm armature and arm meshes as you would do normally. You then need an empty object parented to your hand bone and placed right on top of it. This empty will be your object. It will automatically move with your hand and can be used with any logic brick you want.

After your hand takes the key, you need to make sure the key doesn't fall to the ground or drop into a drain and meet its end next to rusted pennies, cockroaches, and my old yoyo.

As soon as the Collision object (our parented empty) touches the target object, you can set this object to be temporarily parented to this empty (which is then parented to the hand bone). Now, if you keep playing your "picking up key" animation, you will have the target element always "at hand." For more details and instructions please refer to the "Hats Off to Momo and Vice-Versa" tutorial.

In the *Yo Frankie!* game, they use this feature in a similar way. Both main characters—Frankie and Momo—have an empty parented to the wrist bone. When the player tries to catch some nuts or sheep, the game calls a Python script to control that interaction. Internally, a Collision sensor checks to see if the picked object is close to the player, and it parents the picked object to the "Throw Place Carry," the bone-parented empty. In Figure 4.26, you can see Momo's "Throw Place Carry" empty in the middle of the throwing animation.

Figure 4.26
Momo bone-parenting system.
Source: *Blender Foundation.*

SHAPE KEYS

Sometimes bone animation may not give you enough control over the mesh deformation. In those cases, you can animate the mesh directly via shape keys. As in Blender, you can define multiple shape keys representing different poses for your character. Each pose holds the position of all the vertices of your mesh.

The workflow with shape keys is different from armature animations. You start defining your base pose, and on top of that, you create pose variations. If you change your geometry later on, it will be a painful process to merge the change back to all the previously created poses, so make sure your mesh is ready before you create your shapes.

Shape Keys Performance

The level of control that you get from shape keys comes with a price. The performance required for the per-vertex calculation is considerably heavier than regular armature control. Thus, you should not abuse this technique.

When to Use Shape Keys

Use shape keys whenever the animation is too complex for armature animations. That's not the whole story, though. Shape key animations are often integrated with the traditional armature animations, not as something separate. They can work as stand-alone animations, of course; there is indeed an actuator dedicated only to that. However, the greatest application of shape keys is not to replace the bone animation but to complement it.

The most popular usage is for character facial animation. You can create a face pose for every extreme position of your expressions and rely on basic interpolations between the poses to simulate the animation. This can be used for specific applications, such as lip-sync, to general animation, such as expression of moods (happiness, sadness, Monday-ness).

In the game *Yo Frankie!*, both of the main characters used shape key animations together with armatures. Momo used six shape poses to help its animations. The simple ones help with eye blinking. What would our cute monkey be if it couldn't wink at its mates? In Figure 4.27, you can see the Momo base pose and variations of it created by changing only the influence of the four eye poses—eye lids up, eye lids down, eye brows up, and eye brow down.

Figure 4.27
Momo blinking shape key poses.
Source: *Blender Foundation.*

Isn't This Overkill?

You may be wondering if those poses could have been created with regular bone poses. You bet they could. However, the *Yo Frankie!* project has an important educational mission. One of the goals of the project was to demonstrate the multiple features of the game engine. Actually, the support for shape keys in the game engine was implemented specifically for this project. Thus, those files are the first reference that animators studied on how to use them.

The poses left—Smile and Ooh—are a bit more complex. They are opposite extremes of the same shape key animation with the Natural pose in between them. Momo can be smiling, natural, or ooh'ing. Since the latter is not a real verb, take a look at Figure 4.28 to better appreciate all the monkey sex appeal. It would be hard to get those results without adding lots of bones, which would create a system hard to animate. So shape keys are a far more elegant solution.

Figure 4.28
Momo shape keys poses: ooh, basis, and smile.
Source: *Blender Foundation.*

Frankie, the flying squirrel, also uses shape keys for some facial expressions and to control its wings. Like Momo, it would be too hard to control the wings' deformation using only bones. Therefore, a shape pose was created to show how the mesh should be when the wing is tucked in. In Figure 4.29, you can see Frankie in a natural pose and with wings active.

Figure 4.29
Frankie—Ready to fly (left) and a natural pose (right).
Source: *Blender Foundation.*

Those shape keys are not used isolated as an action. Instead, they are used as part of an armature pose, driven by a bone, like all the other animation bones. This bone is used as a driver for the shape action it is intended to control. Like the other bone-over-bone controls with constraints (which we will see next), the driver bone itself is unaware of its role as the shape key controller. Figure 4.30 shows the regular setting of the shape action to a control bone. You will learn more about this later in the tutorial section.

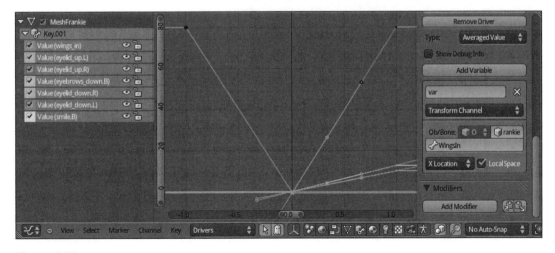

Figure 4.30
Shape key driven by a control bone.
Source: *Blender Foundation.*

Action Actuator

Shape keys can also be used directly by the Action actuator. This is useful when you need to animate your whole mesh exclusively through the vertex manipulation. Although you will probably not use it for your main character, you can make nice groundbreaking effects with this.

TUTORIALS

No keyframes were hurt in the making of these tutorials.

In the following pages, we are going to make a character walk, interact with objects, and have some nice facial expressions for you to play with. For the model, we will be using the monkey, Momo (see Figure 4.31). I cleaned up the original file, removing the shape keys and the animation cycles previously created. You can get Momo in his fresh state in *\Book\Chapter04\tutorials\tutorials_momobase.blend*.

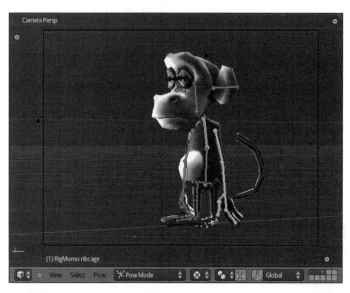

Figure 4.31
Dear Momo, get ready for rock 'n' roll!
Source: *Blender Foundation.*

PRE-TUTORIAL

In this short pre-tutorial, we will the animate the camera rotation and the camera focal length as an opening effect for the game.

The whole tutorial is based on using the Action actuators to control the Momo animations. As we explained previously, there are different action types that can be used. Regardless of the action type, the way to use the actuator is the same. So we will start with a very simple action, and progressively go over more complex topics such as bone and shape key animations.

Open the base file from the \Book\Chapter04\tutorials\tutorials_momobase.blend.

1. Change the current frame to 1.
2. Select the Camera object.
3. In the Camera panel in the Properties Editor, set focal length to 10.0.
4. With the mouse over the value, press I to keyframe it for frame 1.
5. Go to the frame 30.
6. Change the focal length to 100.0.
7. Keyframe the new value for this frame.

What we did was set an initial focal length for the camera to animate over a specific range (90mm over 30 frames ~ 1 second). If you play back the animation in Blender (Alt + A), you can see the camera zoom changing quickly over the initial frames

However, if you enter the game engine, the camera is not animated. We still need to hook this animation with the logic bricks. So with the camera still selected, we need to do the following:

1. Create an Always sensor. Leave the default options so it runs only once.
2. Create an Action actuator. Change the frame range from 1 to 30.
3. Set CameraAction as the actuator Action. (This is the action we created by keyframing the camera lens; it's automatically named by Blender).
4. Connect both bricks. (This will create an And controller.)

The logic brick can be seen in Figure 4.32. There is really not much to it other than to make sure that the animation plays once you run the game.

Figure 4.32
Setting up an Action actuator.
Source: *Blender Foundation.*

If the fast zooming of the lens still doesn't make everyone dizzy, it's time to animate the camera rotation. It's good to remember that while the rotation is a property of the Camera object, the focal length is part of the Camera datablock. As such, these transformations are stored in independent actions. Thus, we will need to create a new action (through keyframing the camera rotation) and set up a new Action actuator.

1. Change the current frame to 1.

2. Select the Camera object.

3. With the mouse over the 3D Viewport, invoke the Keyframe menu (I key) and select Rotation.

4. Advance 5 frames.

5. Change camera rotation along its local Z axis by 60° so it keeps looking forward but spinning (press R + Z + Z + 60).

6. Keyframe the rotation again.

7. Repeat the previous steps until you get (and keyframe) frame 30,which will complete a full loop of 360°.

8. Create an Action actuator. Change frame range from 1 to 30.

9. Set CameraAction.001 as the actuator Action. (This is the new action we created.)

10. Link the And controller with this Action actuator.

You can get this final file on \Book\Chapter04\tutorials\pretutorial_camera_actions .blend.

This effect is a bit annoying if you play the file multiple times to test the animation (as you will soon). So this spinning camera is not included in the base file you will use for the actual tutorial. If, however, you want to bring the camera along, you can append it into your other files. All the logic bricks and actions linked to the Camera object and Camera datablock will follow the Blender object.

ANIMATION CYCLE TUTORIAL

To start, let's open the Momo file and look at the armature. Open the book file \Book \Chapter4\tutorial_walk_1.begin.blend.

We will create a walking cycle for Momo, following these steps:

1. Armature setup

2. Extreme poses

3. Moving forward

4. Between poses

5. Play time

In this tutorial, we will not cover animation extensively. This topic alone could fill a whole book. Instead, we will focus on the workflow of integrating your animation skills with the game engine tools. You'll get some tips you can apply to both Blender and the game engine animations. Both platforms work in a similar fashion.

Armature Setup

The armature is already created, but not yet ready to animate the character. If you go to the Pose mode, you can move the individual bones, as shown in Figure 4.33. As you might already know, bones constraints are useful in posing the armature, so let's create some.

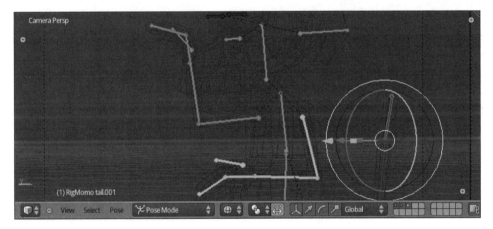

Figure 4.33
Select and move individual bones.
Source: *Blender Foundation.*

For Momo, there are two sets of bone constraints that will help your posing. The Inverse Kinematics, IK, for controlling the bone chains from their extreme bones, and Track To for the eyes.

Inverse Kinematics Bone Constraints

First, let's take a look at the IK bone constraints. IK can be used to pose arms and legs by moving only the hands and feet. The position of the arm and leg bones will be automatically calculated to accommodate the hand/feet position. Not only Momo's human counterparts (arms, legs, etc.) benefit from it, but also Momo's tail is perfect to demonstrate the usage of IK, so let's start with it. With the file open, follow these steps to get to the configuration shown in Figure 4.34.

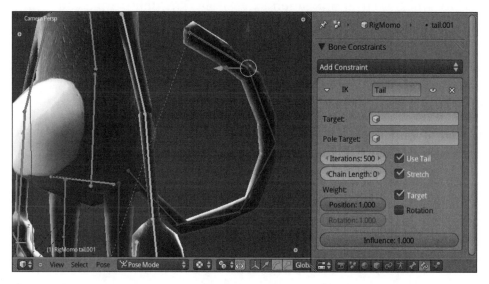

Figure 4.34
Set an IK bone constraint in Momo's tail.
Source: *Blender Foundation.*

1. Select the Armature object.

2. Change to Pose mode.

3. Select the last tail bone (RigMomo.tail.001).

4. Select Bone Constraints in the Property Editor.

5. Add an Inverse Kinematics bone constraint.

Now the setup is almost done. Before we finish, try to move the tail bone around. This results in all sorts of twists and revolving poses just by moving only a single control bone. You can see this early iteration in Figure 4.35, which went a bit too far, however. All you need is to control the chain of bones that this bone belongs to; in this case, all six bones from the tail bone group.

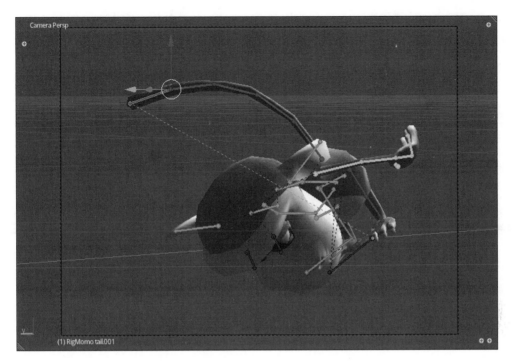

Figure 4.35
IK bone constraint with no limit.
Source: *Blender Foundation.*

In order to constrain the Influence of the bone control, you need to set the chain length in the IK Bone Constraint panel. The default value, zero, makes the chain of influenced bones as long as possible. For the tail, you can set the chain length to be five bones.

There are other IK bone constraints that we want to set. So far we have been seeing only the bones from the first bone layer. Bone layers work like the object layers in Blender. A bone can be in more than one layer, and you can choose which layer to set at a time. The bone layers can be found in the armature Object Data panel in the Property Editor, as seen in Figure 4.36.

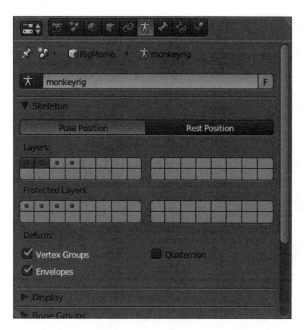

Figure 4.36
Bone layers.

Source: *Blender Foundation.*

If you can turn on the second bone layer, you will see only the hand, foot, and tail bones. They all need IK bone constraints as well. Try copying the steps for the tail bone. To mimic the original file, you need to set the chain length to be two bones for the forearm and the shin bones, and three bones for the feet. These numbers correspond to how many bones are left in the chain of bones. At this point, your file should be like the one on *\Book\Chapter4\tutorial_walk_2.ik.blend.*

Targetless Constraints

Those IK bone constraints are targetless. As explained previously in the bone constraints section, they are a fake IK. They are used only to help in posing and can be removed from the final file once the animation is done.

Track To Bone Constraints

Well, if you haven't looked at the hidden third bone layer, now is a good time to do so. As you see in Figure 4.37, in this layer, we have the eye bones and two other bones to be used as trackers. Sure, you could move the eye bones directly, but again, this is not the ideal workflow.

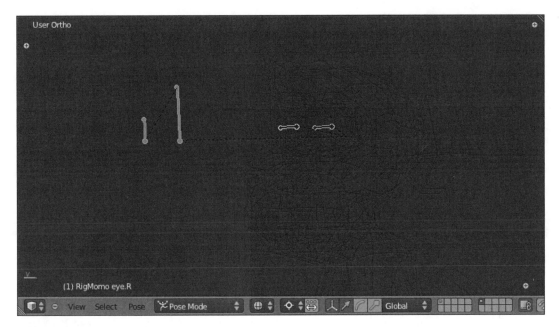

Figure 4.37
Track To bone system.
Source: *Blender Foundation.*

The two bones in front of the eyes are the tracker bones. Each eye bone will need a Track To bone constraint with those bones set as the targets. Think of the bone trackers as the direction in which Momo is looking. For example, if there is a banana on the floor, you can place the trackers right on the fruit. This will make the eyes converge there.

Setting the Track To bone constraint is not much different than setting the other bone constraints. If you follow the steps in the list below, you should see the settings shown in Figure 4.38:

1. Select the Armature object.

2. Change to Pose mode.

3. Select the left eye bone.

4. Select Bone Constraints in the Property Editor.

5. Add a Track To bone constraint.

Figure 4.38
Track To Bone Constraint panel.
Source: *Blender Foundation.*

To finish the setup, select the RigMomo as the target object and eyes.target.L as the target bone. Do the same for the right eye, and you are ready to move the target bones around. The armature is now ready for the first animation. If you just want to have fun animating the character, you can check the current file status at \Book \Chapter4\tutorial_walk_3.trackto.blend.

Extreme Poses

The first thing you need for your animation is the start position of the walking cycle. A good cycle shouldn't have a clear beginning or end, so we'll start with the extreme poses. In general, an extreme pose shows a moment when the animation hits a peak, before it changes direction. For the walking cycle, an extreme pose is when one leg is in its maximum stretch and the other is slightly bent, waiting to transfer its weight to the leg in front of it. We will start from there.

It helps to be able to view images and videos when animating. If you want to spare yourself from a visit to the nearest circus, a drawing or video of a person walking will do just fine.

On the book files, you can find an image of Momo walking in \Book\Chapter4\ *ExtremePoseSide.png* and *ExtremePoseFront.png*.

In Figure 4.39, you can see those images being used as background in a file ready for posing. This Blender file is the same one we built in the previous section with additional reference images as background. Find it in \Book\Chapter4\tutorial_walk_4 .extreme_reference.blend.

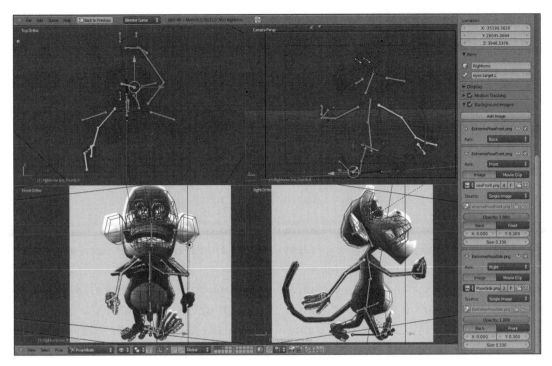

Figure 4.39
Reference image as background.
Source: *Blender Foundation.*

Reference Images

The reference images are used here in the background. If you prefer to see them on top of the view, you have two options. You can use the "Front" option in the Background Images panel. Or you can use empties instead. Add empties with the Display type set to Image. Place them in the desired location and lock their selection in the Outliner.

Try to match your armature to the reference image. In the Pose mode, move and rotate the bones around. (You don't want to change the armature in Edit mode.) Pay special attention to the feet bones to make sure they are well planted in the ground.

After you are done with the initial pose, you can go for a bit of monkey see-monkey do. Follow the steps below. The explanation follows.

1. Change current frame to 1.

2. Select all bones.

3. Keyframe Loc/Sca/Rot (I key).

4. Change frame to 41—this will be the end frame of our animation.

5. Keyframe Loc/Sca/Rot again (with the bones still selected).

6. Change frame to 21—the half of the animation where the second stride begins.

7. Copy all the bone transformations (Ctrl + C or the icon in the 3D View header).

8. Paste them mirrored (Shift + Ctrl + V or the last icon in the 3D View header).

9. Keyframe Loc/Sca/Rot yet again.

10. In the F-Curve Editor, select all bones and change Extrapolation mode to Constant (Shift + E or Channel Menu → Extrapolation mode).

What we just did was first define the animation length for 40 frames (1.3 seconds at 30 fps for one complete set of two strides). The first and last frames need to match; so we copied the transformation of the bones over frame 1 to 41. (You can copy them in the Dope Sheet Editor as well.) We copied to frame 41 and not to frame 40 because we don't want a duplicated frame in the animation. We want the transition from the last frame (40) to the first frame (1) to be the same as from the last frame (40) to the next frame (41), which is outside the loop range.

The extreme poses for the left and the right strides are flipped copies of each other. If you named your bones properly (as we did, using .L and .R for symmetric left and right bones respectively), you can mirror copy/paste them. Therefore, in the middle of our animation (frame 20), we place a copy of the poses.

Finally, the change in the Extrapolation mode ensures that the frames behave as if they were copied over and over in the Dope Sheet. The handlers of the initial key-frames change with the handlers of the final frames and vice versa.

In the Render panel in the Properties Editor, you can set the speed (30fps). The play-back range (1 to 40) can be changed in the Timeline Editor or in the same Render panel if you switch the render engine to Blender Render. With this set, you can play back (Alt + A) your file to see the two extreme poses alternating over time. Before finishing, go to the Dope Sheet Editor, switch from Dope Sheet to Action Editor and rename the previously created action from ArmatureAction to Walking. You can see the panel in Figure 4.40.

The final file can be found in \Book\Chapter4\tutorial_walk_5.extremeposes.blend.

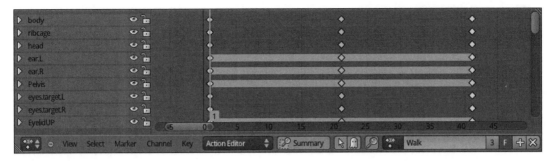

Figure 4.40
Action Editor—first poses ready.
Source: *Blender Foundation.*

Moving Forward

The final walking cycle will have no real forward movement: the character stays in the same place. It's similar to those old Looney Tunes cartoons when the coyote runs past the cliff and keeps running without going anywhere. Then he falls. Nevertheless, you still need to set up a system where you can see the character walking as if you had a Motion actuator attached to it. To help with this, we will look at two methods: using the central bone or moving the environment.

Root Bone

The simplest way to make Momo move is by keyframing the root bone along the way. The root bone is the parent of all the bones. Thus, if it moves, the rest of the armature will follow it. To set the root bone to move, go to Pose mode and do the following:

1. Select the bone. In RigMomo you will find the Bone.main on the floor level.

2. Insert a Location keyframe. This will be the initial position of the bone and armature.

3. Advance from frame 1 to 41.

4. Move the bone forward the distance of one stride—0.23 (see the note below).

5. Keyframe the new bone position.

6. Change the Channel Extrapolation mode of the root bone to Linear Extrapolation.

In the book files, you can see Momo setup with the root bone steps at *Book* *Chapter4\tutorial_walk_6.rootbone.blend.*

How Big Is a Stride?

If your character is walking, eventually you will need to find where its feet will land after each stride. This varies from person to person, and is a function of the leg's size, the speed of the movement (walking, running, jumping), and other factors such as the environment (for example, snow). For this walking cycle, you can use 23cm (or 0.23 Blender units) for the complete two strides.

After you are done with all the animation (past the polishing stage), you then can clean the bone location F-Curve. During the production of your game, you may need to come back for tweaks in your animation cycle. Therefore, instead of cleaning the bone curve you can simply disable the root bone channel in the Graph Editor. In Figure 4.41, you can see the speaker icon you use for that.

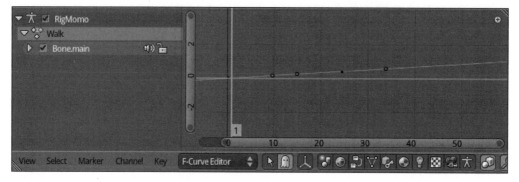

Figure 4.41
Graph Editor—disabling individual bone channels.
Source: *Blender Foundation.*

The downside of this method comes when you need to change the root bone as part of your animation. For example, sometimes you don't want your animation cycle to be uniformly moving forward. Even for Momo's walk, it's better if there is a break every time he rests one of the feet as he gets ready for the next step. As you know, the movement of the character will be decoupled from the animation cycle. And, no, we don't get tired of repeating that. So, in this case, if you look at the character from a constantly moving point of reference, it will seem as if Momo is moving forward, then backward, and then forward again to the original position. To move all the bones at once, nothing is better than the root bone. It's not a good idea to rely on a bone that you plan to disable though.

A work-around for that is to have one root bone to control the external position, and another bone (parented to the root bone) to control the internal position, relative to the object location. To avoid this surplus of global control bones, let's look at our second method.

If Mohamed Won't Go to the Mountain...

...he goes to the beach. Our dear monkey, however, is suntanned enough and might as well stay put. In other words, in this method, Momo never moves. We will instead animate the environment around him.

This method is based on the principle that perception is always relative. For example, on your computer screen, there is no way to distinguish between moving the camera away from the character and moving the character away from the camera. The result will be exactly the same. We will be adding moving placeholders that you can use as a guide to position the feet. Figure 4.42 shows the setup.

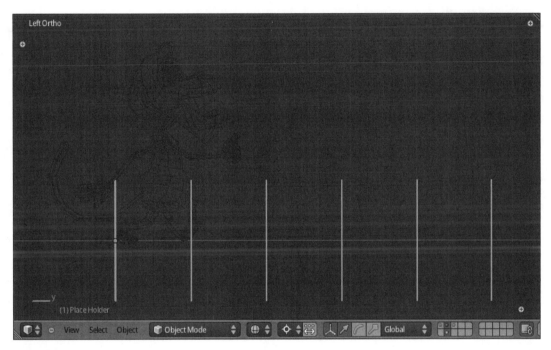

Figure 4.42
Animation feet place holders.
Source: *Blender Foundation.*

This file is on \Book\Chapter4\tutorial_walk_7.placehold.blend. You can't tell from the picture, but if you play back the animation, you will see the placeholders moving against Momo (or would it be the other way around?). In fact, the camera is static so Momo doesn't really move.

1. Create a simple, easy-to-spot object.

2. Create an Array modifier—set the constant offset to be equivalent to one stride and set enough copies to fill the screen.

3. Move the Array object to be aligned with Momo. The feet from your extreme pose should match the position of the array elements.

4. Insert a location keyframe.

5. Advance from frames 1 to 41.

6. Move the Array object forward the distance of two strides—0.46. (See the note on root bone.)

7. Keyframe the new Array object position.

8. In the Graph Editor, change the Array object Extrapolation mode to linear extrapolation.

This method requires a bit more setup than the previous one, but it has a big advantage. To work in the between poses (the next step of this tutorial), you will need to keep track of the foot position while the character moves forward. While the body is constantly moving, the feet are planted on the ground until it's their time to get up and get smashed on the floor again. This will prevent the undesirable effect known as *sliding feet*. This problem will be revisited next when we create the poses between the extremes. Figure 4.43 shows the complete walking cycle in different moments; note that the feet are always in the same place relative to the placeholders.

Figure 4.43
Animation feet placeholders.
Source: *Blender Foundation*.

Between Poses

So far we have only two poses, the extreme left and the extreme right stride poses. By default, Blender interpolates the keyframed poses, creating a smooth transition between them. This mathematic interpolation is of no use for the final animation. That leaves us with 20 frames to fill between those extreme poses.

From traditional animation literature, you can use two main techniques to create those in-between frames: straight-ahead action and pose-to-pose.

Regardless of the advantages of one or another method (you can learn more about them in the material in the reference section of this chapter), we should attend to the differences in their workflows. In straight-ahead action, you animate frames one-by-one as you go. In pose-to-pose, you create sub-extreme poses and fill in the intervals systematically.

In both cases, you need to ensure that the feet are not sliding while you pose them. Use the technique presented in the previous section to prevent this. Sliding feet and feet going under the ground are hallmarks of not enough frames and automatic interpolation. Avoid them at all costs.

Also, although you can create the animation by posing and keyframing the bones in the 3D view, you might want to tweak them in the Graph Editor. That can spare you from creating too many frames and using the handlers for fine-tuning your transitions. The fewer frames you have, the easier it is to change your animation. In Figure 4.44, you can see the current F-Curves edited for this walking cycle.

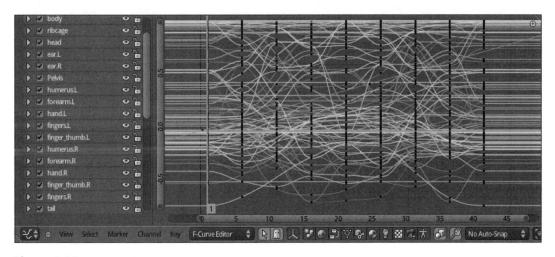

Figure 4.44
F-Curve tweaks.
Source: *Blender Foundation.*

This is no different from the traditional workflow of animation in Blender. It's not even much different from the animation workflow in other 3D software. From the vast amount of techniques and tools available, I used the following for this cycle:

- **IK bone constraints:** Use the IK constrained bones as guides, but remember to keyframe the affected bones as well.

- **AutoKey:** Automatic keyframe insertion in the Timeline Editor header, especially for the straight-ahead action will spare you from a lot of manual keyframing.

- **Show/Hide Handlers (Ctrl+H):** My personal favorite shortcut in the Graph Editor.

- **UV grid:** In the floor to spot feet sliding.

In Figure 4.45, you can see the final result of our take on this. This file is in *Book* *Chapter4\tutorial_walk_8.pose_to_pose.blend*. Play it back to see it animated. From here, you can either keep working out of your file, take it from the book file, or merge both together. An action, as any other datablock in Blender, can be imported and saved over different files (as long as the armature bones don't change their names).

Figure 4.45
Walking cycle complete.
Source: *Blender Foundation.*

Play Time

Now that the animation cycle is done, it's time to bring it from Blender into the game. You need to set an Action actuator to play the walking action and a Motion actuator to make it move accordingly.

Let's start by creating the logic bricks for the armature. With RigMomo selected, follow the steps in order. In Figure 4.46, you can see how the Logic Editor will look.

1. Add an Always sensor and set Positive Pulse on.

2. Add an Action actuator. Set the action created (for example, Walk), the Play mode to Loop End, and the Start and End Frames to 1 and 40 respectively.

3. Link the Action actuator with the Always sensor; this will automatically create an And controller.

4. Add a Motion actuator and leave the values blank for now.

5. Link the Motion actuator with the same And controller.

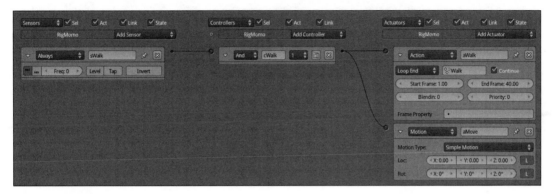

Figure 4.46
Logic bricks for animation playback.
Source: *Blender Foundation.*

To set the value in the Motion actuator, you need to calculate the object speed in Blender and convert it to the game engine. The calculation is simple and is going to give you the precise speed. If, however, you don't feel like doing math today, let trial and error be your guide.

The speed—in Blender units by seconds—is equal to two strides (0.23 × 2) divided by the number of cycles per second–the frame range of your animation cycle (40) divided by the Blender fps playback value. The game engine uses the same frame rate as Blender, to be set in the Render panel to 30 fps. So for Momo, the speed we are working with is 0.35 Blender units per second: 0.46/(40/30).

The value to use in the Motion actuator is the object speed times the frequency on which the Motion actuator is activated. Since we are using an Always sensor triggering every logic tic, the frequency is 1/60 or 0.017. If you change your game to run at 30 logic tics per second, the frequency would be double (2/60 or 0.033). The multiplication of the speed times the frequency is the value you will add to the component of the actuator. The final Loc is [0, −0.0059, 0] X, Y, and Z respectively (see Figure 4.47).

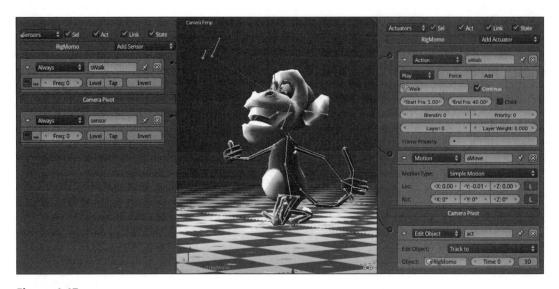

Figure 4.47
Walking Momo.
Source: *Blender Foundation.*

In the end, you might want to set the camera to track Momo during the walk. In the sample file, you will see the camera is parented to an empty with an Edit Object→ Track To actuator to follow Momo. Also, the zoom and rotate camera intro effect was brought back from the pretutorial. A checkerboard pattern on the floor will also help to follow the pace of his progression. The final file is shown in Figure 4.47 and can be found on *\Book\Chapter4\tutorial_walk_9.playtime.blend.*

IDLE ANIMATION

In the latest file, we set up Momo to walk. We never set it up for him to stop walking, though—the Always sensor will play the animation in an infinite loop until you quit the game. To push our animation exercises further, let's create an idle animation for Momo. We will then set up Momo to walk, stop, and walk again. Idle animations are played when the character is waiting for you to make a decision (whether to keep walking, to run, to turn, etc.). So as soon as we stop walking, we will set the character to act accordingly.

Start off by opening the file *\Book\Chapter4\tutorial_idle_1.begin.blend.* This is the same file we made in the previous tutorial, duplicated here for convenience (the spinning camera effect was removed again). Select RigMomo and create a new action in the Action Editor inside the Dope Sheet. You actually have two options here: you can either create a new blank action or use the Walk action as reference (duplicate it and make changes on top of it). To duplicate the existing action into a new one, you have to click in the number by the action name, as shown in Figure 4.48. This is useful when you are creating variations of the same action (different walking styles, different jumps, and so on).

Figure 4.48
Insert a new action.
Source: *Blender Foundation.*

In this case, since the actions are very different, there is not much to recycle from the walking cycle to the idle animation. You want to keep only the first and final frames to guarantee a smoother transition between the two animations. If you don't want to bother deleting keyframes, you can create a new action from scratch, maintaining the initial pose by following these steps:

1. Go to frame 1.
2. Unlink the Walk action from the armature (click the X button).
3. Create a new action (click on the + or New button).
4. Rename your new action "Idle."
5. Select all the bones of the armature and keyframe them.
6. Go to a later frame, which will be the final frame for your idle animation. For example, to make an idle animation of 4 seconds, go to frame 121.
7. Set a keyframe for all the bones again.

Now you have a new, blank action to play with. The only rule you need to follow is to avoid animations that require Momo to move around. The reason is that you may need to interrupt the idle animation at any moment as soon as you get back to walking.

The transition between the walking animation and the idle one can be seamless. In the logic brick section next, we will explain how to make the walk finish its complete cycle before starting the idle animation. Also, this will have to rely on the blend between poses from both actions for a few frames. This will work only if the pose in the current frame of the idle animation is not very distinct from the pose at the initial frame of the walking action. If the poses are extremely different (for example, Momo is facing opposite directions), the automatic calculated in-between poses will be mathematically correct but artistically awful. This is similar to our reasons for making the between poses in the previous tutorial.

As long as your poses are inside the range of the initial and final frames, the idle animation will play fine. Since you want to avoid moving Momo around, it's a good time to learn how to enhance his facial expressions.

Before you finish the idle animation, you need to set up drivers for your shape keys. You can find the current snapshot file at the end of the next section.

Making a Face

Do you know the difference between television and a live performance? In television the director has full control of the framing of the shots. It's common to use and abuse close-ups and strong facial expressions as a replacement for expressive body language. In the live theater, the audience may be sitting close or far away from the stage, and they all need to be pleased. (Sure, people fight over a front seat, but the show still has to make sense to everyone.)

Good artists do fine in both mediums. But a pretty face on your HD television screen can be a very boring, disappointing I-want-my-ticket-back experience in a live theater (been there, done that, and slept).

In a game, we have the best and the worst of both worlds. You still can use directed framing for cut scenes. But for most of the game, you must be prepared to produce good, effective animations for close and far distances.

In the previous tutorial, we covered the techniques for a good, full body-language posing. Add some more classic animation techniques (for example, strong silhouettes, lines of action, and exaggeration), and you are good to go. For facial expression, however, we will look at something new. If you have not been reading these chapters in order, now is a good time to go back and read about the shape keys.

Shape Keys and Bone Drivers

A shape key is like an individual piece of grammar. You need to build a library of poses to use in your animation. Momo already has a few poses previously created. We will use them in our animation posing with the bone-driven technique.

Open the file \Book\Chapter4\tutorial_idle_2.shapekeys_ui.blend. This is the initial file with the UI rearranged to work better with the shape keys.

In Figure 4.49, you can see all the poses in the Mesh data panel in the Property Editor for the MeshMomo object. The different poses were created in pairs: smile and ooh; eyebrowsUP and eyebrowsDOWN; eyelidUP and eyelidDOWN. They are all relative to the basis shape. To see the poses change the value by their names in the shape keys slot—set the influence value to 1.0 and all the other poses to 0.0. If you want to tweak any of the poses, you need to select the shape and go to the Edit mode. You will no longer be working in the basis shape, so any changes will only be applied to this particular shape.

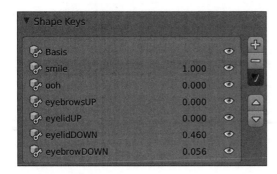

Figure 4.49
Shape smile—Edit mode.
Source: *Blender Foundation.*

The shapes are not exclusive. Often, you will have more than one pose active at the same time. Therefore, each shape has very isolated changes. For Momo, you could have a single pose with both the eyelid up and the eyebrow up shapes. However, this would give you no way to play with their influence individually in different actions. Unlike armatures, you have no way to mask out the shapes by using only a few "bones" (or part of the mesh).

Now you can integrate the shape keys into your idle animation. The first thing you need to do is to set bones to drive the shapes. The idea is to use shape keys as "pose libraries" inside your armature animation workflow. Therefore, you will be using control bones from RigMomo to control the influence of each individual shape.

Select RigMomo and switch to the Pose mode. In the walking tutorial, we looked at the bones in the bone layers 1 to 3. Now you can finally turn on layer 4 to see the last bones of Momo's armature. The bones in this layer are all detached from the main armature, as you can see in Figure 4.50.

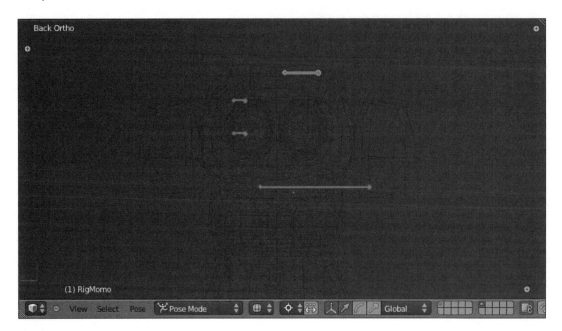

Figure 4.50
Shape key control bones.
Source: *Blender Foundation.*

To hook up the control bones with the shape keys, you need to follow the steps. The final driver in the Graph Editor will look like Figure 4.51.

1. Select the MeshMomo object.

2. Select a shape key (for example, smile).

3. Click with the right mouse button in the Influence value.

4. Select Add Driver.

5. Open the Graph Editor.

6. Switch the Edit mode from F-Curve Editor to Drivers.

7. Inside the "Key" channel, select the curve to edit (for example, Value(smile)).

8. Open the Property panel (N).

9. Change Type from Script Expression into Averaged Value.

10. Delete the F-Curve modifier (created by default).

11. In the Object/Bone panel, set RigMomo and the bone to use as controller (for example, Mouth).

Figure 4.51
Shape key driver.
Source: *Blender Foundation.*

By default, Blender sets the global X coordinate of the bone to drive the shape influence. In the Pose mode, you can move the mouth bone sideways to see the shape influence increasing and decreasing respectively. As with any other bone, you can keyframe the position of this bone controller (mouth) to animate this shape key influence over time.

This is not an effective setup, though. First, it's more intuitive to use the vertical position of the bone to drive this particular shape. Second, it's better if you don't need to move the bone as much as you do now to have significant changes. Sure, these are not deal breakers, but we are here to learn, aren't we?

First, in the Driver panel, change the Transform channel influence from X Location to Z Location and change Space to Local Space. Optionally, you can lock the transformation of X, Y and rotation of the bone—we will be using only its Z movements.

Second, you need to map the bone transformations to shape influence. To keep the bone positions not far away for the rest of the armature, we will use the short distance of a tenth Blender unit to control all the shape influences. That creates a curve with two points, [0.0, 0.0] and [0.1, 1.0]. This will map the shape influence to 0.0 when the bone Z pose location is 0.0, and 1.0 when the location is 0.1.

To move the bone up and down will now drive the shape influence as you want. Your file now should match the book file: \Book\Chapter4\tutorial_idle_3.smile _shapekeydriver.blend.

For the second pose, "ooh," you will use the same bone controller but with a different mapping. We want to set the "ooh" pose when the bone is in −0.1 and "smile" when it's 0.1, as we have. This will allow a smooth transition between those two extreme poses. Repeat the previous steps all the way to the creation of the F-Curve.

This time the curve will be the reverse of the smile, with two points: [−0.1, 1.0] and [0.0, 0.0]. Figure 4.52 illustrates the final arrangement.

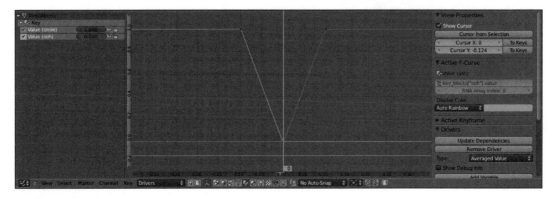

Figure 4.52
F-Curves of shape driver influence.
Source: *Blender Foundation.*

Additionally, you can add a bone constraint to make sure the bone controller is moving only vertically and that it's always inside the range you are using (−0.1 to 0.1).

Finally, you need to set up the remaining poses—eyelid up and down and eyebrow up and down. The setup is the same as for the pair ooh and smile. This time, we will leave them for you, but you can check the final setup file in \Book\Chapter4\ tutorial_idle_4.shapekeysdriver.blend.

Get Your Hands Dirty

With the armature ready to pose, you can complete the idle animation. Once things are set, there is no need to worry about anything but the armature poses. Take the previous file and create the complete cycle.

Our attempt of a fun idle animation can be seen on the book file \Book\Chapter4\ tutorial_idle_5.action.blend. The animation is not (yet) set to play in the game engine, but you can play it back in the 3D view. Also remember to change the end frame in your render panel to match the playback of your animation cycle. This will not affect the game engine, but it will help you preview your work in Blender.

After the tutorial section, you can check out the idle and walking animation made by Moraes Júnior especially for this book. In the meantime, enjoy our take on Momo, the happiest monkey in the world (see Figure 4.53).

Figure 4.53
Momo idle animation.
Source: *Blender Foundation.*

Wiring Up the Logic Bricks

There is only one thing missing. We need to alternate between the two animations: the walking and the idle one. With the latest file open, select RigMomo and in the Logic Editor, make the following changes:

1. Change the Always sensor to a Keyboard sensor with Key set to W.

2. Add a Property Sensor to check whether the frame property is between 39 and 40. Set Invert and turn on Positive and Negative Pulse modes.

3. Connect the Property sensor to the Motion actuator (Move Forward).

These changes can be seen in Figure 4.54. What you are doing here first is to set the action to play when the W key is pressed. Since the Action actuator is set to Loop End, the animation will still play for a few more frames. In order to make Momo keep moving forward, you need to keep the Motion actuator active until the frame played is not the final (40). That way when you release the key, you ensure that the

Momo animation is in the beginning of its animation cycle, ready to blend with the idle action.

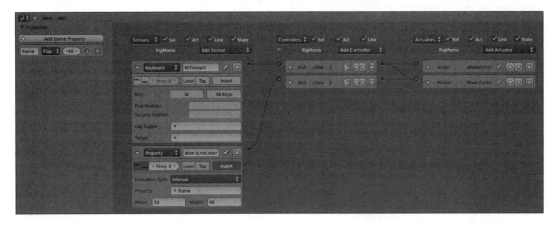

Figure 4.54
Logic brick, Part 1—keep walking.
Source: *Blender Foundation.*

Now all that is left to be done is to play the idle action when Momo is not walking. Add a Nor controller connected to the Keyboard and the Property and connect it to a new Action actuator. The Nor controller will play this actuator only when both sensors are false. The Action actuator and the final logic bricks can be seen in Figure 4.55. The explanation for the parameters follows.

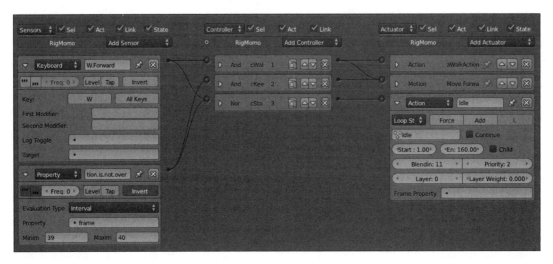

Figure 4.55
Logic brick, Part 2—idle.
Source: *Blender Foundation.*

- **Playback type**: Loop Stop will make the action loop until the Keyboard sensor is active. It will stop immediately after.

- **Priority**: 2—it has to be higher than the walking Action actuator. Lower priority actions have precedence over higher ones.

- **Start/End Frame**: 1 and 160—the range of your animation.

- **Blendin**: 11—If the pose of the initial frame of the idle animation is the same as the walking, you don't need to blend them (Blendin = 0). Otherwise, this parameter will make the transition smooth.

- **Continue**: False—you want the animation to start over from frame 1 every time you stop walking.

The final file is on \Book\Chapter4\tutorial_idle_6.idlewalkforward.blend.

How Many Bricks Does It Take to Turn Momo?

Momo can walk and stop. Now, if only we had a jump, we would be set for a side-scroller platform game (due to copyright restrictions, you will not see a figure of Momo running after a spinning-spiked hedgehog). For a 3D game, however, you need to be able to freely navigate into the levels. And there is no better way than allowing the character to turn around.

The simplest way to make Momo turn is by adding new Motion actuators responding to a new set of Keyboard sensors. Let's use the key A to turn left and D to turn right. To make it turn left, follow these instructions:

1. Add Keyboard sensor—key A.

2. Add Motion actuator with Rot Z 2.5°.

3. Connect sensor with actuator, which creates a new And controller.

4. Change the original Walk controller from And to Or.

5. Connect the new sensor to this controller as well.

6. Connect the new sensor to the Nor controller.

Now do the same for the right rotation, and you will have the logic bricks shown in Figure 4.56. You may notice that I'm using three states for the controllers here. They are always turned on, thus the main purpose is purely for organization.

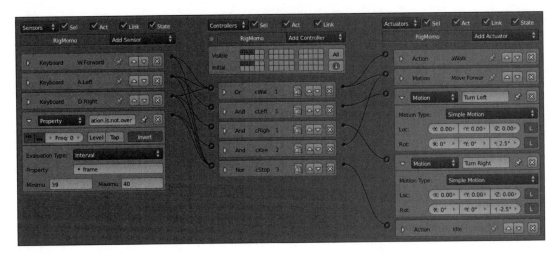

Figure 4.56
Logic brick, Part 3—turning.
Source: *Blender Foundation.*

The final file is on \Book\Chapter4\tutorial_idle_7.turning.blend.

The Dilemma of the Sweet Miso Soup

Once when I was younger, my hand slipped while seasoning the miso soup and, brilliantly, I thought it was a good idea to compensate for the salt by sweetening it. Guess what, it didn't work (and yes, I had to eat it all).

The same goes for animation. No one needs to turn right and left the same way. It can be because of a soccer injury, a shorter leg, you name it.

So sometimes (not always, not now), you need more control over the turning. For the *Yo Frankie!* project, they had specific animations for each side Momo would be turning. Those subanimations make for both good transitions between actions and for more artistic control. It's always a matter of compromising between what you can afford to do and what you can't, which is addressed between the technical and artistic teams. Thus, even though a programmer may insist it is so, an animation for "getting up" is not the same as a "sitting down" animation played backward. For our simple walking cycle, this will do.

Bottomline: a miso soup with sugar is not a break-even—it's bad cooking.

HATS OFF TO MOMO AND VICE-VERSA

Momo is a classy monkey, often seen at parties of the animal kingdom's high society. However, when with his inner circle of friends, Momo is actually a very casual monkey—not much to show, nothing to hide. One character—two quite distinct moments. This is the theme of our animation.

In this tutorial, we will show how to make Momo switch between two kinds of hats: a bouncing hat and a hat that fits tight on its head. We will not only use two different Blender objects, but also animate them differently when worn. Since the objects we want to animate (the hats) are not directly deformed by the armature (like Momo itself), we will need two things: a bone and a parented empty.

The bone, which can be animated as any other bone, will indicate Momo's head location and rotation for every frame. The empty, external to the armature, is parented to the bone, and copies the bone transformations automatically during the game. In this tutorial, this empty, working as a placeholder, will be used to place the hat Momo will be wearing.

Start by opening a variation of the latest walking Momo on the book file *Book* *Chapter4\\tutorial_hat_1.begin.blend*.

If you want to carry these changes to your own working file, you need to append the Hats group into your local file. This also includes the Camera object and an empty where we are running the script to control the hat switch. You can see the hats in Figure 4.57.

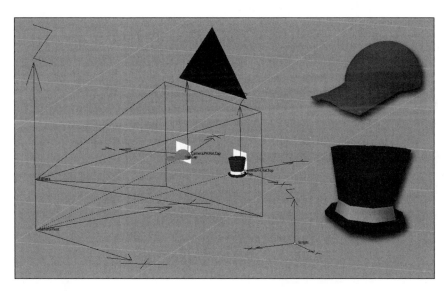

Figure 4.57
Hats for Momo.
Source: *Blender Foundation.*

This is a simple tutorial, focusing on illustrating the bone parenting technique. Thus, most of the components are ready for you to hook up with your file (for example, the scripts). Let's first set up one of the hats.

1. Select the armature and go to Edit mode.

2. Create one bone in the middle of the head named Head.Hat.Steady.

3. Parent the bone to the head bone.

4. Change Armature mode to Pose mode.

5. Go to Object mode and create an empty with the same position/rotation as the Head.Hat.Steady bone. Name the empty Head.PH.Hat.Steady.

6. With the empty selected, select the bone you just created and make it the parent of the empty (Ctrl+P → Set Parent To → Bone).

With those changes, you can already animate the bone Head.Hat.Steady, and the empty placeholder will follow along. The hat will be placed exactly where the empty is. In the current file, both hats are parented to empties/placeholders close to the camera. In order to animate the hat bones, you need to temporarily bring the hat to the position it will be during the game. For that to work with the Head.Hat.Steady bone, you need to bring the Hat.Cap Blender object to the same position/rotation as the empty placeholder and parent the hat object to it (select the hat, select the empty, in the Transform panel in the 3D view, right-mouse click in the values to "Copy To Selected," Ctrl+P to parent). Now you can go to the armature Edit mode and move the bone to make the hat fit the head properly. Figure 4.58 shows the arrangement of Bone + Empty + Hat. The current snapshot can be found in \Book\Chapter4\ tutorial_hat_2.capsetup.blend.

Figure 4.58
Hat + empty placeholder + hat bone.
Source: *Blender Foundation.*

Once the bone is in the right place, you can go over the walking and the idle animations and do some tweaks on its position/rotation over time. For this hat, you don't need to move much. In our case, we only tilted it a bit in the middle of the idle animation to follow the eyebrow raising and some subtle bouncing during the walk. When you now run the game, you will see the hat always in the right place during the animations. To make sure you can follow closely, the file with the animated Hat.Cap can be seen in Figure 4.59 and the book file *\Book\Chapter4\tutorial_hat_3.animatedcap.blend.*

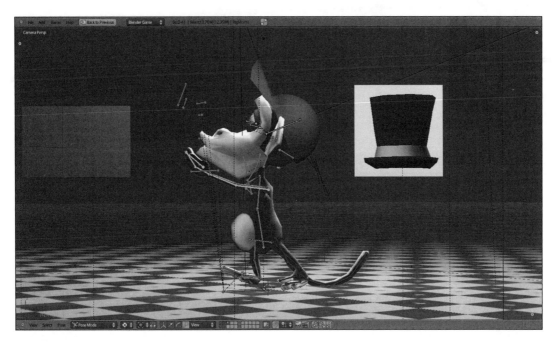

Figure 4.59
Momo walking in the game with the cap on his head.
Source: *Blender Foundation.*

So far so good. Let's now set up the second hat. For this one, you will create a new bone and a new placeholder. The reason is that you will make a different animation for this hat. The classy top hat will be a bit looser, so it should bounce more during the animations.

Start by moving/rotating the Hat.Cap back to its original placeholder by the camera and re-parent it to the empty (Camera.PH.Hat.Cap). Now repeat the same steps you did for the other hat. This time name the bone Head.Hat.Bouncy and the empty Head.PH.Hat.Bouncy. For the animation, make it more exaggerated, with the hat slipping during the walk and the idle actions. Figure 4.60 illustrates one of the moments the hat almost fell off. After moving the Hat.Top object back to its original placeholder (Camera.PH.Hat.Top), your file should be ready for the final adjustments.

Figure 4.60
Classy top hat is too big for Momo's head.
Source: *Blender Foundation.*

Copy Menu Attributes Add-on

As soon as you start parenting your objects, you will see that it's not so easy to copy over transformations. Blender built-in copy tools work only on top of the local transformations, and this is not enough when you want to copy the visual or world transformations. The difference is that the visual transformations (what you see) are an accumulated result from the different local transformations of the chain of parents.

Blender comes with an add-on that allows you to do all sorts of advanced copy operations. Go to the User Preferences, Add-Ons and enable the Copy Attributes Menu add-on.

This add-on was originally intended only to bring over the copy menu (Ctrl+C) from Blender 2.49. Bassam Kurdali, its original developer and maintainer, was kind enough to expand it to help with this tutorial. Kudos to him.

If you don't want to use add-ons, you can go old school with Blender 2.49 work-arounds. Duplicate your empty and do a Clear Parent → Clear and Keep Transformation in the new empty. Now you can use this object to copy the transformations from, delete it, and parent the hat to the original empty.

Now that the animations are done and the armature set up, we can move on to look to the implementation of hats switching on the fly.

Take the final file \Book\Chapter4\tutorial_hat_4.animatedhats.blend.

The interaction is simple: click on a hat to switch to it; click anywhere else to bring it back close to the camera. When you pick a hat, the game engine will have to do as you did to tweak the animations: take the selected hat, move it to the head placeholder position, match their rotations, and parent it to this placeholder.

This is done by a script that is already hooked up for the camera. This Python script is very simple, and you should be able to understand it after the Chapter 7, "Python Scripting." The script accesses the objects—hats and empty placeholders—by their names. Therefore, for your local changes, it's important to follow the names as presented here or tweak the script accordingly.

Mango Jambo Special Animation

The walking cycle you've seen so far is technically correct, and it follows the workflow you can count on, regardless of your animation skills. The bottom line is: with a good method and the understanding of the techniques, although you may not be brilliant, you can't go wrong either.

Now, as the icing on the cake, I've asked the animator Moraes Júnior to do the same thing we did together—a new walking cycle and idle animation using the same base file. For reference, he created Momo for the *Yo Frankie!* project and its original animations. After our using and abusing of Momo in the previous pages, it's only fair to see what his "father" would have done instead. Here you can see and study his work and the final contribution: \Book\Chapter4\mangojambo.blend

To Learn More

Finally, dedicate the proper time to mastering the ways of animation. Learning how to make animation work in Blender is still not the same thing as knowing what to do. Here is a list of classic materials for learning animation—modern references for animation and character control in games and Blender-specific reading.

- *Drawn to Life* by Walt Stanchfield
- *The Animator's Survival Kit* by Richard Williams
- *Cartoon Animation* by Preston Blair
- *3rd Person Action Platformer Hero Animation Graph* by Rune Vendler http://altdevblogaday.org/2011/04/14/3rd-person-action-platformer-hero-animation-graph
- *Character Animation DVD* by William Reynish
- *Blender 2.5 Character Animation Cookbook* by Virgilio Vasconcelos

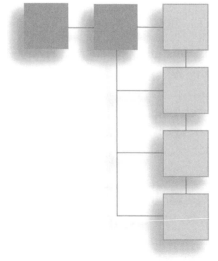

CHAPTER 5

GRAPHICS

Welcome to Chapter 5, where it's all about the visuals! When you play a game, the graphics are usually the first element to make an impression, long before you can form a more rounded opinion of the game based on other aspects like gameplay, story, physics, or sound. Whether it's a screenshot, a video trailer, or a printed poster, graphics is the one element that publishers constantly rely on to draw the public's attention (see Figure 5.1). So it's only fair that we should look at this topic in great detail.

Figure 5.1
Blender game art by Martins Upitis.
© 2014 Chase Moskal and Team.

In a modern game, it is not unusual for the computer to spend the majority of its processing time in rendering the graphics, while game logic, physics, and sound typically take up only a tiny fraction of the total computation time. This fact alone should convince you of the complexity of real-time computer graphics.

In this chapter, we will learn first how to work with the material, texture, and shading systems in the game engine; followed by a quick introduction to GLSL – OpenGL Shading Language, the shading language that would let you further extend the graphic capability of the game engine; and conclude the chapter by showing off some of the more specialized tools and features that can be used in a game.

VISUAL STYLE

For most graphic artists, the ultimate goal of their work has always been photorealism. Photorealism means that the scene looks as believable as possible by replicating all the intricate geometries, light interactions, and surface properties of the physical world. While photorealism is a perfectly valid goal for games that strive to achieve the most realistic graphics possible, many games intentionally employ non-photorealistic styles. Achieving looks such as a cartoon style, anime style, or even a retro 8-bit style is certainly possible within the game engine. With some slight changes in the content-creation process, combined with a good understanding of shading, texturing, and lighting, you'll be able to create stunning artwork of any visual style, as seen in Figure 5.2.

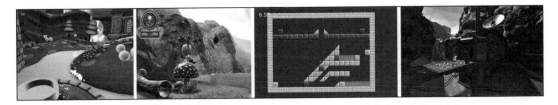

Figure 5.2
Different visual styles of games. These games are all covered in Chapter 10, "Case Studies."
© 2014 Carlos Limon.

DESIGNING FOR REAL TIME

For a typical computer animation, the rendering time is effectively unlimited. A movie studio like Pixar has hundreds of computers working together as a rendering farm to make the images. Games don't have this luxury of rendering time. Because games are interactive, there is no way to pre-render frames ahead of time. Games need to pump out many frames every second (and from a single computer!) in order to achieve interactivity with the player. That means that preparing art assets for games is a bit trickier than for non-real-time animation, where performance usually isn't a concern.

Art Assets

Art asset refers to any piece of work that is used in a game. It includes models, textures, animations, sound, and even shader codes.

Because games are generally distributed to a large audience with a wide range of computer hardware, you need to make sure that the games will run at acceptable speeds on different hardware configurations. This way, you avoid alienating people without top-of-the-line computers. Blender has support for switching between different shading modes to help artists create games that work with different generations of computer hardware. This will be discussed in detail later in this chapter.

Modern graphics cards are surprisingly fast at pushing out high-quality images at astonishing speed, but you still need to keep a few things in mind when making art assets, in order to avoid slowdowns.

Geometry

Geometry is the basis for any 3D scene. You can quantitatively measure the amount of geometry data in a scene using a "polygon count," which refers to the number of faces (triangles or quads, in Blender's case) in a scene. The more geometry data there is, the slower the game will be. So how many polygons are too much? Rather than imposing an absolute limitation, just remember to use polygons sensibly, spend them where they are needed, and don't waste excessive polygons on unnecessary parts that will not be visible to the gamer. Geometry is relatively cheap now. Today's average computer should be able to render a million polygons at an interactive frame rate, so polygon count isn't as much of a concern as it used to be. Figure 5.3 shows the difference between a low-resolution model and a high-resolution model. The high-resolution model is smoother, more detailed, but is slower to render. The game engine also has built-in optimization features that remove hidden objects in order to avoid wasting time displaying them.

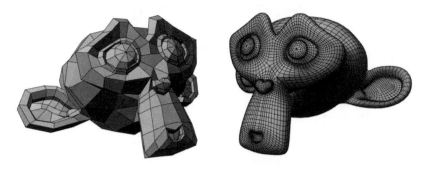

Figure 5.3
Low polygon model vs. high polygon model.
© 2014 Blender Foundation. Art © 2014 Mike Pan.

The supported Blender object types in the game engine are: Camera, Light, Empty, Mesh, and Text.

Non-supported Blender object types are: Curve, Surface, and Metaball. These objects will be hidden during the game.

Materials and Textures

Once the modeling is done, materials and textures, which add visual fidelity, can be applied to the mesh. Using a combination of materials and textures, you can define surface characteristics such as color, shininess, bumpiness, and transparency. Figure 5.4 illustrates the difference between a non-textured model and a fully textured model. Textures also allow you to "bake" certain effects, such as complex light maps and shadows, onto the object, because these effects would otherwise take too long to compute in real time. Due to the importance of materials and textures, a large portion of this chapter will focus on materials and textures. (For a more in-depth discussion on texture baking, refer to Chapter 8.)

Figure 5.4
Oil barrel models without and with textures applied.
© *2014 Mike Pan.*

The Blender game engine implements a subset with some overlapping of all the features found in the regular Blender. Not all options available to the Blender internal renderer are available in the game engine; many advanced graphics features are simply too slow to be implemented in real time. But as you will soon find out, even some of the complex effects like reflection, soft shadows, and ambient occlusion can all be approximated in the game engine using clever tricks on modern graphic cards.

Lights

Lighting not only sets the overall tone of the scene, but it also helps highlight certain details while hiding others. Older games cannot afford to use dynamic lighting for performance reasons, so they often employ precomputed static lighting, which is faster to render, but does not have the flexibility that dynamic lighting offers (such as swinging bathroom lights that cast moving shadows).

In fact, without lighting, the virtual world you create would be pitch black, like Figure 5.5.

Figure 5.5
The effect of lighting on an object.
© *2014 Mike Pan.*

The game engine supports eight real-time lights in Multitexture mode and at least eight in GLSL mode (more on the different shading modes later). But lights are expensive, and more lights will slow the game down significantly. Advanced features such as real-time shadow will slow down the game even more. Light is a very complex phenomenon; effects such as ambient occlusion, bounced light, and volumetric light shafts are all very computationally intensive and simply not feasible for most real-time projects. It is up to the artist to devise ways to fake these effects when needed.

Advanced Shading Techniques

Thanks to the rapid advances in shading language and graphics processing units (GPU), effects such as ambient occlusion, bounced light, and many others that were considered "impossible" are now possible using some very complex shaders. Explaining these advanced techniques is outside the scope of this book, but a selection of sample files is included on the accompanying disk. For advanced shader examples you can look at the book *GPU Gems* from Nvidia.

SHADING MODES

The game engine offers three different real-time shading modes. Think of them as different rendering pipelines—some are more limiting, some are more advanced. In this chapter, you will first be introduced to the most feature-rich shading mode: GLSL. Then we will talk a bit about multitexture and, finally, singletexture.

To switch between shading modes, go to the Render Property Editor. There you should see the options as depicted in Figure 5.6.

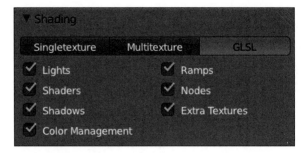

Figure 5.6
Shading mode options.
© 2014 Blender Foundation.

Game Engine Interface

If you are following this chapter on your own without using the supplied template file from the book, remember to set the render engine to Blender Game once you start Blender, as shown in Figure 5.7. This will reveal all the relevant game engine features in the user interface and hide non-relevant interface elements.

Figure 5.7
Engine selector.
© 2014 Blender Foundation.

Table 5.1 shows the advantages and disadvantages of each shading mode. The GLSL mode, despite being the most advanced shading mode in Blender, also happens to be the easiest to use because we can accomplish the effect using the regular Material and Texture panels. Unless backward compatibility with older hardware is a big concern, I strongly recommend using the GLSL shading mode for all your projects. Even if you are not planning on using all the advanced features, it's good to know that they are there if you need them later on.

Table 5.1   Comparison of Shading Modes in the Game Engine

	Singletexture	Multitexture	GLSL
Date of introduction	Pre-2000	2006	2008
Hardware Compatibility	OpenGL 1.0+	OpenGL 1.3+	OpenGL 2.0+
Lighting accuracy	Per vertex	Per vertex	Per pixel
Number of Lights	8	8	8+
Real-time shadow	No	No	Yes
Max texture layer	1	4	16
Texture blending	No	Yes	Yes
Custom shader	No	Yes	Yes
2D Filter	Yes	Yes	Yes
Material nodes	No	No	Yes
Viewport Preview*	Partial	Partial	Full

*Viewport Preview refers to how much of the shading and material can be seen in the 3D Viewport in Textured mode, without running the game
© 2014 Dalai Felinto and Mike Pan.

Because the way to apply materials and textures varies somewhat depending on the shading mode, it is a good idea to decide on a shading mode before you start the project to avoid unnecessary conversion later. An example of what each mode offers is shown in Figure 5.8, followed by a detailed explanation of each.

Figure 5.8
Different shading modes: Singletexture, Multitexture, GLSL.
© 2014 Mike Pan.

GLSL Mode

The GLSL shading mode is the newest real-time shading mode in Blender, added to augment the old Singletexture and Multitexture modes. In a nutshell, GLSL mode tries to emulate the functionality of the internal rendering engine as much as possible. In doing so, it blurs the distinction between the Blender internal renderer and the game engine. In GLSL mode, the artist uses the familiar Material panel and Texture panel to apply shading and texture to an object, as one would normally do when working with the internal renderer. This means materials created for the game engine in GLSL mode can be used for rendering almost without doing any modification.

This is the easiest shading mode to use, since the same materials and textures settings that are used in regular Blender are also used in the game engine.

GLSL Requirements

Being the most advanced shading mode, GLSL requires a relatively modern graphics card that supports OpenGL 2.0 or higher. If you have a computer with onboard Intel graphics, GLSL might not run as expected. It also helps to update your display drivers by visiting amd.com, nvidia.com, or intel.com, depending on your graphic card manufacturer.

Technical Background

GLSL, or the OpenGL Shading Language, is a C-like programming language that runs on the graphics card (as opposed to most other programming languages, which run on the CPU). GLSL lets the artist define custom shaders to achieve more complex animation, material, shading, and texture effects than are possible with traditional fixed-pipeline processing. Blender is capable of generating GLSL codes automatically, so don't get scared just because we mentioned "programming language." Blender converts your settings from the Material and Texture panels into GLSL internally. In fact, the entire process is completely transparent to the artist. The only reason we bring it up now is so that you have a better understanding of what goes on behind the scenes.

Materials and Textures

To help you get to know the material system better, let's play around with a sample file.

Open file \Book\Chapter5\GLSL1.blend. You'll see a very simple scene, with the lights and a monkey head already set up for you as shown in Figure 5.9. Press P to start the game and see what it looks like in-game.

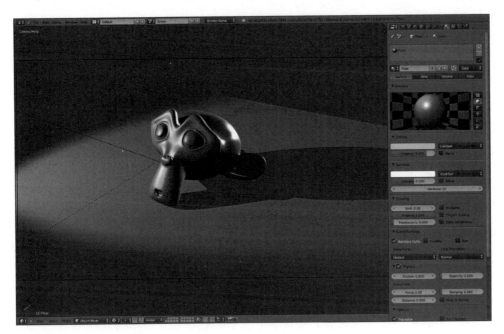

Figure 5.9
Basic material demo setup.
© 2014 Blender Foundation.

Notice the visuals in the 3D Viewport are exactly as in-game. This true "what-you-see-is-what-you-get" is only possible in GLSL mode. This means that as you set up material and texture settings in the Property Editor, changes will be reflected in real time in the 3D Viewport. In fact, as long as the viewport shading is set to Texture, there is no need to run the game in order to preview how the object will really look.

The next two sections will go over each option in the Material and Texture panels, explain what they do, and when to use them. Follow along as we work through the massive list of sliders and options shown in Figure 5.10.

The Material Panel

In GLSL1.blend, you'll see the Material panel on the right side of the 3D Viewport (see Figure 5.10). In the demo setup, the material attached to the floor is shown by default. Recall that this panel was already discussed briefly in Chapter 2, so go ahead and play around with the settings and see how they affect the model in the 3D view in real time.

If you are already familiar with the material system of Blender, you'll be right at home with this section. As an artist, just remember that the game engine supports a smaller subset of the features found in the regular Material panel. Advanced shading

From top: *Elephants Dream*, *Big Buck Bunny*, *Sintel*, *Tears of Steel*, and *Yo, Frankie!*
(as shown in Chapter 1)

Super Blender Galaxy
(as shown in Chapter 10)

Lucy and the Time Machine
(as shown in Chapter 10)

Completed Walking Cycle
(as shown in Chapter 4)

Android Deployment
(as shown in Chapter 9)

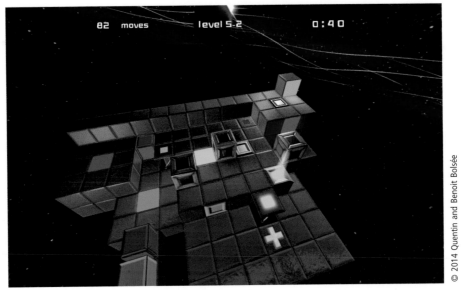

ColorCube
(as shown in Chapter 10)

Tectonic
(as shown in Chapter 10)

Feed the Shark completed game
(as shown in Chapter 2)

The FPS Project
(as shown in Chapter 10)

Different shading modes: Singletexture, Multitexture, GLSL
(as shown in Chapter 5)

Cosmic Sensation
(as shown in Chapter 10)

OceanViz
(as shown in Chapter 10)

Architectural walkthrough example
(as shown in Chapter 7)

Yo Frankie! Graphics with shader effects disabled on the right
(as shown in Chapter 8)

CAVE
(as shown in Chapter 10)

The baked scene (left) vs. the original scene (right)
(as shown in Chapter 8)

features such as ray-traced reflections and refractions and subsurface scattering are not available in the game engine. So they are hidden from the Material panel when Blender Game is selected as the active render engine.

Figure 5.10
The Material panel.
© 2014 Blender Foundation.

Material Management   The very top section of the Material panel lets you manage the material datablocks. Since each object can have multiple materials, the box shows a list of all the materials attached to the active object. Selected materials are highlighted in blue.

To create a first material for an object:

1. In the 3D view, select an object without a material (for example, the monkey in GLSL1.blend).

2. In the Material panel below the Material Slot List, click on the [+ New] icon to create a new material for the object.

3. Since the object has no material, by default the new material will be applied to the entire object.

Multi-Material Objects   If the object has an existing material, you can create another material and assign the new materials to part of the mesh as follows:

1. In the 3D view, select the object.

2. In the Material panel below the Material Slot List, click on the [+ New] icon to create a new base material for the object.

3. In the Material panel, click on the [+] icon to the right of the material slots to create another m.... ....t, followed by clicking on the [+ New] button to create a new material. You will assign this material to the selected part of the object. Figure 5.11 shows this step.

4. Change the color of the newly created material to green just so that you can tell the materials apart.

5. In the 3D view, enter Edit mode for the object using Tab. Select all the vertices that you want to be assigned the new material.

6. With the new material highlighted, press the Assign button to apply the new material to the selected part of the object. Figure 5.12 shows these steps.

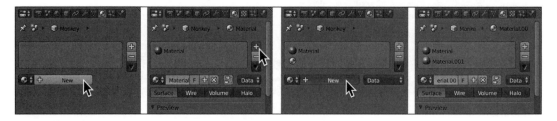

Figure 5.11
The Material panel.
© 2014 Blender Foundation.

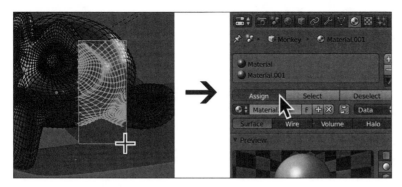

Figure 5.12
The Material panel.
© 2014 Blender Foundation.

Below the Material Slot List is the control for the selected material. You can (and should) rename a material to be more descriptive. This will help you immensely in a large project, since it's usually not very obvious what "Material.001" is, "Orange" is better, "OrangePlastic" is even better, and "MatteYellowishOrangeSoftPlasticWith-SmallBumps" is overdoing it.

A Material datablock can be shared by multiple objects. Clicking on the miniature material icon (labeled as Browse ID Data) will bring up a list of all the existing materials within the current Blender file. To assign an object to an existing material, simply select a Material datablock from that list. Figure 5.13 shows this in action.

Figure 5.13
The Material panel: datablock management.
© 2014 Blender Foundation.

The concept of datablock is very important in Blender: it allows you to effectively organize all the assets into a logical hierarchy. Datablocks are discussed in detail in Chapter 2.

Object vs. Data You might have noticed another pull-down menu beside the New Material button. This link selector controls whether the material is linked to the object or the object data (also known as *mesh*). This distinction is practically negligible for single objects, but if you have an object with shared mesh in the scene, the difference becomes important.

When a material is linked to a mesh (and not the object), duplicating the object using Alt+D to create a copy of the object that shares the same mesh as the original object will result in the material being shared across both objects.

On the other hand, if the material is linked to an object, duplicating the object with Alt+D will result in the material being linked directly to the object. This way, you can assign a different material to each object even if they share the same mesh. Figures 5.14 and 5.15 illustrate the differences between data-linked material and object-linked material.

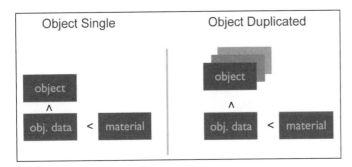

Figure 5.14
Material datablock linked to the mesh.
© 2014 Cengage Learning®. All Rights Reserved.

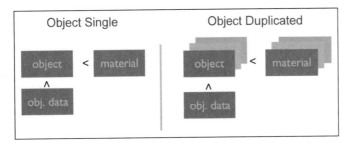

Figure 5.15
Material datablock linked to the object.
© 2014 Cengage Learning®. All Rights Reserved.

Preview The Preview panel shows how the selected material would look if rendered. Because of the generic models and a single light source, the accuracy of the preview is limited if the material relies on a complex lighting setup. You can usually get a more accurate preview directly from the 3D Viewport. Just remember to make sure that Viewport shading is set to Textured by toggling Alt+Z.

Diffuse Diffuse is the soft (matte), reflected component of a surface. Compared to specular highlights below, diffused light is not viewing-angle dependent.

Using the color selector, you can change the diffuse color of the material.

The intensity slider controls how much diffuse light is reflected off the surface—in another words, how bright a surface is when it is exposed to light. Use this in conjunction with the color selector to get the surface color you want. For example, to create a white material, not only do you need to select a white color in the color palette, but you'll also need to crank up the diffuse intensity to 1.0; otherwise, you'll end up with a medium gray. Setting the intensity to 0 instantly creates a black surface, no matter what color is set in the color selector. Figure 5.16 shows the difference between a low diffuse value material and a high diffuse value material.

Figure 5.16
Left: Low diffuse value. Right: High diffuse value.
© 2014 Blender Foundation.

- Lambert is the default diffuse shading algorithm; it is suitable for most surfaces.

- Oren-Nayar better approximates rough surfaces, as it provides a more gradual transition from light to dark than Lambert. Thus Oren-Nayar is generally "softer" looking than Lambert.

- Minnaert is like a regular Lambert shader but with additional processing on the edge of the object where the surface normal is parallel to the camera. It can achieve a somewhat velvety-looking material without the use of a ramp shader.

- Toon shader creates a very distinct banding effect, resulting in a cartoonish look that's suitable for a cell-shaded game.

- Fresnel shader uses the incident light angle to achieve an interesting look that can be best described as "anisotropic," perfect for those brushed metal objects that reflect light in bands or radial patterns.

Of all the diffuse shading algorithms, Lambert is the simplest in terms of shader complexity. So for performance reasons, it is best to stick with Lambert unless you can truly utilize the additional benefits from the other specialized algorithms.

As a different shading algorithm is selected, additional options for that particular mode may appear. Rather than trying to explain these extra settings for each shading algorithm (which is futile without talking about the math behind it), we invite you to try them out yourself and see how they affect the outcome. In the end, all that matters is how it looks.

Specular Specular is the hard (glossy), reflected component of a surface. It is viewing-angle dependent: as the camera, object, or light moves relative to each other, the specular highlight appears to move along the surface. With the color selector, you can change the color of the specular highlight. Most materials (plastic, wood, glass) have a white specular highlight. The only common material that can physically have a colored specular highlight is colored metal, such as gold and copper. Figure 5.17 shows three different specular settings.

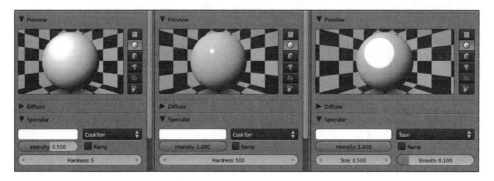

Figure 5.17
From left to right: medium specular intensity and low hardness; high specular intensity and high hardness; specular shader set to Toon.

© 2014 Blender Foundation.

Intensity controls how bright the specular highlight is, while hardness controls the size of the specular hotspot. A high hardness value is useful for shiny material, such as hard plastic or glass. A low hardness value is useful for matte objects, such as rough plastic or plants. For surfaces with almost no visible specular component, such as dry brick walls, dirt, or carpet, you can even disable specular entirely by setting the intensity to 0. This can improve the performance of the game slightly.

Just like diffuse, there are different algorithms to achieve different-looking specular highlights: Wardlso can be used to create very tiny specular highlights, and Toon is used for creating that sharp fall-off often desired in a cartoon. CookTorr is the default algorithm, but Phong is another popular choice. Visually, CookTorr and Phong are very similar.

Ramp Ramp lets you add an arbitrary color gradient to the object. Its power lies in the fact that you can map a color palette onto the object in many different ways. Some common uses for the ramp shader include adding a "peach fuzz" to skin material and adding rim light to objects for dramatic effect. Figure 5.18 shows the Ramp Shader interface.

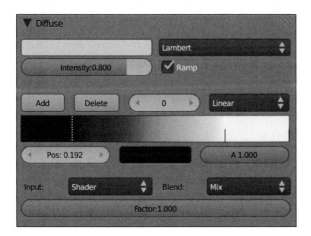

Figure 5.18
The Ramp Shader interface.
© 2014 Blender Foundation.

The top part of the ramp is used to set up the color band. To define a gradient, you can add or delete color stops; each color stop has its own position, color, and alpha value. By default, when you enable ramp, two color stops are created for you. To select a particular color stop, left-click on it. Active color stops are drawn with a dotted line. Once a color stop is selected, you can drag to change its position and alter its color and alpha values using the color selector below it.

The bottom part of the Ramp Shader panel controls how the color band is mapped onto the object. Available input options include:

- **Normal:** The color band is mapped to the surface normal of the object in camera space. Thus, any surfaces perpendicular to the camera (facing the camera) will obtain their color from the right side of the color band, while surfaces that are parallel to the camera (facing sideways) will get assigned the left side of the color band.

- **Energy:** The color band is mapped to the incident energy of all the lamps. High energy areas are mapped to the color band right and vice versa.

- **Shader:** The color band is mapped to the result of the calculated shader intensity. This option is similar to energy, except it also takes the shading model into account.

- **Result:** The color band is mapped to the final resulting material color, including all shading and texture information. Bright pixels are mapped to the right of the color band, and dark pixels are mapped to the left-most color band.

The Blend option controls how the color-band colors are mixed with the existing color, not unlike the layer-blending option in a 2D image-manipulation software such as Photoshop. These blending methods frequently appear in Blender, so you should be familiar with them.

- **Mix:** Uses a combination of both the inputs. A factor of 0.5 means each input contributes exactly half toward the final color. A factor of 1 means one of the inputs completely dominates the other.

- **Add:** The two input colors are numerically added together, often resulting in a brighter image.

- **Multiply:** The two input colors are numerically multiplied together, often resulting in a darker image.

- **Subtract:** One input is subtracted from the other, sometimes resulting in a darker image, and sometimes resulting in a "negative" image where the colors are inverted.

Both diffuse and specular channels can have their own ramp. While the diffuse ramp shader can be visible on the entire object, the ramp for specular is only visible in the region where specular highlights are visible. Other than that, the Ramp Shader panel for specular is exactly the same as the Ramp Shader panel for diffuse.

Shading

- **Emit:** Controls how much light a surface appears to give off. A non-zero value means a surface is visible even when it's completely unlit. Because emit is a material property, and not a real light source, you cannot rely on using emit materials to light up other objects in the scene. Emit is often used to simulate surfaces that give off light on their own.

- **Ambient:** Controls how much influence the ambient color has on the material. Ambient color is a global color that is added on top of all materials, including objects without an explicit material. By default, the ambient color is black, effectively disabling itself. The ambient color can be changed in the World panel. If you want to uniformly lift the brightness of the scene without adding an additional lamp, ambient color is a fast way to achieve this. You can also create a color tint in the world by using a nonwhite ambient color, which is a great way to set the mood of your scene.

Ambient Drawbacks

Ambient does have its drawbacks. Because it adds light to all surfaces uniformly, excessive ambient will reduce the contrast of the scene, making everything look flat and washed out.

- **Shadeless:** When enabled, disables all light calculation for this material. This option bypasses all the complex shading calculations; thus, it can improve performance at the cost of no lighting calculation. This option is useful for situations where you do not want the object to react to light.

- **Cubic Interpolation:** When enabled, gives a smoother transition from light to shadow, at the cost of a slight performance decrease. For certain smooth shapes like spheres, this option helps the shape look more natural.

Game Settings

- **Backface Culling:** When disabled, makes both sides of a face visible when running the game. By default, only the front side of the face is rendered for performance reasons, while the backside of a face is invisible. This is not critical for most new computers, if you are to handle a few faces. However, it's better to take the safe approach and disable backface culling only when you need double-sided faces.

- **Invisible:** When enabled, makes the surface completely invisible. This option is often used for creating hidden Physics Collision objects. Objects can be also made invisible from the Physics panel (see Chapter 6).

- **Text:** When enabled, tells Blender that this object is used to display bitmap text. Using bitmap text in the game engine is covered later in this chapter. Because bitmap text is rather difficult to set up, using the Blender text object is an easy alternative.

- **Alpha Blend:** Selects the way faces are drawn. Options are shown in Figure 5.19a and in details in Figure 5.19b.

  - **Opaque:** Treats the material as a regular solid. This is the fastest draw mode.

  - **Add:** Numerically adds its own surface color with what's behind it, making the combined surface brighter. This option can be used to simulate halo lights, particles, and other "bright" special effects.

  - **Alpha Clip:** Enables binary transparency. Used frequently for texture where there is a very distinct edge, such as tree leaves and a chain-link fence. This is the fastest way to render textures with alpha since there is no alpha blending: a pixel is either fully opaque or fully transparent.

  - **Alpha Blend:** Enables alpha blending between its own color and the background. It is used for truly transparent materials such as glass. One drawback of Alpha Blend is that multiple layers of Alpha Blend surfaces are often not displayed in the correct Z-order. This is a common issue with hardware-accelerated alpha rendering. The solution is to use Alpha Sort, as explained below.

  - **Alpha Sort:** Similar to Alpha Blend, but it solves the Z-sorting issue inherent with Alpha Blend. If you see an alpha-mapped object that is showing through other transparent objects, or if multiple layers of alpha are displayed in the wrong order, then you should use Alpha Sort instead of Alpha Blend. Keep in mind that Alpha Sort is much slower than regular Alpha Blend.

Figure 5.19a
Blending Modes: (from left to right) Add, Alpha Clip, Alpha Blend, and Alpha Sort.
© 2014 Mike Pan.

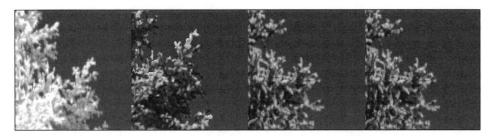

Figure 5.19b
Blending Modes magnified: (from left to right) Add, Alpha Clip, Alpha Blend, and Alpha Sort.
© 2014 Mike Pan.

- **Face Orientations:** Rotates the faces away from their original orientation, as illustrated in Figure 5.20. Note that face orientations are not visible in the Viewport; therefore, to preview the effect of these settings, you need to enter the game mode.

  - **Normal:** The default option. No extra orientation is applied and faces are rendered as normal (see Figure 5.20A).

  - **Billboard:** Forces the X-axis of the object to face the camera while keeping the Z-axis of the object upright. To visualize this, imagine someone is holding a billboard and trying to get your attention by always rotating the billboard to face you. Billboard is used frequently to render simplistic vegetation and trees in architectural visualization, so that a tree can be represented by a single plane that always rotates around its center (see Figure 5.20B).

  - **Halo:** Forces the X-axis of the object to always face the camera. This is similar to the billboard option, but no axis is locked. Halo, as the name implies, can be used to render particles and other non-3D sprites (see Figure 5.20C).

  - **Shadow:** Objects will reposition and reorient themselves so that the center of the object will match the closest object directly below it in the −Z axis. This is used to make an object "fall" and stick to the ground, such as when faking a drop shadow (see Figure 5.20D).

Remember that face orientation is applied after logic and physics calculations. This means that the collision mesh will still be in its original position, so what you see on the screen could be different than the internal physics collision mesh.

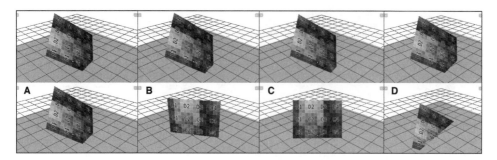

Figure 5.20
Face orientation illustrated. The top-row images show the actual geometry. The bottom row shows the face set to normal(A), billboard(B), halo(C), and shadow(D).
© 2014 Mike Pan.

Physics The physics settings control some of the physics property of the surface. They do not affect the visual property of the object but change the way the object interacts under the physics engine. Jump to Chapter 6 if you want to learn about these settings.

Additional Options

- **Exclude Mist:** Excludes the object from the mist calculation when enabled. Mist is a world setting that can be accessed from the World panel.

- **Face Textures:** Forces Blender to replace the diffuse color of the material with the UV texture. This is an easy way to apply a simple texture onto a material without creating a texture datablock for the material.

- **Face Textures Alpha:** This option is only visible when Face Textures is enabled. It will also override the transparency of the material using the alpha channels of the texture, in addition to replacing the diffuse color of the material.

- **Vertex Color Paint:** Multiplies the vertex color of the mesh on top of the regular material.

- **Receive Shadows:** Makes real-time shadows cast by lamps visible on the surface. Only Spot and Sun lamps cast shadows.

- **Object Color:** Modulates the material color with the object color. Useful for getting different objects sharing the same material to have different colors. The object color can be set from the object Properties Editor.

So far, we have covered all the functionalities of the Material panel. Most of the settings are very intuitive, and their effects can be seen directly in the Viewport, with the exception of the face orientation settings, which require the game engine to be running to see their effects.

The Texture Panel

Texture is the main way to add details to a surface without adding extra polygons. It is done by mapping a 2D image onto the surface of the 3D object. Figure 5.21 illustrates the concept of texture mapping.

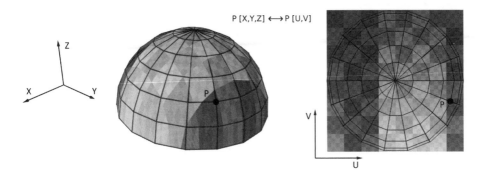

Figure 5.21
How texture mapping works.
© 2014 Dalai Felinto.

Texture Datablocks   Texture datablocks are almost always linked to a material (see note below for exception). Each material can have multiple textures, and through layering and blending of textures, complex effects can be achieved. The top area of the Texture panel shows you all the textures attached to the active material.

Non-Material Textures

The only exception is a "World" texture, which is linked directly to the world settings without a material, and the Brush texture, which is used for painting or sculpting. However, both of them are only supported in the Blender internal renderer and not implemented in the game engine. Therefore, for our game purposes, all the texture datablocks must indeed be linked to a material.

Note that in Blender, texture slots are ordered so that textures further down the texture slots override textures on top of the list. This is opposite from how most image editors treat layers. Figure 5.22 shows the texture slots with two textures active.

Figure 5.22
The Texture panel with two texture slots in use.
© 2014 Blender Foundation.

1. To create a new texture, the object must already have a material. Select the object and add a new material, if necessary.

2. Then, in the Texture panel, click on the [+ New] icon to create a new texture in the first texture slot (see Figure 5.23).

3. For working with the game engine, set the type for the texture to image. (Image texture is what we will be using most of the time.) The only other available texture type option is environment map. Procedural textures, such as clouds and noise, are not supported in the game engine (see Figure 5.23).

Figure 5.23
Using an image texture.
© 2014 Blender Foundation.

Image To load an image as a texture, you can either:

- Load an existing image datablock (one that is already being used in this Blender file).

- Generate a new image directly from within Blender.

- Browse and load an image file from your computer.

The three options are shown in Figure 5.24

Figure 5.24
Create a new image by selecting New or browse for an existing image by selecting Open.
© 2014 Blender Foundation.

Once an image is loaded, you have some options to change the way the color space and alpha channel are interpreted.

- **Input Color Space:** Controls the color space transformation that happens when the image is used. Normally, textures are created in the sRGB color space, so the default setting is sufficient. For color-sensitive work, you can change the Input Color Space to match the image file.

- **View as Render:** Apply an additional color transform in order to take into account the color transform when rendering.

- **Use Alpha:** Uses the alpha channel of an image when available. If enabled, you can also pick between straight alpha and premultiplied alpha. The difference is beyond the scope of this chapter, but if your alpha texture has a dark or bright fringe around the edge, then sometimes switching between straight alpha and premultiplied alpha can solve it.

Image Sampling Panel The Image Sampling panel contains some of the options that change how the image is interpreted inside Blender:

- **Calculate (Alpha):** Ignores the real alpha channel from the image file and instead calculates the alpha channel from the intensity of the image. This treats black pixels as transparent and white pixels as opaque.

- **Normal Map:** Tells Blender to treat the image as a normal map, so that the RGB value is interpreted as surface normal, which can be mapped to the normal channel of the material to create bumpiness on the surface.

Mapping Panel Mapping controls how the 2D texture is mapped onto the 3D object. Available options include global, object, generated, UV, reflection, and normal. The default option, generated, might work in some very simple cases. But most of the time, you will need to use the UV/Image Editor to control exactly how the image is projected onto the object. Using the UV/Image Editor is covered in Chapter 2. When the UV mapping is selected, you can specify which UV channel to use, if there is more than one UV layout for the mesh.

- **Offset:** Translate the texture coordinates.
- **Size:** Changes the scale of the texture coordinates.

Influence Panel This panel controls how the value of the texture is actually applied onto the surface. By default, color is selected with the influence set to 1. This means that the texture completely replaces the diffuse color of the material. A setting of 0 means there is no influence, effectively disabling the texture channel. Any in-between number will blend the current texture with the layer preceding it.

Normal is another commonly used influence setting. By using a normal map, you can create fake but convincing surface irregularities without using massive amounts of geometry. To apply a normal map to an existing material:

1. In the Texture panel, create a new texture slot by pressing the [+] icon.
2. Set the texture type to image and load a normal map image from disk.
3. Enable the normal map option under the Image Sampling panel.
4. Disable texture influence on material color by unchecking color under the Influence panel.
5. Enable the texture influence on material normal by checking normal under the Influence panel. Move the slider to adjust the strength of the effect.

Figure 5.25 shows the effect of a normal map.

Figure 5.25
A model without and with normal map.
© 2014 Mike Pan.

Normal Maps and Height Maps

A normal map is stored as a regular image file, but instead of changing the color of the surface like a regular color texture, normal maps are used to alter the per-pixel surface normal. By altering the surface normal, you can change the apparent bumpiness of a surface.

Internally, a normal map uses the three color-channels (RGB) to store the normal directions (XYZ) of a surface. Because most surface normals are pointing straight up, they have a normal value of (X=0.5,Y=0.5, Z=1.0), which is what gives normal maps that distinct purple color (when in tangent space).

Speaking of tangent space, normal maps can be stored in various different spaces, such as tangent, object, world, and camera space. They affect how the normal maps are interpreted and used in lighting computations. Suffice it to say that tangent space is the most commonly used option.

The other options in the influence section work in the exact way as color and normal. They each influence a different aspect of the material. For example, if you want a texture to influence the alpha value of a material, enable alpha and set the influence to 1. Then, in the Material panel, make sure alpha is set to 0.

- **Blend:** The blend selector is another key setting that controls how textures are mixed with each other. The blend option controls how the texture is mixed with the existing material color.

- **Negative:** Inverts the color of the texture.

- **RGB to intensity:** As the tooltip suggests, converts a RGB image to a grayscale image.

Combined Exercise

If all the checkboxes and sliders seem daunting, don't worry! Now let's put what we just read about material and textures to use. Soon it will become clear how everything fits together.

1. Open \Book\Chapter5\GLSL2.2blend.

2. You will be greeted with a partial car model that we have prepared, as shown in Figure 5.26. Hopefully, you will agree that the model is of decent quality and that all it is lacking is a good material to make it, er, shine.

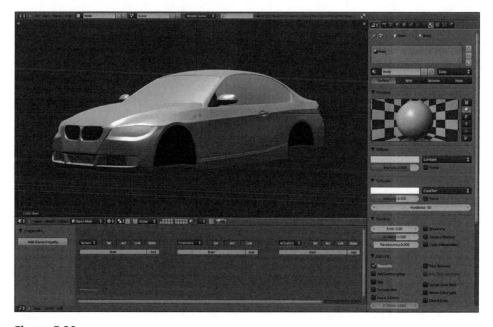

Figure 5.26
A car model with the default materials.
© 2014 Blender Foundation. Art © 2014 Mike Pan.

When working with materials, it is important to make sure there is sufficient lighting to see the model, as the lights can significantly affect the way materials are perceived. In fact, without lighting, everything will be pitch black!

In this car example, since we are trying to duplicate a photo studio setup, we have set up a single Hemi lamp in the scene, pointing straight down over the car body. This basic lighting setup gives a very uniform lighting on the entire surface of the car, without any harsh shadows.

We want to give this sporty machine a shiny metallic finish so that it looks like it just drove out of a car commercial. To achieve this effect, we will need two texture layers: one layer responsible for creating that sparkle found in metallic car paint, and another layer that contains a reflection texture to convey the idea of a glossy finish. The two textures shown in Figure 5.27 are provided online.

Figure 5.27
The two textures (magnified) that will be used for the car body material.

© 2014 Mike Pan. © River Panorama © Sam Schad – blendedskies.com.

3. Select the body of the car (object "Shell") in the 3D Viewport. Notice there is a default material attached to it. But before we spend too much time tweaking the material, let's add the textures first.

4. Go to the texture Properties Editor. Click on New to add a new texture. Notice that the first texture slot is now occupied. Rename the datablock from "Texture" to something more descriptive like "MetallicSpeck."

5. Since procedural textures are not supported in the game engine, we have created our own noise image in an external image-manipulation software. You can find one already made for you online, named Noise.png

6. Change the texture type to image. Then click on Open to reveal the file browser. Navigate to \Book\Chapter5\Textures and select Noise.png. Open it. Now the car should be covered with the texture you just loaded.

   The first problem you'll notice is that the texture is stretched across a certain vertical part of the shell. This is because a proper UV texture layout has not been set up, so Blender is trying its best at using a default texture mapping. So let's first make sure the texture is mapped uniformly across the object.

7. With the car body object still selected, enter Edit mode with the tab key; select all the vertices with a few taps on the A key until all the faces are highlighted.

8. With your mouse still over the 3D Viewport, press the U key to invoke the UV mapping menu. Select Smart UV Project and leave the options as default. This will intelligently project the entire model onto a UV map with minimal distortion. This operation takes a few seconds to complete.

9. Optionally, set one of the window types to UV/Image Editor to see the result of smart project.

10. Don't worry that you can't see the new UV map yet on the 3D model. In the Texture panel, change the mapping coordinates from generated to UV and select UVMap from the drop-down menu, as shown in Figure 5.28. This will tell Blender to use the new UV map that you just created.

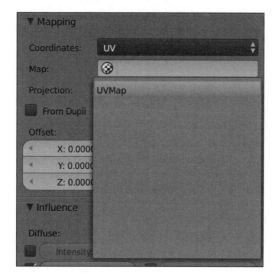

Figure 5.28
Setting the texture mapping to UV.
© 2014 Blender Foundation.

Now the 3D Viewport should look like Figure 5.29.

Figure 5.29
Noise texture with adjusted UV layout.
© 2014 Mike Pan.

11. It is apparent that the noise is way too big to be realistic. To scale it down, change the Size attribute under Mapping from 1.0 to 10.0 for all the X, Y, and Z axes.

To get the metallic shine, you don't want the texture to affect the color channel of the material.

12. Scroll down to the bottom of the Texture panel and locate the Influence panel. Turn off Color. Now, turn on Intensity and Color under Specular. This will make the texture affect only the specular channel of the material. This way, the speckle will only be visible when there is light shining on it, which is exactly what you want. Figure 5.30 shows all the relevant settings in the Texture panel. Settings not shown are left untouched.

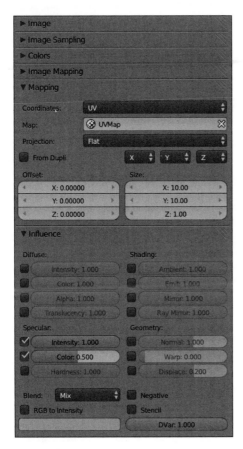

Figure 5.30
Texture options for the noise image texture.
© 2014 Blender Foundation.

13. To add a second texture layer, go back to the very top of the Texture panel and select the topmost empty texture slot from the list. It should be one with a red-and-white checkerboard pattern icon.

14. Click on New to create another texture datablock. This will be your reflection layer. So name it "ReflectionMap."

15. Again, set the texture type to image. Click on Open, navigate to \Book\Chapter5\Textures, and load blendedskies_river.jpg. This image will be used as your environment map.

16. Under Mapping, set the Coordinates to Reflection. This will automatically wrap the texture onto the object in such a way that resembles a real reflection.

17. However, notice that the sparkle you created in the previous texture slot has disappeared. This is because the new ReflectionMap texture is covering the previous texture. To make the reflection less intense, set the color Influence value from 1.0 to 0.75.

18. Change the Blending mode from Mix to Multiply. This will allow the reflection map to look better on base color.

At this point, you should have something that looks like Figure 5.31.

Figure 5.31
The completed car material.
© 2014 Mike Pan.

19. You can now go back to the Material panel and change base color of the car by altering the diffuse color however you wish.

Material Caching

There is a new setting in Blender 2.66 under the Render Properties Editor called *Material Caching*. With this turned on, loading of the game will be faster because GLSL materials are cached. This setting does not work well in Multitexture and Singletexture mode.

Nodes

Node is a new way to work with materials and textures in Blender. Instead of using a panel-style user interface to define a material, nodes allow you to build up materials using basic components. This may seem like a step backward because it will probably take much longer to create a simple material in the Node Editor than using the Material and Texture panels to achieve the same effect. But node offers the artist the freedom to accomplish much more than what is possible using the fixed Material and Texture panels.

Working with Node materials and textures is more of a process, so this section will be presented as a continuous tutorial. Once you have mastered this simple example, you will be able to adapt the workflow to create much more complex effects.

1. Open \Book\Chapter5\GLSL3.blend and familiarize yourself with the scene setup; note there is a sphere object without any material attached. The bottom half of the screen has been changed to the Node Editor.

2. Create a new material by clicking on the New button in the Material panel. Rename the material to NodeMat so we can refer to it later.

3. Click on the Use Shader Nodes button to enable nodes. The Node Editor should now look like Figure 5.32. Notice that the object in the 3D Viewport has turned black; this is because node material has just been activated, but since you have not actually set up a valid node material, the default color is black.

Figure 5.32
The Node Editor.
© 2014 Blender Foundation.

4. Because we don't want to create the material from scratch, we can use an existing material as the basis for the node material. To do that, in the Material node, click on the Browse Material icon and select NodeMat. Now the input material for the node is the material defined in the Material panel on the right side of the screen. Change any of the properties in the Material panel, and you can see the change is reflected in the node material system. Try setting the material color to red.

5. Insert a new Hue-Saturation-Value node in between the input and the output node, and connect them by drawing a line from one yellow dot to the other. The resulting setup should be the same as Figure 5.33.

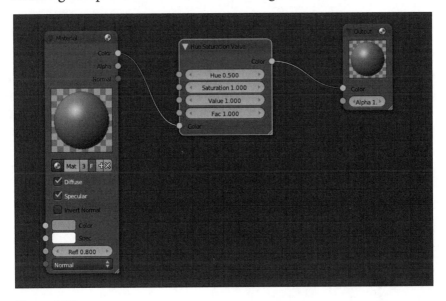

Figure 5.33
The Node Editor—reusing a material.
© 2014 Blender Foundation.

Congratulations! You are using node materials! Although the example we worked through is very basic, the power of the Node Editor is the ability to create almost infinite combinations of looks by only using a few basic building-block nodes.

Some typical uses for node-based materials include:

■ **Mixing multiple materials:** With the Node Editor, you can load multiple materials as input and mix them together to create a meta-material.

■ **More control:** Want the object position to affect the texture brightness? Want lighting intensity to affect the object transparency? With nodes, you can set up almost any effect you can think of.

- **Experimentation:** Using the node system as a sandbox to experiment with different effects is a lot faster than writing shader code to accomplish the same effect. In many cases, you can use the node system as a prototyping platform to build shaders.

MULTITEXTURE

Multitexture is older than the GLSL shading mode, but still far more capable than the singletexture material system.

As outlined in Table 5.1, multitexture uses per-vertex light rather than the per-pixel light of the GLSL. This means that multitexture is generally faster at the cost of less accurate shading.

In Multitexture mode, the artists still use the Material and Texture panels to apply shadings and textures. Compared to GLSL mode, the following material options have no effect in Multitexture mode:

- **Diffuse Shader Model:** The default one will always be used.
- **Specular Shader Model:** The default one will always be used.
- **Cubic Interpolation:** Always disabled because the lighting calculation is per-vertex.
- **Ramp Shaders:** Always disabled.
- **Shadow Settings:** Always disabled. No object casts shadows in Multitexture mode.

Compared to GLSL mode, the following texture options have no effect in Multitexture mode:

- **Blending Mode:** Other than Mix, Add, Subtract, Multiply, and Screen.
- **Influence Setting:** Other than Color and Alpha.
- **Mapping Coordinates:** Other than Global, Generated, Reflection, and UV.

To add a texture for the Multitexture shading mode, you need to use the UV/Image Editor. The Material panel can be used to change some of the surface properties of the model, such as diffuse intensity, specular intensity, and specular hardness.

SINGLETEXTURE

Singletexture is the most basic material setup. It is similar to multitexture, except only one texture is used. Multiple texture blending is not supported. To apply a texture in this mode requires the use of the UV/Image Editor window.

LIGHTS

Lights were covered briefly in Chapter 1. We will revisit them here in more detail.

In GLSL mode, supported lamp types are Point, Sun, Spot, and Hemi. Area lamp is unsupported and will be ignored by the game engine. Spot and Sun lamps are capable of casting dynamic shadows if the Shadow button is enabled. Table 5.2 summarizes the features of the lamps.

Table 5.2 Lights Types			
Type	**Supported**	**Directional**	**Shadow**
Point	Singletexture+	No	No
Sun	Singletexture+	Yes	Parallel
Spot	Singletexture+	Yes	Perspective
Hemi	GLSL	Yes	No
Area	No	Yes	No

© 2014 Dalai Felinto and Mike Pan.

In Multitexture and Singletexture mode, Point, Sun, and Spot are supported, and all other non-supported lamp types will be treated as Point lamps. There is no shadow support in these two modes.

WORLD SETTINGS

From the world Property Editor, you can change things that affect the entire world, such as background color and mist settings:

■ **Horizon Color:** Defines the sky color. In textured view, this color fills the background.

■ **Ambient Color:** Defines the ambient light color. Ambient light is a fill light that illuminates an object evenly from all angles. It makes shadows less dark, at the cost of making everything look "washed out." By default, ambient color is set to black, which is equivalent to the ambient color being disabled.

- **Mist:** Enable mist to add an atmospheric fog to the entire scene. Objects farther away will fade into the sky color (as defined by horizon color).

- **Mist Start:** As illustrated by Figure 5.34, the start distance at which the fog is applied.

- **Mist Depth:** As illustrated by Figure 5.34, the distance at which an object is entirely obscured by the mist color.

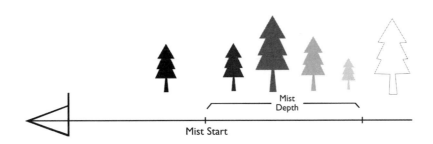

Figure 5.34
Mist distance illustrated.
© 2014 Cengage Learning®. All Rights Reserved.

Smog Can Be Good

Mist can help you hide the boundary of your make-believe world by smoothly blending the far objects into the horizon. Furthermore, fog can increase the atmosphere of the scene by giving a better sense of depth to the scene.

A good example of mist in games is the extremely foggy *Silent Hill* games. Their development team was able to put more details into the models by combining a more aggressive camera clipping with high mist values.

TEXTURE PAINTING

Typically, editing an image texture must be done with external software such as GIMP or Photoshop. Using texture painting, you can edit the texture directly on the model from within Blender (see Figure 5.35). Not only does this give you the ability to see the changes interactively on the model, but brush strokes made on the model will also be automatically projected back onto the image texture. This makes texture painting ideal as a rough outlining tool to mark out some key points on the model for reference or put the finishing touches on the texture. (It's much easier to paint on the model directly than to paint a 2D texture.)

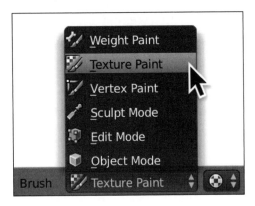

Figure 5.35
Entering Texture Paint mode.
© 2014 Blender Foundation.

To see how texture painting works:

1. Start a new file and set the 3D view to Texture mode (Alt+Z).

2. To paint directly on an object, you will need to set up a UV texture image first. So in the 3D view, make sure the object you want to paint (the initial cube in this case) is selected, and then enter Edit mode by pressing Tab.

3. Make sure that all vertices are selected (toggle A until they are all highlighted).

4. In the 3D viewport, press U to invoke the UV menu. Select Smart UV Project with the default parameters.

5. In the UV/Image Editor, create a new image by clicking on the New button. From the pop-up menu, select UV Grid or Color Grid as the Generated Type and click OK.

6. Notice that the model now has the newly created image texture mapped on it.

7. Switch from Edit mode to Texture Paint mode.

8. Start drawing on the model!

9. You can change options for the tools using the tool shelf on the left of the 3D Viewport.

10. At the time of writing, images updated by texture painting were not saved automatically. So once you are done, be sure to go back to the UV/Image Editor and save the texture by clicking on Image > Save.

11. Optionally, if you are working with the GLSL mode, you will need to create a new texture in the object's material and assign the newly created image to it. In this case, you also need to set UV as Coordinates in the Mapping panel.

CUSTOM GLSL SHADERS

Another way to apply material to an object is to override the game-engine material system completely by applying custom-written GLSL shaders. This will give you the ultimate control over exactly how the object looks, and you can achieve certain effects that are not possible with the built-in Material and Texture panels.

More GLSL?

Custom GLSL shaders are not to be confused with 2D filters, which also use GLSL codes. A 2D filter is GLSL code that is applied to the entire screen as a post-processing effect, while custom GLSL shaders are applied to objects.

Custom GLSL shaders work in the GLSL and Multitexture shading mode; they do not work in Singletexture mode. Custom GLSL shaders are not visible in the 3D Viewport: you must run the game to see them. To use custom GLSL shaders, you will need to use a little bit of Python scripting to link shaders to the object. But first, here is a crash course on GLSL.

GLSL Primer

GLSL is the shading language for the OpenGL graphic API. It has a C-like syntax and is compiled into assembly code by the graphic driver at runtime. It is also cross-platform and vendor-neutral (big words for saying they run on everything: Windows, Linux, Mac, AMD, Nvidia, and Intel). The primary purpose of GLSL is to give artists more control over how they want a surface to look by allowing them to write custom code that changes the way an object is rendered.

GLSL shaders can be divided into three types. They differ in where in the graphic pipeline the codes are executed and what types of data they have access to.

- **Vertex shader:** Operates on vertices, allowing geometry transformation.
- **Geometry shader:** Capable of generating or deleting vertices.
- **Fragment shader:** Operates on each pixel on the screen, allowing texture and shading effects.

All three categories of shaders share the same language construct and follow the same general syntax. The GLSL programs are executed in this order:

vertex shader > geometry shader > fragment shader

Because geometry shader is still relatively new and requires OpenGL 3.2 or higher, Blender does not support it. Only vertex shader and fragment shader can be used within the game engine at the moment.

Rather than wading through all the basics of GLSL, we will assume that you have a background in at least one programming language, and we'll simply outline what makes GLSL unique as a GPU-based language. GLSL is not too different from languages such as C. It has familiar data types such as float (0.5, −3.5), int (0,1,−3), and bool (true, false). Also, because GLSL is designed to work with graphic data, which typically include color information (RGB or RGBA), location data (XYZ or XYZW), and matrices (3×3 matrix, 4×4 matrix), there are many vectorized data types designed just for this purpose.

Consider this snippet of GLSL code:

```
vec4 color1 = vec4(1.0,0.0,0.0,1.0);
vec4 color2 = vec4(0.0,0.5,0.0,1.0);
vec4 final = color1 + color2;
```

vec4 initializes the variable to be a four-component floating point vector. color1 and color2 are the variable names. And finally vec4() can be viewed as a constructor that takes four literal constants and generates a vec4 data type from them.

But what does the code actually do? Here, we first declare two four-component vectors, color1 and color2. The values to the right of the assignment operator (=) are mapped to the red, green, blue, and alpha channels of the vector, respectively. Thus, color1 is initialized to a red color with an alpha of 1; while color2 is initialized to a dark green color, also with an alpha of 1. In the last line of the code, we add color1 to color2, and copy the result to a new variable called *final*, which should have the value (1.0,0.5,0.0,1.0).

The funny-looking swizzling operators of the GLSL language are one of its distinct features. They look like this:

```
vec4 myColor = vec4 (0.0,1.0,0.5,0.6);
float intensity = myColor.r + myColor.g + myColor.b;
```

The dot (.) notation at the end of the color variable is used to select a single component from the four-component vector. In the above case, we took the red, green, and blue components of myColor and added them up to get a sum of the three channels. The result is stored in a variable called *intensity* as a single floating point number. Valid selectors include RGBA, XYZW, and STQR. You can also repeat swizzling operators or rearrange them.

```
vec4 myColor = vec4 (0.0,1.0,0.5,0.6);
vec4 newColor = myColor.ggrr;
```

newColor now has the value (1.0,1.0,0.0,0.0) because the content of `myColor`'s green channel is copied into `newColor`'s red and green channels, and `myColor`'s red channel is copied into `newColor`'s blue and alpha channels. The value of `myColor` is not changed.

GLSL supports basic C-like flow control, such as while loops, for loops, if statements, and function declarations. Although supported, branching with if statements is usually avoided because they are relatively slow.

Using "If"

If you must use "if," be careful with writing your conditions. Floating point values in GLSL are usually not precise enough for an equality comparison operation to work. So instead of writing

```
if (myVar == 1.0)
```

which might never evaluate to true, use the much safer

```
if (abs(myVar - 1.0) < 0.001)
```

This code will look at the absolute difference between the two values it is comparing, and return true as long as the difference between them is small enough (0.001, in this case).

While we know you would enjoy learning about trigonometry, 3D math, matrix, orthogonality, Euclidean vector space, and lerp, teaching GLSL is not the aim of this book. The book *OpenGL Shading Language* by Randi J. Rost does a fantastic job of explaining what GLSL is all about.

GLSL Implementations "Gotchas"

Because GLSL is compiled by the graphic driver, each vendor (AMD, Nvidia, Intel, etc.) does it a bit differently. This means that codes that work on one might not work on another. For example, on Nvidia, the `noise()` function always returns 0. (However, this is technically still within the GLSL specification, which states that the return value for the `noise()` function must be between −1.0 and 1.0.)

Just keep in mind that some drivers are stricter than others, so a GLSL program that works on one computer might not work on another.

Custom GLSL Shaders

So now that you have learned the basics of GLSL, are you ready to tackle your first complete GLSL shader?

```
void main(){
gl_FragColor.rgba = vec4(0.9,0.4,0.2,1.0);
}
```

That's it. This one-line fragment shader will assign each output pixel (a predefined variable by the name of gl_FragColor) the color (0.9,0.4,0.2), which happens to be a pleasant orange. The last value sets the alpha to 1.0, to make sure the face is completely visible.

One of the requirements for any valid GLSL shader is that it contains both a vertex shader and a fragment shader. So, supplying only the fragment shader above is not quite enough; you need a vertex shader as well. But in most cases, you don't want to do anything fancy with the vertices, so a simple

```
void main(){
gl_Position = ftransform();
}
```

is enough. It tells GLSL that you want the vertex to stay in the same position as it would if you used a fixed-transform pipeline.

In Blender, to use custom GLSL shaders as a replacement for any regular material, you need to run a Python script that helps bind the GLSL shader to a material at runtime. A complete script is shown below:

```
01 from bge import logic
02 ShaderObject = logic.getCurrentScene().objects.get("Cube")
03
04 VertexShader = """
05 void main()
06 {
07       gl_Position = ftransform();
08 }
09 """
10
11 FragmentShader = """
12 void main()
13 {
14       gl_FragColor.rgba = vec4(0.9,0.4,0.2,1.0);
15 }
16 """
17
18 for mesh in ShaderObject.meshes:
19       for material in mesh.materials:
20             shader = material.getShader()
21             if shader != None and not shader.isValid():
22                   shader.setSource(VertexShader, FragmentShader, True)
```

If you are feeling faint, don't panic! (Just wait until you get to Chapter 7.) This script has a nice blend of Python and GLSL, but it's not complicated once you break it down.

Python will be formally introduced in Chapter 7. You can skip ahead and read the relevant part first before continuing on from here.

Line 1 loads the bge Python module, which allows us to use the BGE API within the Python script.

Line 2 is equivalent to

```
scene = logic.getCurrentScene()
objects = scene.objects
ShaderObject = objects.get("Cube")
```

One important concept to remember is that the GLSL shader is linked to material. Even though you got the material by referencing an object, the GLSL shader is always replacing a material. This means that if multiple objects share the same material, the shader will run on all the objects.

So you are looking for an object named "Cube" within a list of all the objects in the current scene, and you assign the Cube object to a variable named ShaderObject. So, if an object with the name Cube exists, ShaderObject will now contain a reference to that object. If no object by that name is found, ShaderObject has the value None.

On line 4, VertexShader is simply a multiline Python string. Multiline strings are declared by triple quotation marks. The content of the string is the actual GLSL code. (To clarify, the variable VertexShader is still a Python string object, but the content happens to be another language: GLSL. But it's all the same to Python: the string could be in Chinese and Python wouldn't care.) Notice the vertex shader is wrapped in a `main()` function, just like in C. This is where the execution of the code will start.

Starting on line 11, analogous to the VertexShader, FragmentShader is another multiline Python string containing the fragment shader GLSL code.

From line 18 onward until the end, the Python code is used to invoke the GLSL shader declared above. First, you loop through the internal meshes attached to the object. Then iterating through each mesh, you find all the materials attached to it. Since meshes can have multiple materials (up to 16), iterating through all of them ensures that you replace all the materials on that object with your shader. (Conversely, you can modify the code to apply a unique shader to each material on the same mesh.)

Don't Write This Code!

Since we were trying to keep this example as short and simple as possible, the code has very bad error-handling ability. For example, it would not be good if an object by the name of Cube is not found in the scene, or if the object named Cube isn't a mesh. Do not write code like this in real life!

Line 21 might look a bit convoluted. But in English, it simply means that if there is a shader, the script goes on to check if the shader is valid. If it's not, a new shader is created using the VertexShader and FragmentShader text string as the input. If there is already a valid shader, nothing more is done. (Shaders only need to be compiled and bound once at the start of the game, not every frame. Otherwise, the GLSL compilation will significantly slow down the game)

Save the script as a new text file in Blender. To use the above GLSL shader script, it needs to be invoked once within the game engine. You can easily accomplish this by setting up a simple logic brick chain, as shown in Figure 5.36.

Figure 5.36
Logic brick setup to load a custom GLSL shader.
© 2014 Blender Foundation.

You can try to copy this setup with the provided Blender file at \Book\Chapter5\ GLSL1.blend.

In this case, because there is no object named Cube, you need to modify the script a bit by replacing the line:

```
ShaderObject = logic.getCurrentScene().objects.get("Cube")
```

with

```
ShaderObject = logic.getCurrentScene().objects.get("Monkey")
```

Run the game and enjoy the new orange monkey.

Because GLSL replaces the entire material pipeline with your own code, no shading is applied on the model unless you explicitly tell it to. This is why the monkey head is a flat shade of orange.

Remember that custom GLSL shaders are always applied to each material, not the object, nor the mesh. This means any objects with the same material will all share the same shader.

A Useful Fragment Shader

The first GLSL shader you were introduced to is pretty trivial and nearly useless. Here is a much more useful Lambert diffuse shader:

```
from bge import logic
ShaderObject = logic.getCurrentScene().objects["Monkey"]
lamp = logic.getCurrentScene().objects["MainLight"]

VertexShader = """
uniform vec3 light_position;
varying vec3 light_vec;
varying vec3 normal_vec;

void main(){
        vec3 vert =(gl_ModelViewMatrix * gl_Vertex).xyz;
        light_vec = (gl_ModelViewMatrix* vec4(light_position,1.0)).xyz - vert;
        normal_vec = gl_NormalMatrix *gl_Normal;
        gl_Position = ftransform();
}
"""

FragmentShader = """
varying vec3 light_vec;
varying vec3 normal_vec;
void main(){
        vec3 l = normalize(light_vec);
        vec3 n = normalize(normal_vec);
        float ndotl = clamp(dot(n,l), 0.0, 1.0);

        vec4 color = ndotl * vec4(1.0,1.0,1.0,1.0);

        gl_FragColor = color;
}
"""

mesh = ShaderObject.meshes[0]
for material in mesh.materials:
        shader = material.getShader()
        if shader != None:
                if not shader.isValid():
                        shader.setSource(VertexShader, FragmentShader,1)
                shader.setUniformfv('light_position', lamp.position)
```

This shader uses the Lambert diffuse shading algorithm to apply some basic shading to the object, taking into account the position of the lamp and the surface normal at each pixel. This is still not a terribly useful shader, since the same effect can be achieved without a single line of coding via the Material panel.

We'll leave it to you to discover more complex shaders on your own.

A Useful Vertex Shader

This GLSL shader applies a transformation to each vertex along the X-axis, producing a "wavy" effect, similar to that of leaves swaying in the wind. Using vertex shaders to deform geometry is a fast alternative to using bones.

```
from bge import logic
ShaderObject = logic.getCurrentController().owner

VertexShader = """
uniform float timer;

void main()
{
        //get the first UV layout
        gl_TexCoord[0] = gl_MultiTexCoord0;

        // Fetch the Vertex Position
        vec4 v = gl_Vertex;

        //Displaces each vertex using a sine wave
        v.x = v.x + sin(timer);

        gl_Position = gl_ModelViewProjectionMatrix * v;
}
"""

FragmentShader = """
uniform sampler2D colorMap;

void main(void)
{
        vec4 color = texture2D(colorMap,gl_TexCoord[0].st);
        gl_FragColor = color;
}
"""

mesh = ShaderObject.meshes[0]
for material in mesh.materials:
        shader = material.getShader()
        if shader != None:
                if not shader.isValid():
                        shader.setSource(VertexShader, FragmentShader,1)

                shader.setSampler('colorMap',0)
                shader.setUniform1f('timer',ShaderObject["timer"])
```

This shader introduces yet another new concept, called *uniforms*. Using uniforms is one way to pass data from the Blender world into the shader.

Going Further
Even though GLSL can seem daunting at first, plenty of learning material is available. The accompanying disk has a few more examples of how GLSL can be used; they can be found under \Book\Chapter5\.

2D FILTERS

2D filters are post-processing GLSL shaders that are applied to each frame right before it is displayed. 2D filters can be used to enhance the looks of the image and add special screen-space effects. There are a few built-in shaders that come with Blender to get you started, but 2D filters also allow custom-written GLSL shaders to give you the freedom to do potentially a lot more.

Why Use 2D Filters?

Using 2D filters makes it easy to tweak the mood of your visual, without having to rework the lighting, material, or textures. Because a 2D filter operates on an image (the frame buffer) and not the individual 3D objects, the 2D filter's performance is not dependent on the complexity of the scene, only the number of pixels on the screen and the complexity of the effect itself.

GLSL fragment shader is the language that powers all the 2D filters. Figure 5.37 shows some samples of what 2D filters can do:

The capabilities of 2D filters:

- Apply effects such as sharpen, edge detection, anti-aliasing, and motion blur.
- Alter basic color attributes such as brightness, contrast, and color saturation.
- Add screen-space effects such as Gaussian blur, radial blur, light bloom, and distortion.
- Add cinematic effect such as depth of field, film grain, sepia tone, and lens vignetting.
- Simulate complex lighting effects such as ambient occlusion and light scattering.

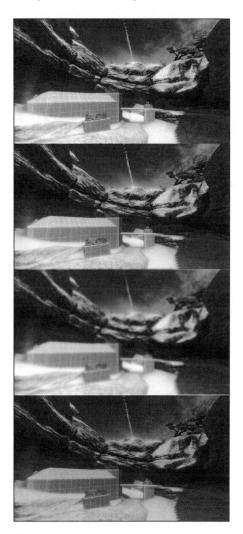

Figure 5.37
Sample Filters: Normal color, grayscale, blur, sepia.
© 2014 Chase Moskal and Team.

How to Use 2D Filters

The 2D filters can be accessed as a standard actuator in the Logic Editor window. If you are rusty on what the Logic Editor does, refer to Chapter 3.

To enable a basic 2D filter, add an Always sensor, an And controller, and a Filter 2D actuator, and link them together. Remember, even though you want the effect to be applied to every frame, there is no need to turn on the "true" pulse in the Always sensor. Because once the shader is bound (initialized), it will stay active until you explicitly disable it. Binding the 2D filter every frame will only slow down the game.

It also does not matter which object the logic brick is attached to; 2D filter is a screen effect and, thus, does not depend on the object it is attached to. You can attach it to any convenient object. Attaching the 2D filter logic to the main camera is a good idea, because it's an intuitive reminder that the 2D filter is a screen effect. Figure 5.38 shows a basic 2D filter setup.

Figure 5.38
Logic brick setup to load a custom GLSL shader.
© 2014 Blender Foundation.

Once you have set up the logic bricks, let's take a closer look at the Filter 2D actuator. The exact function of each option in the Actuator panel is explained in Chapter 3.

The Pass Number at the bottom acts as a "layer" setting where the 2D filter effect resides. Each "layer" can only have one filter, but you can stack filter layers to get a more complex effect. Just make sure that each effect has a unique Pass Number so they don't override each other. Obviously, to set up multiple 2D filter effects, more than one actuator is needed.

In the drop-down menu, you'll see a small selection of predefined effects (Invert, Sepia, Grayscale, Motion Blur). Select one and run the game to see how it looks.

Enable and Disable turn a certain effect on or off. You need to supply a valid Pass Number. Thus, if you bound a 2D filter to Pass Number 5 at one point, you can turn off the effect with Disable and set the Pass Number to 5. Conversely, you can quickly turn the same effect back on by using Enable.

Remove Filter is similar to Disable: it turns off a certain effect on a given Pass Number. Additionally, Remove Filter also completely unbinds the shader, making it impossible to enable the same filter (i.e., Pass number) again.

Custom Filter is used to specify arbitrary shaders. It is useful when the built-in filters can't achieve the effect that you are looking for. To use a custom filter, Blender needs the name of a text file. The text file must be one of the text datablocks stored within the Blender file.

With the pass system, you can make a very robust post-processing stack. You can set up a few filters to be run on an Always sensor to do some basic color correction and add the effects that will always be enabled. Then you can set up a few more filters that are enabled momentarily when you need them.

Custom Filter

A very simple custom 2D filter is shown below:

```
uniform sampler2D bgl_RenderedTexture;
const float contrast 1.5
void main(void)
{
  vec4 texcolor = texture2D(bgl_RenderedTexture, gl_TexCoord[0].st);
  gl_FragColor.rgb = texcolor.rgb * contrast;
  gl_FragColor.a = texcolor.a;
}
```

If the above code looks somewhat familiar, it's probably because a 2D filter is really just a GLSL fragment shader. This shader fetches the color of the current pixel, multiplies it by 1.5, and displays the result. This produces an image with higher contrast than the original.

Limitations

2D filters can be read from the following inputs:

- Frame Buffer Color Image (sampler2D bgl_RenderedTexture)
- Frame Buffer Depth (sampler2D bgl_DepthTexture)
- Frame Buffer Luminance (sampler2D bgl_LuminanceTexture)
- Image Size (float bgl_RenderedTextureWidth, float RenderedTextureHeight)
- Custom Textures as Input (sampler2D)

2D filters are applied per scene, with the effect building one on top of the other. For example, if you have a main scene and an overlay scene, the game engine will proceed as follows:

1. Render the main scene.
2. Apply the filters available on that scene into the screen.
3. Render the overlay scene on top of the already post-processed main scene.
4. Apply the filters on top of this multilayered pixel lasagna.

Text

To display text, you can pre-make a mesh object that has the real geometry of the text or texture map a plane. This method is simple, but is very limiting because the text cannot be changed during the game. To show different text, the artist would need to create a new asset for each text string the game needs.

To display text that can potentially change during the game, there are four ways to display dynamic texts within the game engine. Two of them are useful for only static text: text that doesn't change throughout the game. The other two are dynamic: the text they display can be changed on the fly.

- Static text using real geometry
- Static text using pre-made textures
- Dynamic bitmap text
- Dynamic text object

Static text is not treated any differently than regular Blender objects. For the rest of this section, we will look at ways to create dynamic texts.

Bitmap Text

If the game engine can render hyper-realistic 3D graphics in real time, how hard can it be to render some text onto the screen? Turns out, it's really difficult due to the awkward workflow needed to create the text.

The process involves creating a texture containing all the letters of the English alphabet (plus numbers and symbols)—yes, languages that use a non-Latin alphabet are not supported using this method; UV map the texture onto a plane; turn on the Text option in the material setting; and create a GameLogic property on the text object called "Text." Fill this variable with some string. Once you run the game, Blender will then automatically display content of the "Text" string on the screen. Tada! Hello? Come back!

Okay, let's try that again.

1. Start with an empty Blender file.
2. Select Blender Game from the Render Engine drop-down box.
3. In the top view, add a Plane by clicking on Add > Mesh > Plane.
4. Configure one of the Viewports to be the UV/Image Editor.
5. Select the Plane; enter Edit mode by pressing Tab.

6. From the UV/Image Editor, load the text image texture from the companion files: \Book\Chapter5\Textures\text.png.

7. The image texture deserves a little more attention. This texture is generated by a free tool that can be found at http://www.ashsid.sk/wp/?p=21. It contains the most commonly used characters and symbols arranged so that Blender knows exactly where each character is.

8. Create a material for the object; under the game settings, enable Text. This will tell Blender to treat the image texture you loaded in the above step as a special text image. The plane will now show an @ symbol, the first available character of the text image. This is normal.

9. Configure one of the Viewports to be the Logic Editor.

10. Keep the plane selected. In the Logic Editor, add a new Game Property and name it Text. (This is important! Otherwise, it won't work). And set the data type to String.

11. In the value field, type in anything you want; whatever is stored in this Text property will be displayed as text in the game.

12. Run the game. The content of the Text property will replace the @ symbol.

This method of displaying text does have several drawbacks. For example, because texts are drawn using textures, they might appear blurry when shown at extreme angles relative to the camera. Also, since the character set is extremely limited, international support for non-Latin alphabets and right-to-left languages is impossible to achieve.

Text Object

Using bitmap text is a very confusing process. Text object is an easier way to display text (see Figure 5.39). The same Blender Text object type can be used in-game. Simply create a "Text" object in Blender, and it will be rendered as text inside the game engine. To change the value of the text, you can use logic bricks to change the "Text" property of the Text objects.

Or one can use Python:

```
from bge import logic
logic.getCurrentController().owner.text = "Hello World"
```

Figure 5.39
Text Object: 3D view and in-game.
© 2014 Blender Foundation.

VIDEO TEXTURE

The video texture function allows you to update or replace a texture during the game. Not only does this give you the ability to use a video file as a texture, as the name of the function implies, but video texture can also be used to replace a static texture with the following:

- A video file (useful as animated texture)
- A different image texture (useful if you just want to replace the texture)
- A render from another camera (useful for rendering reflections of mirrors)

Because video texture is a rather advanced feature that requires some Python scripting knowledge, it will be left for your own exploration. The book files contain a few examples of how video texture can be used. You can find them under \Book\ Chapter7\6_texture\.

STEREO

Human eyes are able to perceive depth primarily in three ways:

- Using environmental cues such as haze, lighting, perspective, and existing knowledge of dimensions of common objects. Using this method, you can still get a sense of depth from looking at a flat picture.
- Using the focusing distance of the eye, because things not in focus tend to be blurrier.
- Using the parallax distance between two eyes to see two slightly different images.

The basic idea behind all 3D stereoscopic techniques utilizes the third point on the list above: parallax. That is, to display a different image rendered from a slightly different perspective to each eye. There are many methods used today to make sure the left eye only sees the image intended to be seen by the left eye, and the right eye only sees the image intended for the right eye. Most 3D movie theaters achieve this by using polarized glasses combined with a dual-projector setup. Glass-based 3D TVs for consumers use shutter-glass that quickly alternates between blocking the left and the right eye, synchronized to a fast-refreshing screen that also alternates between right- and left-eye images.

Blender can output stereoscopic renderings in many ways. Figure 5.40 shows how to set it up. But regardless of the final output format, it starts by rendering the scene twice, with a slight horizontal camera offset (controlled by the setting Eye Separation) to mimic the separation between the human eyes. For a typical viewing environment, the optimal eye separation is approximately Focal Distance/30.

The Nitty Gritty Details

Blender uses the zero parallax technique to set up the stereo cameras.

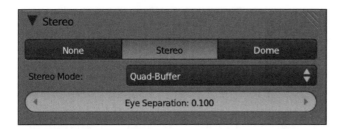

Figure 5.40
Stereo setting panel.
© 2014 Blender Foundation.

When Stereo mode is selected in the Render panel, as shown in Figure 5.40, six Stereo modes become available.

- **V-interlace and Interlaced:** The left and right images are interlaced together. This mode requires additional 3D hardware to see properly.

- **Above-Below:** The left and right images are stacked vertically. This mode also requires additional 3D hardware to see properly.

- **Side by Side:** The left and right images are placed next to each other without overlapping. In this Stereo mode, you should be able to see the 3D effect by crossing your eyes (really!). But this method of viewing 3D is very straining on the eyes. I do not recommend you try this for extended period of time.

- **Anaglyph:** In this mode, Blender filters the left and right images with a different color and then overlays them on top of each other. This mode requires the viewer to wear a pair of 3D glasses with tinted lens. The left eye should be tinted red and the right eye should be tinted cyan. With the glasses on, the colored lens should only allow one image to go through, blocking out the image for the other eye. This way of seeing 3D is less stressful than Side by Side, but requires the monitor to be sufficiently bright relative to the ambient environment for an optimum image. The only downside of this approach is the lack of accurate color representation.

- **Quad-Buffer:** Quad-Buffer is the natural extension to a typical double-buffer rendering system, which is used for single-eye rendering. This mode also requires additional hardware to display the image. Quad-Buffering is a native stereoscopic method supported by OpenGL. Unfortunately, it does not work on consumer-level Nvidia and ATI/AMD graphics cards; only the more expensive Nvidia Quadro and ATI/AMD FireGL support this functionality.

DOME

The Dome mode in the game engine is a great example of how Blender's open source nature makes it the perfect playground for developers to experiment with specialized features that virtually no other game engines on the market have. The Dome mode was implemented by Dalai Felinto as a part-school, part-commissioned work.

Similar to how environment maps are rendered in Blender, the Dome mode works by rendering the scene from many directions, up to six times. This data is then stitched together and mapped onto a new canvas of any arbitrary shape, and finally displayed on the screen. The image generated by the Dome mode is designed for spherical screens like those found in OMNIMAX theaters and planetariums.

Even if you don't have access to the screen of your local OMNIMAX theater (you don't?!), smaller immersive dome screens are also becoming more popular, like the one shown in Figure 5.41.

Figure 5.41
The Dome mode in action.
Photo © Dalai Felinto and Paul Bourke. Club Silo game © Dale Best (Luma).

Even with a flat screen, Dome mode can provide you with a much better viewing experience than the default OpenGL perspective mode at extremely wide angles, as depicted in Figure 5.42. Both cameras are 170 degrees. Notice the heavy distortion on the left image, and the fisheye look that the dome perspective obtains.

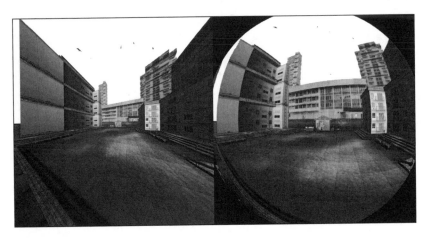

Figure 5.42
Comparison between regular perspective and dome perspective.
© 2014 Mike Pan.

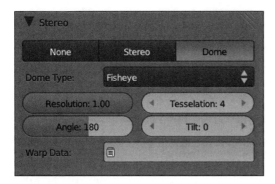

Figure 5.43
Dome settings.
© 2014 Blender Foundation.

Dome settings can be enabled from the Render panel, as shown in Figure 5.43.

- **Dome type:** Controls how the images are mapped onto the screen. Cube Map shows you the raw render done by the dome engine, laid out in such a way to match how Blender stores the environment maps. This is mainly useful for debugging, or if you want to save the cube map for a different purpose. Other options include Spherical Panoramic, Front-Truncated, Rear-Truncated, and Fisheye. These choices warp the images in different ways to fit the screen. Try them out for yourself! Be careful, though—some of these settings can be very disorienting!

- **Resolution:** Sets the dimension of the render-to-texture images; a smaller value will give you better performance at the cost of a lower-resolution final image.

- **Tessellation:** Sets the number of subdivisions of the mesh used for displaying the final image. A larger value means less distortion, but it will also be slower. You can check the effect of this setting by running the game in wireframe view.

- **Angle:** Sets the field of view of the camera.

- **Tilt:** Pitches the view up and down without actually rotating the in-game camera.

Beware of Artifacts!

Because both stereo imaging and Dome mode require the game to reposition or reorient the camera to create multiple views per frame, certain camera-dependent texture and shading functions (such as normal and reflection, and specular highlights) might contain artifacts when rendered in Stereo or Dome mode.

WRAP UP

Before you get carried away with creating the ultimate eye candy, keep in mind that a realistic game isn't just about visual fidelity. As John Carmack (the technical director of id Software, known for *Doom* and *Quake* series) noted at QuakeCon 2009: No matter how good a scene looks graphically, it only takes one frame of awkward animation to completely break the illusion of realism. Many games today have achieved near-photorealistic graphics, but once the character starts to move, it becomes painfully obvious how artificial everything is. So keep in mind that even the most detailed 3D model can't immerse the gamer in a fantasy world if the gameplay, sound, or animation doesn't measure up.

CHAPTER 6

PHYSICS

Welcome to Physics 101! We are going to be your professors for this chapter. Follow along as we dive into a dynamic world of falling apples, run alongside bouncing balls, and soar with flying spaghetti (see Figure 6.1).

Figure 6.1
A physics demo.
© 2014 Mike Pan.

WHAT IS PHYSICS?

In the real world, the laws of physics govern everything from the smallest subatomic particle to the largest galaxy far, far away. Luckily for us, we don't have to understand quantum mechanics, Newtonian physics, or Euclidean space in order to make a fun game. A physics engine handles game events such as collision detection between objects, moves objects in a physically realistic way, and even deforms objects as if they are made up of a soft material.

A physics engine moves things based on a set of predefined rules so that you, the artist, don't have to manually animate every object interaction. Compared to traditional keyframe animations, which are premade, the dynamic nature of the physics engine means that it is inherently non-deterministic—the motion of the object depends on the physical property of the object and its state in the physical world. This unique property makes games that utilize real-time physics fun to play around with, if not unpredictable sometimes.

As usual, this chapter comes with a collection of example files that showcase what the physics engine can do. You can find them in the folder \Book\Chapter6\demos.

OVERVIEW

Because physics is such an integral part of the Blender game engine, physics-related settings are found in many different places. However scattered they might look at first glance, there is a pattern in this chaos.

The physics settings can be broken down into these sections:

- **World settings:** Contain settings that affect the entire scene. Global settings such as gravity strength can be found here. Figure 6.2 shows the World Properties Editor.

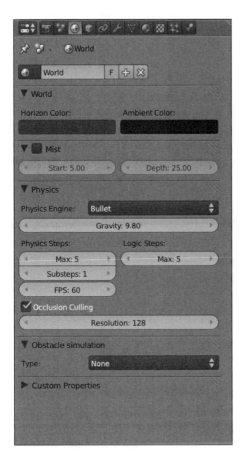

Figure 6.2
World Properties Editor.
Source: *Blender Foundation.*

- **Object Physics settings:** Any game-engine object (Mesh, Lamp, Camera, Empty, and Text) can be turned into a physical object. Once physics is enabled for an object, it starts obeying the rules of the physics engine, transforming the object from a static object into something that falls, collides, tumbles, and deforms. Figure 6.3 shows the Physics Properties Editor.

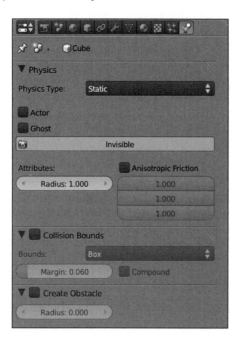

Figure 6.3
Physics Properties Editor.
Source: *Blender Foundation.*

■ **Material Physics settings:** The Material panel is not only a place where all the graphic magic happens; it also contains additional physics that control how the surface of the object behaves. Settings such as surface friction can be found here. Because an object can have multiple materials, material physics settings allow the artist to assign different surface materials for different parts of a single object. Figure 6.4 shows the Material Properties Editor.

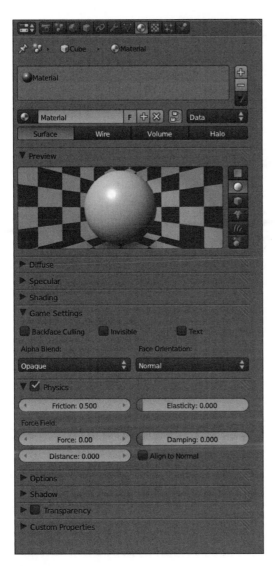

Figure 6.4
Material Properties Editor.
Source: *Blender Foundation.*

■ **Object constraints:** When you were young, your parents probably set out certain rules that you needed to abide by. If any of the rules were broken, bad things happened. Physics constraints work in roughly the same way (without all the drama and door slamming). They allow you to set up simple rules that the objects follow, rules such as tracking one object to another or limiting their range of motion. With constraints, it's possible to realistically represent many of the structures that have a limited degree of motion, such as hinges, wheels, and chains. Figure 6.5 shows the Object Constraints Properties Editor.

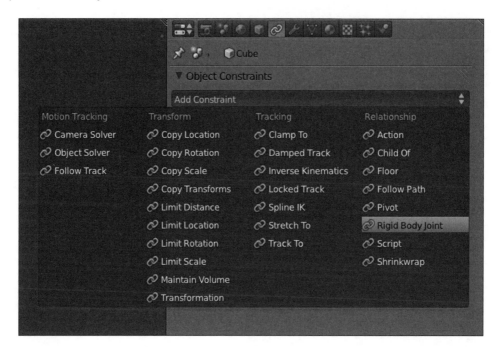

Figure 6.5
Object Constraints Properties Editor.
Source: *Blender Foundation.*

■ **Physics sensors and actuators:** Except for maybe the case of a Rube Goldberg machine, where everything happens in a predetermined manner, most games would be pretty boring if there were no way to make an object move at a user's command or to trigger a reaction when two objects collide. Actuators and sensors fulfill these two roles, respectively. Actuators are part of a logic brick that carries out an action (such as applying a force to the object to make it move). Sensors are triggers that detect when something happens in the game, such as when two objects touch. A combination of sensors and actuators makes a game truly interactive, by giving the game engine the ability to make decisions. Figure 6.6 shows the Logic Editor. In case you forgot, Chapter 3 is all about logic bricks.

Figure 6.6
Logic Editor.

Source: *Blender Foundation.*

■ **Python:** In addition to all the physics settings one can access from the graphic user interface, an extensive Python API is at your disposal. The Python API gives you programmable control over many aspects of the physics engine. With Python, you can dynamically set many of the physics options while the game is running. It even allows you to accomplish a few things that are not possible from the graphic interface. For instance, Python can be used to create realistic vehicle physics. Figure 6.7 shows the Text Editor with a Python script open.

```
244  for row in data:
245      if row["attribute"]:
246          vehicleAttribute[row["attribute"]] = row["value"]
247
248  ## instantiate car python object ##
249  G.car = vehicleClass(vehicleAttribute, cont.owner, vehicleAttribute["name"])
250
251  ## setup vehicle physics ##
252  vehicle = PC.createConstraint(G.car.obj.getPhysicsId(),0,11)
253  G.car.cid = vehicle.getConstraintId()
254  vehicle = PC.getVehicleConstraint(G.car.cid)
255
256  ## attached wheel based on actuator name ##
257  act1 = cont.actuators["wheel1"]
258  wheel1 = act1.owner
259  wheelAttachPosLocal = [G.car.wheelBaseWidth , G.car.wheelFrontOffset,G.car.wheelHeight]
260  vehicle.addWheel(wheel1, wheelAttachPosLocal,G.car.wheelAttachDirLocal,G.car.wheelAxleLocal,G.car.suspensionLength, G.car.wheelRadius,1)
261
262  act2 = cont.actuators["wheel2"]
263  wheel2 = act2.owner
264  wheelAttachPosLocal = [-G.car.wheelBaseWidth , G.car.wheelFrontOffset,G.car.wheelHeight]
265  vehicle.addWheel(wheel2, wheelAttachPosLocal,G.car.wheelAttachDirLocal,G.car.wheelAxleLocal,G.car.suspensionLength, G.car.wheelRadius,1)
266
267  act3 = cont.actuators["wheel3"]
268  wheel3 = act3.owner
269  wheelAttachPosLocal = [G.car.wheelBaseWidth , G.car.wheelBackOffset,G.car.wheelHeight]
270  vehicle.addWheel(wheel3, wheelAttachPosLocal,G.car.wheelAttachDirLocal,G.car.wheelAxleLocal,G.car.suspensionLength, G.car.wheelRadius,0)
271
272  act4 = cont.actuators["wheel4"]
273  wheel4 = act4.owner
274  wheelAttachPosLocal = [-G.car.wheelBaseWidth , G.car.wheelBackOffset,G.car.wheelHeight]
275  vehicle.addWheel(wheel4, wheelAttachPosLocal,G.car.wheelAttachDirLocal,G.car.wheelAxleLocal,G.car.suspensionLength, G.car.wheelRadius,0)
276
277  ## set vehicle roll tendency ##
278  vehicle.setRollInfluence(G.car.suspensionRollAmount,0)
279  vehicle.setRollInfluence(G.car.suspensionRollAmount,1)
280  vehicle.setRollInfluence(G.car.suspensionRollAmount,2)
281  vehicle.setRollInfluence(G.car.suspensionRollAmount,3)
282
283  ## set vehicle suspension hardness ##
284  vehicle.setSuspensionStiffness(G.car.suspensionStiffness,0)
285  vehicle.setSuspensionStiffness(G.car.suspensionStiffness,1)
286  vehicle.setSuspensionStiffness(G.car.suspensionStiffness,2)
287  vehicle.setSuspensionStiffness(G.car.suspensionStiffness,3)
```

Figure 6.7
Text Editor.

Source: *Blender Foundation.*

So now that you have an overview of what physics is all about and where to find all the settings, the rest of the chapter will explain how to use these settings in combination to achieve various effects.

WORLD PROPERTIES

World Properties Editor is generally the first place to visit when setting up physics, simply because the settings here are truly global: they affect the entire scene.

In the World Properties Editor, there are numerous global physics settings that affect how the scene behaves. Again, remember that game-specific settings are only visible when the engine selector is set to Blender Game, as shown in Figure 6.8.

Figure 6.8
Set engine to Blender Game to see the relevant game settings.
Source: *Blender Foundation.*

Physics Engine

Under the Physics section of the World Properties Editor, you are presented with a choice to select a physics engine. A physics engine is the underlying computer algorithm that drives all physics simulation. Blender uses Bullet Physics, which is a powerful and open-source physics library developed by Erwin Coumans and others. Not only is Bullet used in Blender, but it is also used by other commercial games, as well as movie productions, as part of the visual effects pipeline.

When the engine selector is set to none, all physics calculation is disabled. Dynamic objects will not move when a force is applied, and collisions will not be detected. Most games will use some degree of physics, so keep physics turned on unless you are absolutely sure you don't need it. If you choose to disable physics, the majority of the features mentioned in the rest of this chapter will not work.

Figure 6.9 shows the World Physics settings.

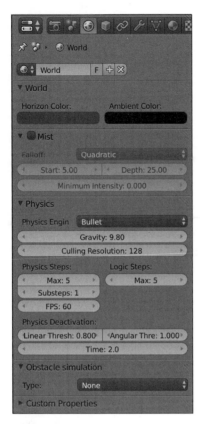

Figure 6.9
World Physics settings.
Source: *Blender Foundation.*

Disabling Physics

Some functions that seem to be unrelated to the physics engine, such as the raycast and mouseover sensors, also use the physics engine to detect objects. Therefore, disabling physics will break these functions as well.

With the physics engine set to Bullet, you can set the world gravity value. The higher the number, the faster an object falls. The default value of 9.8 corresponds to acceleration due to gravity on Earth; for comparison, Mars has a gravity of 3.7 m/s^2.

World and Scene Gravity Settings

There are two separate gravity settings in Blender. One in the World panel—which controls gravity for the game physics, and one in the Scene panel—which controls gravity for the non-game aspect of Blender physics (fluid, particles, and smoke simulation). They are only visible in their respective engines (Blender Game and Blender Render or Cycles Render, respectively). When working with games, make sure you adjust the right setting under World.

Hands-on: World Settings for Multiple Scenes

Because Blender supports multiple scenes and each scene can have its own World datablock, the physics settings can be set independently per scene. This means it is possible to create multiple worlds (or *levels*, as they are commonly called in games), each with different physics settings, all contained within one Blender file. For example, one could create a game with two scenes, one taking place on Earth and another taking place on Mars. By altering world settings such as sky color, mist depth, and the gravity strength for each scene, you can easily convey the idea of a foreign planet.

To create a game with two scenes:

1. Open \Book\Chapter6\earthMars.blend. When the game is running, you are in control of a first-person-shooter-style camera, which can be moved with the W, A, S, and D keys and rotated with the mouse. Cubes are generated out of thin air and they fall to the ground according to gravity.

2. First, rename the default scene from "Scene" to something more descriptive, such as "Earth," by clicking on the Scene datablock and typing in a new name, as shown in Figure 6.10.

Figure 6.10
Renaming the scene.
Source: *Blender Foundation.*

3. Go to the World Properties Editor; set the Horizon color to a light blue, as shown in Figure 6.11. This way, you can easily tell which scene is which.

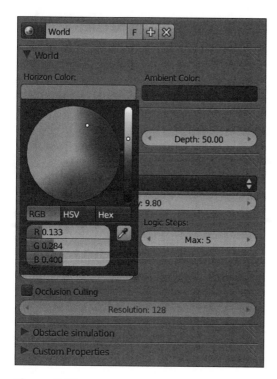

Figure 6.11
Changing the color of the world.
Source: *Blender Foundation.*

4. To make another world, you create a copy of Earth scene by clicking on the +
   sign beside the scene browser. From the drop-down list, select Full Copy, as
   shown in Figure 6.12. This will be the scene for your second world.

Figure 6.12
Making a full copy of the scene.
Source: *Blender Foundation.*

5. Rename the new scene you just created from "Earth.001" to "Mars."

6. Go to the World Properties Editor; set the Horizon color to a dark orange (see Figure 6.13).

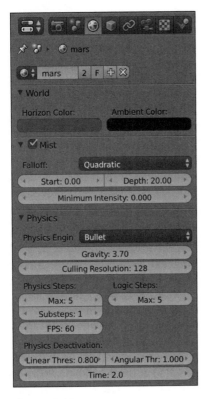

Figure 6.13
"Mars" world settings.
Source: *Blender Foundation.*

7. Lower the gravity from 9.8 to 3.7, which is the gravity on Mars.

8. To toggle between the two scenes, you need to add a simple logic brick to both of your scenes, so that when the spacebar is pressed in the Earth scene, it will jump to the Mars scene, and vice versa. Set up the logic brick as shown in Figure 6.14. In this case, it doesn't matter which object the logic brick is attached to because the action it carries out is global. The camera is used in our example to host the logic brick.

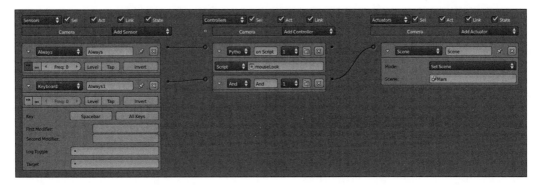

Figure 6.14
Logic brick setup.
Source: *Blender Foundation.*

9. Recreate the logic brick in the other scene as well. Set it to load the corresponding scene.

10. Now press P to play the game. Jump between the two scenes using the spacebar. Notice that the gravity and the sky color changes depending on which scene you are on.

11. That's it! The finished game can be found under the name earthMars-finished. blend. To extend this game, you can play around with the physics properties of the cube, which is hidden in layer two.

Culling Resolution

Occlusion culling skips the rendering of objects that are out of view or behind an Occluder object. By not drawing these objects, you can speed up the display performance of the game. Occlusion culling used to be an option that could be turned off by the user, but in the most recent versions, occlusion culling is always turned on.

Occluder objects must be manually defined. For more information on how to set up occlusion culling, refer to Chapter 8, "Workflow and Optimization."

The culling resolution setting controls how fine the occlusion test is. Higher value leads to slower performance, but it gives more accurate culling of smaller objects that might otherwise be missed by a low-resolution occlusion buffer. The default value of 128 is optimum for most cases.

Not Visible but Still There

Occlusion culling only skips the display of an object. The object would still be processed by the logic and physics engine. So any physical interaction, logic brick setup, or Python script attached to the object will run as usual even when the object is culled from the display.

Physics Substeps

The Physics Steps and Logic Steps are two settings that control the behavior of the physics engine. They are considered advanced tweaks that generally should not be tinkered with. And even if you do, the effect might not be obvious at first. This section tries to demystify those settings. Refer to Figure 6.15 as you follow along.

When physics simulation is not accurate enough, you might see objects going through each other, especially when objects are moving very fast relative to each other. To increase the accuracy of the physics simulation, you can force Blender to break down the physics simulation into a smaller slice of time. You do so by increasing the value of the subset in the interface. Essentially, a substep accounts for the number of physics iterations we have per frame. So 1 substep stands for one interaction per frame, 2 substeps is two iterations (thus twice the physics calculations), etc. A higher number makes the physics simulation run with better accuracy, at the cost of a dramatic decrease in performance for physics-heavy scenes.

If you run into any physical instability, you might be tempted to immediately raise the substep value. Avoid this impulse: do not rely entirely on substeps to hide a badly designed physics setup; the physics engine is designed to run with a substep of 1 or 2. Use other ways to stabilize the physics as described later in the chapter. Only raise the substep value when all else fails.

Bottom Line

Generally speaking, a value of 1 is sufficient for slow-moving games; 2 is optimum for fast-moving arcade games and action games with lots of physics interactions; driving games might require a 3 or a 4 (well, depending on how fast the car can go); do not use 5 unless your game contains supersonic objects.

On the Issue of Time

For the following discussion, the word *realworld-time* refers to the flow of time in the real world, the world that we live in. Relativistic physics aside, real time is always constant for our purpose. There are no magic devices, fabled incantations, or speeding DeLoreans to alter the flow of time.

The term *game-time* refers to the flow of time in the virtual game world. The flow of game-time is generally constant as well, except for special cases where slow motion or time lapse is used.

Why is this important? For most games, the game-time should be directly proportional to the realworld-time and completely independent of the frame rate. So that no matter how high or low the frame rate is, the game-time will always flow at a constant rate. Having the game-time independent of the frame rate has many benefits. A game that runs on a constant game-time does not slow down when the frame rate is low, nor does it speed up when the frame rate is high. This is to ensure that people with different computers can enjoy the game at the same speed. You wouldn't want to play a driving game that makes the car go faster on a fast computer but slows down to a crawl on a slow computer!

It turns out that ensuring a constant game-time despite fluctuations in the frame rate is hard! The following few settings are used to control how the game-time is tied together with the frame rate.

Physics Steps

The Max Physics Steps control how many consecutive physical simulation frames the game engine is allowed to run for each rendered frame. A high value (5) is more physically accurate, because it gives the physics engine enough time to complete the physics calculation, regardless of the game frame rate, therefore yielding a more consistent game-time that is independent of the frame rate, at the cost of taking up more processing time. A low value (1) can increase the frame rate of the game slightly by reducing the number of consecutive physical simulation frames the game engine is allowed to run every frame, but at the cost of inaccurate physics behavior, because the game-time would be linked to the frame rate.

Bottom Line

If you are still confused, just set the Max Physics Steps to 5. This ensures that the game-time is as constant as possible, no matter what the frame rate is.

Logic Steps

Very similar to the Max Physics Steps, the Max Logic Steps control how many consecutive game logic tics the game engine is allowed to run for each rendered frame. When the game frame rate is lower than the nominal FPS setting, a high value (5) is more accurate because it makes sure the logic step always gets enough time to finish all the logic computation. Conversely, a low value (1) will yield slightly better performance at the cost of a fluctuation in game-time. So this means that when the frame rate is high, the game will run normally, but if the frame rate drops, the game will appear to slow down.

Bottom Line

The default value of 5 means that the logic always gets enough time to run, no matter what frame rate the game runs at. This ensures that the game-time does not slow down when the frame rate is low.

FPS

Frames per second is the Holy Grail of performance benchmarking. For a video game, a high frame rate is always desired because it means smoother action and faster response to user input. Frame rate is a function of the complexity of the scene and the speed of the computer. Unfortunately, the setting here only acts as a frame rate cap, not the actual frame rate the game is guaranteed to run at. The default value of 60fps means that each second, the game engine evaluates the game logic 60 times. This particular number is chosen since most LCD monitors do not refresh faster than 60Hz, so, any extra frame rendered by the computer will just be wasted.

Internally, fps sets the number of logic tics and physics tics the game engine runs at. So as you lower the fps setting, the number of logic and physics tics performed by the game will decrease accordingly. This has the effect of slowing down the game-time. In another word, if the fps is set too low, not only will the game feel choppy, but it will actually appear as if it's running in slow motion.

Bottom Line

The default value of 60 is good for most game applications. Setting this value higher does not give you better performance. It is also customary for some games to set the fps to a lower value such as 30. The idea is that a game running at a constant 30fps feels smoother than a game that is fluctuating between 30fps and 60fps. Additionally, you can set vsync in your graphic card to force a frame rate ceiling. You don't have control over that in the player's computer, though.

Physics Deactivation

The values Linear Threshold, Angular Threshold, and Time all control how aggressively the physics engine puts objects to "sleep" in order to reduce the load on the game.

Setting the deactivation time to 0 effectively disables this optimization. Since sleep can also be disabled per object from the Physics Properties Editor, it's generally not recommended to disable deactivation here.

Lower the Linear Threshold if an object comes to a stop earlier than expected.

Lower the Angular Threshold if an object comes to a stop from spinning earlier than expected.

PHYSICS PANEL SETTINGS

So now that you are familiar with the World Properties Editor, which contains settings that apply to all physical objects indiscriminately, let's take a look at the Physics Properties Editor. From here, you can alter the physical characteristics of individual objects.

Physics settings apply to all game objects types, including Mesh, Empty, Lamp, and Camera.

Physics Types

How do you decide which physics type to pick for an object? That largely depends on the role of the object in the game. Table 6.1 shows all the physics types that are available in Blender and their corresponding characteristics.

Table 6.1   Physics Types

Type	Collision	G,F,T	Roll	Typical Use
No collision	No	No	No	Effects, high-resolution mesh
Static	Yes	No	No	Buildings, immovable structures
Dynamic	Yes	Yes	No	None
Rigid Body	Yes	Yes	Yes	Movable barrels, crates, general objects
Soft Body	Yes	Partial	Yes	Hair, cloth, rubber ducky
Occluder	No	No	No	Walls for performance optimization
Sensor	Yes	No	No	Event triggers
Navigation	No	No	No	Pathfinding helper
Character	Yes	No	No	Designed specifically for characters

Collision: Whether the object detects collision.
G,F,T: Whether the object can be moved by Gravity, Force, and Torque.
Roll: Whether the objects roll and tumble when they are on an incline.
Source: © 2014 Dalai Felinto and Mike Pan.

To familiarize yourself with the different physics types, open the demo file available from \Book\Chapter6\demo\physicsTypes.blend. It shows some of the common physics types and their behavior, as shown in Figure 6.15.

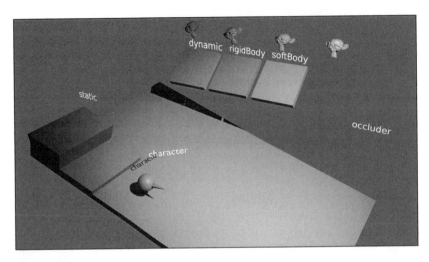

Figure 6.15
Different physics types visualized.
Source: *Blender Foundation.*

Let's look at the settings in more detail.

No Collision

No Collision skips all physics calculation. The objects will be effectively invisible to the physics engine. Other objects will not be able to detect collision with the object, nor collide with it. No Collision objects can still be moved using the Motion actuator. Use this for objects that you don't intend to interact with at all during the game, such as leaves of vegetation.

Collision Proxy

Setting an object to No Collision completely skips collision detection on the object, which can speed up the game considerably on a high-polygon mesh. A common practice is to set the high-polygon mesh to No Collision and then manually create a simplified "collision proxy" mesh object that approximates the shape of the high-polygon mesh. Then attach the high-polygon mesh to the collision proxy using parenting. This way, the low-polygon mesh will be used for all collision calculation, which is fast, and a high-polygon version of the object will be used for display, which is visually nicer. As this is an optimization technique, a step-by-step tutorial on creating a collision proxy is covered in Chapter 8.

Static

Static objects are the default physics type for objects. They do not fall due to gravity, nor do they move by external impact, such as another object striking them. By default, the mesh itself is used as the collision mesh, which can be slow if the object has a lot of polygons. Static objects never move on collision with another object. Use this setting for objects that require collision but don't move, such as buildings and fixed structures.

Dynamic

Dynamic objects are different from Static objects in that they have a defined mass and follow the basic Newtonian law of mass and acceleration. They fall due to gravity and react when another object collides with them. By default, the collision bound for Dynamic objects is a sphere for performance reasons. Sometimes this is sufficient, but most of the time, it's better to use another shape as the collision bound. More on collision bounds in Chapter 8. Moreover, because Dynamic objects do not roll, their usefulness is limited. If you want to simulate a realistic 3D object, Rigid Body is what you want.

Rigid Body

Rigid body behaves very similarly to a Dynamic object: they have a defined mass, accelerate due to gravity, and react to collisions. On top of that, Rigid Body objects have the ability to tumble when needed, whereas a Dynamic object will slide awkwardly down a ramp without rotating.

If the Suzanne model in the aforementioned sample Blender file is set to Rigid Body, it will behave like a real object, fall toward the ground, and come to rest on one of its ears.

Avoid DLoc Movement

When using a dynamics based object (Dynamic, Rigid Body, and so on), you should use physics-based options, such as force and linear velocity for movement, and not change its location directly by dLoc.

Soft Body

Whereas all the previously described physics types operate on the objects by moving and rotating them around without changing the underlying geometry, Soft Body physics uses a mass-spring system to apply deformations to the actual geometry. With Soft Body, you can create convincing cloth and other soft objects. Although it is very cool to play around with, Soft Body is very computationally intensive compared to the other physics types, and not as stable, so use it sparingly.

As seen in the Suzanne model in the sample file, it will fall due to gravity, and once it hits the ground, it collapses as if it's made of a rubber shell. This is the power of Soft Body physics.

Apply Scale

The physics engine works more reliably when the objects have a scale of 1. Thus, it is highly recommended to Apply Scale by pressing Ctrl+A on most of the objects before you run the game. This will prevent a lot of the strange issues that might crop up later.

Occluder

Occluder objects do not react to gravity and collision. Their only function is to make any objects behind them invisible. Occluder objects are used to help the game engine decide when to remove objects from view to speed up the rendering performance. Strategically-placed occluders can significantly increase the performance of the game.

Figure 6.16 explains how occluders work.

From left to right, the first image shows the scene setup of \Book\Chapter6\ PhysicsOccluder.blend. The second image shows what the camera sees. Notice the monkey head is not visible because the plane is blocking it. The third image is the view from the same camera while in-game, in wireframe mode. Notice that even though the monkey head is behind the wall, it is still being rendered, thus wasting precious computing time. The last image is the same in-game view as the previous image, but with the wall set to Occluder, the monkey head is not displayed.

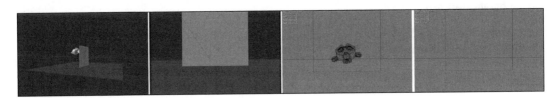

Figure 6.16
Occluder culling.
Source: *Blender Foundation.*

Sensor

Similar to Static Object, a Sensor object detects collision with another object. It is usually used as a replacement for the "radar" or "near" sensor because a Sensor object can be made into any arbitrary shape. Furthermore, Sensors will detect collisions, but they do not register a response. In other words, they behave like ghost objects. Additional logic bricks are needed to utilize a Sensor object effectively.

Navigation Mesh

This setting turns an object into a helper object that is used for pathfinding navigation.

Since Blender 2.6, the game engine has a fully automated AI pathfinding routine. It can be used to direct an AI character through the 3D world, reaching a target, while avoiding obstacles.

Hands-on Tutorial: Navigation

1. Open \Book\Chapter6\navigation.blend.
2. This scene is set up with four objects (excluding the lamp and the camera).
3. *Monkey* is our main character; it will be navigating through the maze (the VisualMesh) to get to the Target. To aid its quest, we have created a simple helper geometry that outlines where the character can walk. This object is known as the *NavMesh*. Figure 6.17 shows the initial setup.

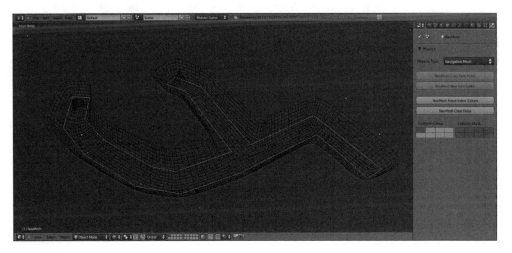

Figure 6.17
Navigation system.
Source: *Blender Foundation.*

4. A navigation mesh is a helper object (invisible while the game is running) that is used to help guide other objects along a path. The NavMesh object is a regular mesh object that defines the shape of the accessible area for the pathfinding routine.

5. There are two ways to create a navigation mesh. One is to manually model a geometry that covers all the areas that are accessible to a character. This is what we have done with NavMesh.

6. Another option is to ask Blender to create a navigation automatically. It might be easier for larger maps, but the result is far less predictable. We will cover this functionality at the end of this hands-on tutorial.

7. Make sure that the NavMesh object is selected and change its physics type to Navigation Mesh. The NavMesh will turn into a colorful grid, but don't be alarmed—this is normal. It means the object now can be used to aid in navigation. Navigation meshes becomes invisible when the game is running.

8. Select the Monkey object and add a "Steering" actuator to it, as shown in Figure 6.18. Define the Target and Navigation Mesh object, as shown in Figure 6.19.

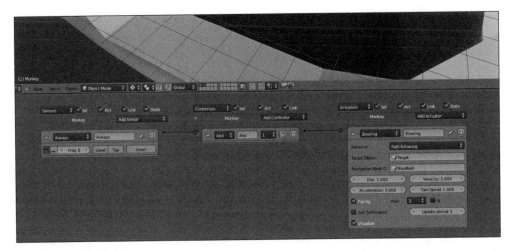

Figure 6.18
Steering actuator setup.
Source: *Blender Foundation.*

9. And you are done! Start the game and watch the monkey seek out the cone. The Steering actuator contains additional options that you can explore.

10. Figure 6.19 shows the finished game running in the Blender game engine. You can check out navigation-finished.blend.

Figure 6.19
Finished.
Source: *Blender Foundation.*

11. As promised, another way to create a navigation mesh is to use the automatic generator. To do this, delete the NavMesh object first so you can start with a clean slate.

12. Select the object you want to use as the guide in creating the navigation mesh. In this case, you need to select VisualMesh. Blender will build a new navigation mesh based on this mesh.

13. Go to the Scene tab of the Properties Editor, as seen in Figure 6.20. You should see a "Build Navigation Mesh" button, along with a whole slew of settings.

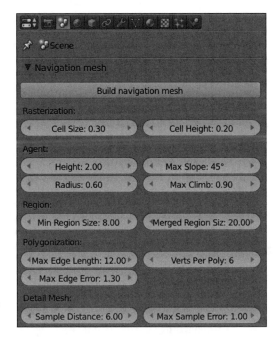

Figure 6.20
Automatic Navigation mesh generation.
Source: *Blender Foundation.*

14. Pressing the aforementioned button will create a navigation mesh automatically from the visual mesh.

15. If the result isn't optimal, play with the settings. Agent Radius is a good place to start.

Characters

This is a specialized physics type that is designed specifically for player-controlled characters. This physics type follows the basic rules of kinematics, while ignoring some of the other physical rules in order to make the object's behavior more predicable. For example, the Character object type doesn't bounce off walls or slide on ramps. PhysicsType.blend has an example of a playable Character object that walks around. Try to move it with the arrow keys.

Common Settings

Whew. With all the physics types out of the way, let's look at some of the shared settings common to most of the physics types described earlier.

- **Actor:** Makes the object part of the physics evaluation loop. An object not marked as an actor is ignored by the Near and Radar sensors, although it will still obey the laws of physics.

- **Ghost:** Makes an object not react to collisions such that it will pass through another—like a ghost. Collisions are still detected for ghost objects, so any sensors that detect collision between two ghost objects will still fire, but the objects will not bounce apart as they normally would.

- **Invisible:** Skips rendering of the object while still calculating all the physics and logic. This is useful for creating invisible walls and edges of maps to prevent players from visiting places you do not want them to go.

- **Mass:** Sets the mass of the object. A heavier object requires more force to move. Contrary to intuition, a heavier object does not fall faster than a lighter object (see note, "Hammer and Feather"). So increasing the mass will not make your object fall faster. To make objects fall faster, lower the damping on the object or increase the gravity in World settings.

Hammer and Feather

A hammer and a feather fall at the same rate in vacuum! In air, the drag force will slow down a lighter object more than a heavier object, so a heavier object indeed falls faster than a lighter object. But since Blender does not model air friction, object mass does not affect how fast they fall. This is not a bug!

Just as an 18-wheeler truck hitting a bunny won't have a happy ending (for the bunny), the physics engine works best when the objects interacting have masses of a similar magnitude. When an object with a very large mass collides with an object with a very small mass, instability might be created in the physics engine. As a general rule, keep all objects within 2 magnitudes of mass to each other. So, if an object weighs 1.0, it shouldn't interact with an object that is much heavier than 100.0.

- **Radius:** Controls the radius of the collision sphere. If a collision bound other than Sphere is selected, this setting has no effect.

- **No sleeping:** By default, the physics engine automatically suspends the physics calculation for an object when its motion is sufficiently slow. This is known as "sleeping." Putting the object to sleep can free up the CPU cycle and increase game performance until another object interacts with it again. Putting objects to sleep can cause some odd-looking behaviors, such as slow-moving objects coming to a sudden stop. "No sleeping" disables this optimization. The downside is that "no sleeping" might lead to some odd, jittery behavior for objects that are not perfectly stable.

  Additionally, there are options for controlling when objects go to sleep in the World properties under the "Physics Deactivation" label. This settings can be used to change the global delay before objects are deactivated.

- **Damping:** Applies a drag force on an object. A damping of 0 corresponds to no friction at all, just like a spherical cow traveling in a vacuum. A damping of 1.0 corresponds to a drag force so strong that the object will be unable to move. Translational damping slows down an object's movement; rotational damping slows down an object's spinning.

- **Anisotropic Friction:** Controls the friction force per axis. You can use this to mimic objects that have different coefficients of friction, depending on the orientation of the object. For example, a skateboard slides easily along its length, but is almost unmovable sideways.

- **Form Factor:** The tooltip says this setting "scales the inertia tensor." Make sense? No? Well, aren't you glad you have this book! Form factor controls the tendency for an object to roll. The bigger the value, the less likely an object will roll and tumble. A smaller value makes the object much more likely to rotate. Set the value too low, and the object will become unstable. The default value is a good balance between physics stability and realism.

- **Collision Bounds:** This is the shape of the object as it appears to the physics engine. This might sound surprising, but the shape of the object used for physics calculation is not always the same as the one that is displayed. The distinction is important because, for performance reasons, a rough proxy shape is often used in place of the actual geometry. This way, the user still sees a fully detailed object on the screen, but the physics engine can run a lot faster using a simplified collision bound. It is important to try to use the simplest collision bounds possible in order to keep the game engine's performance fast.

■ **Capsule, Box, Sphere, Cylinder,** and **Cone:** These are some of the basic primitives that can be used to approximate different collision bounds (see Figure 6.21). Their shapes are self-explanatory. To see exactly how the bounding box is applied to your model in-game, turn on "Show Physics Visualization" in the Game Options screen.

When the collision bound is set to Convex Hull, the collision bound takes the shape of the object, but with all the concave areas filled in. Convex Hull can accurately approximate an object of any shape as long as it doesn't have any "negative" space, such as holes. For example, a doughnut-shaped rigid body object set to Convex Hull will be treated as if the hole isn't there.

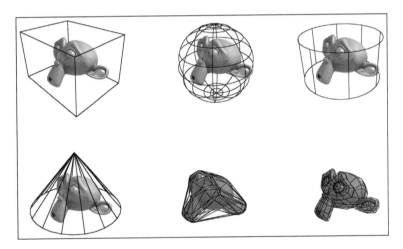

Figure 6.21
Collision bounds visualization: Top row: Box, Sphere, Cylinder; Bottom row: Cone, Convex Hull, Triangle Mesh.
Source: *Blender Foundation. Art: © 2014 Mike Pan.*

■ **Triangle Mesh:** This is the most robust collision bound type. It will create a collision bound that is an exact duplicate of the actual mesh. If you want to ensure that the collision bound matches the visual mesh exactly, this is the setting to use. So why don't we use this setting all the time? The reason is performance and stability. The physics engine is far better optimized for simple primitives, such as a box, than an arbitrarily shaped triangle mesh.

Visualizing Collision Bounds

Once the collision bound is set, you should notice that the collision bound is visualized as dashed lines in the 3D Viewport. This helps you visualize the relationship between the collision bounds and the visual mesh.

To visualize the collision bounds in-game, turn on "Show Physics Visualization" in the Game Options screen and run the game.

- **Collision Margin:** The Bullet Physics Engine SDK Manual explains that the collision margin is an internal setting that improves the performance and stability of the collision detection by giving thickness to each face. It is highly recommended that you do not adjust this setting outside its normal range (0.05). In some cases, too high of a value will result in a tiny air gap between colliding objects. Too small of a value will increase the chance of missed collisions between objects.

- **Compound:** The compound setting makes objects linked together by parent-children relationships behave as if they are a single physics entity.

But, why use compound when you can just join your objects together with Ctrl+J? Apart from the fact that there might be times when you need to control individual objects (so joining them might not be an option), using compound collision bounds made up of simple primitives is actually recommended over using one Triangle Mesh collision bound. The reason is again that a combination of simple primitives is faster to compute than a Triangle Mesh.

Hands-on Tutorial: Creating Compound Objects

To create a compound Physics object (see Figure 6.22):

1. Open \Book\Chapter6\compound.blend.

2. Run the game. Notice that even though the three objects are parented together, they do not react to the ground plane in a convincing way. Only the parent object collides with the ground.

3. To change that, from the Physics Properties Editor, turn on Compound for each of the three objects.

4. Run the game now and notice that all objects contribute to the kinematics of the group.

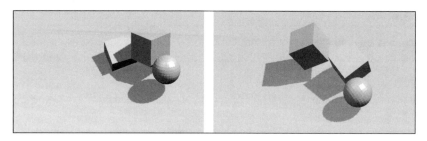

Figure 6.22
Compound Physics objects.
© 2014 Cengage Learning®. All Rights Reserved.

MATERIAL PANEL PHYSICS SETTINGS

By adding a material to the object, you enable additional options that give you finer control over some of the physical properties of the surface. Figure 6.23 shows the physics settings found in the Material panel.

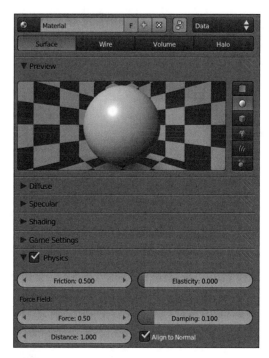

Figure 6.23
Material physics settings.
Source: *Blender Foundation.*

■ **Friction:** Controls the force that slows down a moving object when it comes in contact with another object. The effective friction force between two objects is dependent on the friction settings on both objects. So if one object with a high friction setting comes in contact with another object with low friction, the effective friction force would be somewhere in the middle of the two values.

■ **Elasticity:** Controls the "bounciness" of the objects when they collide with another. An object with low elasticity does not bounce away as far after a collision; an object with high elasticity loses almost no momentum in a collision and bounces away at almost the same speed as it came in. The effective elasticity between two colliding objects takes both objects into account. A tennis ball hitting a hardwood floor would be an example of an elastic object colliding with another elastic object. A tennis ball hitting carpet would be an example of an elastic object colliding with a non-elastic object.

■ **Force Field:** The next set of settings controls what Blender calls *force field*. When the force and distance are set to non-zero, a force field is generated on all the faces so that any object that comes within range (as specified by the distance setting) is pushed away with a certain force (as specified by the force setting). The result of this is that any object that comes close to a force field surface will be repelled. The effect on the object is exactly as the name implies: it mimics a magnetic field. The damping setting slows down the object.

Once Force Field is enabled in the Material panel, you will need to tell individual objects to respect that setting by going into the Physics Properties Editor and turning on Use Material Force Field.

Hands-on Tutorial: Force Field Water Surface

Force field can be used to create a convincing—you guessed it!—force field effect, where an object moving toward a force field seems to be slowed down by invisible energy. This is very different from the usual Rigid Body interactions, which are always hard collisions.

As you might imagine, the Force Field setting is used to simulate the realistic interaction of floating objects on a calm water surface. To do this:

1. Open \Book\Chapter6\water.blend.

2. Select the *Cube*. You want this object to behave like a basic wooden crate, a crate that bounces, tumbles, and floats in water. So let's add some dynamics to it. Go to the Physics Properties Editor and set the Type from Static to Rigid Body.

3. For extra fun, let's make a lot of these crates! But instead of manually creating them, we'll dynamically add them in-game on the player's command.

4. Select the Camera object in the Logic Editor panel and add a new Keyboard sensor, a new And controller, and an Edit Object actuator, as shown in Figure 6.24.

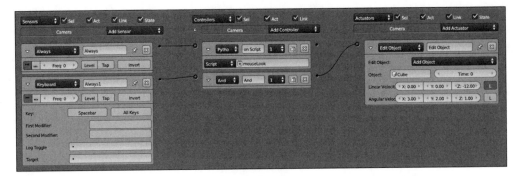

Figure 6.24
Logic bricks.
Source: *Blender Foundation.*

5. To make sure that the Cube objects get instantiated when you run the game, you need to hide the original Cube object. To do this, simply move the Cube to the second layer by pressing M and then 2.

6. With only layer one selected, run the game now. Notice how the cubes all collide with the ground plane, but because the ground plane is hard, the motion is rather jarring. It doesn't look like objects floating on water at all.

7. To make the ground plane have a water-like property, we will turn on Force Field. First, select the object called *WaterPlane.*

8. Head to the Material Properties Editor and create a new material. Then simply copy the force field physics setting, as shown in Figure 6.25.

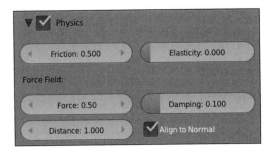

Figure 6.25
Material physics settings.
Source: *Blender Foundation.*

9. Et voilà! Start the game, press the spacebar, and watch the crates tumble into the ocean.

10. For added realism, create a No Collision Plane on top of the WaterPlane to act as the water surface.

CONSTRAINTS

Constraints are frequently used to create joints and mechanical linkages, indispensible components of many games. The Constraints Properties Editor is shown in Figure 6.26.

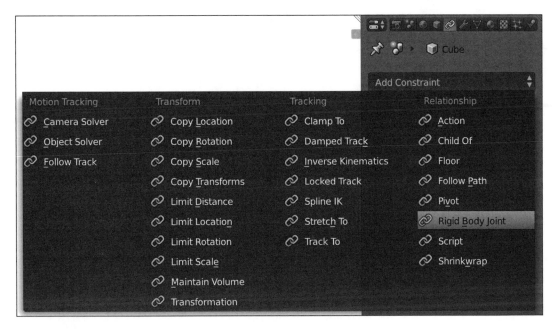

Figure 6.26
Adding a Rigid Body Joint in the Constraints Properties Editor.
Source: *Blender Foundation.*

The only supported object constraint is the Rigid Body Joint. It is used to connect two objects together using a user-defined joint.

Figure 6.27 illustrates the variety of pivot types.

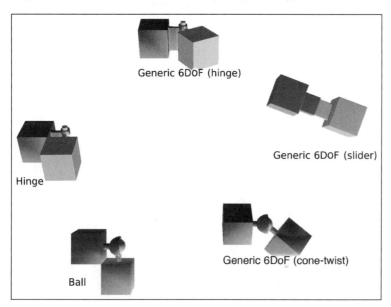

Figure 6.27
Constraints illustrated.

- **Ball:** Joins two objects together using a ball-and-socket joint. This type of constraint is free to rotate around all three axes.

- **Hinge:** Joins two objects together using one axis—the hinge axis. This constraint is often used to simulate a door hinge or a wheel on an axle.

- **Cone-twist:** This is an extension of the Ball constraint that supports limiting the angle of rotation. This is especially useful for animating limbs using ragdoll physics. You can set the individual angle limits for each of the three axes.

- **Generic 6 DoF:** If none of the above constraints meet your needs, chances are this generic constraint will give you enough control to accomplish any mechanical linkage you can dream up.

Once you have decided on the pivot type you need, you'll need to set the Target object. The Target object is the object that the current object will be linking to.

The rest of the settings should be very self-explanatory. Refer to \Book\Chapter6\demo\constraints.blend to see each constraint type in action.

- **Extending Constraints:** While one constraint might not be too useful, constraints can be daisy-chained to simulate many different objects. See ConstraintsChain.blend, ConstraintsWaterMill.blend and ConstraintsTrampoline.blend for examples of how to set up multiple constraints.

VEHICLE PHYSICS

The Blender physics engine has built-in support for vehicle physics. It is a very stable physics constraints system that provides easy-to-set-up car physics. The result is a fast-performing vehicle physics engine with easily tweakable settings that maps well into a real vehicle (steering, suspension length, suspension stiffness).

Of course, you can also try to create a car physics setup without using the built-in physics constraints; however, it will be far more time-consuming. This section will demonstrate how to set up a playable car object in the game engine using the built-in Bullet engine and a bit of Python scripting.

Hands-on Tutorial: Vehicle Physics Using Python

To get started, open \Book\Chapter6\vehicle\car.blend.

Rather than presenting this as a step-by-step tutorial, we will dissect a fully working, pre-made file.

Our basic car is composed of a body object and four wheel objects. The wheels are separate from the car for now. The physics engine will be responsible for keeping the wheels attached to the body, so the location of the wheel objects does not matter at this point. In this file, they are placed close to the car body for convenience.

Because attaching the wheels to the body will be done by a script, it is crucial for the rotation of the wheel to be correctly set; otherwise, the wheel will be linked to the car in the wrong orientation once the physics engine takes over. In the sample file, notice that the wheel objects all have their rotation set to [0,0,0]. This is important because the local rotation on the objects will interfere with the physics engine and confuse the game engine, resulting in unexpected behavior when you try to attach the wheels to the car. If a wheel needs to have its rotation reset, press Ctrl+A to apply any rotation.

Also notice that the car body is a Rigid Body object with Ghost turned on. This setting is crucial for the car physics to run correctly.

That's pretty much it—a car body object and four tires make up the vehicle.

As already mentioned, the actual vehicle physics relies on some Python script to function. Figure 6.28 shows all the logic bricks that are attached to the car body object. Notice that script plays a big part in it.

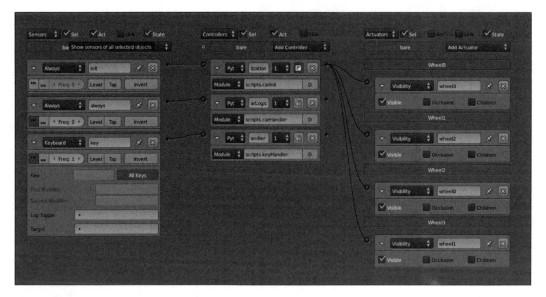

Figure 6.28
Vehicle logic brick setup.
Source: *Blender Foundation.*

The `script.carInit()` functionality is run when the game is started. Here, it initializes the car as a "vehicle constraint," also known as constraint type11, and stores it as a Python object called *vehicle*. The same script then looks for the four wheels by accessing an actuator with specific names (in this case, wheel1, wheel2, etc.), and then the script attaches the wheels to the car body using the settings specified in the script. Variables such as RollInfluence, SuspensionStiffness, and TyreFriction can all be set on a per-tire basis once the vehicle object is created. The job of `carInit()` is now done. Your car body is now considered to be a vehicle by the game engine, and it will behave like one.

The second most important function, `script.carHandler()`, is run every frame. This script does the actual moving of the car, and it applies engine force and steering to the vehicle object. But this script gets the user input (Keyboard sensor inputs) from another source (see below). The vehicle wrapper has built-in methods such as `applyBreaking()`, `applyEngineForce()`, `getWheelRotation()`, and `getNumWheels`, which you can call.

Every time a key is pressed, `script.keyHandler()` is run. It figures out which key is pressed and sets the intermediate variable so that the `scripts.carHandler` function will know how much throttle to apply, which way to steer, and so on. This script is separated from `scripts.carHandler()` not because of technical limitations but by design, so that it's easier to manage the code.

With these three Python functions, the car comes alive.

GAME SETTINGS

Game settings are global settings that affect the running of the game. These settings are shown in Figure 6.29 and can be found in the Render panel.

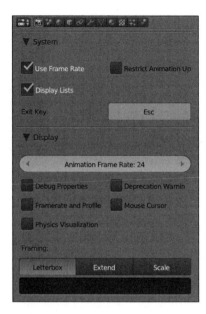

Figure 6.29
Additional game settings.
Source: *Blender Foundation.*

- **Animation Playback Speed:** Closely related to the frame-rate setting is the animation playback speed. This setting controls the speed of the F-Curve and armature animation. By default, the value is set to 24, meaning all F-Curve and actions will be played back as if they are running at a 24fps timebase. This setting can be found in the Render panel.

- **Debug Property:** Shows the value of the Game Properties that are marked with the Debug flag. This can be useful when you want to keep an eye on the values of certain variables while the game is running.

- **Frame Rate and Profile:** Shows the frame rate and other performance statistics in-game. These statistics will be displayed in the top-left corner of the screen in-game.

- **Physics Visualization:** Visualizes the internal computation of the physics engine. This can help you see what the physics engine is really doing when the game is running.

Rigid Body objects are displayed in white, and sleeping objects are drawn in green.

■ **Deprecation Warning:** Gives warnings about outdated Python API called in the console (see Chapter 7).

■ **Mouse Cursor:** Draws the mouse cursor in-game. This is useful if the game uses mouse-input. Mouse cursor can also be turned on and off via Python.

STABILIZING PHYSICS

The Bullet physics engine is good. Really good. But as with anything that is powered by a computer, it is still possible to get into a situation where things go haywire.

Okay, so what is unstable physics anyway? When you see objects jitter around when they are not supposed to, or when objects go through each other when they are supposed to collide, you know it's time for a reality check.

Here are some tips to help you regain control of your game. All of the settings here are already covered in the chapter; this list is simply a collection of the most common actions to take to stabilize physics.

■ **Avoid Extremes:** Avoid interaction between an extremely heavy object and an exceptionally light object. Avoid interaction between extremely fast objects. Avoid interaction between objects of very different sizes, especially if neither object is static.

■ **Physics Substeps (World Properties Editor):** Crank it. Higher will be slower but gives a much more accurate physics simulation result.

■ **Bounding Box (Physics Properties Editor):** Try to use collision primitives (Sphere, Cube, Cylinder) rather than mesh-based collision boxes (Triangle Mesh or Convex Hull). The former will be more stable and perform faster.

■ **Form Factor (Physics Properties Editor):** Controls the rotational tendency of an object. Setting this too small will make moving objects extremely unstable. Increasing the form factor usually helps calm down the object, at the cost of making the object feel sluggish on collision.

■ **No Sleeping (Physics Properties Editor):** By default, this option is off, meaning objects "freeze" when their movement falls below a certain threshold for a certain time. Keeping the option off improves physics stability and performance.

■ **Object Damping (Physics Properties Editor):** For non-static objects, Translational Damping and Rotational Damping can be used to slow objects down.

Setting this to a non-zero value ensures that objects eventually will slow down to a stop, which might help with stability.

■ **Margin (Physics Properties Editor):** If objects go through each other when they are not supposed to, and you've exhausted the other options listed above, increasing the object collision margin might help.

CHAPTER 7

PYTHON SCRIPTING

Congratulations, you finally arrived at one of the most technical parts of the book. Keep that in mind in case you get lost.

The Blender game engine was once famous for letting you create a full game without touching a single piece of code. Although this may sound attractive, it also leads to a very limited game-making experience. Logic bricks, as presented in Chapter 3, are very handy for quick prototyping. However, once you need to access advanced resources, external libraries and devices, or simply optimize your application, a programming language becomes your new best friend.

Through the use of a scripting language called *Python*, the game engine (as Blender itself) is fully extensible. This programming language is easy to learn, although extremely powerful. Be aware, though, that you will not find a complete guide to learning Python here. There are plenty of resources online and offline that will serve you better. However, even if you are not inclined to study Python deeply now, sooner or later you will find yourself struggling with script files. So, it's important to know what you are dealing with.

Yes, You Can

For those experienced Python programmers (or for those catching up with the reference learning material), always remember: if you can do something with Python, chances are, you can do it in the game engine.

After the brief overview in the Python basics, we will explain how to apply your knowledge of Python inside the game engine. You'll also learn how to access the Python methods, properties, and objects you'll be using.

WHY SCRIPT WHEN YOU CAN LOGIC BRICK IT?

We can compare logic bricks with real bricks. On the one hand, we have strong elements on which to build our system, but, on the other hand, we have a system as flexible as a blind wall.

There are many occasions when the same effect can be achieved in different ways. Different phases of the production may also require varied workflows. The reason for picking a particular method is often personal. Nevertheless, we present here a few arguments that may convince you to crack a good Python book and start learning more about it:

- Sane replacement for large-scale logic-bricked objects.
- Better handling of multiple objects.
- Access to Blender's advanced features.
- Use features that are not part of Blender.
- Keep track of your changes with a version control system.
- Debug your game while it runs.

Logic Brick, the Necessary Good

You can't ever get away from logic bricks. Even when using Python exclusively for your game, you will need to invoke the scripts from a Python controller. The ideal is to find the balance that fits your project.

Sane Replacement for Large-Scale Logic-Bricked Objects

It's always good to have an excuse to show an image in a programming chapter, and here it is. In Figure 7.1 you see the logic bricks for Frankie, the main character of the open game *Yo Frankie!*

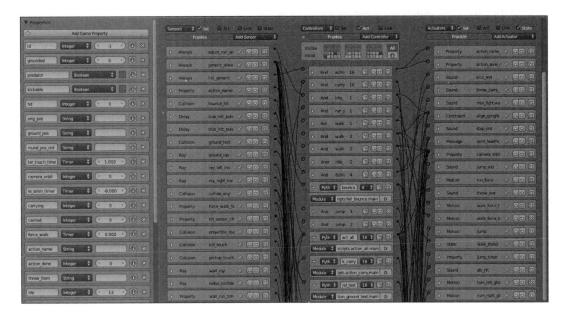

Figure 7.1
Chapagetti.
Source: *Blender Foundation.*

This system is well organized: different actions belong to different states and sensors; controllers and actuators are properly named. Nevertheless, it's not hard to lose yourself trying to understand which sensor connects to which controller. One of the reasons for such a complex project to rely on logic bricks is because *Yo Frankie!* serves as a didactic project for artists wanting to start with the game engine. Anyone with a little programming experience can take the files and expand the game freely. (Have you tried it yet?)

However, you often aim for performance and workflow. Having everything centralized in a single script file can save you a lot of time.

Another important aspect while working is to document your project. It's easy to open a file only a few months old and find yourself completely lost. Script files, on the other hand, are naturally structured to be self-documented. To document logic bricks, you need to rely on text files inside or outside your Blender files (and neat image diagrams). It's definitively not as handy as inline comments along your code. (Code diagrams can still be useful, but that's a different topic.)

For the Artist Behind the Programmer Façade

Please resist the temptation to create ASCII art while documenting your scripts.

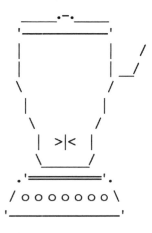

Better Handling of Multiple Objects

Big projects lead to multiple files—this is an inevitable truth. Even when you use external linking and libraries, it's crucial to optimize the time spent in changing multiple sets at once. This is one of the weaknesses of logic bricks—they make it hard to automatically change a big range of elements at the same time.

If you need to change a property name or initial value of an object, you will need to repeat that change in other instances of the same. We have ways to make it easier by using copy and paste of logic bricks/properties between objects or even through logic sharing. Nevertheless, you will still have to update all the Property sensors, controllers, and actuators that may rely on the old value. That's especially true for objects with logic bricks across them—as we saw, the game engine allows you to link logic bricks from different objects. However, self-contained objects/logic bricks are easier to work with (and with less spaghetti).

If you thought that Figure 7.1 was a mess, try to make sense of Figure 7.2. Here we have the logic bricks of *Frankie,* plus the objects that have logic bricks connected to it. As you recall, you can restrict the visible logics through the Show Panel option, but this illustrates how difficult it is to get a global view of your system.

Figure 7.2
Spaghetti.
Source: *Blender Foundation.*

Once you start to work with scripts, you will see how easy it is to assume control over all your scene elements in a global way. It will give you lots of benefits in the long run.

Access to Blender's Advanced Features

You will be happy to know that the game engine has a powerful set of features beyond those found in the logic brick's interface. Also, almost all the functionality found in the logic bricks can be accomplished through an equivalent method of the game engine API (which will be covered in the section "Using the Game Engine API—Application Programming Interface"). The API ranges from tasks that could be performed with logic bricks, such as to change a property in a sensor or to completely remove an object from the game, all the way to functionality not available otherwise, such as playing videos and network connection.

We Never Forget the First Patch

The ability to directly end an object from Python was introduced in Blender 2.47. This is a good example of how convenient script methods can be. And here comes a bit of history … back in August 2008, the project we were working on, OceanViz (read more about it in the Case Studies in Chapter 10), required a huge amount of objects to dynamically pop up and die. The game engine simulation had critical performance issues, and optimization was not a luxury there. At that point, we had reduced ending objects by having a simple Property sensor that would trigger an Edit Object → EndObject actuator. So far, so good. However, one extra sensor running every frame for every single object in the scene was costing us some performance we could use elsewhere. (We are talking about hundreds of objects here.)

When blaming our software didn't help (it may eventually), it was time to get our hands dirty. After some hard work and some online help, we had our first patched version of Blender game engine working right in front of us. We didn't need those multiple sensors anymore because a simple

```
myobjects.endObject()
```

was doing the job now. (Where is the champagne?)

To be allowed to extend our own version of Blender in that way was cool. To submit the patch and have it implemented in the core of Blender was memorable.

There are a few reasons for not having all the methods accessible through logic bricks. First, a graphic interface is very limited for complex coding. You may end up with a slow system that is far from optimized. Second, having methods independent from the interface allows it to be expanded more easily and constantly (from a development point of view). Some advanced features, such as mirroring system, dynamic load of meshes, OpenGL calls, and custom constraints would hardly fit in the current Blender game engine interface. They would probably end up not being implemented because of the amount of extra work required. Other things you will find in the game engine built-in methods are: make screenshots; change world settings (gravity, logic tic rates); access the returned data from sensors (pressed keys, mouse position); change object properties (camera lens, light colors, object mass); and many others we will cover in the course of this chapter.

Use Features That Are Not Part of Blender

No man is an island. No game is an island either (except *Monkey Island*). And the easiest way to integrate your Blender game with the exterior world is with Python. If you want to use external devices to control the game input or to tie external applications to your game, you may find Python suitable for that task.

Here are some examples that showcase what can be done with Python external libraries:

- Grab data off the Internet for game score.
- Control your game with a Nintendo Wiimote controller.
- Combine head-tracking and immersive displays for augmented reality.

These possibilities go with the previous statement that almost everything that you can do with Python, you can do in the game engine. And since Python can be used with modules written in other languages (properly wrapped), you can virtually use any application as a basis for your system.

Cross-Platform, Yes; Cross-Version, No

To use external libraries, you must know the Python version they were built against. The Python library you are using must be compatible with the Python version that comes with your Blender. It's also valuable to check how often the library is updated and if it will be maintained in the future.

Keep Track of Your Changes with a Version Control System

If you take a Blender file in two different moments of your production, you will have a hard time finding what has changed between them. This is because Blender's native file format is a binary type. Binary files are written in a way that you can't get to them directly—they are designed to be accessed by programs and not by human beings.

Scripts, on the other hand, are plain text files. You can open a script in any text editor and immediately see the differences between two similar files. Finding those differences are vital to going forward and backward with your experimentations during work. Actually, if you don't want to check for differences manually, you may want to consider using external script files with a version control system such as Git, SVN, Mercurial, or CVN.

And the Catch Is …

This works only for scripts maintained outside Blender. This is one of the strong reasons to prefer Python Module controllers as opposed to Python Script controllers.

A version control system allows you to move between working versions of your project files. It makes it relatively safe to experiment with different methods in a destructive way. In other words, it's a system to protect you from yourself. In Figure 7.3, you can see an application of this. Someone changed the script file online while we were working locally on it. Instead of manually tracking down the differences, we could use a tool to merge both changes into a new file and commit it. We were using TortoiseSVN for Windows here, a graphic interface to use with a SVN system. For Linux systems, SVN command-line plus the software "Meld" work just as well.

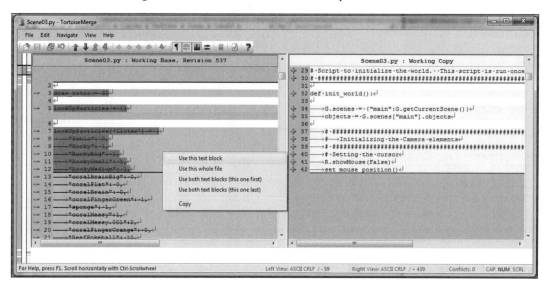

Figure 7.3
TortoiseSVN merging.
© 2014 Stefan Küng.

Debug Your Game While It Runs

Interpreted languages (also known as scripting languages) are slower than compiled code. Therefore, to speed up their performance they are precompiled and cached the first time they run (when you launch your game). This is not mandatory, though, and if you are using external Python scripts (instead of those created inside Blender), you can use the debugging button to have them reloaded every time they are called.

In Figure 7.4, we have the scripts.reload_me module that will be reloaded every frame. That way you can dynamically change the content of your scripts, variables, and functions without having to restart the game. Try it yourself: copy the content of the folder \Book\Chapter7\1_reloadme to your computer and launch debug_python.blend. Play your game, and you will see a spinning cube. The speed of the cube is controlled by the 14th line of the file script.py, found in the same folder.

```
# edit the speed value and you will see the rotation changing
# (try with values from 0.01 to 0.05)
speed = 0.025
```

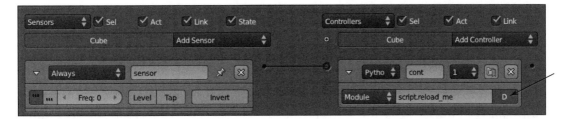

Figure 7.4
Python Module controllers.
Source: *Blender Foundation.*

Without closing Blender or even stopping your game, open the file script.py in a text editor, change this line to 0.05, for example, and save it. You will see the speed changing immediately. Your game is literally being updated at runtime, and you can change any module that's been called with the debug option on.

Turn It Off When You Leave

Remember to turn debugging off when you are done with this script. Reloading the script every frame can drastically reduce your performance.

So What Exactly Is Python?

Now that you are aware of all the benefits of using Python, it's time to understand what Python is. Once again, we can't go over all the aspects of the language here. Nevertheless, a general overview is still desirable to help you understand the examples presented in this book.

To study your scripts, you must be aware of the following aspects:

- Flexible data types
- Indentation
- OOP—Object-Oriented Programming

Flexible Data Types

Whenever you write a program, you have to use variables to store changing values at runtime. Unlike languages such as C and Java, Python variables are very flexible: they can be declared on the fly when you first use them; you can assign different data types for the same variable; and you can even name them dynamically:

```
for i in range(10): exec("var_%d = %d" % (i,i))
```

This snip of code is the equivalent to the following:

```
var_1 = 1
var_2 = 3
var_3 = 3
(...)
```

As you can see, the variable names are created at runtime. Therefore, if you name your objects correctly in the Blender file, you can store them in variables named after them. The following code snip assigns the scene objects (retrieved from the game engine) to variables named after their names.

```
(...)
for object in scene.objects:
    exec("%s = \"object\" " % (object.name))
```

Although we have flexible data types, we must respect variable types while manipulating and passing/returning them to functions. Here you can see a list of the data types you will find in the Blender game engine API:

- **Integer:** This is the most common of the numerical types. It can store any number that fits in your computer memory. You can perform any regular math operations on it, such as sum, subtraction, division, modulus, and potency.

    ```
    my_integer = 112358132134
    ```

- **Float:** This type is very similar to integers, but has a range of numbers that includes fractions. If you divide an even number by its half, Python will automatically convert your integer to a float number.

    ```
    simple_float = 0.5
    phi = (1 + math.sqrt(5)) / 2 # ~1.618
    ```

- **Boolean:** As simple as it sounds, this data type stores a true or a false value. It can also be understood as an integer with the value of 1 or 0.

    ```
    i_am_enjoying_the_book = True
    i_am_understanding_the_book = i_am_enjoying_the_book - 1
    ```

- **List:** A list contains a conjunct of elements ordered by ascending indexes. Although the size of a list can change on the fly, you can't access a list index that wasn't created yet (this will crash Python). Lists can have mixed elements such as integers, strings, and objects.

    ```
    my_list = [3.14159265359, "PI", True]
    ```

- **Tuple:** This is another kind of list where elements can't be overwritten. As with lists, you can read them using indexes. But it's more common to access all the values at once, assigning them to different variables.

```
t,u,p,l,e = (1,2,3,4,5) # works as: t = 1, u = 2, p = 3, ...
```

- **String:** Whenever you need to store a text, you will use strings. As words are a combination of individual letters, a string consists of individual characters. Indeed, strings can be understood as a list of characters because you can access them using their location index, though you can't overwrite them (like in a tuple).

```
python = "rulez"
```

- **Dictionary:** Like a list, a dictionary can store multiple values. Unlike a list, a dictionary is not based on numerical index access. Therefore, we have strings working as "keys" to store and retrieve the individual variables. In fact, anything can be a key to a dictionary, a number, an object, a class ...

```
_3d_software = {"name ": "Blender", "version": 2.6}
```

- **Custom Types:** These are things such as vectors and matrices. The game engine combines some of the basic data types to create more complex ones. They are mainly used for vectors and matrices. That way you can interact mathematically with them in a way that basic types won't do.

```
mathutils.Vector(1,0,0) * object.orientation # the result is a Matrix
```

Indentation

Indentation—the amount of white spaces or tabs you leave before a new line.

When coding in a particular programming language, it's mandatory to follow its general syntax. In that regard, Python is one of the most restricted languages out there. Think of this as a tough grammar exam. You won't be able to score high unless you follow all the pre-established grammar rules. Now imagine that it could be even worse—as bad as a written legal document. We are talking about strict paragraphs, indentation, information hierarchy, and similar rules.

As in a legal document, those rules have a raison d'etrê. With strict form/syntax, you can focus more on the content of the text. And ambiguity in the context of code making is fatal.

Indentation is the most important aspect of Python syntax. Python code uses the indentation level to define where loops, functions, and general nesting start/end. Take a look at this example:

```
1 def here_i_am(): # definition of the first function
2     print("I'm inside the first function.")
3 print("I'm outside the function.")
4 def but_I'm_not_here(): # definition of the second function
5     print("For you can't see me!")
6 print("I'm still outside the function.")
7 here_i_am() # calling the first function
```

Here we are defining a function (1–2), calling a built-in print function (3), defining another function (4–5), calling another built-in print function (6), and finally calling the first function we declared (7).

The output of such script will be:

```
I'm outside the function.
I'm still outside the function.
I'm inside the first function.
```

The first thing you may notice is that Python runs from top to bottom. Therefore, you must define your function before you call it. Secondly, you can see that the second function is never called. So how can the code interpreter determine which print statements to call? The answer is: indentation! Whenever you change the indentation level (lines 1–2, 2–3, 4–5, and 5–6), you determine the hierarchical relation between the elements. Therefore line 2 belongs to the function defined in line 1, line 5 to line 4, and the other lines are all at the same level.

Whether to use spaces or tabs in your scripts is a matter of personal preference. But be consistent—it makes it easier to copy and paste your code for reutilizing it.

Pound Sign, I (Finally) Love You

If, like me, you never understood the reason for the number/pound sign key (#) on your phone, you will eventually find it very useful. In Python, any text to the right of a pound sign is ignored by the interpreter. Therefore, the pound sign is used to add commentaries to your code or to temporarily deactivate part of it.

OOP—Object-Oriented Programming

Since games deal with 3D world objects, it makes sense to use a language that is oriented to them. The game engine itself is written in C++, a very strong and object-oriented language, and Python OOP capabilities let you handle the game data in a

Python-native way. It reflects in the game engine objects having their own set of functions and variables directly accessed from a Python API (to be explained later in this chapter in the section "Using the Game Engine API—Application Programming Interface").

In the Python code, you can (and will) create your own classes, modules, and elements. For example, you may want to control some 3D elements as a group defined by your code. It will make it easy to get to all of them at once. Therefore, you can have a custom class that will store all the related objects you want to access and preserve some properties as a group.

Open the book file: \Book\Chapter7\2_oop\oop.blend

The first script that runs in this file is the init_world.py. Here we are creating two groups to store different kind of elements (cube and sphere). In order to sort the objects between the groups, we go over the entire scene object list and check for objects with a property "cube" or "sphere" and append them to their respective lists.

```python
# ############# #
# init_world.py #
# ############# #
import bge
from bge import logic as G
from bge import render as R

# showing the mouse cursor
R.showMouse(True)

# storing the current scene in a variable
scene = G.getCurrentScene()

# define a class to store all group elements and the click object
class Group():
    def __init__(self, name):
        self.name = name
        self.click = None
        self.objects = []

# create new element groups
cube_group = Group("cubes")
sphere_group = Group("sphere")

# add all objects with an "ui" property to the created element
for obj in scene.objects:
    if "cube" in obj:
        cube_group.objects.append(obj)
    elif "sphere" in obj:
        sphere_group.objects.append(obj)
```

```
    elif "click" in obj:
        exec("%s_group.click = obj" % (obj["click"]))
G.groups = {"cube":cube_group, "sphere":sphere_group}
```

After storing them in the global module bge.logic, we wait for the user to click in the cube or sphere in the middle of the scene. When that happens, it will toggle the value of the on/off property of the cube or sphere. The following script (which runs every frame) will then hide/unhide the group's objects accordingly.

```
# ################### #
# visibility_check.py #
# ################### #
from bge import logic

# defines a function to hide/turn visible all the objects passed as argument
def change_visibility(objects, on_off):
    for obj in objects:
        obj.visible = on_off

# retrieve the stored groups to local variables
cube_group = logic.groups["cube"]
sphere_group = logic.groups["sphere"]

# read the current value of the "on_off" property in the cube/sphere
cube_visible = cube_group.click["on_off"]
sphere_visible = sphere_group.click["on_off"]

# calls the function into the group object with the visibility flag
change_visibility(cube_group.objects, cube_visible)
change_visibility(sphere_group.objects, sphere_visible)
```

And we are done with this interaction. Play with the file by adding new elements (tubes, planes, monkeys) and make them interact as we have here. A few copies and pastes should be enough to adapt this code to your new situation. Remember to note the current indentation used.

Where to Learn Python

If you have previous experience with another programming language, you will learn Python in no time. If you go over some basic Python tutorials, look at some script examples, and check the Blender game engine API, that might be enough. But if learning Python is your first step into coding experience, don't worry. Take the time to read through the basics of the language, start with the simplest tasks, and never give up.

Usually, a good way to start is tweaking ready-to-use scripts, which doesn't require you to understand all the aspects of the language before your first experiments. Also, it gives you a good motivational boost by producing quick results for your efforts. We recommend you first learn Python and then focus on its application in the game engine. But you may be more comfortable messing with game engine files first and then later learning Python more deeply.

Online Material

Below are some websites where you can learn more about Python.

www.python.org

Learn about new Python versions, API changes, and module documentation.

www.blender.org/documentation/blender_python_api_2_66_release/#game-engine-modules

Official BGE API Documentation—all the built-in modules that can be used with the game engine.

www.blenderartists.org/forum

Blender Artists forum—you can find good script examples in the Python section (general Blender Python) and in the Blender game engine section.

www.diveintopython3.net

Dive Into Python 3 covers Python 3 and its differences from Python 2. A complete book available online.

Offline Material

Here are some other resources to help you learn Python.

Learning Python, by Mark Lutz and David Ascher, published by O'Reilly Media

You can learn Python in a week with this book. You can also find it as an e-book, which is useful for searching quickly. Try to get the newest edition of the book you can find. Different Python series (2.x, 3.x) have certain particularities you don't want to have to deal with.

Before Buying a Book

If you are going to buy a Python book, be aware of its target audience. Some books are written for people with absolutely no previous knowledge in programming languages, while others assume otherwise. And make sure the book covers the Python version that is included in Blender (at the time of writing, Python 3.2).

Yo Frankie! DVD www.yofrankie.org

An open game made with the game engine by the Blender Foundation. You can download all the files of this project for free and go over their scripts. Although this can be confusing for someone in the first phases of learning Python, it's good reference material for later on.

Python Built-in Help

You can also access help directly in Python.

```
dir(python_object)
```

The Python function "dir" creates a list with all the functions/modules/attributes available to be accessed from this object.

```
help(python_function)
```

This built-in function reveals the official documentation for this module or data type.

PYTHON AND THE GAME ENGINE

This whole chapter is organized into three main parts: why, what, and how. Thus, if you have read from the beginning, you already have solid reasons to start using scripts for your project, and you understand what Python is. The final part of this chapter will cover how to use your Python knowledge inside the game engine. This part is divided into four submodules:

- Integrating Python in the game engine.
- Writing your Python scripts.
- Designing your script.
- Using the Game Engine API.

Integrating Python in the Game Engine

In the game engine, the script interface is controller-centric by design. Therefore, you can consider the Python script simply as a more complex controller to replace the Expression or the Boolean controllers. In those cases, the script will be responsible for controlling how the sensors are related with the actuators of a given object. In fact, the sensors, actuators, and even the object where you are calling the script from are all attributes of the controller.

As we mentioned earlier, with a Python script you can control external devices, control multiple objects at once, and much more. However, you will never be free from using a logic brick framework. And from the combination of logic bricks, individual sensors, global sensors, and actuators, the elegance of your system will arise.

In the first example, you will find a very simple case study of how to make your Python controller work. It will cover the basic behavior of receiving sensors' input in the script and triggering actuators from it.

Open the file \Book\Chapter7\3_template\abracadabra.blend.

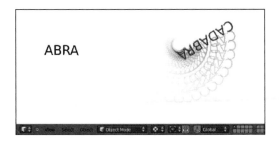

Figure 7.5
Abracadabra.
Source: *Blender Foundation. Art © 2014 Cengage Learning®. All Rights Reserved.*

Launch the game and keep the spacebar pressed. In Figure 7.5, you can see the result before and after you press the key. Can you read the spinning text? It may not be impressive, but it certainly is didactic. Here is the script behind this effect:

```
1    import bge
2    from bge import logic
3
4    cont = logic.getCurrentController()
5    owner = cont.owner
6
7    scene = logic.getCurrentScene()
8    objects = scene.objects
9    text_obj = objects["Text"]
10
11   sens = cont.sensors['my_sensor']
12   act = cont.actuators['my_actuator']
13
14   if sens.positive:
15       cont.activate(act)
16       text_obj.text = "CADABRA"
17   else:
18       cont.deactivate(act)
19       text_obj.text = "ABRA"
```

This script is triggered from a keyboard sensor, runs from a controller in the Camera object, activates an actuator in the camera itself, and changes a property in the Text object. Figure 7.6 shows logic bricks for this one.

Figure 7.6
Simple logic bricks with a Python controller.
Source: *Blender Foundation.*

Let's look at it from the beginning:

```
1    import bge
2    from bge import logic
```

The first lines import the module bge and then the submodule logic. No big deal here. We actually don't need to explicitly import the bge module since we are importing a submodule directly. However, it doesn't hurt to do it. Lines 4 and 5 will store the current controller in a variable and create a pointer to the object where it was called from (known as *owner*). We are not using the owner variable here, but it's good to be familiar with it. You will be using it a lot.

```
4    cont = logic.getCurrentController()
5    owner = cont.owner
```

The following lines get more elements from the game to be used in the script: scene will give you direct access to the current scene; objects is the current list to be used later; text_obj is one element of the objects list (accessed by its name in Blender).

```
7    scene = logic.getCurrentScene()
8    objects = scene.objects
9    text_obj = objects["Text"]
```

Remember when we said that the game engine is controller-centric? All the sensors and actuators are accessed from the controller, not from the object they belong to (its owner), as you might expect. Lines 11 and 12, respectively, read the built-in sensor and actuator list to get the ones we are looking for.

```
11      sens = cont.sensors['my_sensor']
12      act = cont.actuators['my_actuator']
```

In a way similar to how logic bricks work, we are going to activate the actuator if the sensor triggers positive and deactivate it otherwise. The deactivation happens in the frame after the sensor ceases to validate, for example, the key is unpressed or the mouse button is released.

```
14      if sens.positive:
15          cont.activate(act)
17      else:
18          cont.deactivate(act)
```

We are not restricted to controlling only actuators, though. Lines 16 and 19 change the text of the object when you press/release the spacebar:

```
16      text_obj.text = "CADABRA"
19      text_obj.text = "ABRA"
```

This file can be simple, but holds the essence of the game engine architecture design. Now is a good time to go over the three game engine template files that come with Blender. Go to Text Editor → Templates → Python → GameLogic and spend some time studying those examples. You can also get them on the book files under \Book \Chapter7\3_template\.

Writing Your Python Scripts

If you haven't started your own scripts, now is a good time to do so. You will need a text editor, the API modules documented, and a good way to test your files.

Text Editors   It's important to find a script editor that you find pleasant to work with. The most important features you will be looking for are: syntax coloring and highlighting, auto indentation, and auto completion. You can find editors with even more features than these, so experiment with different alternatives and decide what's best for you.

Notepad? Notepad++

Most of the scripts presented in this chapter were coded using Notepad++. This Windows-based open source text editor is not Python specific, but handles Python syntax highlighting well. You can download Notepad++ from their website:

```
http://notepad-plus.sourceforge.net
```

If you are using Linux or OSX, there are plenty of native alternatives that may serve you even better.

Blender Text Editor   As you probably know, Blender has its own internal text editor (see Figure 7.7). Although it may not be as powerful as software designed exclusively for this particular task, it can be very convenient. It's useful for quick tests, small scripts, or when you want to keep everything bundled inside the Blender file. Here are its main features:

- Syntax highlighting

- Dynamic font sizes

- Indentation conversion (spaces to tabs and vice versa)

- Line counting and navigation

- Search over multiple internal files

- Sync with external files

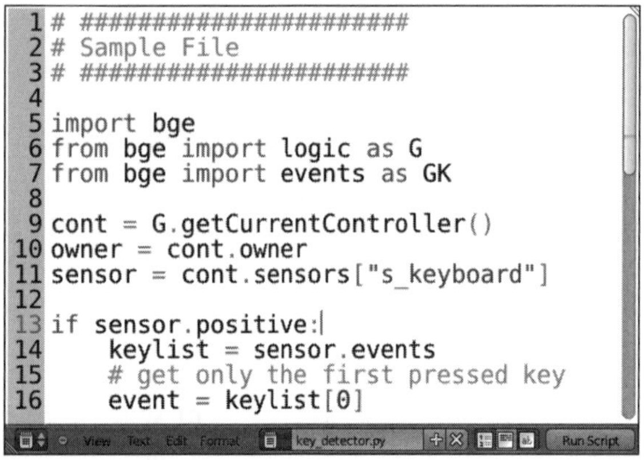

```
1 # ######################
2 # Sample File
3 # ######################
4
5 import bge
6 from bge import logic as G
7 from bge import events as GK
8
9 cont = G.getCurrentController()
10 owner = cont.owner
11 sensor = cont.sensors["s_keyboard"]
12
13 if sensor.positive:|
14     keylist = sensor.events
15     # get only the first pressed key
16     event = keylist[0]
```

View Text Edit Format   key_detector.py   + X   Run Script

Figure 7.7
Blender internal text editor.
Source: *Blender Foundation.*

Reference Material and Documentation

Since the game engine Python API is available online, you have an official excuse to keep a Web browser open while you work. It's not a bad idea to keep an offline version of it, too. (You can find it on the book files.) Use it when you need to be more productive and the Internet is getting in your way (as in, always).

It's good if you can start to gather example materials from the Internet and keep them organized. If you use the append feature in Blender to navigate to and import text files from your "collection," you will not even need to open another Blender application. Also, if you are consistent with your naming style, indentation rules, and file structures, you will find it easy to reuse your own scripts.

Testing Your Scripts

It doesn't matter how easy Python is, you will spend evenings testing and retesting your scripts before you have them working properly. The more complete way to test your script is to play it inside the game engine. However, you may not want to load your game every time you need to be sure of some Python syntax, data types' built-in functions, or simply to check if the math of a result is correct.

In those cases, you can use an interactive interpreter to help you. If you have Python installed on your system, you have it already. If you are using Windows, this will be the python.exe application in your Python installation directory (C:\Python31\ by default, considering the installation of Python 3.1), as seen in Figure 7.8. In Linux or OSX, you have to type "python" in any console and you are good to go.

Figure 7.8
Python IDE.

You can also use the Blender Python console. Change one of your current windows into the console, and you should see the screen shown in Figure 7.9.

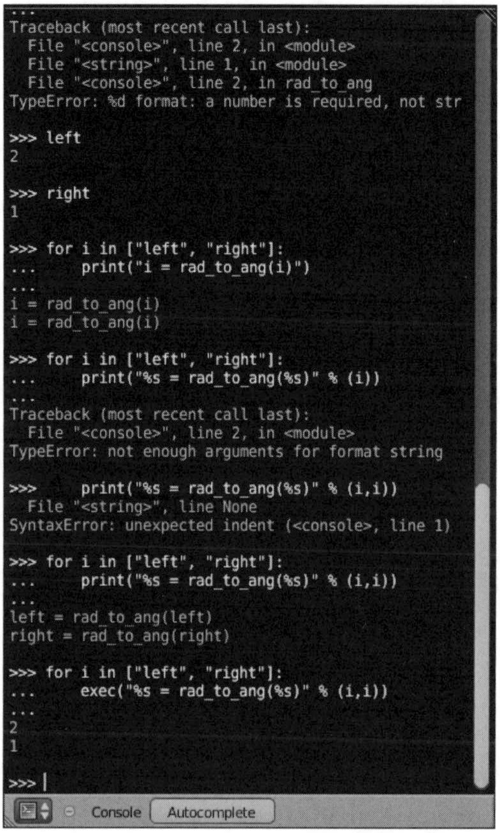

```
...
Traceback (most recent call last):
  File "<console>", line 2, in <module>
  File "<string>", line 1, in <module>
  File "<console>", line 2, in rad_to_ang
TypeError: %d format: a number is required, not str

>>> left
2

>>> right
1

>>> for i in ["left", "right"]:
...     print("i = rad_to_ang(i)")
...
i = rad_to_ang(i)
i = rad_to_ang(i)

>>> for i in ["left", "right"]:
...     print("%s = rad_to_ang(%s)" % (i))
...
Traceback (most recent call last):
  File "<console>", line 2, in <module>
TypeError: not enough arguments for format string

>>>     print("%s = rad_to_ang(%s)" % (i,i))
  File "<string>", line None
SyntaxError: unexpected indent (<console>, line 1)

>>> for i in ["left", "right"]:
...     print("%s = rad_to_ang(%s)" % (i,i))
...
left = rad_to_ang(left)
right = rad_to_ang(right)

>>> for i in ["left", "right"]:
...     exec("%s = rad_to_ang(%s)" % (i,i))
...
2
1

>>> |
```
Console   Autocomplete

Figure 7.9
Blender Python console.
Source: *Blender Foundation.*

Now you can use it to type simple codes, or to run a help or a dir into any of the Python modules. Unfortunately, only Blender modules have the auto-complete working from there.

Another important strategy is to keep the development of new functionalities outside the main file. For example, if you need to develop a navigation system (as we will soon), you don't need to use your real big, high-textured scenario. Definitively not for the early tests. If you keep independent systems that work together, you will be able to identify errors faster and easier and even to port fixes over to other projects smoothly.

Designing Your Python Script—Study Example

We are now going to dive into an example of writing and planning a Python script for the game engine from scratch. We will assume that you have already covered all the basics of Python scripting and the general understanding of game engine internals so we can move on to its real usage. More specifically, we are going over the writing process of a camera navigation system for an architectural visualization walkthrough. This study case is actually the system developed for a commercial project for an Italian book project. In general, we needed to implement a system to navigate and interact in a virtual model of an Italian Doric temple. Here, however, we are going to develop it under a sandbox and reapply it into another file, emulating what you could do with your own projects.

Unlike gaming cameras, a virtual walkthrough can use a very simple navigation system compound of (1) an orbit mode to look at the exterior of the building; (2) a walk mode to navigate inside the building with gravity simulation and collision; (3) and a fly mode to freely explore the virtual environment with collision only. The other requirement was to make the system as portable as possible, and with the least amount of logic bricks.

All of those aspects must be considered from the first phases of the coding process. With a well-defined design, you can plan the most efficient system in the short and long run.

Pencil and Paper, Valuable Coding Assets

One of the most remarkable moments during my coding studies was at Blender Conference 2008. I was still in my first steps of learning C++ and OpenGL coding, and I got the chance to explain a game engine bug to Brecht van Lommel—a really experienced and acknowledged Blender coder and a very inspiring person. The bug itself was hard to explain through the Internet; it's the one behind the implementation of canvas coordinates for 2D filters presented in Chapter 5. I was pleased enough to have his input on this, but even more impressive was seeing him code a partial solution right in front of me.

At this point, I learned an important lesson. It doesn't matter how advanced and technical the coding is that you are working on; you can always have a great time sketching your ideas and plans with old-fashioned pencil and paper. This is how he solved the problem, clearly laying down the ideas and organizing them logically. I never forgot that—thanks, Brecht!

The system will consist of one camera for the orbit mode, and one to be used for both the fly and walk mode. Each mode works as described in Table 7.1.

Table 7.1 Comparison of Different Navigation Cameras

	Orbit	Walk	Fly
Vertical Rotation Angle (Z)	−200° to 200°	Free	Free
Horizontal Rotation Angle (X)	10° to 70°	−15° to 45°	Free
Moving Pivot	None	Empty*	Empty
Horizontal Rotation Pivot	Empty	Empty and Camera	Camera
Vertical Rotation Pivot	Empty	Empty	Empty

*Empty is an Empty object the camera is parented to.

Source: © 2014 Dalai Felinto and Mike Pan.

Try It Out

In order to illustrate it better, you can see the working system demonstrated in the book file: \Book \Chapter7\4_navigation_system\camera_navigation.blend.

To switch modes press 1, 2, or 3. This will change the mode to orbit, walk, and fly, respectively. To navigate, you can use the mouse and the keys WASD.

3D World Elements

Open up the file \Book\Chapter7\4_navigation_system\camera_navigation.blend.

You will find two cameras and different Empty objects in the first layer:

```
scripts--an empty to call all the scripts.
CAM_Move--the camera for the walk and fly mode.
CAM_Orbit--the camera for the orbit mode.
CAM_back, CAM_front, CAM_side, CAM_top--empties to store the position and orientation
for the game cameras.
MOVE_PIVOT--the pivot for the walk and fly camera.
ORB_PIVOT--the pivot for the orbit camera.
```

In the second layer, you will find the collision meshes—the ground and the vertical elements. Everything is very simple here, since we only need to test the system, and for that a few low poly obstacles work fine.

Understanding the Code

\Book\Chapter7\4_navigation_system\camera_navigation.py

This program is divided into five different parts: (1) Global Initialization, (2) Event Management, (3) Internal Functions, (4) Game Interaction, (5) More Python.

The diagram in Figure 7.10 illustrates how they relate to one another. Now let's take an inside look at each of them.

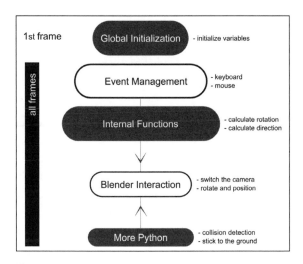

Figure 7.10
Script architecture.
© 2014 Cengage Learning®. All Rights Reserved.

Global Initialization

```
camera_navigation.init_world()
```

There is one function that is loaded once at the beginning of the game; we call it "init world"—init_world inside scripts.py. We are going to check the priority option in the Python controller to make sure this script runs on top of all the others. In this function, you will first find the global initialization. We are going to store in the global module logic all the elements we are going to reuse over the scripts. That way we don't need to get the object list every time we need a particular object. A common technique is to store the scene object as well. Therefore, for every scene, you can run a script at the beginning of the game that stores a reference to the current scene globally:

```
33 G.scenes = {"main":G.getCurrentScene()}
34 objects = G.scenes["main"].objects
```

Save and Load a game with GlobalDict

Since the module logic is accessible from all the functions and all the scenes, it can be used to store "global" objects. If you need to preserve those objects and variables between game sessions (i.e., after you close your game), you can store them inside the dictionary `logic.globalDict` and use `logic.saveGlobalDict()` and `logic.loadGlobalDict()` to save and load it.

To store the camera information, we are first going to create a global dictionary named cameras. We will use it to store the Camera objects, their pivot, and the original orientation of the orbit pivot:

```
43    G.cameras = {}
44    # orbit camera
45    camera = objects["CAM_Orbit"]
46    pivot = objects["ORB_PIVOT"]
47    G.cameras["ORB"] = [camera, {"orientation":pivot.worldOrientation}, pivot]
48    # fly/walk camera
49    camera = objects["CAM_Move"]
50    pivot = objects["MOVE_PIVOT"]
52    G.cameras["MOVE"] = [camera, {"orientation":pivot.worldOrientation,
      "position":pivot.worldPosition}, pivot]
```

Now that we have our objects instanced, we can set the initial values for our functions, such as the camera rotation restrictions. We don't want the cameras to look under the ground; thus, we need to manually set our limits. Although we could set those limits directly in the orbit and look functions, having all the parameters in the same part of code is easier to tweak (and slightly faster since they don't need to be reassigned every frame).

External Settings File

Another common workflow is to have a separate Python file (for example, settings.py) with all the variables set. Then in your working script, you simply have to import settings.py and use e.g. settings.left.

```
      # Camera Orbit settings:
58    # angle restriction in degrees
59    left      = -220.0
60    right     = 220.0
61    top       = 70.0
62    bottom    = 10.0
63
64    # convert all of them to radians
65    left = m.radians(left)
      (...)
70    # store them globally
71    G.orb_limits = {"left":left, "right":right, "top":top, "bottom":bottom}
72
      # Camera Walk/Fly settings:
      (...)
```

Last, but not least, we need to create the variables we are going to read and write between the functions. Initializing them here allows us to read them since the first frame of the game. This is especially important for variables that are going to be used in the event management functions—for different values of nav_mode and walk_fly, we are going to run different functions for the camera movement.

```
103 G.walk_fly = "walk"
104 G.nav_mode = "orbit"
```

Event Management

```
camera_navigation.mouse_move
camera_navigation.keyboard
```

Apart from the Always sensor needed for the camera_navigation.init_world() function, there are two other sensors we need—a Keyboard and a Mouse sensor. All the interaction you will have with this navigation system will run through those functions.

scripts.mouse_move   Let's first take a look at the Mouse sensor controlling system:

```
210 def mouse_move(cont):
211     owner = cont.owner
212     sensor = cont.sensors["s_movement"]
213
214     if sensor.positive:
215         if G.cameras["CAM"] == "ORB":
216             orbit_camera(sensor)
217         else:
218             look_camera(sensor)
```

It looks quite similar to the script template we saw recently. A difference is that instead of activating an actuator, we are calling a function to rotate the view. Actually, according to the current camera (orbit or fly/walk), we will have to call different functions (orbit_camera and look_camera respectively). Also, you can see that the function gets the controller passed as an argument. The game engine passes the controller by default for the module when using the Python Module controller. The argument declaration in the function is actually optional. So you could replace line 210 of the code with the following two lines, and it would work just as well:

```
def mouse_move():
    cont = G.getCurrentController()
```

scripts.keyboard   The second event management function handles keyboard inputs. This function takes the sensor input and calls internal functions according to the pressed key. If the pressed key is W, A, S, or D, we move the camera. If the key is 1, 2, or 3, we switch it.

```
110 def keyboard(cont):
111     owner = cont.owner
112     sensor = cont.sensors["s_keyboard"]
113
114     if sensor.positive:
115         keylist = sensor.events
117         for key in keylist:
118             value = key[0]
119
120             if G.cameras["CAM"] == "MOVE":
121                 if value == GK.WKEY:
122                     # Move Forward
123                     move_camera(0)
124                 elif value == GK.SKEY:
125                     # Move Backward
126                     move_camera(1)
127                 elif value == GK.AKEY:
128                     # Move Left
129                     move_camera(2)
130                 elif value == GK.DKEY:
131                     # Move Right
132                     move_camera(3)
133
134             # CAMERA SWITCHING
135             if value == GK.ONEKEY:
136                 change_view("orbit", "orbit")
137             elif value == GK.TWOKEY:
138                 change_view("front")
139             elif value == GK.THREEKEY:
140                 change_view("top", "fly")
    (...)
```

For a World with Fewer Logic Bricks

If you don't want to use a Keyboard sensor, you can use an internal instance of the keyboard module. You can read about this in the "bge.logic" part of the "Using the Chapter Engine API" section later in this chapter, or on the online API page: *http://www.blender.org/documentation/blender_python_api_2_66_release/bge.logic.html#bge.logic.keyboard*.

Internal Functions

```
scripts.move_camera
scripts.orbit_camera
scripts.look_camera
```

These three functions are called from the event management functions. In their lines, you can find the math responsible for the camera movement. We're calling them "internal functions" because they are the bridge between the sensors' inputs and the outputs in the game engine world.

scripts.move_camera   The function responsible for the camera movement is very simple. In the walk and fly mode, we are going to move the pivot in the desired direction (which is passed as argument). Therefore, we first need to create a vector to this course. If you are unfamiliar with vectorial math, think of vector as the direction between the origin [0, 0, 0] and the vector coordinates [X, Y, Z].

```
336 def move_camera(direction):
338     if not G.cameras["CAM"] == "MOVE": return
339     MOVE = 0.25 # speed
340
341     if direction == 0: # Forward
342         vector = M.Vector([0, 0, -MOVE])
344     elif direction == 1: # Backward
345         vector = M.Vector([0, 0, MOVE])
347     elif direction == 2: # Left
348         vector = M.Vector([-MOVE,0,0])
350     elif direction == 3: # Right
351         vector = M.Vector([MOVE, 0, 0])
    (...)
356     # now that we calculated the vector we can move the pivot
357     # to be continued in the Game Interaction section
```

Here the vector is the movement we need to apply to the pivot in order to get it moving. The size of the vector (MOVE) will act as intensity or speed of the movement.

scripts.orbit_camera   We decided to use different methods for the walk/fly camera and the orbit one. In the orbit camera, every position on the screen corresponds to an orientation of the camera.

If you want to study this part of the script in particular, you can turn on the Mouse Cursor in the Render Panel. That way, you can see that the same cursor position will (or should) always generate the same view.

```
224 def orbit_camera(sensor):
228      # Get screen size, attributes from the sensor and global variables
229      screen_width  = R.getWindowWidth()
230      screen_height = R.getWindowHeight()
231
232      win_x, win_y = sensor.position
233
234      # G.orb_clamp is in radians
235      orb_limits    = G.orb_limits
236      left_limit    = orb_limits["left"]
237      right_limit   = orb_limits["right"]
238      bottom_limit  = orb_limits["bottom"]
239      top_limit     = orb_limits["top"]
240
241      # Normalizing x to run from left to right limits
242      x = win_x / screen_width
243      x = left_limit + (x * (right_limit - left_limit))
244
245      # Normalize y to run from top to bottom limits
246      y = win_y / screen_height
247      y = top_limit + (y * (bottom_limit - top_limit))
248
249      # Flip the vertical movement
250      y = m.pi/2 - y
251
254      # Calculate the new orientation matrix
255      mat_ori = G.cameras["ORB"][1]["orientation"]
256
257      mat_x = M.Matrix.Rotation(x, 3, 'Z')
258      mat_y = M.Matrix.Rotation(y, 3, 'X')
259
260      ori = mat_x * mat_y
261
262      # now we can use ori as our new orientation matrix
264      # to be continued in the Game Interaction section
         (...)
```

The first lines that deserve our attention here are the normalizing operation. To normalize a value means to convert it to a range from 0.0 to 1.0. In our case, it can be understood as the mouse pointer coordinates relative to the screen dimensions (width and height):

```
242      x = win_x / screen_width
```

Even Fewer Logic Bricks and Normalized Mouse Coordinates

It's important to always use normalized coordinates for your screen operations. Otherwise, different desktop resolutions will produce different results in a game. As a counter edge case, you may need the absolute coordinates for mouse events if you want to assure minimum clickable areas for your events.

You don't always need to normalize the mouse coordinates manually. Like the Keyboard sensor, you can replace the Mouse sensor by an internal instance of the mouse module.

The coordinates from bge.logic.mouse run from 0.0 to 1.0 and can be read anytime. (You can even link your script to an Always sensor, leaving the Mouse sensor for the times where you are using more logic bricks.)

You can read about this in the "bge.logic" section in this chapter or on the online API page: *http://www. blender.org/documentation/blender_python_api_2_66_release/bge.logic.html#bge.logic.keyboard.*

Now a simple operation to convert the normalized value into a value inside our horizontal angle range (−220° to 220°):

```
243      x = left_limit + (x * (right_limit − left_limit))
```

We run the same operation for the vertical coordinate of the mouse. Though you must be aware that the canvas height runs from the top (0) to the bottom (height), this is different from what we could expect (or from OpenGL coordinates, for example). In order to better understand the flipping operation (line 257), you can first comment/uncomment the code to see the difference.

Next find in the .blend file the pivot empty (ORB_PIVOT) and play with its rotation in the X axis. The rotation is demonstrated in Figure 7.11. Therefore, if we subtract our angle from 90° ($\pi/2$ in radians), we get the proper angle to rotate the pivot vertically.

```
250      y = m.pi/2 − y
```

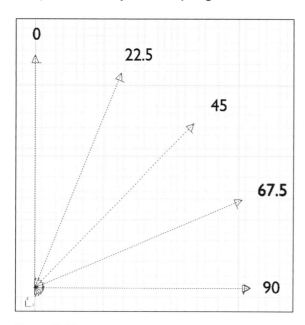

Figure 7.11
Orbit pivot rotation.
© 2014 Cengage Learning®. All Rights Reserved.

scripts.look_camera The function to rotate the walk/fly camera is quite different from the orbit one. We don't have a direct relation between mouse coordinate and camera rotation anymore. Here we get the relative position of the cursor (from the center) and later force the mouse to be re-centered—to avoid continuous movement unless the mouse is moved again.

In order to get the relative position of the cursor, the normalizing function needs to be different. This time we want the center of the screen to be 0.0 and the extreme edges of the canvas (border of the game window) to be -0.5 and 0.5.

```
291     x = (win_x / screen_width) - 0.5
292     y = (win_y / screen_height) - 0.5
```

The values of x and y can be used directly as radians angles to rotate the camera. However, when we are walking, we want to restrict the view vertically. This design decision means that we need to limit the view angle to a maximum and minimum range. Sure, this turns tying your shoes into a circus challenge. Though it may seem like overkill, this limitation helps add a better sense of reality to our navigation system.

The solution is to get the current camera vertical angle and see if by adding the new angle (i.e., vertical mouse move) we would end up over the limit of 45°. If so, we clamp the new angle to respect this value. To get the vertical angle, remember that the camera pivot (an empty object) is always parallel to the ground. Therefore, the vertical angle can be extracted from the camera's local orientation matrix. If that still doesn't make sense to you, try to find some 3D math tutorials online).

```
302    # limit top – bottom angles
303    if G.walk_fly == "walk":
304        angle = camera.localOrientation[2][1]
305        angle = m.asin(angle)
306
307        # if it's too high go down. if it's too low go high
308        if (angle + y) > top_limit: y = top_limit – angle
309        elif (angle + y) < bottom_limit: y = bottom_limit – angle
```

For the actual project this was originally designed for, we ended up moving the orbit camera code to be a subset of the walk/fly. Having the mouse always centered comes in handy when you have a user interface on top of that, and it needs to alternate between mouse clicking and camera rotating. Although the methods are different, the results are the same.

Game Interaction

```
camera_navigation.change_view
```

And the outcome of the functions:

```
camera_navigation.move_camera
camera_navigation.look_camera
camera_navigation.orbit_camera
```

In the previous section, we saw how the angles and directions were calculated with Python. However, we deliberately skipped the most important part: applying it to the game engine elements. It includes activating actuators (as we do in the change_view() function) or directly interfering in our game elements (cameras and pivots).

Outcome of the functions: scripts.move_camera, scripts.look_camera, and scripts.orbit_camera Let's put the pieces together now. We already know the camera future orientation and position. Therefore, there is almost nothing left to be calculated here. Nevertheless, there are distinct ways to change the object position and orientation.

In move_camera(), we are going to use an instance method of the pivot object called applyMovement (vector, local). This is part of the game engine methods (another one is applyRotation you will see next) we explain later in this chapter in the "Using the Game Engine API" section. This built-in function translates the object using the vector passed as a parameter. It can either be relative to the local or world coordinates:

```
336 def move_camera(direction):
      (...)
356     # now that we calculated the vector we can move the pivot
357     pivot = G.cameras["MOVE"][2]
358     pivot.applyMovement(vector, True)
```

In a similar way in the look_camera() function, we will apply the rotation in the camera object. This has the advantage of sparing the hassles of 3D math, matrices, and orientations. Also, instead of manually computing the new orientation matrix in Python, we can rely on the game engine C++ native (i.e., fast) implementation for that task.

```
269 def look_camera(sensor):
      (...)
314     if G.walk_fly == "walk":
315         # Look Up rotation
316         camera.applyRotation([y,0,0], 1)
317
318         # Look Side rotation
319         pivot.applyRotation([0, -x, 0], 1)
```

Although we are leaving the math calculation to the game engine, we should still be aware of how it works. The applyRotation() routine works with Euler angles (as a gimbal machine). The effects for the walk and the fly modes are very similar. The only difference is whether the rotation is local or global and the axis to rotate around:

```
322     else: # G.walk_fly == "fly"
323         # Look Side rotation
324         pivot.applyRotation([0, 0, -x], 0)
325
326         # Look Up rotation
327         pivot.applyRotation([y, 0, 0], 1)
```

In the orbit_camera() function, we calculated the orientation matrix of the pivot. This matrix is no more than a fancy mathematical way of describing a rotation. Since we already have the matrix, all we need to do is to set it to our pivot orientation.

The orientation is a Python built-in variable that can be read and written directly by our script. We will talk more about this in the "Using the Game Engine API—Application Programming Interface" part of this chapter.

```
223 def orbit_camera(sensor):
      (...)
261      # now we can use ori as our new orientation matrix
262      pivot = G.cameras["ORB"][2]
263      pivot.orientation = ori
```

scripts.change_view   After the user presses a key (1, 2, or 3) to change the view, we call the `change_view()` function to switch to the new camera (with a parameter specifying which camera to use). This function consists of two parts: first, we set the correct position and orientation for the camera and pivot; secondly, we change the current camera to the new one.

Decomposing the View Orientation

Keep in mind that the desired orientation (stored in the empty and accessed through the G.views dictionary) represents the new view orientation. In our system, this view orientation is the combination of the parent object (pivot) orientation with the child one (camera).

Let's start simple and build up as we go. First the orbit camera: in the orbit mode the camera is stationary—its position never changes. All we need to do is reset the pivot orientation to its initial values. Its orientation was globally stored back in the `init_world()` function. So now we can retrieve and apply it to the pivot:

```
155      dict = G.cameras["ORB"]
157      pivot = dict[2]
158      pivot.orientation = dict[1]["orientation"]
```

The fly camera is slightly different. In this case, the camera orientation contains no rotation (i.e., an identity matrix). Therefore, it's up to the pivot orientation to match the view orientation. In other words, the pivot orientation matrix is exactly the same as the view orientation matrix:

```
169      pivot.position = G.views[view].position
170      pivot.orientation = G.views[view].orientation
171      camera.orientation = [[1,0,0],[0,1,0],[0,0,1]]
177      if G.walk_fly == "walk":
178          fly_to_walk()
```

For the walk camera, we have yet another situation. The mode we are coming from (fly) has the camera pivot orientation (same as `camera.worldOrientation`) as the current view orientation. However, for the walk mode, the pivot needs to be parallel to the ground.

For that, we need to rotate it a few degrees to align with the horizon. The camera now will be looking to a different point (above/below the original direction). In order to realign the camera with the view orientation, we need to rotate the camera in the opposite direction. This way, the pivot and camera rotations void each other (with the benefit of having the pivot now properly aligned with the ground).

```
190 def fly_to_walk():
      (...)
194     view_orientation = camera.worldOrientation
195     euler = view_orientation.to_euler()
196     angle = euler[0] − (m.pi/2)
197
198     pivot.applyRotation([-angle,0,0],1)
199     camera.applyRotation([angle,0,0],1)
```

Reasoning Behind the Design

There is another reason for keeping this as a separate function. Originally, I was planning to switch modes (walk/fly) while keeping the same camera position and view. Although I dropped the idea, I decided to keep the system flexible in case of any turn of events (clients—who understands their minds?).

Now that the new camera and pivot have the correct position and orientation, we can effectively switch cameras. For that, we first set the new camera in the Scene → Set Camera actuator. Next, we activate the actuator and the camera will change:

```
181     act_camera.camera = dict[0]
182     cont.activate(act_camera)
```

More Python

```
scripts.collision_check
scripts.stick_to_ground
```

The script system shown so far handles all the interaction from the game engine sensors to the 3D world elements. Even though this covers most parts of a typical script architecture, I'd be lying if I said this is all you will be doing in your projects. Very often, you will need a script called once in a while that deals directly with the game engine data. In our case, we will have two "PySensors" to control the collision and to stick our camera to the ground while walking.

We could have them both working attached to an Always sensor. However, this would not be too efficient. Since we only need them while walking and flying, they can be integrated with the Keyboard sensor pipeline. The stick_to_ground() function will be called after any key is pressed if the current mode is "walk":

```
142          if G.nav_mode == "walk" and G.walk_fly == "walk":
143              stick_to_ground()
```

The collision system can be used even more specifically. Inside the move_camera() function, we will use the collision test to validate or discard our moving vector:

```
353          # if there is any obstacle reset the vector
354          vector = collision_check(vector, direction)
```

If the collision_check() test finds any obstacle in front of the camera, it returns a null vector ([0, 0, 0]). Otherwise, it leaves the vector as it was set, which will then move the camera.

The code of these functions is very particular to this project; therefore, we're not going into more detail here. (You are encouraged to take a look at the complete code in the book file, though). Nevertheless, the key point is to understand the role of these functions in the script architecture. These scripts can complement the functionality of other functions, to rule your game in a global and direct way, or simply to tie things together.

Reusing Your Script

One of the reasons this system was designed so carefully is because of the need for portability. You don't want to rewrite a navigation system every time you have a new project. This is not particular to this script example. Very often, you will be recycling your own scripts to adapt them to new files. Let's go over some principles you should know.

File Organization—Groups and Layers   The first thing to have in mind is how your final file will look. Do you want the script system to be merged with the rest of the existent Blender file? Do you want to keep them in separated scenes (very common for user interfaces)? Will you need to access/edit the script system elements later?

In our case, there is no need for an extra scene. However, we need to make sure that the navigation system elements are easy to access (especially the empties with the cameras' positions). If you can afford to dedicate one layer exclusively to the navigation system elements, do it. Make sure that the desired layer is empty in the model file and that all the objects you want to import are contained in this layer.

If it's not possible to have all your elements in a single layer, you can create a group for them. That way, you can always quickly isolate them to be listed in the outliner and selected individually. The other advantage of using groups is during importing. It's easier to select a group to be imported than to go over all the individual objects, determining which one should be imported and which one is part of the test environment (which usually doesn't have to be imported).

Tweaks and Adjustments—Getting Your Hands Dirty   Open the file \Book\Chapter7 \4_navigation_system\walkthrough_1_base\walkthrough.blend.

This small file is part of the presentation of an architectural walkthrough of an urban project (see Figure 7.12) that I (Dalai) did. It's an academic project and only my second project using the game engine. As you can see, there are absolutely no scripts in it—all the interaction is done with logic bricks. I didn't use Python for this project mainly because I had absolutely no knowledge of Python at all back then (and the project was done in six days).

Figure 7.12
Architectural walkthrough example file.
© 2014 Dalai Felinto.

It's time for redemption. Let's replace its navigation system with the Python system we just studied. For convenience, this file was already organized to receive the navigation elements (cameras, empties, and so on.).

Organize and Append Your File   In this case, we decided to group all the navigation elements in a group called NAVIGATIONSYSTEM and to make sure they are all in layer 1. You can use the Outliner to make sure you didn't miss any object out of the group. Leave the lamps and the collision objects out of the group.

To see a snapshot of the file at this moment, you can find it in the book files at: \Book \Chapter7\4_navigation_system\walkthrough_2_partial\camera_navigation.blend.

Now open the walkthrough file again and append the NAVIGATIONSYSTEM we created. It's important not to link the group but to append it. Linked elements can only be moved in their original files; thus, you should avoid them in this case.

1. Open the Append Objects Dialog (Shift+F1).

2. Find the NAVIGATIONSYSTEM group inside the camera_navigation file.

3. Make sure the option "Instance Groups" is not checked. (This would insert the group, not the individual elements.)

4. Click on the "Link/Append from Library." (This will add the group.)

5. Set CAM_Orbit as the default camera. (Tip: Use the Outliner to find the object; it's inside the ORB_PIVOT.)

A snapshot with these changes can be found at:

\Book\Chapter7\4_navigation_system\walkthrough_2_partial\walkthrough.blend.

Now if you run the application, the navigation system should work—kind of (see Figure 7.13).

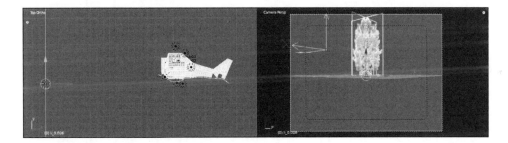

Figure 7.13
Still not there.
Source: *Blender Foundation. Art © 2014 Dalai Felinto.*

Adjustments in Loco As you can see in Figure 7.13, the new camera system looks absurdly wrong. There are two main reasons for that: the walkthrough file elements are far away from the file origin [0, 0, 0], and the cameras are not prepared for a project with this magnitude (their clipping parameters are way too low). We will need to move the objects to their new correct places, adjust the camera parameters, and do a small intervention in the script file:

All the elements from NAVIGATIONSYSTEM group (layer 1):

Move them 2000 in X and 350 in Y.

Empties:

CAM_front and CAM_back—These empties will hold the position for walk cameras. Make sure their position from the ground is at the human eyes (~1.68).

CAM_top and CAM_side—These empties will be used in Fly Mode. Here, we should also make sure their initial orientation looks good. The easiest way to do that is by using the Fly Mode (select the object, set it as current camera, and use Shift+F).

The one thing missing for the camera is to increase the clipping distance. That way, we can see all the skydome around the camera (see before and after in Figure 7.14).

Cameras:

CAM_Orbit—Adjust initial Z, change clip ending to 1000.

CAM_Move—change clip ending to 1000.

A snapshot with these changes can be found at:

\Book\Chapter7\4_navigation_system\walkthrough_3_partial\walkthrough.blend.

Figure 7.14
Camera clipping of 400 in the left and 1000 in the right.
© 2014 Dalai Felinto.

Make Sure That Collision Is Set Properly

All the houses, the ground, and the other 3D objects already have collision enabled in this file. In other situations, however, you may need to change the Collision objects, enabling or disabling their collisions accordingly. The Python raycast uses the internal Bullet Physics engine under the hood. In order to prevent the camera from going through the walls and the ground, set enough collision surfaces (but not too much, so that you don't compromise the performance of your game).

Script Tweaks   Finally, it's good to fiddle a bit with the script. Due to the particularities of this project (mainly its scale), you may feel that everything happens a bit too fast. It's up to you to change the settings in the `init_world` function. Also, it would be interesting to explore multiple viewpoints for this presentation. We have already positioned the side and back empties. Although we were not using them previously, their names are present in the script as part of the available cameras list:

```
93      available_cameras = ["front", "back", "side", "top"]
```

The difference now is that we will make the camera actually change to the side and back views when you press the keys four and five respectively. As you can see here, it's really easy to expand a system like this. Try to create a fifth camera (add a new empty) and see how it goes. To enable the "side" and "back" cameras, the only code we have to add is:

```
110 def keyboard(cont):
        (...)
new             elif value == GK.FOURKEY:
new                 change_view("side")
new             elif value == GK.FIVEKEY:
new                 change_view("back", "fly")
```

There is not much more to be done here. This is a simple script, but its structure and the workflow we presented are not much different from what you will find in more complex systems you may have to implement or work with. There are different ways to implement a navigation system. This one was designed focusing on a didactic structure (clean code as opposed to a highly optimized system that is hard to read) and robustness (easy to expand). Try to find other examples or, better yet, build one yourself.

The final file is on the book files as:

\Book\Chapter7\4_navigation_system\walkthrough_4_final\walkthrough.blend.

USING THE GAME ENGINE API—APPLICATION PROGRAMMING INTERFACE

The game engine API is a bridge connecting your Python scripts with your game data. Through these modules, methods, and variables you can interact with your existent logic bricks, game objects, and general game functions.

The official documentation can be found online in the Blender Foundation website:

http://www.blender.org/documentation/blender_python_api_2_66_release.

We will now walk through the highlights of the modules. After you are familiar with their main functionality, you should feel comfortable to navigate the documentation and find other resources.

Game Engine Internal Modules

- Game Logic (bge.logic)
- Game Types (bge.types)
- Rasterizer (bge.render)
- Game Keys (bge.events)
- Video Texture (bge.texture)
- Physics Constraints (bge.constraints)

Stand-Alone Modules

- Audio System (aud)
- Math Types and Utilities (mathutils)
- OpenGL Wrapper (bgl)
- Font Drawing (blf)

bge.logic

The main module is a mix of utility functions, global game settings, and logic bricks replacements. Some of those functions were already covered in the tutorial, but they are here again for convenience sake. We will look at some of the highlights.

getCurrentController()

Returns the current controller. This is used to get a list of sensors and actuators (to check status and deactivate respectively), and the object the controller belongs to:

```
controller = bge.logic.getCurrentController()
object     = controller.owner
sensor     = controller.sensors['mysensor']
```

If you are using Python modules instead of Python scripts directly (see Python Controller in Chapter 3), the controller is passed as an argument for the function:

```
def moduleFunction(cont):
    object = cont.owner
    sensor = cont.sensors['mysensor']
```

getCurrentScene()

This function returns the current scene the script was called from. The most common usage is to give you a list of all the game objects:

```
for object in bge.logic.getCurrentScene().objects: print(object)
```

expandPath()

If you need to access an external file (image, video, Blender, etc.), you need to first get its absolute path in the computer. Use single backslash (\) to separate folders and double backslash (\\) if you need to refer to the current folder:

```
video_absolute_path = bge.logic.expandPath('//videos/video01.ogg')
```

sendMessage(), addScene(), start/restart/endGame()

These functions copy the functionality of existent actuators. They are Python replacements for those global events when you need a direct way to call them, bypassing the logic bricks.

LibLoad(), LibNew(), LibFree(), LibList()

There are cases when you need to load the content of an external Blender file at runtime. This is known as *dynamic loading*. The game engine supports dynamic loading of actions, meshes, or complete scenes. The new datablocks are merged into the current scene and behave just like internal objects:

```
bge.logic.LibLoad("//entities.blend", "Scene")
```

Beware of Lamps

New Lamp objects can be dynamically loaded from external files. However, in GLSL mode, they will not work as a light source for the material shaders, since the shaders would need to be recompiled for that.

---

globalDict, loadGlobalDict(), saveGlobalDict()

The bge.logic.globalDict is a Python dictionary that is alive during the whole game. It's a game place to store data if you need to restart the game or load a new file (level) and need to save some properties. In fact, you can even save the globalDict with the Blender file during the game and reload later.

```
bge.logic.globalDict["password"] = "kidding, kids never save your passwords in files!"
bge.logic.saveGlobalDict() # save globalDict externally
bge.logic.loadGlobalDict() # replace the current globalDict with the saved one
```

keyboard

You can handle all the keyboard inputs directly from a script. The usage and syntax are very similar to the Keyboard sensor. You need a script running every logic tic (Always sensor pulsing with a frequency of 0 or every time a key is pressed; Keyboard sensor with "All Keys" set) where you can read the status of all the keys in the bge.logic.keyboard.events dictionary. If instead of inquiry for the status of a particular key (e.g., if spacebar is pressed), you want to list all the pressed keys, you can use the dictionary bge.logic.keyboard.active_events.

The keys for both event dictionaries are the same you use with the Keyboard sensor (see the bge.events module). The status of each key (whether it was pressed, released, kept pressed, or nothing) is the value stored in the dictionary. The keys values are defined in the bge.logic module itself:

```
keyboard = bge.logic.keyboard
space_status = keyboard.events [bge.events.SPACEKEY]
if space_status == bge.logic.KX_INPUT_JUST_ACTIVATED:
    print("space key was just pressed.")
elif space_status == bge.logic.KX_INPUT_ACTIVE:
    print("space key is still pressed.")
elif space_status == bge.logic.KX_INPUT_JUST_RELEASED:
    print("space key was just released.")
else: # bge.logic.KX_INPUT_NONE
    pass
```

A sample file can be seen at \Book\Chapter7\5_game_keys\key_detector_python .blend. This shows the more Python-centric way of handling keyboard. For the classic method of using a Keyboard sensor, look further in this chapter into the "bge.events" section.

mouse

Similar to the keyboard, this Python object can work as a replacement for the Mouse sensor. There are a few differences that make it even more appealing for scripting—in particular, the fact that the mouse coordinates are already normalized. As we explained in the tutorial, this helps you get consistent results, regardless of the desktop resolution. The available attributes are:

■ **events:** A dictionary with all the events of the mouse (left-click, wheel up, and so on) and their status (for example, bge.logic.KX_INPUT_JUST_ACTIVED).

■ **position:** Normalized position of the mouse cursor in the screen (from [0,0] to [1,1]).

- **visible:** Show/hide the mouse cursor (can also be set in the Render panel for the initial state).

joysticks

This is a list of all the joysticks your computer supports. That means the list is mainly populated by None objects, and a few, if any, Joystick Python objects. To print the index, name, number of axis, and active buttons of the connected joysticks, you can do:

```
for i in bge.logic.joysticks:
    joystick = bge.logic.joysticks[i]
    if joystick and joystick.connected:
        print(i, joystick.name, joystick.numAxis, joystick.activeButtons)
```

For the complete list of all the parameters supported by the Joystick Python object, visit the official API: *http://www.blender.org/documentation/blender_python_ api_2_66_release/bge.types.SCA_JoystickSensor.html.*

A sample file can be found on \Book\Chapter7\joystick.blend.

Others

There are even more functions available in this module (setMist, getLogicTic Rate, and setGravity, for example). Make sure that you visit the online documentation (or the documentation included on the book files) to see them all.

bge.types

Objects, meshes, logic bricks, and even shaders are all different game types. Every time you call an internal function from one of them, you are accessing one of those functions. This happens when you get a position of an object, change an actuator value, and so on.

Each one of the classes has the same anatomy. You can access instance methods and instance variables. In order to explain their use properly, we will go over one of the most commonly used modules, the game object.

Some of the variables will only work inside the correct context. Therefore, you can't get the mouse position of a Mouse sensor if the sensor was not triggered yet. Be aware of the right context and the game type.

Class KX_GameObject

If you run a print(dir (object)) inside your script, you will get a very confusing list. It includes Python internal methods, instance methods, and instance variables. Most of them are common to all objects, so we are going to talk about them first. However, lamps and cameras not only inherit all the game object methods but also extend them with specific ones.

The Truth Is Out There

In order to see all available methods, please refer to the documentation. We are only covering a few of them here.

Python Internal Methods

__class__, __doc__, __delattr__ ...

Most of these methods are inherited from the Python object we are dealing with. However, given the nature of the Python classes presented in Blender, some of these methods may not be fully accessible. It's unlikely you will be using them. So for now it's safe to ignore any method starting and ending with double underlines (__ignoreme__).

Instance Methods

endObject(), rayCast(), getAxisVect(), suspendDynamics(), getPropertyNames() ...

If it looks like a function, it should be one. Every game engine object provides you with a set of functions to interact with them or from them to the others. Here are some methods you should know about:

rayCast (objto, objfrom, dist, prop, face, xray, poly) *"Look from a point/object to another point/object and find first object hit within dist that matches prop."*

This method is a more complete version of the rayCastTo(). It has so many applications that it becomes hard to delimitate its usage. For instance, this was the method used to calculate the collision in the navigation system script we studied previously.

getPropertyNames() *"Get a list of all property names."*

Once you retrieve the list of property names, you can use it to see if the object has a specific property before using it. To get individual properties, you can use *if "prop" in object:* or *object.get("prop", default=None).*

A Use for Properties

Properties have multiple uses in the game engine. One of those uses is to mark an object to be identified by the Python script. Why not use their names instead? While names work fine to retrieve individual objects, properties allow you to easily mark and access multiple objects at once. Frankly, it's easier to create an organized, named, and tagged MP3 collection than it is to find time to properly name all your Blender datablocks—objects, meshes, materials, textures, images, and so on.

endObject() *"Delete this object can be used in place of the EndObject Actuator."*

This method is one of the functions that mimic existent actuators. You will also find this design in methods such as `sendMessage()`, `setParent()`, and `replaceMesh()`.

applyRotation() *"Set the game object's movement/rotation."*

There are a few methods that will free you from doing 3D math manually. This particular one is a replacement for multiplying the object orientation matrix by a rotation matrix. (If you are "old school," you can still set the orientation matrix directly though.)

Other methods are `applyMovement()`, `applyForce()`, `applyTorque()`, `getDistanceTo()`, `getVectTo()`, `getAxisVect()`, and `alignAxisToVect()`.

Instance Variables *name, position, mass, sensors, actuators ...*

Last but definitely not least, we have the built-in variables. They work as internal parameters of the object (for example, name, position, orientation) or class objects linked to it (for example, parent, sensors, actuators). In Blender versions prior to 2.49, these variables were only accessible through a conjunct of `get` and `set` statements (`setPosition()`, `getOrientation()`, and so on). In Blender 2.5, 2.6 and on, they not only can be accessed directly, but also manipulated as any other variable, list, dictionary, vector, or matrix you may have:

```
obj.mass = 5.0
obj.worldScale *= 2˘
obj.localPosition [2] += 3.0
obj.worldOrientation.transpose()
print(obj.worldTransform)
```

position, localPosition, worldPosition Position is a vector [X, Y, Z] with the location of the object in the scene. We can get the absolute position (worldPosition) or the position relative to the parent of the object (localPosition). And what about accessing the position variable directly? This is deprecated, but you may run into it in old files you find online. If you access the position variable directly, you get the world position on reading and set the local position on writing. Confusing? That is why this is deprecated. ;)

orientation, localOrientation, worldOrientation   This variable gives you access to a matrix 3×3 with the orientation of the object. The orientation matrix is the result of the rotation transformation of an object and the influence of its parent object. As with position, the orientation variable will give you the world orientation on reading and set the local orientation on writing. As with position, you should always specify whether you want the local or world orientation.

visible   We have different ways to set the visibility of an object. If your material is not set to invisible in the game panel, you can use this method. To change the visibility recursively (to the children of the object), you must use the method setVisibility.

sensors, controllers, actuators   All the logic bricks of an object can be accessed through these dictionaries. The name of the sensor/controller/actuator will be used as the dictionary key, for it's important to name them correctly.

Sub-Class KX_Camera   Not all the objects have access to the same methods and variables. For example, an Empty object doesn't have mass, and a Static object doesn't have torque.

When the object is a camera, the difference is even more distinct. The Camera object has its own class derived from KX_GameObject. It inherits all the instance variables and methods and expands it with its own. You will find some screen space functions (`getScreenPosition()`, `getScreenVect()`, `getScreenRay()`), some frustum methods (`sphereInsideFrustum()`, `boxInsideFrustum()`, `pointInsideFru stum()`), and some instance variables (lens, near, far, frustum_culling, world_to_ camera, camera_to_world).

Sub-Class KX_Lamp   Like cameras, lamps also have their own subclass. It inherits all the instance variables and methods, and only expands the available variables.

The parameters that can be changed with Python include all that can be animated with the Action actuator: energy, color, distance, attenuation, spot size, and spot blend. Additionally, you can change the lamp layer in runtime.

bge.render

If we compare gaming with traditional 3D artwork, rasterizer would be the rendering phase of the process. Internally, it's when all the geometry is finally drawn to the screen with the light calculation, the filters applied, and the canvas set. For this reason, the Rasterizer module presents functions related to stereoscopy, window and mouse management, world settings, and global GLSL material settings.

Window and Mouse:

`getWindowWidth() / getWindowHeight()`

Get the width/height of the window (in pixels).

`showMouse(visible)`

Enable or disable the operating system mouse cursor.

`setMousePosition(x, y)`

Set the mouse cursor position (in pixels).

World Settings:

`setBackgroundColor(rgba), setAmbientColor(rgb)`

Set the ambient and background color.

`setMistColor(rgb), disableMist(), setMistStart(start), setMistEnd(end)`

Configure the mist (fog) settings.

Stereo Settings:

`getEyeSeparation() / setEyeSeparation(eyesep)`

Get the current eye separation for stereo mode. Usually focal length/30 provides a comfortable value.

`getFocalLength() / setFocalLength(focallength)`

Get the current focal length for stereo mode. It uses the current camera focal length as initial value

Material Settings:

`getMaterialMode(mode) / setMaterialMode(mode)`

Get/set the material mode to use for OpenGL rendering. The available modes are:

`KX_TEXFACE_MATERIAL, KX_BLENDER_MULTITEX_MATERIAL, KX_BLENDER_GLSL_MATERIAL`
`getGLSLMaterialSetting(setting) / setGLSLMaterialSetting(setting, enable)`

Get/set the state of a GLSL material setting. The available settings are:

`"lights"`, `"shaders"`, `"shadows"`, `"ramps"`, `"nodes"`, `"extra_textures"`

Others:

`drawLine(fromVec, toVec, color)`

Draw a line in the 3D scene.

`enableMotionBlur(factor) / disableMotionBlur()`

Enable/disable the motion blur effect.

`makeScreenshot(filename)`

Write a screenshot to the given filename.

bge.events

The Keyboard sensor allows you to set individual keys. As you can see in Figure 7.15, it can also be triggered by any key once you enable the option "All Keys." This is very useful to configure text input in your game or to centralize all keyboard events with a single sensor and script.

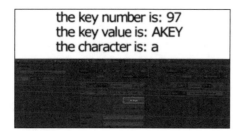

Figure 7.15
Key codes visualizer.
Source: *Blender Foundation.*

In this case, every key pressed into a Keyboard sensor will be registered as a unique integer. Each number corresponds to a specific key, and finding them allows you to control your actions accordingly to the desired key map. In order to clarify this a bit more, try the file in \Book\Chapter7\5_game_keys\key_detector_logicbrick.blend.

This file is similar to the key_detector_python.blend we used to demonstrate bge.logic.keyboard. However, this file is using the Keyboard sensor directly, instead of its wrapper.

```
from bge import logic
from bge import events

cont = logic.getCurrentController()
owner = cont.owner
sensor = cont.sensors["s_keyboard"]

if sensor.positive:
    # get the first pressed key
    pressed_key = sensor.events[0][0]

    text = "the key number is: %d\n" % pressed_key
    text += "the key value is: %s\n" % events.EventToString(pressed_key)
    text += "the character is: %s" % events.EventToCharacter(pressed_key, 0)

    # press space to reset the initial text
    if pressed_key == events.SPACEKEY:
        text = "Please, press any key."
    owner["Text"] = text
```

This script is called every time someone presses a key. The key (or keys) registers as a list of events, each one being a list with the pressed key and its status. In this case, we are reading only the first pressed key:

```
pressed_key = sensor.events[0][0]
```

This line stores the integer that identifies the pressed key. However, we usually would need to know the actual pressed key, not its internal integer value. Therefore, we are using the only two functions available in this module to convert our key to an understandable value:

```
text += "the key value is: %s\n" % events.EventToString(pressed_key)
text += "the character is: %s" % events.EventToCharacter(pressed_key, 0)
```

After that, we are checking for a specific key (spacebar). bge.events.SPACEKEY is actually an integer (to find the other keys' names, visit the API page):

```
if pressed_key == events.SPACEKEY: text = "Please, press any key."
```

And, voilà, now we only need to visualize the pressed key:

```
owner["Text"] = text
```

Key Status

The status of a key is what informs you whether the key has just been pressed or if it was pressed already. The Keyboard sensor is always positive as long as any key is held, and you may need to trigger different functions when some keys are pressed and released. The status values are actually stored in bge.logic:

```
0 = bge.logic.KX_INPUT_NONE
1 = bge.logic.KX_INPUT_JUST_ACTIVATED
2 = bge.logic.KX_INPUT_ACTIVE
3 = bge.logic.KX_INPUT_JUST_RELEASED
```

bge.texture

The texture module was first discussed in the Chapter 5, "Graphics." With the texture module, you can change any texture from your game while the game is running. The texture can be replaced by a single image, a video, a game camera, and even a webcam stream.

Let's look at a basic example. Please open the file: Book\Chapter7\6_ texture\basic_texture_replacement.blend.

This file has a single plane with a texture we will replace with an external image. Press the spacebar to change the image and Enter to return to the original one. The script responsible for the texture switching is:

```python
from bge import logic
from bge import texture
def createTexture(cont):
 """Create a new dynamic texture"""
    object = cont.owner

    # get the reference pointer (ID) of the texture
    ID = texture.materialID(obj, 'IMoriginal.png')
    # create a texture object
    dynamic_texture = texture.Texture(object, ID)\

    # create a new source
    url = logic.expandPath("//media/newtexture.jpg")
    new_source = texture.ImageFFmpeg(url)

    # the texture has to be stored in a permanent Python object
    logic.dynamic_texture = dynamic_texture

    # update/replace the texture
    dynamic_texture.source = new_source
    dynamic_texture.refresh(False)
```

```
def removeTexture(cont):
  """Delete the dynamic texture, reversing it back to the original one."""
    try: del logic.dynamic_texture
    except: pass
```

It's a simple script, but let's look at the individual steps. We start by getting the material ID (that can be retrieved for an image used by an object, hence the prefix IM) or a material that uses a texture (with the prefix MA).

```
ID = texture.materialID(object, 'IMoriginal.png')
```

With this ID, we can create a Texture object that controls the texture to be used by this object (and the other objects sharing the same image/material).

```
dynamic_texture = texture.Texture(object, ID)
```

The next step is to create the source to replace the texture with. The bge.texture module supports the following sources: ImageFFmpeg (images), VideoFFmpeg (videos), ImageBuff (data buffer), ImageMirror (mirror), ImageRender (game camera), ImageViewport (current viewport), and ImageMix (a mix of sources).

```
new_source = texture.ImageFFmpeg(url)
```

Now we only need to assign the new source to be used by the object texture and to refresh the latter. The refresh function has a Boolean argument for advanced settings. A rule of thumb is: for videos, use refresh (True); for everything else, try refresh (False) first.

```
dynamic_texture.source = new_source
dynamic_texture.refresh(False)
```

For the image to be permanent, we have to make sure the new dynamic_texture is not destroyed after we leave our Python function. Therefore, we store it in the global module bge.logic. If you need to reset the texture to its original source, simply delete the stored object (for example, *del logic.dynamic_texture*).

Since this is a simple image, you don't need to do anything after that. If you are using a video as source, you need to keep refreshing the texture every frame. Videos also support an audio-video syncing system. To make them play harmoniously together, you first play the audio and then query its current position to pass as a parameter when updating the video frame (for example, *logic.video.refresh(True, logic.sound. time)*). The audio can come from an Audaspace object or even a Sound actuator.

In the book files, you can find other examples using different sorts of source objects:

Basic replacement of texture:

Book\Chapter7\6_texture\basic_texture_replacement.blend.

Basic video playback with Sound actuator:

\Book\Chapter7\6_texture\basic_video_sound.blend.

Video player with interface controllers:

\Book\Chapter7\6_texture\player_video_audio.blend.

Basic video playback with Audaspace:

\Book\Chapter7\6_texture\video_audaspace.blend.

Mirror effect:

\Book\Chapter7\6_texture\mirror.blend.

Render to texture:

\Book\Chapter7\6_texture\render_to_texture.blend.

Webcam sample:

\Book\Chapter7\6_texture\webcam.blend.

bge.constraints

The Bullet Physics engine allows for advanced control over the physics simulation in your game. Using Bullet as a backend, this module (formerly known as *Physics Constraints*) allows you to create and set up rigid joints, dynamic constraints, and even a vehicle wrapper. The constraints' functionalities make sense only when you understand the context in which they are to be used (with Physics Dynamic objects). Therefore, this module is covered in the previous chapter on game physics.

Mathutils—Math Types and Utilities

Mathutils is a generic module common to both Blender and the game engine. There are a lot of methods to facilitate your script in handling 3D math operations. You won't have to reinvent the wheel every time you need to multiply vectors or transpose matrices. Simply using the mathutils classes and built-in methods frees you to invest your time in something far more important: relearning all of the long-forgotten math lessons you skipped.

Unless your background is in math, physics, or engineering, you won't use this module any time soon. For those already familiar with the passionate secrets of math, you'll be glad to know that this module's functions are mainly self-explanatory. Names such as cross, dot, slerp (what?), and a quick look at their specifications will be all you need to know to start working with them. Nevertheless, newcomers often use this module without even knowing it. Every time you change an object position, get the vector from an object, or apply a rotation, you are using mathutils classes and methods. Therefore, it's good to have this module as a reference for further studies and more advanced coding. (We all get there eventually.)

We are going to present the four available classes in this module: vector, matrix, Euler, and quaternion. For a list of the available methods, refer to the API documentation.

Vector

This class was already present in the KX_GameObject class and in the script example. It behaves like a list object, with some advanced features (for example, swizzle and slicing) expanded with its instance methods. Some of those methods are: reflect, dot, cross, and normalize.

A recurring problem that new Python programmers have is with list copying. If you forget to manually copy the list when assigning it to a new variable, you end up with two variables sharing the same list values forever (each of the variables becomes a pointer to the same data).

The same behavior happens with vectors. Look at the differences:

```
new_vector = old_vector
```

If you change new_vector you will automatically change old_vector (and vice-versa).

```
new_vector = old_vector[:]
```

So, new_vector is a new independent list object initialized with the old_vector values.

```
new_vector = vector.copy()
```

And new_vector is a new vector, an independent copy of the old_vector object.

Matrix

While vectors behave similarly to lists, matrices behave similarly to multidimensional lists. A multidimensional list is a list of a list, organized either in columns or rows.

While in Python, a list of a list is always the same:

```
matrix_row = [[1,2,3], [4,5,6], [7,8,9]]
```

In a mathutils.Matrix, the data can be stored differently, accordingly to the matrix orientation (row/column). Following you can see how the order of the elements in a matrix changes, according to its orientation (note, this is not actual Python code):

```
matrix_row_major    = [ [1 2 3]
                        [4 5 6]
                        [7 8 9] ]
```

```
            [1][4][7]
matrix_column_major = [ |2||5||8| ]
            [3][6][9]
```

It's important to be aware of the ordering of your matrices; otherwise, you end up using a transposed matrix for your calculations. Since all the game engine internal matrices (orientation, camera to world, and so on) are column-major oriented, you will be safer sticking to this standard.

If your matrix represents a transformation matrix (rotation, translation, and scale) you can get its values separately. `Matrix.to_quaternion()` and `Matrix.to_euler()` will give you the rotation part of the matrix in the form you prefer (see next section), and `Matrix.to_translation()` and `Matrix.to_scale()` will give you the translation and the scale vector, respectively.

Euler and Quaternion

Euler and quaternion are different rotation systems. The same rotation can be represented using Euler, quaternion, or an orientation matrix.

Guerrilla CG

You can find two great video tutorials on the Guerrilla CG vimeo channel that explain and compare the two rotation system:

Euler Rotations Explained: http://vimeo.com/2824431.

The Rotation Problem: http://vimeo.com/2649637.

When you convert an orientation matrix to Euler (`Matrix.to_euler()`), you get a list with three angles. They represent the rotation in the X, Y, Z axes of the object. In the navigation system script example, we are using this exact method to determine the horizontal camera angle. You can find this usage in the function `fly_to_walk()` (lines 190 to 199 of navigation_system.py or in the early pages of this chapter).

Conversion Between Different Rotation Forms

You can convert an orientation matrix to Euler, an Euler to a quaternion, a quaternion to an orientation matrix, and on and on and on:

```
original_matrix=mathutils.Matrix.Rotation(math.pi, 3, "X")
converted_matrix=original_matrix.to_euler().to_quaternion().to_matrix().to_euler()
.to_matrix().to_quaternion().to_euler().to_matrix().to_quaternion().to_euler().
to_quaternion().to_matrix()
```

In this example, converted_matrix ends up as the same matrix as original_matrix.

aud—Audio System

This module allows you to play sounds directly from your scripts. There are three classes you will be working with: device, factory, and handle.

The audaspace module in a nutshell: you need to create one audio device per game. You need one factory per audio file (which can also be any video file containing a sound track). And every time you need to play a sound, a new Handle object will be generated from the factory (this is where its name comes from).

Example: Basic Audio Playback

```
import aud

device = aud.device()
# load sound file (it can be a video file with audio)
factory = aud.Factory('music.ogg')

# play the audio, this returns a handle to control play/pause
handle = device.play(factory)
# if the audio is not too big and will be used often you can buffer it
factory_buffered = aud.Factory.buffer(factory)
handle_buffered = device.play(buffered)

# stop the sounds (otherwise they play until their ends)
handle.stop()
handle_buffered.stop()
```

We start by creating an audio device. This is simply a Python object you will use to play your sounds. Next, we create a Factory object. A factory is a container for a sound file. When we pass the Factory object into the device play function, it will start playing the sound and return a handle. Handles are used to control pause/ resume and to stop an audio.

When Will This Music Stop?

After you initialize a sound, you can get its current position in seconds with the handle.position Python property. This is especially useful to keep videos and audio in sync. If you need to check whether or not the audio is ended, you shouldn't rely on the position, though. Instead, you can get the status of the sound by the property handle.status. If you are using the sound position to control a video playback, the sound status will also tell you if the video is over (handle.status = aud.AUD_STATUS_INVALID).

The possible statuses are:

```
0 = aud.AUD_STATUS_INVALID
1 = aud.AUD_STATUS_PLAYING
2 = aud.AUD_STATUS_PAUSED
```

bgl—OpenGL Wrapper

This module is a wrapping of OpenGL constants and functions. It allows you to access low-level graphic resources within the game engine. You can use this module to draw directly to the screen or to read OpenGL matrices and buffers directly.

Sometimes, you will need to run your OpenGL code specifically before or after the game engine drawing routine, so you can store your Python function as a list element either in the scene attributes pre_draw and/or in the post_draw. This will be demonstrated in our first example.

To Learn OpenGL

You can find good OpenGL learning material on the Internet or in a bookstore. *The Official Guide to Learning OpenGL* (also known as *The Red Book*) is highly recommended, and some older versions of it can be found online for download.

Example 01: Line Width Changing

Open the file \Book\Chapter7\7_bgl\line_width.blend.

(Run it in wireframe mode.)

```
from bge import logic
import bgl

def line_width():
    bgl.glLineWidth(100.0)

scene = logic.getCurrentScene()
if line_width not in scene.pre_draw:
    scene.pre_draw.append(line_width)
```

This code needs to run only once per frame and will change the line width of the objects. Be aware that the line is only drawn in the wireframe mode.

You will find on the book files another example where the line width changes dynamically—\Book\Chapter7\7_bgl\line_width_animate.blend.

Example 02: Color Picker

Open the file \Book\Chapter7\7_bgl\color_pickup.blend.

In this file, you can change the light color according to where you click.

```
from bge import logic
from bge import render
import bgl
```

```
cont = logic.getCurrentController()
lamp = cont.owner
sensor = cont.sensors["s_mouse_click"]

if sensor.positive:
    width = render.getWindowWidth()
    height = render.getWindowHeight()

    viewport = bgl.Buffer(bgl.GL_INT, 4)
    bgl.glGetIntegerv(bgl.GL_VIEWPORT, viewport);

    x = viewport[0] + sensor.position[0]
    y = viewport[1] + (height - sensor.position[1])

    pixels = bgl.Buffer(bgl.GL_FLOAT, [4])

    # Reads one pixel from the screen, using the mouse position
    bgl.glReadPixels(x, y, 1, 1, bgl.GL_RGBA, bgl.GL_FLOAT, pixels)

    # Change the Light color
    lamp.color = [pixels[0], pixels[1], pixels[2]]
```

There are three important bgl methods being used here. The first one is bgl.Buffer. It creates space in the memory to be filled in with information taken from the graphics driver:

```
viewport = bgl.Buffer(bgl.GL_INT, 4)
pixels = bgl.Buffer(bgl.GL_FLOAT, [4])
```

The second one is the bgl.glGetIntegerv. We use it to get the current Viewport position and dimension to the Buffer object previously created:

```
glGetIntegerv(bgl.GL_VIEWPORT, viewport);
```

The buffer coordinates run from the left bottom [0.0, 0.0] to the right top [1.0, 1.0]. The mouse coordinates, on the other hand, run from left top [0, 0] to the right bottom [width, height]. We need to convert the mouse coordinate position to the corresponding one in the buffer.

```
x = viewport[0] + sensor.position[0]
y = viewport[1] + (height - sensor.position[1])
```

The third one is bgl.glReadPixels. This is the method that's actually reading the pixel color and storing it in the other buffer object:

```
bgl.glReadPixels(x, y, 1, 1, bgl.GL_RGBA, bgl.GL_FLOAT, pixels)
```

And, finally, let's apply the pixel color to the lamp:

```
lamp.color = [pixels[0], pixels[1], pixels[2]]
```

blf—Font Drawing

If you need to control text drawing directly from your scripts, you may need to use this module. Be aware, though, that this module is a low-level API that has to be combined with the OpenGL wrapper to handle texts properly.

The blf module works in three stages:

1. Create a new font object.
2. Set the parameters for the text (size, position, and so on).
3. Draw the text on the screen.

Example: Writing Hello World

Open the file \Book\Chapter7\8_blf\hello_world.blend.

In the init function, we load a new font in memory and store the generated font ID to use later.

```python
def init():
    """init function - runs once"""
    # create a new font object
    font_path = bge.logic.expandPath('//fonts/Zeyada.ttf')
    bge.logic.font_id = blf.load(font_path)

    # set the font drawing routine to run
    scene = bge.logic.getCurrentScene()
    scene.post_draw=[write]
```

The actual function responsible for writing the text is stored in the scene post_draw routine. Apart from the OpenGL calls, the setup for using the text is quite simple.

```python
def write():
    """write on screen - runs every frame"""
    width = bge.render.getWindowWidth()
    height = bge.render.getWindowHeight()

    # OpenGL calls to re-set drawing position
    bgl.glMatrixMode(bgl.GL_PROJECTION)
    bgl.glLoadIdentity()
    bgl.gluOrtho2D(0, width, 0, height)
    bgl.glMatrixMode(bgl.GL_MODELVIEW)
    bgl.glLoadIdentity()
```

```
# blf settings + draw
font_id = bge.logic.font_id
blf.position(font_id, (width*0.2), (height*0.3), 0)
blf.size(font_id, 50, 72)
blf.draw(font_id, "Hello World")
```

On the book files, in the same folder, you can find two other examples following the same framework: *hello_world_2.blend* and *object_names.blend*.

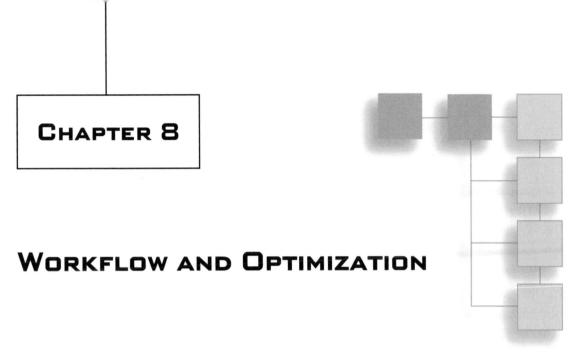

CHAPTER 8

WORKFLOW AND OPTIMIZATION

We were once told that making a video game is a constant struggle between four elemental forces:

- Quality
- Performance
- Development time
- Monday-morning meetings

Okay, so maybe the last item shouldn't be on the list, which Figure 8.1 reflects. But the point is that it's easy to make a visually impressive game when performance is not an issue. Conversely, it's also easy to make a game perform well if the game has very basic graphics. The difficult part is achieving both at the same time. Luckily, this can usually be accomplished by investing more development time in the project. Finally, if you have worked in a team environment, you undoubtedly know that Monday-morning meetings do not guarantee a better game, but are guaranteed to end in frustration and spilled coffee.

Figure 8.1
The holy trinity of game development.
© 2014 Cengage Learning®. All Rights Reserved.

In this chapter, we'll talk about some of the techniques used to improve the performance of the game, speed up development, and how to survive Monday-morning meetings to keep the upper management happy.

Optimization Basics

Making a video game is both a science and an art. The creative aspect of a game can't be realized without technology, and the technology alone is useless without the creative work.

When we play a game, we rarely think about the hundreds of program functions that are invoked each second, nor the millions of lines of codes that are executed every frame, nor the billions of transistors that change state every nanosecond to make all that happen. We don't think of all these things because our game runs on a game engine, which runs on top of the operating system, which in turn manages all the low-level hardware. So as the developer, you can focus on making the game fun.

Understanding Hardware

That said, having a good understanding of computer hardware is essential in the game-creation process, because it allows you to manage the limited hardware resources efficiently. Making the most of the available hardware enables the game to perform as fast as possible.

The key components of a modern computer are listed below:

- **CPU** (central processing unit), or processor, is often aptly called the brain of the computer. Everything is controlled by the CPU, with the exception of graphics, which are handled by the graphics card. A faster CPU allows more complex logic and physics, as these things are calculated on the CPU. Today, many CPUs are multicore, so they can do multiple tasks simultaneously without slowing down. However, a multicore CPU does not automatically make a game run faster; the software needs to be multithreaded in a way that utilizes multiple cores. Currently, Blender's game engine is not optimized to take advantage of multiple cores. So having even a quad-core processor does not increase the game's performance significantly.

- **RAM** (random-access memory), or memory, is a place to store temporary data for running programs. The more complex the scene, the more RAM will be used. With most computers having 4GB of RAM or more, we usually don't have to worry about running out of memory unless the game is exceptionally large. For a small-to-medium-scale game, memory size is effectively not an issue.

- **GPU** (graphics processing unit), or graphics card, is a processor that is specially designed to display 3D graphics. Blender uses the GPU to render the 3D world, so a faster graphics card definitely helps make the game perform faster. Generally speaking, a faster GPU would allow the game to have more complex geometry, more lights, and more complex graphic effects.

Performance Target

If you are a PC gamer, you are no doubt familiar with the (perhaps frustrating) notion of minimum system requirement. Unlike video game consoles, which have a fixed set of hardware, computers vary a great deal in capacity and performance. Minimum system requirement is a way to guarantee that the game will run at a sufficiently acceptable performance level given a certain hardware configuration.

One of the questions that you should ask yourself before starting any project is: Who is your target audience?

For example, if you are making a casual Web-based online game, you probably want to keep the system requirements relatively low, so that a larger number of casual gamers can enjoy it. On the other hand, if your game is a full-blown action game, then there is a higher chance that your game will be enjoyed by "serious" gamers with relatively fast computers. Figure 8.2 illustrates the difference in graphics between one of the first video games and a modern 3D game made in Blender.

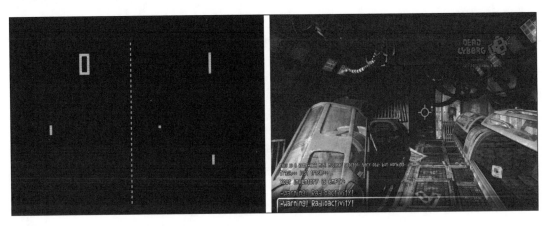

Figure 8.2
Pong (1972) vs. *Dead Cyborg* (2010).
Pong Source: Atari, Inc. Dead Cyborg © 2014 Endre Barath.

Blender on the Web

Publishing a Blender game as a browser game is mentioned in Chapter 9, "Publishing and Beyond."

Once a minimum system target is set, you can start creating your game knowing exactly how much detail and complexity you can put into it. You can compromise details to achieve the performance you are looking for. Luckily for us, lowering the overall level of detail usually means the artists have less work to do.

Performance Scaling

After a performance target has been decided, most game studios still have to think about how the game will run on hardware that is significantly faster or slower than the target platform.

Big, commercial PC games are excellent at scaling. They accomplish this by giving the user the options to change the game settings to fit a wide range of computers. However, making a game run well on a wide range of computers is time consuming, because additional development time is necessary to make sure the game works well at every combination of settings. For example, you don't want the game to leave out a graphic effect that is crucial to the gameplay just because the user has a slower computer.

Blender has some built-in support for disabling certain advanced graphical features, which can help you in adapting the game to older computers. Figure 8.3 shows *Yo Frankie!* running at different levels of detail.

Figure 8.3
Yo Frankie! graphics with shader effects disabled on the right.
Source: *Blender Foundation.*

When running in GLSL mode, advanced shader effects can be turned off to reduce the workload on the graphics card. These settings can be found in the Render Properties Editor, as shown in Figure 8.4.

Figure 8.4
Render Properties Editor.
Source: *Blender Foundation.*

- **Lights:** Disables all GLSL lighting calculation. Has the largest impact on performance as well as visuals.

- **Shaders:** Disables advanced GLSL surface shaders, only basic diffuse and specular shaders will be used.

- **Shadows:** Disables shadows cast by lamps.

- **Ramps:** Disables Ramp Material shaders.

- **Nodes:** Disables Node Material shaders.

- **Extra Textures:** Disables textures that are not mapped to the diffuse channel of a material. So, in effect, this will disable any specular map, normal map, or emit texture, and only keep the diffuse texture on the surface.

All of the above options are only changeable in GLSL mode. In Singletexture and Multitexture mode, the game engine will always render everything in exactly the same way.

Apart from tinkering with graphical features to influence the performance of the game, many commercial games also vary the object level of detail, reduce particle effect density, and even change the audio quality in order to make the game play smoother on older hardware. Some of these techniques are explained in this chapter.

When to Optimize

Throughout the development process, you will have to make high-level decisions that will affect how the game performs, so it's important to keep performance in mind at all times. On the other hand, doing micro-optimization too early will only slow down your workflow, leading to bugs and sometimes making the game hard to maintain, which is all bad.

An example of premature optimization is to compress all the textures to JPEG so that they take up less space. Why is it bad? JPEG is a lossy compression—every time you open and resave a JPEG file, some data is lost. So by constantly editing a JPEG file, its image quality will decrease considerably. During development, it is always better to save files in lossless formats, such as TGA or PNG. This applies to audio files as well; editing should always be done on lossless formats such as WAV.

Figure 8.5 shows JPEG compression artifact vs. TGA, which compresses losslessly.

Figure 8.5
Lossless TGA (left) vs. highly compressed JPEG (right).
© 2014 Mike Pan.

The Tale of Two Tabs

For the underwater marine visualization project Dalai Felinto and I were involved with at the University of British Columbia, I was given the task to "see if you can squeeze more fish into the scene and make it run faster"—a typical request from a Monday-morning meeting. Because this BGE visualization already contained hundreds of objects in the scene, I just assumed that Blender wasn't good at handling a large number of separate objects. But despite the hunch (which proved to be so very wrong), I kept trying different scenarios, turning objects on and off, turning off Python scripts, playing with physics, and culling settings. Then I found a script that, when disabled, would speed up the game performance by five times! When 12fps suddenly became 60fps, I knew I'd found the proverbial silver bullet. But being the author of the script, I was not convinced that a 70-line script could slow down the game by that much, so I dug further, until I finally realized that there was an error in the code that made an inner loop run way more than it should.

So, after two hours of profiling, the only finding was a badly nested Python loop. The fix took all of two seconds and involved unindentation of the offending code. But the end result was spectacular, to say the least.

Silly bugs like this might not be present in your project. Without finding a bug like this, you'll never increase your performance five-fold by fixing a few indentations in the code. But never assume you know where the problem is—always profile.

How to Optimize

As obvious as it sounds, the first step in optimization is locating the bottleneck. A bottleneck is the point in the game where it is taking the longest time to compute. Focusing on the bottleneck will make sure that the work you do in optimizing the game will have the largest impact on performance.

Common wisdom in the programming world says never assume you know where the bottleneck is. Experience might tell you where the slowdown should be, but if there is an unexpected bug somewhere, the bottleneck might not be where you think it is. Always make sure that you locate the bottleneck before trying to remove it. The performance profiler in Blender can give you some very insightful information about the performance of the game and where the bottleneck might be.

The Performance Profiler

Blender has a basic performance profiler available to you. It gives you timing information on how long a frame takes to update, as well as the breakdown of how long the game engine spent on specific tasks.

To turn it on, go to the Render Properties Editor and check Framerate and Profile under Performance, as shown in Figure 8.6.

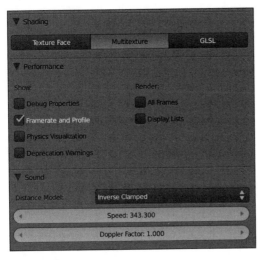

Figure 8.6
Performance options in the Render Properties Editor.
Source: *Blender Foundation.*

The profiler can also be accessed from the top menu under Game.

Once that's enabled, you will see a text overlay as depicted in Figure 8.7 in the top-left corner when running the game.

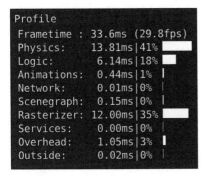

```
Profile
Frametime : 33.6ms (29.8fps)
Physics:    13.81ms|41%
Logic:       6.14ms|18%
Animations:  0.44ms|1%
Network:     0.01ms|0%
Scenegraph:  0.15ms|0%
Rasterizer: 12.00ms|35%
Services:    0.00ms|0%
Overhead:    1.05ms|3%
Outside:     0.02ms|0%
```

Figure 8.7
Framerate and Profile information overlay.
Source: *Blender Foundation.*

The Profiler

The most common measurement of performance for a real-time application is frames per second; that's how many images the computer can render per second. This number is shown at the very top of the profiler in two ways. First, as "swap," which refers to the time it takes to swap out the previous frame for the new one, expressed in milliseconds. Secondly, as a more readable "frames per second" value, expressed in hertz.

Moving down, you can see that the number in the first column is the time it took to complete the operation in milliseconds; the second column is the same value expressed as a percentage of the total time.

To understand the profiler, simply look at the relative percentage of time it takes to complete all the operations. The table below shows you the meaning of each.

Table 8.1 Profiler Breakdown

Label	Meaning	Hardware Used	Typical Ratio
Frametime	Combined time	Entire system	100%
Physics	Bullet physics time	CPU	10%
Logic	Game logic time	CPU	5%
Animation	Animation time	CPU	5%
Network	Network time	Network	0%
Scenegraph	Scene setup time	CPU	10%
Rasterizer	Rendering time	Graphics card	65%
Services	Misc. time	CPU	2%
Overhead	Misc. time	CPU	2%
Outside	Idle time	CPU	0%

© 2014 Dalai Felinto and Mike Pan.

It is impossible to say what would be an ideal profiler-time ratio. The typical ratio is only meant to give you a very rough idea of how an "average" game will perform. Each application is different. A fast-action game with lots of physics could easily spend 25 percent of the time on physics, a graphic-intense cut scene might spend 95 percent of the time on rasterizer, while a scientific visualization might use 40 percent of the time on logic.

The "outside" time deserves special mention. This time represents the idle time that is not spent actively doing anything. So do not be alarmed if the outside value is too high, especially when the framerate is capped at 60.

Furthermore, the ratios change depending on the computer hardware. For example, a computer with a fast graphics card would breeze through the rendering in almost no time, making the rasterizer-time ratio much smaller. Because of this, the profiler works best when it is run on a computer with hardware that matches the intended target audience. Otherwise, it might give you a false sense of where the bottleneck is.

For a detailed analysis of what each of the components do, Mitchell Stokes has written a very comprehensive article on the subject. It can be found at http://wiki.blender.org/index.php/Doc:2.6/manual/Game_Engine/Performance/Display/Framerate_and_Profile.

Quick 'n Dirty Optimization Techniques

Once you've located the slowest portion of the game by looking at the profiler, here are some things you can try to speed up the game:

- **Disable physics for non-essential objects:** If physics is taking a large portion of the CPU time, then maybe consider disabling collision for non-essential objects. By default, all objects in the scene have collision detection turned on, so this can be slow. Changing the physics type from static to no collision will make the physics engine work less. Setting is found in the Physics Properties Editor for the object.

- **Switch to simple collision shapes:** The more complex the collision bounds, the harder the physics engine has to work. Consider using simple shapes that approximate the models by switching to a different bounding box. Setting is found in the Physics Properties Editor for the object.

- **Use display list:** When enabled, display list caches the geometry data on the graphics card so that they do not have to be sent to the graphics card every frame; this significantly increases the performance of games that contain complex geometry. Setting is found in the Render Properties Editor. There is almost no downside to this feature. Some very old graphics cards might not support it, but at the time of writing, display list works for almost all the computers in use.

- **Use power-of-two textures:** Older graphics cards expect textures to have dimensions that are powers of two. For example, 512×512 pixels, 2048×2048 pixels, and 512×64 pixels are all good sizes. Traditionally, non-power-of-two textures are automatically extended to the next highest power of two, so a 513×513 pixel texture will take up as much memory as a 1024×1024 image texture when the game is running. Even though most newer graphics cards do not impose this requirement on image sizes, it's always a good idea to manually save all your images in a more compatible size.

- **Use DDS-compressed textures:** If your game contains a lot of high-resolution texture maps, they will take up a lot of video memory. File formats such as PNG, JPEG, or TGA are compressed on the file level, but when these images are loaded into Blender, they are uncompressed into a raw format so that the graphics card can quickly decode them. This makes estimating texture memory usage based on file size very difficult, since 40MB worth of JPEG might take up 200MB of real texture memory on the graphics card. If a game has a lot of textures, it might be worthwhile to look into DirectDraw Surface (DDS) compressed textures.

DDS is a common name that refers to a set of compressed image formats (specifically DXT1 through DXT5) that is designed for real-time use. In Blender, DDS textures remain compressed even after they are loaded into memory. Therefore, they take up significantly less memory than a conventional image texture.

Popular image editors such as Photoshop and GIMP have plug-ins that support the loading and saving of DDS files.

- **Reduce the number of dynamic lights:** If rasterizer is taking up too much time on the profiler, consider reducing the number of dynamic lights. Dynamic lights are wonderful. When skillfully placed and animated, they contribute so much realism to the scene. Unfortunately, they come at a hefty cost to the graphics card: more lights mean slower performance. So use them sparingly. Generally speaking, it's best to keeping the number of lights under four. Remember, you can accomplish a lot by prebaking the light effects, discussed later in the chapter. Lights with real-time shadows are even slower.

- **Reduce the number of objects:** It goes without saying that fewer objects are faster. Sometimes, even just by batching up all the static objects into one, you can achieve an impressive performance boost. A large number of objects usually causes the scenegraph time in the profiler to be unusually high.

- **Use instancing:** If your game world is populated by hundreds of identical objects, make sure they share one mesh. This is done by pressing Alt+D to duplicate the object, rather than the usual Shift+D. Datablock sharing makes the game load and run faster. When using instancing, Object Color can be a handy way to add some variation to the material without having to create multiple materials.

- **Play with window size:** If by resizing the 3D Viewport to a smaller size, you get a larger increase in performance, it means your game is limited by the fill-rate performance of your graphics card. Transparent objects, complex shaders, and 2D filters are all fill-rate heavy. Reducing these effects will make the game run faster on slower graphics cards.

- **Use Blenderplayer:** Blenderplayer, the stand-alone game engine of Blender, can be a bit faster than Blender. So if you are looking for one last bit of performance out of the game, try switching to Blenderplayer. In fact, it's always a good idea to use Blenderplayer when publishing your game anyway.

- **Watch the console:** By default, the Blender console window is hidden on all operating systems. Turn on the console and see if there are any error messages being printed. Error messages generally indicate a much greater problem with the game. Not to mention that an excessive amount of console printing can slow down the game significantly.

To turn on the console window on Windows: Go to Main Menu → Window → Toggle System Console

To run Blender with a console window on OS X or Linux, launch the application from the command line.

■ **Try another version of Blender:** When all else fails, consider the possibility that there is a bug in Blender that's causing the slowdown. (This has happened before.) Try your file with another (older or newer) version of Blender and see if the performance problem is still there. If you believe something is abnormally slow when it shouldn't be, file a bug report so the developers can have a chance at fixing it. This might not only solve your problem, but it makes the program better for everyone else, too.

ADVANCED OPTIMIZATION TECHNIQUES

Here are some other, more advanced, optimization techniques to try.

Think Small

If you are making a large game, instead of making a sprawling million-acre landscape, consider separating the map into many smaller pieces and using cleverly designed tunnels, elevators, or entryways to trigger the loading of a new section of the map. Half-Life 2 is a wonderful example of this; their massive terrain is actually made up of many zones. This way, the computer doesn't have to load and render nearly as many assets at once.

Additionally, if the level chunks are kept in different files, as opposed to different scenes in the same file, you could also have multiple people working on the levels and not cause version control issues.

Once the level is broken up into different sections, each can occupy a scene. You can use the Scene actuator to switch between scenes, as shown in Figure 8.8.

Figure 8.8
Using the Scene actuators to load a different level.
Source: *Blender Foundation.*

Collision Proxy

While it is justifiable to spend hundreds, if not thousands, of polygons on a model to make it look nice onscreen, the collision mesh used for physics rarely needs to be as detailed as the visual representation. Because of this, a common technique used in games is to approximate physics meshes with built-in primitives, such as cubes or spheres. These are the fastest to compute.

If more definition is needed, you can create a collision proxy for a complex object. A collision proxy is a simplified, invisible shell that occupies the same space as the visual model but is only used for collision detection. Figure 8.9 explains.

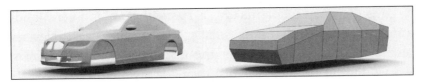

Figure 8.9
Collision proxy: visual mesh (L) vs. collision mesh (R).
© *2014 Mike Pan.*

To use collision proxy:

1. Open \Chapter8\collisionProxy.blend.
2. The scene contains a high-polygon model of a tree. Start the game and notice that all of its faces react to collision. You can confirm this by pressing the spacebar to throw balls at the tree. Notice that no matter where the ball hits the tree, it will detect the collision.
3. If you have a slower CPU, also notice that the physics is taking a large amount of the time, mainly because of the complexity of the tree mesh.

4. To further visualize what's going on, enable Show Physics Visualization from the top menu. All the faces that have collision enabled will be outlined in green when the game is running.

5. If we have to build a collision proxy for the tree object manually, it would involve modeling out a mesh that has the rough shape of the tree, but using much less detail. For this exercise, a simplified version of the tree has been created for you. In layer 2 of the file, you will find a collision proxy that fits over the tree. The model consists of the main tree trunks, combined with a sphere to approximate the canopy.

6. Turn on both layers 1 and 2: Press the 1 key, then, while holding down Shift, press the 2 key.

7. To link the high-detail tree model to the low-detail tree model, we will parent them together. First, right-click on the treeHigh object to select it; then while holding down the Shift key, right-click on the treeProxy object to select that as well. Now simply parent the treeHigh object to the treeProxy object by pressing Ctrl+P. Note that the order in which we selected the two objects is important!

8. Right now, both objects still have collision and display turned on. If you were to play the game right now, the game engine would have a difficult time trying to resolve the collision between two objects that are occupying the same space, and display a mess of colliding polygons.

9. To remove the collision property on the treeHigh: Select treeHigh. In the Physics Properties Editor, set the physics type to No Collision.

10. To disable the visibility of the treeProxy, Select treeProxy. In the Physics Properties Editor, enable the Invisible button.

11. Run the game now to see how the collision is handled by treeProxy, while the treeHigh gets displayed.

12. Keep in mind that since the treeProxy is the parent of treeHigh, any logic brick should be attached to the proxy object. treeHigh is simply a collision-less, logic-less, nice-looking model.

Figure 8.10
Collision proxy: visual mesh (L) vs. collision mesh (R).
© 2014 Cengage Learning®. All Rights Reserved.

So that's collision proxy in a nutshell. As you can see, a lot of steps are involved with this approach, which makes using collision proxy suitable only for very complex models that have a unique shape. Otherwise, it is much easier (and efficient) to use one of the predefined collision bound primitives.

Partial Collision

Another alternative to collision proxy is to simply turn off collision on part of the model. This can be done in the Material Properties Editor. By adding multiple materials, you can control which part of the model is collision detected and which part is ignored by collision detection.

---

1. Open \Chapter8\collisionMultiMaterial.blend.

2. Start the game and notice that the entire tree object reacts to collision. You can confirm this by looking at the wireframe physics visualization.

3. In order to make the game run better, let's disable collisions for the smaller tree branches.

4. Select the tree object and go to the Material Properties Editor.

5. Select the material slot named *Trunk* and make sure that the Physics checkbox is turned on.

6. Select the material slot named *Branches* and disable collision by unchecking the Physics checkbox. The resulting file should look like Figure 8.11.

7. Run the game again and notice that the smaller branches will now be ignored by the physics engine. Not only will this free up some physics computation, but it will also make the game more realistic by letting objects go through leaves.

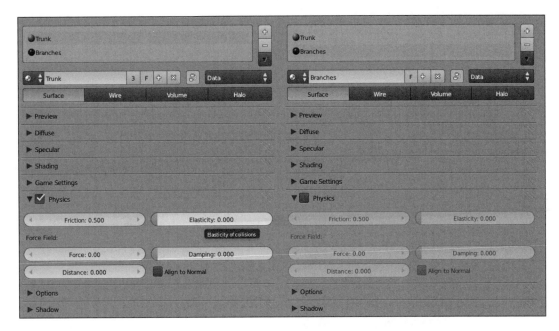

Figure 8.11
Material Properties Editor.
Source: *Blender Foundation.*

Texture Baking

The Blender rendering engine is capable of creating some stunning effects. Don't you wish you could have that level of graphic quality in your game? With texture baking, you can! Texture baking is the process of rendering effects such as shadow map, ambient occlusion, and lightmaps onto a texture, so they do not have to be computed in real time.

Texture baking requires the material to be set up so that it can be rendered by the internal rendering engine. Then, with a few more clicks, the renderable material will be baked onto an image texture that can be used in-game.

The entire workflow can be summarized as:

1. Make object material compatible for rendering.

2. UV unwrap object.

3. Bake.

4. Reassign the baked texture onto the object.

Let's try this out:

1. Open \Chapter8\TextureBaking.blend.

2. Run the game and notice that this interior scene is very flat, and the lighting isn't very realistic.

3. Quit the game and press F12 to do a render of the scene. This is what we want our scene to look like in-game. Close the rendered image by pressing F11.

4. To bake texture, you need to first UV unwrap the scene so that the baked texture has a place to go. To do this, right-click to select the room object. Enter Edit mode with a quick tap on the tab key. Press U key to invoke the UV Unwrap menu. Select Lightmap Pack.

5. In the pop-up menu shown in Figure 8.12, make sure that the New Image checkbox is enabled; this will ensure that an empty image texture is created for you. Click OK to unwrap the model.

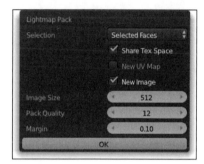

Figure 8.12
Lightmap Pack UV dialog box.
Source: *Blender Foundation.*

6. For a more complex model, it might be necessary to manually UV unwrap a model, but for this exercise, the automated unwrapping is sufficient. Keep in mind that for texture baking to work correctly, the UV layout should not have any overlapping region. Otherwise, the baking will render to the same texture coordinate multiple times, causing an artifact.

7. To bake texture for the room object, go to the bottom of the Render Properties Editor, where the Bake function is found, as shown in Figure 8.13.

Figure 8.13
Bake panel.
Source: *Blender Foundation.*

8. The Bake Mode selector controls what will be baked to a texture. Full Render will bake the full color, light, shadow, and texture onto the texture. Ambient Occlusion is another commonly used one.

9. Select Full Render for this project and click on Bake. This might take a few minutes, depending on the complexity of the model. As the texture is getting rendered out, you can see the baked texture filling up the Image Editor on the bottom of the screen.

10. When the texture baking is finished, it should look something like Figure 8.14

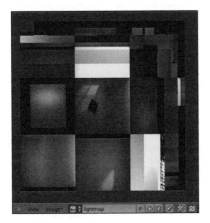

Figure 8.14
The baked texture.
Soruce: *Blender Foundation. Art © 2014 Cengage Learning®. All Rights Reserved.*

11. Now that the baking is finished, quit out of Edit mode by toggling the Tab key.

12. Finally, you need to tell the game engine to use the texture you just baked, instead of the old materials. The easiest way is to delete all three materials from the object by clicking on the [-] button in the Material Properties Editor. This is a cheap and fast way to force Blender to use the texture you just created.

13. Run the game now. Notice that all the light and color you saw in the render are visible in real time. However, specular effects, such as specular highlights and reflections, cannot be baked. Therefore, those are still not visible.

14. The lightmap image is not automatically saved. To save the image, click on Image → Save As from the Image Editor. You can also save the image by pressing F3 with the mouse over the image editor.

15. Figure 8.15 shows the finished version, which can be found at \Chapter8\TextureBaking-finished. blend.

Figure 8.15
The baked scene (left) vs. the original scene (right).
© 2014 Cengage Learning®. All Rights Reserved.

Limitations of Texture Baking

As with anything that "sounds too good to be true," there is usually a catch.

■ With texture baking, only view-independent lighting effects can be baked. So while diffuse color can be baked to a texture because diffuse color is not linked to the camera-view angle, specular highlights and reflections are ignored during texture baking because specular highlights are view-dependent lights; there is no way to bake them onto a static texture.

■ Texture baking is an act of sacrificing flexibility for performance. Once a scene is baked, the scene becomes rather static. For example, moving an object after you baked the lightmap might result in a black spot and some odd-looking phantom shadow. So usually light baking is limited to the static environment only.

- Every object has to be UV mapped in a non-overlapping manner. If two areas of an object share the same texture coordinate, they will not display properly.

- Keep in mind that Blender doesn't save image files automatically, so make sure you manually save the baked texture file by clicking on Image → Save.

Despite the limitations, texture baking is a popular method that is widely used to include fancy light effects in real time. In addition to baking full renders, it is also possible to bake just an ambient occlusion map. The baked ambient occlusion texture can then be used as a secondary texture to influence the surface shading of an object.

Normal Map

Baking a normal map is actually just a special case of the texture baking. Normal map baking is commonly used to generate a tangent normal map from a high-resolution model to map onto a low-resolution model.

So what is a normal map?

A normal map is a regular image file, but instead of influencing the color of the surface like a regular color texture, normal maps are used to alter the per-pixel surface normal. By altering the surface normal, you can change the apparent bumpiness of a surface. The effect of a normal mapped object is one that has far more apparent fidelity than the actual underlying mesh. Figure 8.16 shows the effect of a normal map.

Figure 8.16
From left to right: Original high-resolution model, low-resolution model, low-resolution model with normal map.
© 2014 Mike Pan.

There are two ways to create a normal map:

1. A normal map can be created in an image-editing tool, such as Photoshop or GIMP. Plug-ins are available that can convert a black-and-white height map into a normal map.

2. Use Blender's built-in tool to bake a normal map from a high-polygon model to a low-polygon model.

To bake a normal map from a high-polygon model to a low-polygon model:

1. Open \Chapter8\NormalMap.blend.

2. Notice that we have two objects of the same model: a high-resolution model that we'll use as the input, and a low-resolution model that we will bake the normal map to. They occupy the same space because this is necessary for the normal map-baking process to work properly.

3. As with lightmap baking, you first need to UV unwrap the model so that the texture baking knows where to place the texture. Select the low-resolution model (since that's the one you are baking to). Go into Edit mode, press U, and select Unwrap.

4. Because no image texture is created for you automatically, manually create a new image texture datablock by clicking on the New button in the Image Editor. A resolution of 1024 is sufficient for this example.

5. Now comes the tricky part. First, select the high-resolution model; then hold down Shift to add the low-resolution model to the selection. This way, both objects should be selected, with the low-resolution model being the active object. You can select the object from the Outliner to make the process simpler.

6. From the Render Properties Editor, select Normal from Bake mode and then click on Bake.

7. Once the baking is done, the baked texture should have a purple hue to it. If the color is off, check to make sure that you are baking a normal map into the correct normal space (tangent), as shown in Figure 8.17.

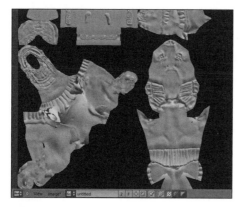

Figure 8.17
Baked normal map.
Source: *Blender Foundation. Art © 2014 Mike Pan.*

8. At this point, you have no use for the high-resolution model anymore. Move the object to a different layer or delete it.

9. To use the normal map, create a material and image texture for the low-resolution model, as shown in Figure 8.18.

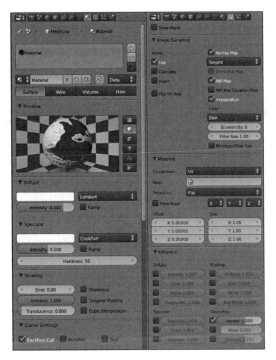

Figure 8.18
Normal map material.
Source: *Blender Foundation.*

10. The final result should look like the file Chapter8\NormalMap-Finished.blend.

If you are curious, a normal map uses the three color channels (RGB) to store the normal directions (XYZ) of a surface. Because most surface normals are pointing outward, they have a normal value of (X=0.5,Y=0.5, Z=1.0), which is what gives normal maps that distinct purple color.

Normal Map Utilities

The two most popular normal map utilities seem to be Gimp-NormalMap for (you guessed it!) GIMP (http://code.google.com/p/gimp-normalmap) and NVIDIA Texture Tools for Photoshop (http://developer. nvidia.com/nvidia-texture-tools-adobe-photoshop).

Level of Detail

Level of detail (LOD) is a general term referring to ways to adjust the complexity of the object, depending on its perceived size. The idea is that objects farther away are smaller and generally less significant to the gameplay. Therefore, they can often be removed or simplified.

Ideally, LOD requires computing the size of the object on the screen. Because this is usually very difficult to achieve, LOD is commonly done by looking at the distance between the camera and the object.

For a complex mesh, you can create multiple copies of the same model, with decreasing complexity. So when an object is a certain distance away from the camera, you can ask Blender to swap the mesh to a less detailed version. Additionally, as the object gets further away, you can even set the object to invisible, which avoids rendering that object completely.

Unfortunately, Blender does not have built-in support for LOD, so you have to create your own with Python.

A reference implementation of a LOD system can be found at \Chapter8\LoD.blend. This implementation uses a small script that keeps track of the distance of the object to the camera, and replaces the mesh with a less detailed one as the distance increases. Figure 8.19 shows the script-based LOD system.

Figure 8.19
LOD system.
Source: *Blender Foundation.*

The script should be a good place for you to start tinkering with your own LOD implementation.

Object Culling

To make the game run as efficiently as possible, objects that are not visible should not be rendered. While it might be obvious that everything behind a solid wall should not be processed, the computer will need a bit more help to accomplish that.

To help the game engine cull objects, set up occluders to hide part of the scene from view. For example, occluders can be used to mark the separation between an indoor scene and an outdoor scene. A sample file is provided at \Chapter8\culling.blend. The effect of culling is shown in Figure 8.20.

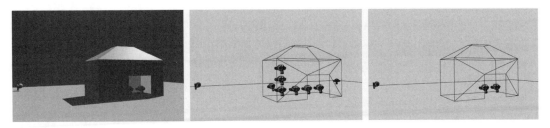

Figure 8.20
Object Culling: game view (left), no occluder (center), house as occluder (right).
© *2014 Cengage Learning®. All Rights Reserved.*

To see the effects of occlusion culling, make sure that you are in wireframe view.

First, run the sample file. Notice that everything inside the house is visible, even when the camera is outside. This is because there is no Occluder object.

Now, set the WallOccluder object to be an occluder and rerun the game. Notice that the wall effectively hides objects inside the house until the camera is inside.

Keep in mind that culling is done on a per-object basis. Blender will not hide part of the model. Therefore, occlusion culling is effective only when there are many small objects in the scene hiding behind a large object.

SCENE MANAGEMENT

Optimization isn't just about making your game fast; it is also about keeping the project organized and easy to manage. As the game project becomes larger, it gets progressively harder to keep everything organized. Here are some things you can do to maintain your own sanity:

Linked Libraries

The size of a single Blender file is virtually unlimited, so in theory, you can make a massive game with everything stored in a one Blender file. However, this approach is not practical for many reasons. Only one person at a time can edit a Blender file. So how do you spread a large project out so that multiple people can work on different aspects of it at the same time, without overwriting each other's work?

The answer is Blender's library system. You have already been exposed to linking and appending in Chapter 2. It's a system that allows you to bring in datablocks (such as a character model) from other Blender files into the current file. This way, each asset can be worked on at the same time separately. This also makes reusing of assets easier.

The game *Yo Frankie!* (available for free online) is a great example of how a large game project is organized. In it, each entity (for example, tree, character model, and rocks) has its own Blender file, which can be linked into a master file, which makes up the game level.

Linking vs. Appending

Both functions import datablocks in Blender from an external file. The difference is that append makes a copy of the datablocks, and in doing so, severs the ties with the original library file. Once an append operation is done, you can edit, move, or even delete the library file without any consequences on the appended object.

Link does not make a new copy of the datablock, but instead references the library file every time the master Blender file is loaded. This way, changes made to the linked object will be propagated to the master file.

Linking is generally preferred over appending since it doesn't replicate the datablocks.

Relative Path vs. Absolute Path

Once you start referencing external files (such as image textures and audio files) into a project, you need to decide if you want Blender to point to that file using a relative file path (the default option) or an absolute file path. Generally, keeping paths relative means it's easier to move a whole project around, as long as the overall folder structure is maintained. If multiple people are working on a project jointly using a file-share or source-management system, using relative path is absolutely crucial.

Blender has some helpful tools under the File → External Files menu that can let you manage file paths.

StreetLamp vs. Cube.001

A scene teeming with objects with unhelpful names like Cube.001, Cylinder.87, and Material.002 would be a nightmare to manage. First, scripts that refer to objects by their name will be harder to understand if object names aren't clear. By keeping everything named, you reduce the time it takes searching for something.

Assigning proper names is not only limited to objects. All datablocks in Blender can be renamed. This includes objects, object data, lamps, materials, textures, and Image datablocks. Renaming everything might seem like a lot of work, even borderline OCD, but once you are used to it, it really does make the project easier to manage. Think of the poor intern who has to pick up your project six month later!

Layers

Not unlike the layer functionality in a 2D image-editing program, the layer functionality in a 3D program is mostly there to keep the scene organized. Blender provides 20 layers for you to work with. How these layers are utilized is up to the artist. Since you cannot assign names to layers, it will be up to you to keep track of, and perhaps document, how the layers are being used.

Beauty Trumps Complexity

Armed with these newly acquired optimization methods, you might be tempted to beef up the game with more details. More polygons! Higher-resolution textures! Larger explosions! (Cough—Michael Bay—Cough.) It's easy to lose sight of the big picture. A visually beautiful game does not have to be photorealistic, nor does it have to be crammed to the brim with details. Sometimes, simple visuals can be just as powerful.

Below are a few games that are faithful to the adage that "less is more":

- **Journey:** http://thatgamecompany.com/games/journey/
- **Limbo:** http://limbogame.org/
- **Love:** http://www.quelsolaar.com/love/

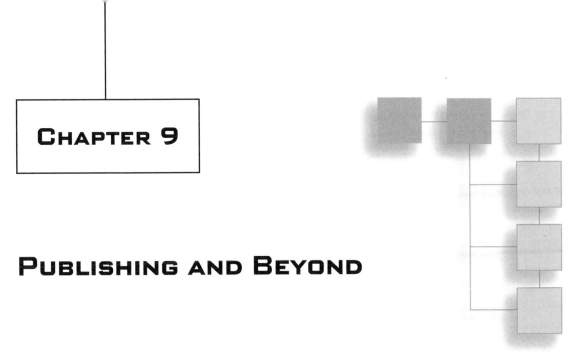

CHAPTER 9

PUBLISHING AND BEYOND

You've made it this far! By now you should have a solid understanding of everything it takes to make a game. Now the question is: How do you get that game into the hands of the public?

This chapter will focus on publishing the game, including how to package your game, using the stand-alone Blenderplayer, and understanding the licensing issues related to using Blender. We will also explore alternatives to the Blender game engine while still using Blender as the main content-creation tool. Even though this is a Blender-specific book, we encourage you to familiarize yourself with other game engines and to understand their pros and cons so you can decide for yourself what is the best publishing platform to use for a particular game.

GETTING READY FOR PUBLISHING

You finished your game, now what? Apart from stress-test, promote, and polish it, there are a few technical things you need to do in order to deploy your project. They apply to almost any of the options discussed in this chapter, and even if you are using external engines, you should take them into consideration.

Resources

Generally speaking, for other users to run a game created by Blender, they will need all of the following files:

- **Blender file:** This is a .blend file that contains your 3D scene and game logic.
- **Resources:** These include image textures, audio, fonts, and scripts.
- **Blender binary (or executable):** This can be the Blender or Blenderplayer binary that is needed to run the game for people who don't already have Blender installed.

This list is simplified. For example, in a larger project, instead of a single Blender file, a game could be composed of multiple Blender files, but there will always be one file that acts as an entry point to start the game. Resources are external files that are used in the game. Resources can be packed, which basically copies these files into the Blender file. Finally, Blender binary is also not usually a single file. It contains libraries and scripts that Blender will need. It is usually a good idea to include the binary with the release, because unless the game is distributed exclusively within the Blender community, the user probably will not have Blender (or the correct version of Blender) installed to run the Blender file.

The Theory of Relativity

The first rule of deployment is to remember that because we have no control over the user's computer, it is impossible to predict where our game will be installed. If that is not bad enough, different operating systems (Windows, Mac, Linux) handle file paths differently. The only way to ensure compatibility across different systems is to make sure all file paths used in the game are relative and nested to the root folder of your game.

Some relative file paths:

//textures/color.png

//audio/music/background.mp3

Some bad relative file paths (avoid them):

//../../../Fonts/ComicSans.ttf

//../../Downloads/textures/floor.png

Some absolute file paths (avoid them):

C:\Users\Documents\Peter\MyBlenderProject\textures\color.png

/home/desktop/DownloadedFromInternet/audio/music/background.mp3

As you can see, not only does an absolute file path reveal a lot of things you probably don't want others to see, but an absolute file path simply wouldn't work on another computer unless it has the same folder setup as you and a compatible operating system.

By default, Blender references all external assets (such as image textures, audio files, and linked Blender files) using a relative path. The file path is always relative to the Blender file.

Because all relative paths are relative to the currently opened Blender file, in order for the relative path to work, the Blender file should be saved before any external assets are loaded.

If you are using Python scripts to load a file from the computer, you should always use the "os" module (os.path.sep, os.path.join, …) to handle these files' locations.

It's Never Too Late to Make It Right

If you forgot to save your file before appending assets, or missed the "Relative Path" option in the load menu, don't worry. There is an option in the file menu that helps rearrange the assets' file paths:

File → External Data → Make all Paths Relative

Packing

If you don't want to deal with external files, Blender also offers another helpful tool to simplify the distribution of a game—packing. Packing makes the Blender file self-sufficient by collecting all external assets such as images, sounds, and fonts into the current Blender file.

To pack a file, click on File → External Data → Pack into .blend file.

Needless to say, packing will make the Blender file increase in size. Packing is a very crude way to hide the file structure of your game from casual observers, but in no way does packing ensure the security of these files. It is easy for someone to unpack the files and have access to the entire game asset you created. Packing is a convenience tool, not an encryption method.

Unpacking does the reverse of packing; it takes all the packed data from a Blender file and writes them out as separate files.

For the Lazy and Unorganized

When you start a project, use external data from wherever on your computer, with no regard to its location. When you feel like getting organized, simply do a pack operation, and then immediately follow it with an unpack operation (with the Unpack to Current Directory option). This will first pack all the images into Blender and then unpack them neatly into a directory called *textures*. This way, there is no need to manually move stuff around. All the external data used will be automatically moved to a single folder for easy distribution. Images in their original location are untouched.

BLENDERPLAYER

One of the strengths of the game engine is its tight integration with Blender and the almost instantaneous feedback you get when starting a game inside the Blender Viewport. This mix of level editor, character design, and general asset management is indeed a trend in the game industry nowadays. Often, we see game engines that have been brought inside the 3D editing tools. There needs to be a distinction between the editing tool and the deployment tool, though. Your game, once published, needs to be a software application on its own. The player shouldn't be aware of the tool you are using—not that magicians never reveal their tricks. (You can include a good description of your tools in your credits if that pleases you.) But to go through the Blender interface to open your game will certainly break the spell.

Export as Runtime

As we mentioned earlier, Blenderplayer is a way to play back your files independently of Blender. The first step is to make sure the "Save As Game Engine Runtime" add-on is enabled. The next is to run it through the menu File → Export → Save As Game Engine Runtime. See Figure 9.1.

This will open up a dialog for you to choose where to save your binary file, which works differently in different operating systems:

Figure 9.1
Export as Game Engine Runtime.
Source: *Blender Foundation.*

- **Windows:** A few files will be copied to the folder you exported the runtime to. The main file is an executable (.exe) that you will be using to launch your game. The name of the file is the one you choose in the Export dialog. It contains both your Blender file (.blend) and Blenderplayer (.exe) bundled together. A few libraries (.dll) are presented as well. They are needed to play your game, so make sure to bring them with your executable wherever it goes (copy, zip, pack). Finally, something that is present in all operating systems, you will find a folder that contains the files needed to run Python scripts. The folder is named after the current Blender version (for example, 2.66\python\).

- **Linux:** In Linux (and Mac OSX), the Blenderplayer binary is static-linked to the libraries. That means that you have one single executable file that contains almost everything you will need. The newly created file (named from the Export as Runtime dialog) already has the proper user permission to be run by any user.

  Just like the Windows runtime, in Linux we have a folder with the files needed for the Python scripts. Even if the system already has Python installed, Blenderplayer (and Blender for that matter) relies on one particular version of Python for its execution. This prevents your games from running into compatibility issues with different Python versions that may exist on the user's system. This also allows you to use compiled Python scripts as we will soon see.

- **Mac OSX:** In this case, the Export as Runtime creates an executable (.app) that you can run by double-clicking on it. This executable is named from the Export dialog, but it's no more than a folder you can explore via the command line. This folder contains the Blenderplayer executable, the Blender file (game.blend), the Python libraries, and the icons used for game file.

Using Blenderplayer Without Exporting Your Game

You don't need to export your game every time you want to test it in the Blenderplayer.

In the same folder where you installed Blender, you can find the Blenderplayer executable. Run it from the commandline/console with your file as argument:

Blenderplayer.exe C:\MyFileWindows.blend

./blenderplayer.app/Contents/MacOS/blenderplayer ~/myFileOSX.blend

./blenderplayer ~/myFileLinux.blend

If you run it with the argument "-h," you can see all the options available through the command-line. Another option is to use the Start button in the Stand-alone Player tab in the Scene menu to launch the current file in Blenderplayer (see "Interface Options" later in this chapter).

Resource Files

Often, your game will need more than you've enclosed in Blender. For example, if you decided not to pack the textures into your file, you will need to copy them to the same folder structure as they were originally. The same applies for sounds, fonts, movies, Python scripts, and so on.

For Linux and Windows, you simply need to copy them to the same folder of the exported executable. In other words, you need to keep the same file structure as you were using from inside Blender.

For Mac OSX, you need to copy them to "mygame.app/Contents/Resources/." This is the base folder (for example, textures go in mygame.app/Contents/Resources/textures/").

Interface Options

In the Render panel, you can find a few specific options for Blenderplayer, as shown in Figure 9.2.

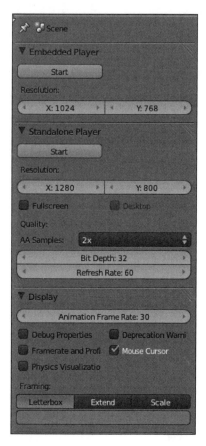

Figure 9.2
Blenderplayer and other options.
Source: *Blender Foundation.*

- **Start:** A quick way to launch your game in Blenderplayer. It will open it in a new window, You need to save your file first. Don't mistake this with the Start button in the Embedded Player tab, which plays the game inside Blender.

- **Width and Height:** The width and height of the Embedded Player determines the aspect ratio of the camera. The ones in the Blenderplayer panel change the actual size of the screen.

- **Full-Screen and Desktop:** If you want to launch your game in full-screen, you can use this option. If you set the Desktop option, the game engine will use the current computer screen resolution for the Full-screen mode. Otherwise, the Blenderplayer resolution will change the desktop resolution.

- **AA Samples:** For smooth rendered edges, you can turn on anti-aliasing. If the computer running the game does not support a specific level of AA or doesn't support AA at all, the game engine will fall back to the maximum supported parameter.

- **Bit Depth and Refresh Rate:** The color depth and the refresh rate for the graphics.

- **Framing:** What can you do when the screen is scaled? Choose one of those three options: Letterbox, Extend, and Scale. Scale will stretch the frame to the new screen size (expect some aspect ratio distortions); Extend will reveal more of the frame, as if you had changed the Blenderplayer and the Embedded Player resolution at the same time. Letterbox will fill any difference between the camera aspect ratio (Embedded Player resolution) and the screen size with the color you choose in the color box (black by default).

FILE SECURITY

Because Blender is available for free to everyone, if you distribute your game as a Blender file (.blend), there is really no way to prevent people from firing up Blender and taking a peek at your Blender file. Even if the game is packed and made into a runtime in the form of a single executable, it is still relatively easy for someone with a bit of technical skill to extract the game data. The bottom line is that packing, compressing, and making runtime are just conveniences for you; a Blend file is never secure against a curious (and determined) evil mind.

No Cheating

If the game involves multiple players connected across the Internet, the only way to make sure that the game is tamper-proof is to do rigorous checking on the server. Any client-side Python code to ensure integrity can be easily modified by the user, and so it is effectively useless. For example, for a shooter game, the game server should keep track of the remaining ammunition for each player; this way, a malicious player would not be able to cheat by altering his own ammunition count.

The part of your program you can easily protect is the Python scripts. Although the plain text .py file is easy to be read by anyone, a compiled script is an unintelligible blob of binary code. To compile your script, all you need to do is run it once, and the game engine will generate a .pyc file for you. This file can be found in the same folder as your original scripts in a subfolder called __pycache__. Now all you need to do is to replace the original script files (.py) by their compiled version (.pyc). Alternatively, you can use Python from the command line to generate the .pyc files: python –m compileall –b <folder-with-scripts>.

Even though your production files will be exposed, this is not the end of the world. Your work is still protected under the licensing rights. Which happens to be our next topic—what are the odds?

LICENSING

It's true that 11 out of 10 people haven't read a single software EULA (End User License Agreement) in their lives. You know, that box full of text you have to agree to before installing a program. To enlighten your mind and relieve your guilty conscience, try not to skip this section.

Just like a document you composed in Word rightfully belongs to you, and not Microsoft, any Blender file you created is entirely yours. You are free to distribute, sell, and publicly show the Blender file as much as you want.

The game engine has a catch, though. Blender and Blenderplayer are licensed under the GNU General Public License (GPL). In a nutshell, it means that any executable file that is derived from one of those binaries needs to follow the same original license. And from that legal perspective, a game exported as a runtime is considered to be a derived binary.

In other words, you need to ensure that all the files you don't want to license under the GPL are not bundled within the Blenderplayer. The option for Export as Runtime can still be used, but your initial file (the one incorporated inside the Blenderplayer) will have to be licensed under GPL.

A simple way to keep your files separated from the Blenderplayer is to create an initial load file. This file will have a Game actuator that only then will load your real main file. This way, all your actual game files can be kept external to the binary. Your file doesn't even need to end in ".blend" for the Game actuator to work.

Why the Blender Game Engine Won't Run on iOS

There is a downside of the GPL license when publishing in some distribution platforms. For legal (and perhaps economic) reasons, most distribution game platforms do not accept GPL code in their components. That means it will be hard to get the game engine ported over to consoles and some more restrictive mobile and portable devices.

WEB PUBLISHING: BURSTER

www.geta3d.com

Burster is a plug-in that allows you to publish and play your games in a Web browser. The plug-in was developed and is supported by a third-party company, independently of Blender Foundation. The plug-in contains a slightly modified version of Blenderplayer that runs as fast as if it were installed natively.

Not all Python modules are supported (for security reasons), but external assets (for example, textures and videos) work pretty well. Additionally, Burster offers a protection system for your work through online on-the-fly decryption of your Blender files. This does not violate the GPL and can provide the necessary security that some commercial works demand.

If you are considering using the Web as a publishing platform, you can find updated information on the Burster website. Make sure you test your game extensively. Even though most of the features are supported, more advanced resources can get a bit tricky (for example, video texture is supported, but the only way to play videos is with external URLs in a server that supports streaming).

Beyond Packing

For Web deployment and mobile, you need to include all the external dependencies into the main file. While textures can be incorporated with the Packing option, the files and scripts need to be merged in manually.

If you are using Python scripts follow these advanced instructions:

- Open all the external scripts (e.g., originally in //scripts/) in the Blender Text Editor.
- Remove all the "from." from the scripts.

∎ Fix all the Python Module controllers by copying this into the Blender Text Editor and running it as a script (in Blender, not inside the game engine):

```
import bpy
for obj in bpy.data.objects:
    for cont in obj.game.controllers:
        if cont.type == 'PYTHON' and cont.mode == 'MODULE':
            cont.module = cont.module.replace('script.', '')
```

MOBILE PUBLISHING: ANDROID

wiki.blender.org/index.php/Doc:2.6/Manual/Game_Engine/Android

Although it is too early to know how far this will go, the Android deployment for the game engine is starting to get in shape. An experimental branch of Blender, "soc-2012-swiss_cheese" makes an Android-compatible Blenderplayer that can open simple .blend game files. Animation, physics, GLSL materials, and mouse interaction are already supported.

In Figure 9.3, you can see the final sample file from Chapter 4 running in an Android phone. To see this in action go to: http://youtu.be/bF1m5b4jEKs.

Figure 9.3
Android deployment.
Source: *Blender Foundation.*

To run your game, you can download the Blenderplayer Android app and open the game from it. As of the time of writing, the app is not yet on the Android market. You can download it from this BlenderArtists forum thread: http://blenderartists.org /forum/showthread.php?255746.

A mobile platform is a limited deployment target. The phones and tablets are getting more powerful every day, yet they still lack in hardware horsepower compared to gaming PCs. As such, you need to be especially careful with optimizing your games.

Some general guidelines:

- Simplify the geometry.
- Chop down big objects into small parts.
- Use occlusion culling when possible.
- Work with power of two textures.

OTHER TOOLS

The Blender game engine can be used for prototyping, before the game is fully developed in another game engine. Or, another common situation, you can use Blender only for asset making for an external engine, and the Blender game engine for previewing the animation playbacks and basic interactions. In those cases, you will not be using the logic components of the game, but mostly making sure your assets (objects, materials, animations) can be transferred easily to other engines.

Exchange File Formats

When your engine does not support Blender files directly, you have to find the best format to export from Blender. There is one format in Blender intended for games. It supports not only mesh and texture, but also animation, shading, and physics.

Collada is an open exchange file format maintained by Khronos consortium (the same group behind the well known OpenGL, OpenCL, and others). Although the support for it in Blender is not complete yet, it's getting there.

Another format broadly used is FBX. This is a proprietary format created and maintained by Autodesk with proper support in Blender going on and off in the past releases.

Even when you are using Blender only to build your assets, the game engine can be of great value. It should be simple to create test levels for your character animations, test ideas, and, in some cases, even build a whole game prototype before migrating to another engine.

In the next chapter, you will learn about some projects that used the game engine in one way or another. One of these projects is *Cubic World*, originally created in the game engine for a game contest. The project was so well received that the main developer decided to port it to the iPhone, writing a specific engine from scratch. Whether you are building your own engine, porting it to an open or commercial alternative, or deploying with the game engine, be aware of the alternatives to better support your decisions. This is an ever-changing topic. New technologies come and go, and it's up to you to keep yourself updated on the subject. Sign up for newsletters, visit forums, and go to conferences (and although it may eventually help, we don't mean wandering around on Twitter or Facebook).

GameKit

www.gamekit.org

GameKit is a "basic game engine that allows fast prototyping built around open source software free for commercial use." GameKit uses Bullet for physics, Ogre for rendering, OpenAL for sound, Lua for scripting, and AnimKit for animation (a stand-alone library created specifically for this engine but open for use elsewhere). It reads Blender files and supports all of its logic bricks.

This modular approach makes it quite interesting for indie developers who often need to design their own engine from scratch. You can borrow their support for Blender files and Render engine and implement a unique logic system, for example.

One of its key benefits over the Blender game engine is that GameKit fully supports non-PC platforms such as Android and iOS. GameKit also uses a non-viral license, meaning the games you create can have any license you want.

As of the time this book went to press, GameKit is still in its early stages. Nevertheless, it's generating some hype in the Blender game community. We are following this project closely and recommend you do the same.

Unity, SIO2

While GameKit stands out for its tight integration with Blender, there are other engines with strong supports for the Blender native file.

SIO2 is an engine targeted exclusively to the mobile market. It currently supports both Android and iPhone devices. It also supports native Blender files, so there is no need to fiddle with export file types.

If your market does not use only portable devices, then Unity3D is another commercial engine that works with Blender files; it's as simple as drag-dropping them inside the editor.

Unity3D has been broadly used by the indie industry. They support mobiles to desktops, and by the time you read this, they can probably deploy for all the main consoles on the market. You still need to rework your materials once you import them inside the engine, but changes in the original file can be merged into the Unity3D editor.

BLENDER DEVELOPMENT CYCLE

The development of the game engine is tied to the development cycle of Blender itself. Although improvements in different parts of the software are done separately, the release of new versions of the game engine happens as part of the Blender releases.

Once a week there is an online developers' meeting—Blender Sunday Meeting. At the meeting, they deliberate on pending issues, present current development from coders, and trace plans for the upcoming weeks and months. The meetings happen in the #blendercoders channel in the Freenode IRC network every Sunday at 4 p.m. Amsterdam time.

For topics that require longer discussions and a larger audience, the developers use a mailing list hosted at the Blender Institute servers: bf-committers@blender.org.

To subscribe to this list or visit its archives, go to: *http://lists.blender.org/mailman /listinfo/bf-committers*.

Proposals and roadmaps are presented and discussed in both channels. Some long-term projects end up resting in the Blender wiki, which in turn can be incorporated at the official development documentation page: *http://www.blender.org/development/*.

Approximately every two months, a new release cycle starts. In the first week, the proposals for what features should be in the trunk (official Blender code) are presented, discussed, and, if necessary, voted in or out of the upcoming Blender release.

This is especially applicable for big features developed on branches (code not incorporated into the trunk yet). Developers may go for long periods of time coding, testing, and calling for feedback, before the code ever gets incorporated into Blender's main source.

To follow new developments, to help beta-test new features, and to make sure we keep the game engine backward compatible, you can keep track of the branches, which are always announced in the Blender Sunday Meetings and in the mailing lists.

Additionally, if you want to talk with Blender game engine coders directly, or follow our discussions, the #bgecoders IRC channel (also on Freenode) is a place where development is discussed.

How to Report Bugs

All software has bugs. Make no mistake about that. For those unfamiliar with this technical terminology, a bug is a problem in the software. Think about the last time you swore at a computer. Behind your lost hours of work lies a bug (and the imprudence of not saving your work; haven't you learned anything from playing video-games?).

Blender has a webpage dedicated solely to report and track bugs from users: http://projects.blender.org.

The guidelines for bug reporting are simple:

- Make sure you can reproduce the bug several times.
- Re-create or isolate the bug in the simplest file you can think of.
- Report the environment you are working in if it's relevant (OS, hardware, version).
- Be patient. Reporting a bug can be a very-time consuming task. And a fix may take a long, long time with some further tests and interactions with you and the coders.

And remember, the more time you spend on making a good report—with good sample files, concise descriptions, and so on—the more you free a developer to work on fixing the bug itself.

Do It Yourself

As a provocative final thought, have you considered literally expanding the game engine yourself? We haven't been giving enough attention to the fact that the Blender source code is open and available to everyone. That may not be the reason you got into the software, but it's interesting to explore its potential.

Blender and the game engine are partly maintained by the Blender Foundation and partially by online volunteer coders. Most of the coders started as users, implementing specific features required for their projects. In the short term, that leads to solutions that make life easier and a project more complete. In the long term, it helps build the community that dedicates energy to the game engine project.

If nothing else, you can try building Blender and replacing the splash screen (see Figure 9.4). It's definitively the first step to looking cool and impressing your boss:

http://wiki.blender.org/index.php/Dev:Doc/Building_Blender.

Figure 9.4
Custom splash screen.
Source: *Blender Foundation. Art © 2014 Mike Pan and Dalai Felinto.*

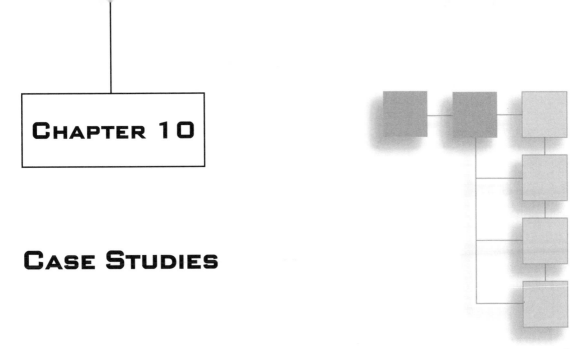

CHAPTER 10

CASE STUDIES

By now you should have a very good command of the Blender game engine. Armed with this newfound skill, no doubt you are bursting with ideas. Whether you are working alone or with a team, completing a game from start to finish is a lot of work. It is also a lot different from the examples and tutorials we used in the book, which are often stripped down to the most basic in order to be didactic. Real-world productions usually involve many more files, which are larger, more complex, and messier. This chapter tries to ease the transition between the classroom and the real world by showcasing other people's finished work.

The Blender-made games selected for this chapter represent some of the best work in quality, gameplay, and visuals. Some are also selected for their interesting use of the game engine in non-traditional ways. By seeing what is possible with Blender, we hope you will be inspired to learn from these masters of the Blender game engine. By showcasing some of the different uses for the game engine, we hope you will realize that the game engine is not just a video-game production machine, but also a sandbox that allows you to do almost anything.

All the games mentioned here can be found on the book website for you to play, and when the authors are willing, the .blend source files are also provided so that you can freely explore the file on your own. You will notice that each artist has a unique style in file organization, scene structure, techniques, and tricks. Most of these tricks might be invisible to the player when the game is running. But by looking at the source file, you can gain much insight into how the game is made.

Blender Versions Clash

We worked hard with the authors of these games to make sure that all the included games on the disk are playable in the latest version of Blender; however, due to limited time, some games might require a different version of Blender to run. Refer to the readme.txt file within each game folder for system requirement.

SUPER BLENDER GALAXY

Carlos Limon

Figure 10.1
© 2014 Carlos Limon.

Figure 10.2
© 2014 Carlos Limon.

Figure 10.3
© 2014 Carlos Limon.

Super Blender Galaxy wooed the Blender community with its fantastic artwork and slick gameplay. Carlos Limon is a relatively new member to Blender, but he wasted no time in single-handedly creating a stunning game that took home a very well deserved first place in the 2010 Blender Game competition.

Based on Super Mario Galaxy, Super Blender Galaxy was inspired by the art and gameplay concept from the classic Nintendo title. Of course, Carlos had to remake all the artwork from scratch. It took eight months of hard work to get the game ready, an impressive feat considering it was a one-man production.

What strikes us about this game is its attention to detail: every component of the game just feels polished right from the introductory screen. Objects look like they fully belong in this fictional universe, the effects are superb, and the gameplay is just what you'd expect from a Mario game.

Carlos explains how the game was made:

> "It wasn't till around 2009 that I found Blender. I have never had experience with any kind of 3D software. I actually stumbled onto Blender when I was trying to learn how to make those stereogram images that look like a mess of stuff that you have to cross your eyes to see.
>
> I picked Blender up pretty quickly. I've always had artistic talent so modeling, texturing, and animating was easy. Learning the Blender interface was the hard part. Once I got over this hump, I decided to tackle the game engine. I made some small demos here and there, but nothing as polished as Super Blender Galaxy [SBG]. The one thing that set SBG apart from all my other games was that I taught myself Python over the duration of the production. I still consider myself a Python newbie, but I pulled off what I needed for the game. There were close to 100 different Python scripts in SBG, and getting them to all work seamlessly was no easy feat.
>
> I started on SBG in March of 2010, and it took me eight months to get this demo out. There really was no planning when I started out. I kind of just kept moving forward. Once I modeled, textured, and animated Mario, I focused on all of his functions and smart cameras. I had to watch a lot of Mario stuff to see how the controls and camera systems worked; then I actually duplicated everything I saw. This was extremely difficult for me, considering that I'm just one person, and I'm trying to match what the professionals are doing.
>
> Once I got this done, I kind of hit a brick wall. I had no ideas for level design. I did get a lot of help from my girlfriend (Alexis F. Porter) in this department. She had some off-the-wall ideas, such as antlers on Yoshi, a sleigh ride race, and of course Skunk Mario. I ended up just replicating Puzzle Plank Galaxy to rush things through.
>
> The Blender community helped me throughout the process, although no one knew what they were helping me with as far as the project goes. When I ran into problems with code, I would post a snippet of my problem, and overnight people would respond with an answer or point me in the right direction. I am very appreciative of that."

Carlos aspires to become a game developer and is currently studying Game Development and Computer Programming in San Antonio, Texas. A playable version of the game is available on the accompanying disk.

Lucy and the Time Machine

Vitor Balbio, Bernardo Hasselmann

Figure 10.4
© 2014 Vitor Balbio.

Figure 10.5
© 2014 Vitor Balbio.

Figure 10.6
© 2014 Vitor Balbio.

Every year the Blender community hosts game engine contests that invite people to create and share their Blender skills. As a response to the contest, in 2010, Vitor Balbio teamed up with Bernardo Hasselmann, who contributed to the concepts, story, and level design. Together, they created a perfectly executed platform-puzzle game that forever raises the bar for Blender-made games. The result is a game with a rich story that involves Jules Verne, a time machine, and a robot sidekick, all taking place in a beautifully rendered 3D environment.

The game is notable for being one of the most professional-looking Blender games out there. It was produced by just two people over the course of four months. The game makes heavy use of the Bullet Physics engine and relies entirely on logic bricks. No Python is used at all. We can't think of a better way to show off the power of the game engine.

Vitor Balbio explains in detail the making of the game:

"Bernardo and I were very rigid in adhering to our work plan. We followed a strict design workbook known as our 'Game Bible' that contained all workflow, game planning, concepts, and notes. This allowed us to see what was doomed to fail early in the project—way before ideas materialized into pixels. The Blender community was also quite receptive to the project. Those factors were fundamental for us to complete our creation.

The game aims to be an enjoyable experience for the player, in part accomplished by visuals—matching the quality standards of an indie game—and its strong plot. The gameplay was based on platform games with puzzles closely connected to the cinematic and time control of the game. The games Trine *and* Braid *were a big inspiration for our work.*

Lucy and the Time Machine *was created entirely with logic bricks. While this made our lives easier on many occasions, this also constrained us a lot. Without using Python, one of the biggest limitations was not being able to animate the values of the Motion actuators. The high number of logic bricks quickly became hard to manage. Thus, we had to rely on strict documentation for naming conventions and other internal rules.*

A few months after the demo release, we started working on a second version of the game (not yet released). This time we were using Python scripting for some of the tasks. Thanks to that, we already had the following: save and load, checkpoint, and better animations.

For this project, the most limiting aspect of the Blender game engine was the lighting. Our inability to dynamically add lights and their slow performance affected some of our design decisions. Sound also proved to be an issue in 2.49 when it came to cross-platform support. Luckily, it's working smoothly in Blender 2.5.

Despite its limitations, I see Blender as an excellent tool for diverse goals. In the field of prototyping, commercial and scientific visualization, virtual walkthrough … I don't know a tool with a better trade-off between robustness and ease of use. The integration with Blender and the logic brick system allowed us to produce fantastic results in a short window of time. I'm also unaware of another open game engine with a better and easier material system (which is my favorite reason for working with Blender).

Our future plans are to port Lucy for other publishing platforms, such as WebPlayer and iOS. Our goal is to stick to Blender for prototyping though.

Keep Blending!"

Vitor Balbio's previous work includes a stunning-looking demo scene called "Ruínas" (Ruins), which competed in the graphics category in an early edition of the same competition. Information about *Lucy and The Time Machine* can be found on Vitor's blog (in Portuguese): *http://obalbio3d.wordpress.com/.*

The FPS Project

Chase Moskal, Geoff Gollmer, Martins Upitis, Mitchell Stokes, Daniel Stokes, Lonnie Ralfs, Fleeky Flanco, Thomas Lobig

Figure 10.7
© 2014 Chase Moskal and Team.

Figure 10.8
© 2014 Chase Moskal and Team.

The *First-Person-Shooter Project* was an attempt to create a solid online multiplayer shooter in the game engine. It began a few years ago with Chase and his good friends, Geoff and Lonnie. All three had played around with the game engine for years, and had always wanted to make an FPS, a goal that certainly aligned with the interests of many gamers and game developers alike. The project took off with enthusiasm and energy. Unfortunately, high self-expectations led to a loss of focus as the project progressed— the project lost steam as the game's complexity spiraled out of control. This all-too-familiar story is unfortunately common to many amateur game developers. The *FPS Project* is currently undergoing a refactoring, and Chase hopes that this time, by keeping the project goals clear and reasonable, the project will not reach the same fate as last time.

Chase wants to share their story so that you won't repeat the same mistakes as they did:

"Just a month or so into the start of the project, Martins Upitis spontaneously contacted Geoff, Lonnie, and me. He had checked out our previous project, Nanoshooter *(a top-down multiplayer shooter, which was more or less a precursor networking test for the* FPS Project*), he was very impressed, and explained how he'd like to make an FPS with us. We were ecstatic, as Martins was our favorite artist of the Blender community.*

We were soon joined by more talented people, including Daniel and Mitchell Stokes, Fleeky Flanco, and Thomas Lobig. With the help of Mitchell and Geoff, I began developing the code base. Online multiplayer is a lot more than just transferring data over sockets: the entire game engine needs to be structured in a way that is conducive to multiplayer. Concepts like GameState and entity management are not built into the game engine, so we improvised them with Python scripting. It really felt like building a game engine within a game engine.

An early challenge was figuring out how to best organize the project's source. We eventually settled on a system that uses Blender's ability to dynamically link objects in from one blend file to another. Environments (levels) are kept in individual blends. All of the game's programming was external from the game engine, and it all ran from one master script called "mainloop.py." Each level linked in the game's programming (which is in its own blend file) that ran the mainloop script every frame. This system kept the programming separate from the levels, and let us organize the game's programming in any way that we wanted. To play the game, the main menu just started up the chosen level's blend file, passing information such as the server's address.

We used Google Docs to collaborate on our plans, to-do lists, and just about anything else. It's an invaluable tool for collaboration, as is Subversion and Google Code. Tools like these are absolutely essential to manage a project of almost any magnitude.

Despite getting a lot of cool work done and learning a ton in the process, it didn't quite work out. Unfortunately, being an inexperienced project manager, I failed to keep us focused on achieving realistic goals. Our team's goals for the project grew out of control: not only did we want a multiplayer shooter, but soon we had plans for a co-op survival mode with hordes of bots; character classes and weapon customization; vehicles and even drop-ship insertions. Before long, the network code became too complex to work on, and our team's motivation declined to nothing.

I'm sure this story sounds familiar to hobbyists of any kind. Most Blender users I've talked to bear the psychological scars of an abandoned beloved project. It's important to set realistic goals. You need enough ambition to inspire initiative, but you must be careful because motivation can easily drown in over-ambition.

It's not all doom and gloom, though. After a long stretch of inactivity, Geoff and I have rebooted the project, but this time vowing to keep things simple. We've stripped away unnecessary ambition, and we're hoping to finish the project as a multiplayer template to be released as open source to the Blender community."

As the project is undergoing a restructuring, no file is available to the public yet. You can learn more about the FPS project at *https://code.google.com/p/fps-project/*.

Whip Frog

David Thompson, Campbell Barton, Daniela Hammer, Alex Fraser, Luca Pavone

Figure 10.9
© *David Thomson, Campbell Barton, Daniela Hammer, Alex Fraser, Luca Pavone.*

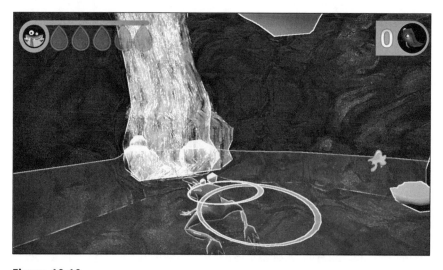

Figure 10.10
© *David Thomson, Campbell Barton, Daniela Hammer, Alex Fraser, Luca Pavone.*

How fast can you build a game? A month? A week? What would you do if you only had 48 hours to make a game with a group of five people? This is the premise of Global Game Jam, an annual event that invites developers and artists to come together to create games from scratch within 48 hours. Alex Fraser participated in the 2011 Game Jam with Blender developer Campbell Barton and three other artists. During those two days, they each slept only a few hours per night, each accomplishing the equivalent of a full week's worth of work by the end of the Jam.

This game shows one area of Blender that is great for game development: rapid prototyping. Thanks to logic bricks, a fully functional Python API, and the integrated workflow, a team can build a game in no time. However, Blender isn't without its downside. The team expressed concern over the lack of version control or collaborative tools within Blender. Without this, only one person can work on the file at a time, which can be frustrating when working under such a tight deadline.

Despite the pressure, the result is a game that is visually unique and fun to play.

Here is Alex Fraser and Daniela Hammer's retrospective on the intense 48 hours:

"The original idea for the gameplay came from Campbell Barton. He had the idea on the way to the competition, and then we just had to extend it to make it fit with the theme of this year's event: Extinction.

We spent the entire allowed time—48 hours—to build the game. The team consisted of 1.5 artists, 1 programmer, 1 integrator, 1 musician and 0.5 designers. Only half of the allocated time was actually used to develop the separate pieces for the end product of the game. Almost as much time was used for test-playing and discussion between group members. This involved keeping constant track of what each team member was creating and making sure that individual team members were up to speed with the rest of the team. While this method demanded a significant portion of time, it ensured that we worked efficiently and allowed us to catch many potential problems in their infancy.

An example of this would be during some of the early game mechanics testing, where we soon found out a horizontal approach for movement was more difficult and less enjoyable than a vertical approach. Were we to only play-test at the end of the game, we would have ended up with a very different and potentially much less enjoyable product.

For us, asset management was hard. We were passing files around on USB sticks. The big problem was that only one person could work on a Blender file at a time. If only we could merge blend files like you can with programs. Or perhaps Verse (a collaborative networking solution that allows multiple people to collaborate on one file at the same time) would help. So we had Campbell doing pretty much full-time integration of the assets that the artists were making with the main game.

We loved the tight integration of the game engine with Blender. It's such a great way to develop something, given the time constraints we had.

Everyone agrees that the biggest challenge during the Game Jam is forcing yourself to walk away from development to go to sleep."

You can learn more about this game at *http://globalgamejam.org/2011/whip-frog.*

Tectonic

Andrew Bentley

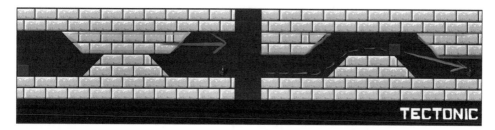

Figure 10.11
© *2014 Andrew Bentley.*

Figure 10.12
© *2014 Andrew Bentley.*

Being a 2D game that looks like something ported from the Nintendo 64 era, *Tectonic* might not look like a groundbreaking game at first glance. But after trying it out, you will be thoroughly impressed with the innovative gameplay mechanics and progressively harder levels that have many of the hallmarks of a professionally made game. If you take it one step further and dive into the source code of the game, you will be impressed as well by the design and programming behind the game's puzzle engine.

For Pythonistas interested in extending their programming skills, this game is a treasure box. Andrew used Python extensively for the game. The game also made use of Mitchell Stokes' BGUI module, which is a Python module for Blender that helps in the creation of user-interface in the game engine.

Despite the extremely late start, Andrew made an impressive puzzle game that won third place in the 2010 Blender Game Competition.

Andrew explains how he made the game in three days:

> "I first got the idea for Tectonic three days before the competition deadline. I was attempting to solve the Rubik's Cube when I thought "hey, this could make a pretty cool mechanic in a game" and "oh hey, there's a game competition on right now." So I guess the game competition and stiff schedule really made me work hard on it. I wanted to get something playable out before the deadline, sort of like a prototype. So I jumped on Blender and dived straight into it. I didn't do any planning or anything; I just wanted to get some sort of Rubik's Cube-esque 2D game mechanic working inside Blender, which didn't take long at all. What I had was a grid of tiles that could be slid around, and that was it.
>
> So I decided I probably needed to figure out what I wanted to do before moving on. I was intending for it to be a top-down perspective at first, so you could see a lot of variables called "y" defining a lot of z ordinates in the code. I still didn't really do any solid planning. I just decided on what the gameplay was going to be. Thinking back, I probably should have thought out the game in a little more detail. I'm still actively developing the game, and still haven't done any planning. I find that once I finished adding a feature or fixing a bug, I just sat there playing in the menu and thinking "what now?" It's a lot of wasted time, but the way I structured the game was quite future-proof, so if I suddenly get an idea I can just add it in. I don't have to spend hours fiddling in the code trying to make it accept the new changes. As well as my structure, I probably have Python to thank for making it so easy.
>
> Structure is something I really worked on in Tectonic. Not so much in the three days leading up to the competition, but definitely after it. I read someone who once said that you should never use prototype code in a finished game. I took that advice and spent most of January recoding the game, although at a much slower pace than those first three days, since the pressure was off. I've been frustrated at the Blender API in the past, especially in the pre-2.49 days, but I think it has come a long way. I was able to implement some OOP, especially when handling the game objects, which was nice. It allowed a better structure and control of everything from a Python point of view.
>
> I used sfxr to make the sound effects. It's a nice, small, open source utility. It also has a flash port."

Andrew (19-years-old) lives in Melbourne, Australia and is attending university. He started using Blender about four years ago for its game engine. Andrew also made *Pit Monsters*, another quite successful game.

sfxr is a simple sound synthesizer, which can be found at *https://code.google.com/p/sfxr/*.

BGUI is maintained by Mitchell Stokes (Moguri) and can be found at *https://code.google.com/p/bgui/*

Sintel The Game

Jonathan Buresh, Noah Summers, Malcolm Corliss, David Barker, James Raymond, David Jogoo, Carlo Andreacchio

Figure 10.13
© 2014 Jonathan Buresh and Team.

Figure 10.14
© 2014 Jonathan Buresh and Team.

Sintel is Blender Institute's third open movie project, after *Elephants Dream* and *Big Buck Bunny*. *Sintel*, like its predecessors, is unique because all the production files used in the film were released under a Creative Commons License. This encourages remixing and reusing of the character, storyline, and the asset files. *Sintel The Game* takes advantage of this by taking story inspirations and characters from the movie. It is an adventure role-playing game that is set in the Sintel universe.

The development team consists of five main developers, with additional contributions from many artists, including David Revoy, the art director for Sintel. The dedication of these Blender hobbyists and encouragement from many supporters has kept the project going. *Sintel The Game* is still under development.

The team gives a behind-the-scenes look at how they are doing:

"We all know each other from working on other Blender-related endeavors and game projects. During the summer of 2009, we were looking to start a new game project. Then the Blender Foundation announced Sintel, and we decided to jump into it. We started writing a script and throwing ideas around in September of 2009. Our team works on Sintel The Game *in our free time (as most of us are attending college and another is in the Air Force). We collaborate via the Internet. It's like a hobby project. This method of development is easier to work around, but makes it pretty difficult to meet deadlines. Unfortunately, the unpredictable nature of our working schedule also means that dates can rarely be set for development milestones, such as release dates.*

As well as support from the Blender community, we have also received offers of help from individuals and groups who have been able to enhance or fill in gaps that our core team is not well versed in. For instance, Philippe Rey has create some fantastic and immersive music for the game; and a group called Digital Bard are working with us to bring our characters to life by contributing voice talent.

We are using models and textures from the movie. Although not every model and texture is game ready (due to the high level of detail), there are plenty of useful assets. Not only does this take a load off our shoulders, but it also makes use of the open source nature of the film.

The original decision was to use the Blender 2.4 game engine. Everyone on the team was more familiar with Blender 2.4. However, after testing the new Blender builds, the many new features that 2.5 could bring to the table proved irresistible. Initial tests of running the game in 2.5 went surprisingly well. No major changes were needed for the code to run with the new Blender API.

Even though the game engine does suffer from limitations, it is always improving. There are many small improvements in the new 2.5 engine that make game production in Blender less daunting. For example, logic bricks now updates when you change the name of an object, and a drop-down menu shows you a nice list of all the available objects, properties, and scripts. It's small helpful features like these that are turning the Blender game engine into a fantastic beginner's tool."

The development team of *Sintel The Game* is not affiliated with the Blender Institute. *Sintel The Game* is still under development. You can watch their progress, support them, or contribute at *http://sintelgame.org/*.

CAVE

Jorge Gascón Pérez

Figure 10.15
© 2014 Jorge Gascón Pérez.

CAVE stands for Cave Automatic Virtual Environment, and it is a cubical room where all the ceiling, floor, and walls are screens. Used for virtual reality applications, a participant standing in a CAVE would be completely surrounded by projected images. Each wall shows the image cast by a video projector, and each in turn is driven by a computer. For this project, the game engine is used to create the virtual reality world displayed by the CAVE. However, unlike most virtual reality applications where the display is a single screen, the CAVE is made up of many screens, each with a field of view of 90 degrees. So a special arrangement is required to set up the game engine to render the scene from multiple angles at the same time. In this particular installation, Jorge put together a system that allows multiple instances of Blender to run on different computers in order to provide a unique view of each wall of the CAVE. This approach requires a method to synchronize the game state across multiple computers so that the image outputted by each instance of Blender is completely synchronized with the others.

Jorge explains how Blender is used in this project:

> *"In our implementation, we have a Blender instance running in each computer. Each instance has loaded the same Blender scene, but each one uses a different camera as an active one. All of these instances need to communicate with each other; for that we have developed a network communication protocol in Python. The communication architecture follows the Master-Slaves approach—the master node is the instance that drives the front screen directly; and in addition, only this instance needs external control peripherals mouse and keyboard so far.*
>
> *In order to synchronize each instance, network protocol was developed. This protocol is event-based, which means that when the user (users) presses a key or moves the mouse, it generates one or more events that are sent to the other instances. Each instance processes all of these events using standard logic bricks.*
>
> *For matching screen borders, each scene in Blender has one camera per screen, and these cameras are configured to be perpendicular to each other, and all of them are parented to the "same" virtual user. (We call it "Virtual Camera Cluster.") The user can move and look around in a first-person view with the master instance, and all the cameras are translated and rotated with it.*
>
> *Although the Blender game engine has no network capabilities (yet), it is really flexible, and it allows the use of complex Python scripts."*

BlenderCave is an ongoing research project. You can follow its progress and download source code at *http://gmrv.es/~jgascon/BlenderCave/index.html*.

ColorCube
Quentin Bolsée, Benoit Bolsée

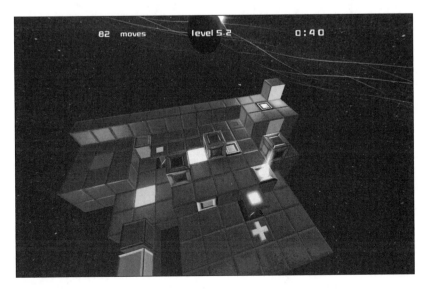

Figure 10.16
© 2014 Quentin and Benoit Bolsée.

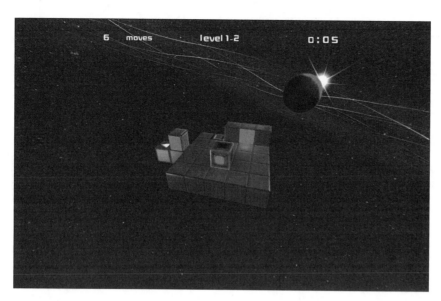

Figure 10.17
© 2014 Quentin and Benoit Bolsée.

What do you get when you combine an original gameplay idea, a talented artist, and the Blender game engine? Something that might look like *ColorCube*.

ColorCube is an addictive puzzle game that requires the user to flip a cube onto a series of targets, while "painting" the floor underneath it with the matching color the cube picked up from elsewhere. While the game mechanics might sound confusing on paper, it's very intuitive once you see the game in action. This is a great example of a "casual game" design: the game mechanic is easy to learn, but challenging at the same time as the levels gets progressively harder.

An iPhone version of the game is also available, which uses a 3D engine written from scratch by Benoit Bolsée, who is Quentin's father, as well as an active Blender developer.

Quentin was 14-years-old when he started working on the game two years ago:

"The first version of my game was only made with logic bricks. It was for a competition on the BlenderArtist forum. I won second place, but a lot of people said to me that I had to make it commercial. So I did. I wanted to have a level editor, so I had to learn Python. It was complicated at first, and I needed help from my father. The new version was finished a few months after I started it. I didn't make any plan; I just worked day by day on it until it was finished. I also created a website to promote the game.

The game engine is really powerful for this kind of game. You can easily produce nice graphics using GLSL. The problem was that it's a bit slow and doesn't work on every computer, so I had to create a version of my game running without GLSL, because too many users were complaining.

Another problem with the game engine, in my opinion, was the lighting system. I had to simply give up with the shadows. And if you want to create lights during the game, you will also get into trouble. Here's the thing: adding the same light multiple times doesn't work. I had no solution for my game, because the bug is visible if you pick up the same color twice with your cube. But I suppose it's just a detail."

ColorCube is available as a trial and commercial game for Windows, Mac, Linux, and iPhone from *http://www.colorcubestudio.com/*.

A demo version of the game is available from the accompanying online material.

JOGO DA COLETA—RECYCLE IT 2.0

Diego Rangel

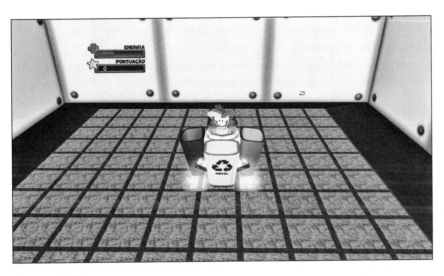

Figure 10.18
© 2014 Diego Rangel.

A game doesn't have to be complex or epic. There is a huge market for casual games—games that you can play from a smartphone or a Web browser without having to sit through endless cut scenes and cinematic storytelling. *Recyle It* is one such game that is simple to play, but carries a strong message.

Diego explains:

"The Recycle It *game was initially developed as an educational tool for the project 'Ambientação'— conceived by the state of Minas Gerais in Brazil. The goal of this game project was to raise environmental awareness of the workers in governmental buildings regarding the recycling procedures.*

The game had as its primary goal to collect the maximum amount of recyclable garbage by using the correct trash cans. (In Brazil. the different recyclable materials are collected in bins with a specific color code.)

In order to achieve that, the player must use mouse clicking and movement to translate and rotate the recycle bins into place to catch the falling objects.

This new version is an upgrade over the original one developed as a personal project. It's a complete revamp with new models and a different dynamic to make it more entertaining. Despite the refactoring, the game maintains the same goal: to collect garbage using the recycle bins properly.

The game contains only one single level, which gets harder as more garbage is correctly collected. When the player fails to collect the garbage (or puts it into the wrong bin), its energy decreases. When the energy ends, the game is over and hopefully a new record is set.

All the gameplay logic was planned ahead of the modeling and programming stages. This helped a lot, since it avoided drastic changes later in the development process. The production time, from its conception to the final game, took no more than a week. The speed was due to the size of the project, which spared me from doing highpoly artwork and complex programming—and because Blender is great software for quick prototyping and development of small projects.

During the course of this game development, the Blender game engine met all my requirements. The logic brick system allowed for quick implementation of ideas. Furthermore, the speed gain from having the game engine integrated with a full asset creation package (for example, Blender itself) was wonderful. The Blender game engine fulfilled its duties for this project. It seemed especially attractive for small and medium projects, in particular for one-man projects like this."

World Cup Stadiums

Chico Ortiz, Yorik van Havre, Maíra Zasso

Figure 10.19
© 2014 Chico Ortiz and Team.

Figure 10.20
© 2014 Chico Ortiz and Team.

World Cup Stadiums is a project that used Blender to create an interactive showcase of the sports venues at the 2010 World Cup. The interactive kiosk allows people to explore the different football stadiums and their surroundings using just a mouse. Furthermore, you can view the stadium from the perspective of the field, a view that most of us rarely have an opportunity to experience in real life. Two kiosks were installed at a Brazilian Cultural Center in São Paulo, Brazil during the game.

Chico writes:

"During South Africa's 2010 World Cup, we were asked to deliver an installation for the SESC Cultural Center in São Paulo, Brazil. The initial idea was to make real models using rapid prototyping. But our client then reached the conclusion that they didn't have a site to store the models after the exhibit was over. So we ended up doing a real-time, virtual reality version of the installation using Blender.

One of the main goals of this project was to make an application that worked using only a mouse. Furthermore, we needed to consider that this piece was not meant to be seen in a personal computer but in a public space. That required care to be taken so that users couldn't shut down the file using the mouse, and the game needed to reset if there was nobody using it.

Considering our time budget of only two months, we decided to create something that visually resembled the old school 3D arcade of our childhood: 'Daytona USA' by Sega. By forfeiting photorealistic graphics, it made the application look cleaner, and gave us more time to focus on the interaction and other aspects of the game. Also, due to time constraints, we decided to run the game directly in Blender instead of using the Blenderplayer binary because there wasn't enough time to track down and resolve the differences between the two.

We are really grateful to the Open Source and Creative Commons communities. It would be untrue to say that our crew was only five persons strong. All Blender coders were part of our crew, because without their contribution, this project would not have been possible."

Chico, Maíra, and Yorik are all architects who are big fans of open-source software, and they have a long history of using Blender for their work. Maíra and Yorik's work can be seen at *http://www.uncreated.net*.

The original project was made in Blender 2.49, but was ported to Blender 2.5 later. More information on this project is available from: *http://yorik.uncreated.net/ guestblog.php?2010=89*

OceanViz

Dalai Felinto, Mike Pan, Stephen Danic

Figure 10.21
Oceanviz © UBC Fisheries Centre. Blender work © 2014 Dalai Felinto, Mike Pan, and Stephen Danic.

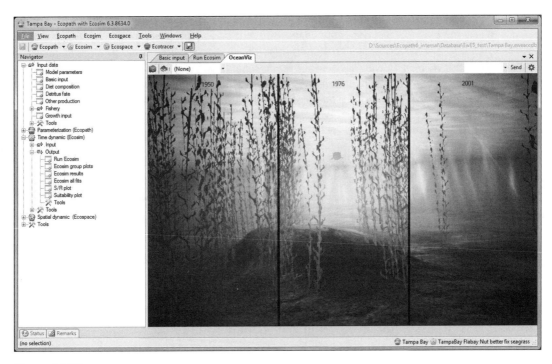

Figure 10.22
© 2014 Dalai Felinto, Martins Upitis, and Mike Pan.

Blender was used extensively at the Fisheries Centre at the University of British Columbia as a visualization and media production tool. Using 3D visualization to aid in the display of scientific data at the Fisheries Centre was first implemented by a small team of artists led by Stephen Danic from the Centre for Digital Media in Vancouver. Both authors of this book got involved in the project later on, and worked to produce a number of short films and interactive applications over the past four years.

Mike explains the project:

"The first project, nicknamed OceanViz, is an interactive underwater visualization made with the Blender game engine. The goal of this visualization was to accurately display the amount of marine life in the sea, based on a scientific modeling program called Ecopath with Ecosim (EwE). EwE would use a set of user-defined inputs to interpolate and predict the future. By playing the 'what-if' game, scientists and policy makers could test out different scenarios and see how their decisions today would impact tomorrow's oceans. A large portion of this project focused on the 3D visualization, which is what the users will ultimately be seeing. By replacing complex data and charts with realistic animated underwater scenes, users will be better able to appreciate the impact of their decisions.

The development of the visualization spans over two years, and we started the project with Blender 2.46 and eventually ported the visualization to Blender 2.5. Python was used extensively to drive the entire visualization, and it was responsible for populating the virtual world with fishes, controlling their movements, and handling all of the user-inputs.

One of the biggest roadblocks for OceanViz was balancing the performance and realism of the visualization. As it turns out, the Blender game engine was not very well optimized for rendering a large number of objects. Framerate would drop sharply as the number of objects on the screen increased. To assign each fish its own intelligence routine would undoubtedly lead to better behavior, but at the cost of much higher computation requirements. A compromise was reached by joining a large number of fishes into one object, thus reducing the need to control individual objects separately. This worked out surprisingly well. When there is a large school of fish, it is almost impossible to tell that the fishes are, in fact, batched together."

The *OceanViz* project was presented at the 2008 Blender conference; sample files and slides are available from *http://www.blender.org/community/blender-conference/blender-conference-2008/proceedings/*.

In its current iteration, *OceanViz* is implemented as a plug-in for the Ecopath with Ecosim (EwE) desktop software, using the embedding capabilities of the Blenderplayer.

The *OceanViz* project was conceived by professor Dr. Villy Christensen. The EwE development team that supports *OceanViz* consists of Jeroen Steenbeek and Joe Buszowski, with past support from Sherman Lai and Sundaran Kumar.

Cosmic Sensation

Dalai Felinto, Martins Upitis, Mike Pan

Figure 10.23
© 2014 Dalai Felinto, Martins Upitis, and Mike Pan.

Figure 10.24
© 2014 Dalai Felinto, Martins Upitis, and Mike Pan.

Somewhere in the Netherlands, there was a Blender project that involved cosmic particle detectors, a 30-meter tall immersive dome, a three-day party with Euro-disco music, and lots of beer. We worked on that project.

Every second, billions of harmless muon particles from outer space bombard the earth. Using particle detectors developed at Radboud University in Nijmegen, we were able to use this inflow of particles to drive an immersive audio-visual experience inside a 30-meter tall immersive dome installation. The event used Blender to generate real-time graphics of the muon particles hitting the sensor, and it painted the entire dome using six high-power projectors using visualizations generated in real-time by Blender. Thanks to our team's familiarity with Blender, the game engine turned out to be the perfect tool for us to use for a generative graphic art installation like this.

Mike recalls:

> *"Being the mastermind behind the project, Dalai brought Martins and me on board the project. We arrived on location 10 days prior to the event and started working. The goal was to create real-time visualizations that were driven by an external "beat"—the muon particles. The challenge was the massive size of the display. Instead of a typical flat TV screen that is usually less than a meter across, the graphics would be displayed on the inside of a 30-meter hemisphere that had a total resolution of 3840 × 1080 pixels.*

> *We wanted to create artwork in a Tron-like style, with a dark background and glossy glass, accented by colorful neons. Armed with only a vague concept of what we wanted to create, we started experimenting. The resulting visualization can be seen in the photos above.*

While Martins and I worked on the artwork, Dalai was busy patching the game engine's dome mode to support the projection mapping required. To output a 360-degree panorama of the scene to the projectors, it involved making Blender render the scene from multiple angles of each frame, stitching them together to form one massive image, and then wrapping the image to fit the projection mapping required by the projection software. It was a rather complex task that involved some mind-bending math and a good knowledge of the GPU. The task was further exacerbated by the lack of time and the strict performance requirement—after all, we didn't want the framerate of the visualization to drop anywhere below 30fps.

One technical limitation that hindered our creativity was that we had to keep the visualization dark— because if a bright image were projected onto one side of the dome, white light would reflect off the screen and light up the other side. This reduced the contrast of the overall projected image in the dome. (This is exactly the same reason why a movie theater is kept dark.) So in order to keep the ambient light level to a minimum, we had to make the visualization black-dominant and be careful to use only brighter areas sparingly. This ensured that we always had a good, high-contrast image.

With two days left, and the main visualization completed, we started considering other "fun" stuff to make. What better way to show off a huge dome than to play a classic game of Breakout on it? Using the incoming cosmic particles as projectiles, they would fire down from above to slowly destroy the rotating bricks' layers. From inception to finish, it took us less than a day to create the game.

During those 10 days, there were a lot of sleepless nights and way too many energy drinks. But in the end, we pulled off a wonderful show, and had fun while doing it. Isn't that what it's all about?"

The Cosmic Sensation project was an initiative of professor Dr. Sijbrand de Jong from the Radboud University along with Barney Broomer, producer and full-dome specialist.

Videos, photos and description of the event can be found at *http://www.dalaifelinto. com/?page_id=445.*

INDEX